Transcontinental
Railway Strategy, 1869-1893:
A study of businessmen

Transcontinental Railway Strategy, 1869-1893:

A study of businessmen

by Julius Grodinsky

PHILADELPHIA
UNIVERSITY OF PENNSYLVANIA PRESS

© 1962 *by The Trustees of the University of Pennsylvania.*

Published in Great Britain, India, and Pakistan
by the Oxford University Press
London, Bombay, and Karachi.

Library of Congress Catalog Card Number: 61-6624

7268

Printed in Great Britain
by Charles Birchall & Sons, Ltd
Liverpool and London

Preface

THIS VOLUME is an examination of the work of businessmen in the transcontinental railway industry. It is a record of their successes and failures, their trials and tribulations, their hopes and frustrations. It is a tale of fortunes gained and fortunes lost—all this on a field of open competition.

The story is typical of a growing industry in its pioneering stage. Competition then and now works itself out in a similar fashion. Some businessmen gain, some lose—but the public benefits. It got the railroads.

JULIUS GRODINSKY

Bibliographical Note

1. *American Railroad Journal.* In the eighteen sixties and seventies this source made available a large number of railroad Annual Reports and other documents pertaining to the railroad industry.

2. *Burlington Archives.* The records of the Chicago, Burlington and Quincy Railroad throughout the period under consideration in this volume are deposited with the Newberry Library in Chicago, Illinois. They are a significant and valuable source of study, not only for American railroad historians but also for students of American history in a variety of aspects. These papers reflect far more than views, actions, and policies of an individual businessman—a description which characterizes most collections of business papers. In the Burlington archives are found expressions of conflicting views of officials of the Burlington and of many other railroads, some of them friendly and some unfriendly to the Burlington. Furthermore, these views are not screened, as are those normally presented before public investigating bodies. These papers reflect hurried business judgments forged on the anvil of red-hot necessity, as well as calm and deliberate judgments slowly matured over the course of years. They reflect no censorship or selection of material to disclose favorable and eliminate or minimize unfavorable conclusions. The dynamic aspects of a large and growing American business enterprise are presented in this unique collection of business documents.

3. *Commercial and Financial Chronicle.* This weekly publication, beginning in 1865, reflected the opinions of the financial community. Its editorials were frequently critical of the policies of particular railroad managements. There were from time to time, particularly in the late seventies and eighties, detailed studies of individual railroads, with emphasis on

earning power and on financial strength and financial weakness. Beginning in the late seventies, the *Chronicle*, more than any other source, made available full or slightly abridged texts of railroad Annual Reports, as well as many other significant documents such as reorganization plans and reports of investigating committees.

4. *Dodge Papers*. The papers of General Grenville M. Dodge, deposited with the Iowa State Historical Society in Des Moines, Iowa, throw considerable light on the building program of the Texas and Pacific in the middle eighteen seventies; on the expansion of the Mexican railroads through the use of American capital; on the strategic problems of the Union Pacific in the latter years of the administration of Charles Francis Adams, Jr.; and on the relationships between Charles Francis Adams, Jr. and Henry Villard in the latter years of the eighteen eighties.

5. *Henry Villard Papers*. The papers of Henry Villard are deposited in the Houghton Library of Harvard University. They throw light on many of the business activities of Villard and disclose in detail the conflict over control of the Kansas Pacific (1875 to 1879) between Villard and Gould. The papers also illustrate the way in which large amounts of foreign funds were attracted to the American railway industry through the initiative of American promoters and investment bankers. They also throw light on the combination of investment and speculative motives that characterized the raising of funds for a growing industry in a dynamic economy.

6. *Railway Journal*. Herapath's *Railway Journal* is an English periodical devoted largely to the affairs of the British railroads. Because of the investments made by English investors in American railroads, the coverage also includes numerous American railroads. Aside from a number of documents made available from this source, the *Journal* is interesting because of its record of almost continuous optimism over the future of American railroads. Its analysis of financial prospects is on the whole superficial and reflects the kind of reasoning usually found in stock brokers' letters.

7. *Joy Papers*. The papers of James Frederick Joy are deposited in the Burton Historical Collection in the Detroit Public Library, Detroit, Michigan.

8. *Library of the Mariner's Museum, in Newport News, Virginia*. The letters between Collis P. Huntington, Charles Crocker, Leland Stanford, Mark Hopkins, and David D. Colton, are deposited in this Library. These letters bear upon the relationship between Gould and Huntington

in the middle eighteen seventies and again in 1881. References to Huntington's opinion of Gould in the early period and to the business conflicts between the Central Pacific and the Union Pacific are of value; and the letters between Huntington and Crocker in the latter period reveal their determination to thwart Gould's ambitions to invade the Pacific Coast. These letters are helpful in tracing the unique methods used by Huntington in financing the Southern Pacific's expansion program in the middle seventies, the Central Pacific's critical financial problems in 1872 and 1873, and the subsequent growth of the Southern Pacific's system between late 1878 and 1883.

9. *Northwestern Archives*. A collection of letters in the eighteen seventies and eighties were found in the accounting offices of the Chicago and Northwestern in Chicago, Illinois. They reflect, though on a minor scale, many pressing business problems of the company. Probably through some oversight, these letters were later destroyed. This author has photographic reproductions of some of them and typewritten copies of many others.

10. *Northern Pacific Archives*. A collection of letters deposited in the files of the Northern Pacific in St. Paul, Minnesota. These letters throw some light on the relationship between Henry Villard and Frederick Billings prior to Villard's capture of control of the Northern Pacific in 1881. They are also instructive in clarifying a number of the business problems confronting Villard and his operating officials in the business reversals that culminated in Villard's expulsion from the affairs of the Northern Pacific late in 1883.

11. *Railroad Gazette*. This periodical probably represents the most complete coverage of the affairs of the railroad industry in the eighteen seventies and eighties and in the early nineties—the period covered by this study. The periodical's discussions of the traffic problems of American railroads are the best available in secondary sources. Many of its editorial analyses cast interesting lights on significant phases of American railroad development. Its obituary notices on American railroad leaders are also valuable.

12. *Railway Review*. This magazine was published in Chicago. Its discussions of the affairs of western railroads were frequently illuminating. The journal's value in reflecting western railroad affairs increased with the passage of time and the coverage was more complete in the eighties than in the seventies.

13. *Railway World.* This successor to the *United States Railroad & Mining Register* began publication in 1875. In its earlier years it supported the views of the Pennsylvania Railroad and of its president, T. A. Scott, especially in the Huntington-Scott struggle over the Southern 32nd Parallel transcontinental route in the seventies. During the eighties the *Railway World* published little that is not covered in the *Railroad Gazette*.

14. *United States Railroad & Mining Register.* The contributions and opinions of this ably edited periodical were valuable in the late sixties and the early seventies. The paper suspended publication in 1875.

Other sources used are newspapers in New York, Philadelphia, Chicago, Boston and San Francisco, and a number of periodicals. These are footnoted. The most valuable of the periodicals is *Bradstreet's*, which began publication in 1879. A number of congressional documents were useful, and these, too, are all footnoted.

Abbreviations Used in Footnotes

Am. R. R. Journal—*American Railroad Journal*

Burlington Archives—Papers of the Chicago, Burlington and Quincy in the Newberry Library, Chicago.

Chron.—*Commercial and Financial Chronicle*

Credit Mobilier—Select Committee on *Credit Mobilier*, Report No. 77, House of Representatives, 42nd Congress, 3rd Session, 1873.

Dodge Papers—The papers of General Grenville M. Dodge, Iowa State Historical Society, Des Moines, Iowa.

Evans—Cerinda W. Evans, *Collis Potter Huntington* (Newport News, Virginia: The Mariner's Museum, 1954).

Gould—Julius Grodinsky, *Jay Gould* (Philadelphia: University of Pennsylvania Press, 1957)

Hedges—James Blaine Hedges, *Henry Villard and the Railways of the Northwest* (New Haven: Yale University Press, 1930).

H.V.P.—The papers of Henry Villard, in the Houghton Library, Harvard University.

Iowa Pool—Julius Grodinsky, *Iowa Pool* (Chicago: University of Chicago Press, 1950).

Joy Papers—The papers of James Frederick Joy, in Burton Historical Collection, Detroit Public Library.

Larson—Henrietta M. Larson, *Jay Cooke* (Cambridge: Harvard University Press, 1936).

M.M.—Collection of letters in the library of the Mariner's Museum, Newport News, Virginia.

Northern Pacific Archives—Letters of this road in St. Paul.

Northwestern Archives—Papers of the Chicago & Northwestern.

Overton—Richard C. Overton, *Gulf to Rockies* (Austin: University of Texas Press, 1953).

Pac. Ry. Commission—United States Pacific Railway Commission, Testimony, Executive Document No. 51, U. S. Senate, 50th Congress, 1st Session, 1887.

Pyle—Joseph G. Pyle, *The Life of James J. Hill* (New York: Doubleday, Page, 1917).

Report No. 778—Report No. 778, U. S. Senate, 54th Congress, 1st Session, 1896.

R. R. Gazette—Railroad Gazette.

Ry. Review—Railway Review.

Ry. World—Railway World.

Southern Pacific—Neill C. Wilson and Frank J. Taylor, *Southern Pacific* (New York: McGraw-Hill, 1952).

Waters—L. L. Waters, *Steel Rails to Santa Fe* (Lawrence, Kansas: University of Kansas Press, 1950).

Abbreviations of Railroads

Name	Abbreviation
Atchison and Nebraska	A. & N.
Atchison, Topeka and Santa Fe	Atchison
Burlington, Cedar Rapids and Northern	Cedar Rapids
Burlington and Missouri River in Nebraska	B. & M.
Chicago and Alton	Alton
Chicago, Burlington and Northern	Burlington and Northern
Chicago, Burlington and Quincy	Burlington
Chicago and Northwestern	Northwestern
Chicago, Milwaukee and St. Paul	St. Paul
Chicago, Rock Island and Pacific	Rock Island
Chicago, St. Paul and Kansas City	Stickney Road
Chicago, St. Paul, Minneapolis and Omaha	Omaha
Colorado Midland	Midland
Denver and Rio Grande	Rio Grande
Denver and Rio Grande Western	Rio Grande Western
Denver, South Park and Pacific	South Park
Galveston, Harrisburg and San Antonio	San Antonio
Gulf Colorado and Santa Fe	Gulf
Hannibal and St. Joseph	Hannibal
International Great Northern	International
Kansas City, St. Joseph and Council Bluffs	Council Bluffs
Minneapolis, St. Paul and Sault Ste. Marie	Soo
Missouri, Kansas and Texas	Kansas and Texas
Oregon and Transcontinental	Transcontinental
Oregon Improvement Company	Improvement

Oregon Railway and Navigation Company   Navigation
St. Joseph and Denver City   St. Joseph
St. Louis and San Francisco   Frisco
St. Louis, Fort Scott and Wichita   Wichita
St. Louis, Iron Mountain and Southern   Iron Mountain
St. Louis, Kansas City and Northern   Kansas City and Northern
St. Paul, Minneapolis and Manitoba   Manitoba
Sioux City and Pacific   Sioux City
Southern Railway Security Company   Security Company
Texas and Pacific Railway   Texas and Pacific

Dramatis Personae (1869-1893)

Names of railroad officials appearing repeatedly in the text, and their positions. The full name is used when they are first mentioned in the text. Thereafter, only the surname is used.

Name	Position
Adams, Charles Francis, Jr.	President, Union Pacific, 1884–1890.
Ames, Frederick L.	Director, Union Pacific, 1869–1893 also large Union Pacific stockholder
Blackstone, T. B.	President, Chicago and Alton, 1869–1893.
Billings, Frederick	President, Northern Pacific, 1878–1881. Director, 1869–1889.
Cable, Richard R.	General manager, Chicago, Rock Island and Pacific, 1877–1883; President, 1883–1893.
Colton, D. D.	Associate of the Huntington Group, 1873–1878.
Crocker, Charles	Vice-president, Central Pacific, 1869–1888
Dillon, Sidney	President, Union Pacific, 1874–1884, 1890–1892

Dodge, Grenville M.

Chief Engineer, Texas Pacific, 1872–1879; President of Gould's southwestern construction companies, 1879–1883; adviser to Charles Francis Adams, Jr. on Union Pacific problems, 1886–1890

Dows, David

Director, Chicago, Rock Island and Pacific, 1869–1890.

Endicott, William J.

Associate of Henry Villard in the Northern Pacific, Oregon and Transcontinental, and Oregon Railway and Navigation Company, 1877–1884.

Forbes, John M.

Leading personality in the Chicago, Burlington and Quincy, variously chairman and president, 1869–1893.

Gould, Jay

Chief figure in the Missouri Pacific and controlled and affiliated lines, 1879–1892, in control of Union Pacific policies, 1874–1884, 1890–1892.

Harris, Robert

General superintendent, Chicago, Burlington and Quincy, 1869–1875; president, 1875–1878, president, Northern Pacific, 1884–1889.

Hill, James J.

General manager, St. Paul, Minneapolis and Manitoba, 1879–1882; president, 1882–1889; president, Great Northern, 1889—1893.

Hopkins, Mark

Associate of Huntington in the Central Pacific, 1869–1878.

Hughitt, Marvin

General manager, Chicago and Northwestern, 1877–1887; president 1887–1893.

Huntington, Collis P.	Chief figure in the Central Pacific and Southern Pacific and allied and controlled companies, 1869–1893.
Keep, Albert	President, Chicago and Northwestern, 1874–1887.
Merrill, Shelburne, S.	General manager, Chicago, Milwaukee and St. Paul, 1869–1884.
Miller, Roswell	President, Chicago, Milwaukee and St. Paul, 1887–1893.
Mitchell, Alexander	President, Chicago, Milwaukee and St. Paul, 1869–1887.
Nickerson, Thomas	President, Atchison, Topeka and Santa Fe, 1874–1881.
Oakes, Thomas F.	Associate of Henry Villard, 1879–1893; vice-president, Northern Pacific, 1881–1889; president, 1889–1893.
Palmer, William J.	President, Denver and Rio Grande 1870–1883; president, Denver and Rio Grande Western, 1883–1893.
Perkins, Charles E.	Vice-President, Chicago Burlington and Quincy, 1876–1881; president 1881–1893.
Porter, H. H.	Promoter and leading figure in the Chicago, St. Paul, Minneapolis and Omaha, and predecessor companies, 1873–1884.
Riddle, Hugh	General superintendent, Chicago, Rock Island and Pacific, 1869–1873; president, 1873–1883.
Sage, Russell	Associate of Jay Gould; director of Gould companies—Missouri Pacific and Union Pacific in periods of Gould control.

Scott, Thomas A.   President, Texas and Pacific, 1872–1879.

Scott, Walter L.   Director, Chicago and Northwestern 1870–1890.

Vanderbilt, William H.   Director, Chicago and Northwestern, 1879–1885; large stockholder in Chicago, Burlington and Quincy, Chicago, Rock Island and Pacific, and Union Pacific at various times between 1880 and 1884.

Villard, Henry   Leading personality in the affairs of the Oregon Railway and Navigation Company, 1879–1884, and in the Northern Pacific, 1881–1884, 1887–1893.

Contents

xix

Maps and Tables

Transcontinental Railway Strategy, 1869-1893:

A study of businessmen

I

Introduction

THE COMPLETION in May, 1869 of the first transcontinental railroad route was a notable physical success—as a transportation facility. It was built quickly and finished a number of years before the time limit set by the Congress. It was not, however, a financial success. There were two corporations and two sets of promoters and security holders. The eastern section of the route (the Union Pacific) extended from Omaha to Ogden, and the western end (the Central Pacific), from Ogden to Sacramento. The line from the latter point to the Pacific Coast was owned by another road acquired soon after its completion by the Central Pacific. The stockholders of the Union Pacific had received a substantial dividend in 1867, while the stockholders of the Central Pacific had received none. The Union Pacific in 1869 was short of working capital. The proceeds realized from the sale of its first mortgage bonds and from the borrowed United States Government bonds for a thirty-year term had all been spent. The road at that time had a floating debt of more than $15 million. For two years it had been raising funds in a manner characteristic of an approach to bankruptcy. Bank loans were incurred at interest rates of $2\frac{1}{2}$ per cent per month. New bond issues junior to the first-mortgage bonds were unsaleable. They were pledged for loans between 25 and 50 cents on the dollar. Securities bought by directors and leading stockholders were pledged to secure bank loans. By the end of 1870 declines in security prices had destroyed the equity in these loans. One of the leading promoters thereby lost his personal fortune and others dropped out in 1871.

Oakes Ames, a large stockholder, was the bankrupt; D. C. Durant, another substantial stockholder, suffered heavy losses, while three others were also heavy losers. Upon their retirement from the management in January, 1871, the company was left with a three-month maturing debt of $5 million secured by collateral with a market value of approximately one-third lower than the loan. There were also second-mortgage Land-Grant Bonds and $10 million in 10 per cent Income Bonds. The end of the promoters' regime was featured by a decline in the price of the Land-Grant Bonds to 53, the Income Bonds to 32, and the common stock to 9. Interestingly enough, the official clothed with the responsibility of watching the company's affairs, in order to protect the government investment was certain that the stock was worthless. The stockholders' interest in the spring of 1869, according to this observer, had "so far vanished already that it is scarcely worth considering"; and that because of its debts, "the chances of the stockholders to realize anything from their investments are so remote that the science of mathematics is not equal to their calculations."[1]

The Central Pacific, unlike the Union Pacific, was financially supported by a single dominating personality. Collis P. Huntington was a resourceful financier; shrewd in trading, skilful in borrowing, and indefatigable in establishing and maintaining continuous contacts with capitalists both in this country and abroad. As a promoter and financier of the Central Pacific he was aided by Mark Hopkins, a master of accounting detail; Charles Crocker, an energetic railroad builder; and Leland Stanford, the smooth-talking politician and publicity agent. Stanford was president and Huntington vice-president. Upon Huntington fell the responsibility of raising funds. The Central Pacific, like the Union Pacific, had by 1869 spent the proceeds of government bonds borrowed for a thirty-year term and its own first-mortgage bonds. Additional cash was needed to pay corporate obligations. These sums had to be borrowed and Huntington did the borrowing, acting variously as agent of the Central Pacific, of the construction company—the Contract and Finance Company—and, not infrequently, borrowing on his own personal credit and on that of his associates.

Huntington and his associates, together with a few scattered stockholders, owned a majority of the stock. Huntington had been unsuccessful in interesting capitalists in subscribing to the stock. Moses Taylor, president of the National City Bank and a large stockholder in coal, iron, and railroad enterprises, Commodore Garrison, a capitalist with large commitments in steamship ventures, and a number of others on the West

Coast refused to buy. "The risk is too great," Garrison told Huntington, "and the profits, if any, are too remote."[2]

Little was raised by stock sales. Neither could substantial sums be realized through the pledge of the stock as collateral for loans. The Central Pacific had earnings, but the earnings were needed to improve the road. Huntington wrote early in 1870 that he did not see how interest could be paid from earnings. "There should not be a dollar spent that could possibly be avoided . . . beyond keeping the track and rolling stock in order."[3] No dividends were paid. The stock was not well known; no annual report had (by 1869) been issued. "I do not believe," insisted Huntington, that the stock in 1869–1870 "could have been sold in New York for 5 cents on the dollar."[4] A contemporary capitalist, speaking from memory in 1887, was even more emphatic. "I would not have been willing at the time the Central Pacific road was finished," he declared, "to take a block of the stock as a gift and be liable for the debts as they then existed."[5]

The company's financial requirements were met from earnings and by the creation of junior debts—that is, by obligations subordinate to the two mortgage bonds. Most of the debt instruments were delivered to Huntington's office in New York City. Few of the junior bonds were sold. They were used largely as collateral for loans, and interest rates ranged from 7 per cent to 12 per cent. In 1869 and 1870 there was only a slight demand for debts of railroads in process of construction or of completed roads. The capital markets were flooded with such bonds. In the spring of 1870, according to Huntington, there were forty railroads offering bonds in New York, "at almost any price for ready cash."[6] And in July, Huntington tried vainly to raise $2 million. It is "almost impossible to borrow money here on railroad bonds on incompleted roads..."[7]

In the face of this competition, Huntington still managed to borrow large sums for the Central Pacific. Major financial aid at this time came from a banking house—Fisk and Hatch. This firm had the contract for the sale of the road's first-mortgage bonds. The profits from that business were substantial. By early 1870, it had advanced the road about $3 million. Additional sums were borrowed on the Pacific Coast. "We owe here," (that is, New York City), wrote Huntington to Hopkins, "over $3 million and how much you owe there you and your God may know but I do not."[8] Through Fisk and Hatch, Huntington was introduced to a relatively new investment banking institution with German affiliations.

Through this house, Speyer and Company, Huntington was able to place some bonds on the German market. As the months rolled on in the summer of 1870, Huntington borrowed heavily, secured largely by Central Pacific bonds. The cost of capital was high. Fisk and Hatch grew nervous; Huntington was unable to pay maturing loans. Fisk and Hatch became an unwilling partner with Huntington. The firm, asserted Huntington, had "made money out of us" and would make more. Therefore, he declared, the firm "must expect now and then to have to turn a sharp and hard corner. . . ."⁹

The arrangements between Huntington and his associates constituted a unique venture in financial history. There were no written understandings. By informal and verbal understandings their personal funds were pooled with Huntington and were spent by him as he thought necessary to promote the common interest. And the common interest was associated largely with the Central Pacific. By 1870 all California roads, with but two exceptions, had been acquired by the Central Pacific. These roads, like the Central Pacific, were short of cash. They could not raise the cash but Huntington could; and that ability spelled the difference between their failures and his success. His philosophy was all-embracing. ". . . It is about as well to fight them [the California roads] on all the railroads in the state as on our road, as it is not much more fight and there is more pay," he wrote to Hopkins in 1868.¹⁰ Huntington raised the cash largely by skilful borrowing. To borrow it was necessary to maintain a reasonable price for the Central Pacific bonds. This in turn required Huntington to raise more money, again through borrowing. The financial problem was well illustrated by an experience late in 1870. A large New York trader publicly declared that the Central Pacific bonds were not worth 50 cents on the dollar. Accordingly he sold short, and Huntington to sustain the market bought approximately $700 thousand of bonds. "I do not believe," wrote Huntington, "we shall be troubled again for sometime with the bears."¹¹ If Huntington had not bought these bonds, his borrowing power would have been impaired. It was at this time that the Union Pacific's securities dropped to the low level already noted. Huntington's buying, however, made the Central Pacific's accounts "fearfully overdrawn."¹²

The status of both the Central Pacific and the Union Pacific reflected the progress of pioneer companies in growing pioneering industries. The profits of such companies are uncertain and speculative. Their prospects are excellent but time must elapse before they can be converted into profits. The profits of the Union Pacific were garnered by a new group under the leadership of Jay Gould, and those of the Central Pacific were realized gradually throughout the 1870's and early 1880's through the financial genius of Huntington.

The newly established Union Pacific–Central Pacific transcontinental line terminated at the Missouri River. Between the Missouri River at Omaha and Chicago the route was served by three railroads; the Chicago, Burlington and Quincy, the Chicago, Rock Island and Pacific, and the Chicago and Northwestern. The first-named property was under the leadership of a group of Boston capitalists headed by John Murray Forbes. Though Forbes was active in the formulation of policies and the raising of funds, he was not the adminstrator. The executive responsibilities of the railroads, fed with capital under Forbes's leadership, were James Frederick Joy's. The Joy roads—those roads organized under the Joy leadership—included the Burlington with a line from Chicago to a small point in Western Iowa; the Kansas City, St. Joseph and Council Bluffs, owning a line between Kansas City and Council Bluffs and affording the Burlington entrance into the City of Council Bluffs, thereby making the connection with the Union Pacific; the Hannibal and St. Joseph, connecting with the Burlington at Quincy, and giving that line a short connection with Kansas City; and the Burlington and Missouri River in Nebraska, affording the Burlington an outlet into southern Nebraska competing there with the Union Pacific, and making connections with that road at Kearney. In 1869–1870 the Burlington capitalist group under the Forbes-Joy leadership was carrying on a program of expansion through the acquisition and construction of branch lines and main-line extensions into new territory. Joy thought it essential to acquire unproductive roads in the hope that thereby he would avoid, or at least minimize, competition. By the diversion of their traffic to the main line of the Burlington, he could make the acquisition of the smaller lines profitable. Joy personally was not a man of means, but he enjoyed the support of a group of capitalists, including, among others, Forbes, Nathaniel Thayer, a private banker in Boston and a member of the Burlington finance committee, and Taylor, president of the National City Bank of New York. Taylor was an ardent admirer of Joy. For his own personal account, for the bank, and for his iron and coal companies, Taylor bought millions of dollars of railroad bonds recommended by Joy. He made little study of his own prior to the purchase of the Joy securities. On one occasion, for example, he was asked to purchase the bonds of the Missouri, Kansas and Texas, then projecting a line from the Missouri River through the Indian territory into northern Texas. Taylor refused to buy without consulting Joy.[13]

On the other hand, Taylor purchased bonds of short roads with uncertain futures but carrying Joy's recommendations. When Joy offered the bonds of the Chicago and Iowa, a property owning a small mileage in northern Illinois and designed to serve as part of a line to enable the Burlington to compete with the Northwestern, Taylor had his doubts. He, nevertheless, deferred to Joy's judgment.

Joy was a pioneer railroad builder. His roads penetrated new territories, so that for a number of years they had no competition. His early successes, particularly with the Michigan Central and the Burlington, gave him an enviable reputation. Joy was not a careful administrator. His responsibilities were heavy and as the executive of many railroads and other properties he was unable to give to each the attention necessary for the successful conduct of enterprises in a rapidly growing industry. He did not permit his executive officials to handle many of the administrative details. He thus had many problems to examine, he was usually short of time, and his decisions were inclined to be immature and subject to misinterpretation.

The leadership of the Rock Island fell upon John F. Tracy—a man who, though as vigorous and aggressive as Joy, confined his operations to a smaller geographical area. Under the Tracy leadership the Rock Island built across Iowa to Council Bluffs for a connection with the Union Pacific. Tracy, unlike Joy, was a capitalist in his own right. He had ample means and he conducted several successful trading operations in the New York security markets. His financial supporters came largely from New York. The most important was David Dows, a member of the brokerage fraternity with a considerable capitalist following. The Rock Island was in sound financial condition, and in 1869 succeeded in selling $1 million of stock to its stockholders on a privileged-subscription basis. This venture was unique in an era characterized by railroad bond financing, with stock normally distributed either as bonuses to bondholders or as compensation for services rendered by railroad promoters.

The Northwestern, the third road connecting Chicago with the Missouri River, was originally promoted by Chicago capitalists. In 1870 they sold out their interests, and Tracy with a number of associates and with borrowed funds bought a controlling interest. The Northwestern had been built as a local property. Its extension to the Missouri River was facilitated by the lease of a number of roads promoted by John I. Blair. Blair, with the aid of leading capitalists including Taylor and one of the Ames brothers active in the Union Pacific, had acquired numerous roads in Illinois, Iowa, and Nebraska. A number of these were leased to the Northwestern at high rentals.[14]

In 1870 Tracy was appointed president of the Northwestern. He was, therefore, the policy maker of both this road and of the Rock Island. In Illinois and Iowa these roads were competitors. Tracy found it difficult to harmonize their rivalries. Both competed with the Burlington, and they competed between themselves for business exchanged with the Union Pacific and also for local traffic. There was also rivalry in the southwestern business. This developed in 1869 when the Rock Island guaranteed the bonds of a Tracy-promoted line from southeastern Iowa to Atchison and Leavenworth on the Missouri River. By the summer of 1869 a number of rate wars had already developed. Joy, having operated for such a long period under a stabilized rate structure, had a lively fear of the losses arising from rate rivalries. He therefore suggested that the three roads between the Missouri River and Chicago pool their business and divide the revenues from the transcontinental business between Council Bluffs and Chicago. After brief consideration the idea was accepted. There thus was established the famous Iowa pool that successfully operated throughout the 1870's and into the early 1880's.

The central transcontinental route terminating at Omaha was only one of the potential rail routes to the Pacific Coast. For many years others had been discussed. On the North, a line between the Great Lakes and Puget Sound had been the subject of public debate, both in and out of Congress. Another, from St. Louis via the 35th Parallel and crossing the Colorado River in northern Arizona, was under consideration. And still another route, from the lower Mississippi Valley parallel to the Mexican boundary to Los Angeles and San Diego, had long been advocated. By 1869 the genesis of these routes had already been sketched. The northern route was promoted under the leadership of Jay Cooke with the assistance of capitalists associated with the Pennsylvania Railroad. Cooke was an investment banker. He rose to leadership in that business in the Civil War years, when he negotiated for the government the sale of United

States government bonds. He continued in the post-Civil War years to buy and sell government bonds; but he also utilized his talents in the field of railroad securities. In a ten-year period Cooke's firm handled business of approximately $5 million which, according to reliable opinion, was "a larger amount than was ever handled in the same time by any house in the world."[15]

After long hesitation, Cooke decided to promote and finance the construction of a railroad between Duluth and Puget Sound with a branch to Portland, Oregon. The project was incorporated under the name of the Northern Pacific. Cooke agreed to advance the new enterprise $500 thousand, and to buy the road's 30-year 7.3 per cent first-mortgage bonds at 88 in legal-tender currency. He also guaranteed the sale within thirty days of $5 million of the new bonds. In return, the Cooke firm was appointed the fiscal agent of the road and for a small consideration received a majority of its stock. To aid in construction, Congress gave the company a munificent grant of land.

The Duluth connection of the road was made by the Lake Superior and Mississippi Railroad. This road had also been built under Cooke leadership and with the enthusiastic support of the Pennsylvania railroad interests. J. Edgar Thomson, president of the road, had "inspired the necessary confidence to capitalists" to supply the funds. "Draw on me for $40,000 to commence this work, and the balance shall be forthcoming," declared Thomson.[16] Philadelphians responded well to this lead. The bonds of the new road were taken up in that city "in such parcels as as they [investors] could carry and buttoned them up beneath their shad-bellied coats . . . ."[17] The combined Northern Pacific-Lake Superior and Mississippi route, in conjunction with lake transportation from Duluth, was hailed enthusiastically in Philadelphia. One editorial expected the route to give Philadelphia "such advantages for transportation to and from the West as can be secured by no other city. . . ."[18]

Philadelphia and Pennsylvania Railroad support also appeared in the southernmost transcontinental route along the 32nd Parallel. Here by 1869 a number of enterprises had already been established to connect eastern Texas with the Pacific Coast. One was the Memphis, El Paso and Pacific under the leadership of General John Charles Fremont. A few miles had been built along the eastern end, and property rights had also been obtained on the western end in San Diego. The road was grievously mismanaged, and in 1870 it fell into receivership. Another road with transcontinental ambitions was the Southern Pacific Railroad Company of Texas. This road in 1869 was sold in foreclosure. In 1871 these properties were taken over and merged into a new corporate entity under the name of the Texas and Pacific Railway. The leadership appeared to be of the best. T. A. Scott and Thomson, vice-president and president respectively of the Pennsylvania Railroad, were behind the enterprise. The influence of these two personalities on the progress of the American railway system has been underestimated. Neither of them produced any dramatic climaxes of the kind that, for example, characterized the career of Cornelius Vanderbilt or Gould. They did not appear before many congressional committees. Thomson did his work quietly. He was an engineer and accomplished his task by careful building and unpublicized negotiations. Scott had a greater flair for security trading and corporate manipulation. He appeared occasionally before investigating committees, both in Pennsylvania and in Washington. He attracted national publicity in his contest with Huntington over the building of the southern transcontinental route. In the earlier and more creative phases of his career, however, Scott's activities produced little legislative or judicial climaxes.

Still another transcontinental route—this one along the 35th Parallel —was set up under an act of Congress in 1866 as the Atlantic and Pacific Railroad. The line was to begin at Springfield, Missouri (though it was later pushed farther east to Pacific, thirty miles west of St. Louis), to extend west to the Colorado River, there to join another line to the Pacific Coast. The Act also authorized the Southern Pacific Railroad of California to build east from San Francisco to join the Atlantic and Pacific near the Arizona-California boundary. Both the eastern and western arms of this route received federal land grants. Building was carried on actively, and by early 1871 it had reached a point in the Indian Territory, 361 miles west of St. Louis.

There were therefore, in operation in 1869–1870, at the time of the completion of the Union Pacific-Central Pacific route, the beginnings of three major rival routes. Another line destined to emerge as a leading transcontinental rival had by then also been organized under inauspicious circumstances, as a local property in Kansas. This road—the Atchison, Topeka and Santa Fe—had encountered the usual financial difficulties associated with pioneering railroads. The original promoters sold out in 1869.

Another local line destined to become the basis for a transcontinental route in the 19th century was a small property in Minnesota—the St. Paul and Pacific. The road was built largely with the support of Dutch capital. One line was projected from St. Paul to the Red River, and two other lines north from Minneapolis were destined for a connection with a Canadian line at the Minnesota-Canadian border. The road also connected with the Northern Pacific and indeed was acquired by that road in 1872.

All these lines—those with transcontinental ambitions as well as those for specific local purposes—were built in sparsely settled areas. The traffic was light, the overhead and capital expenses were heavy, and the cost of transportation reflected in freight rates was correspondingly high. Railroad properties could become profitable only with an increase in population and traffic. The railroads were indeed pioneers in the American frontier area. To serve their own interests, to increase their earnings, and to attract capital essential to their development, they established immigration agencies. Through these agencies the railroads competed for immigrants into the territories served by their lines. As the population and the traffic increased, it became essential to build lines into new areas and to improve existing lines. New funds derived from the investing public had to be raised. Existing earnings were inadequate to finance improvements and extensions. The cost of capital was high. In the post-Civil War era the limited supply of funds was actively bid for by numerous groups engaged in the creative task of building up a strong productive capacity in a rapidly growing economy. Farmers in Nebraska and Kansas paid between 10 and 15 per cent for mortgage money. In Illinois and Iowa the rates were somewhat lower, averaging between 8 and 10 per cent, while in the Dakota territory, loans, including substantial commission charges, averaged from 17 to 18 per cent. The railroads also competed for funds with rapidly growing cities in need of municipal improvements. Other demands upon the limited capital supply came from industries: coal, iron, steel, lumber, farm equipment, copper, and an increasing variety of manufacturing and fabricating enterprises.

High interest rates reflected both strong demands and high risks. Relatively little institutional money—money raised from the savings of the masses—was available for western railroad investment. Even seasoned, hard-bitten capitalists hesitated to commit their funds to western railroads. That this skepticism was justified was shown by the extensive

Table I

COST OF OBTAINING BOND MONEY BY PIONEERING
RAILROADS, 1869–1873

Railroad	Name of Bond	Interest Rate	Sales Price	
Atchison, Topeka & Santa Fe	Income Bonds	12% (Currency)	100	a
Atchison, Topeka & Santa Fe	Second Mortgage	7% (Gold)	50	b
Atchison, Topeka & Santa Fe	Land Grants	7% (Currency)	73	c
Burlington, Cedar Rapids & Minnesota	First Mortgage	7% (Gold)	90	d
California & Oregon	First Mortgage	6% (Gold)	79½	e
Chesapeake & Ohio	First Mortgage	7% (Gold)	70	f
Denver & Rio Grande	First Mortgage	7% (Gold)	66	g
Elizabethtown & Paducah	First Mortgage	8% (Gold)	85	h
Northern Pacific	First Mortgage	7.3% (Gold)	83	i
Oregon & California	First Mortgage	7% (Gold)	72	j
San Joaquin Valley	First Mortgage	6% (Gold)	74¼	k
St. Paul & Pacific First Division	First Mortgage	7% (Gold)	65	l
St. Louis, Iron Mountain & Southern	Second Mortgage	7% (Currency)	79	m

Railroad	*Name of Bond*	*Interest Rate*	*Sales Price*
St. Louis, Iron Mountain & Southern	Consolidated Mortgage	7% (Currency)	71 n

a   *Chron.*, Dec. 20, 1873, 834.
b   *Ibid.*
c   L. L. Waters, *Steel Rails to Santa Fe*, (Lawrence, Kansas: University of Kansas Press, 1950), p. 239.
d   *Chron.* Jan. 21, 1871, p. 25.
e   *R. R. Gaz.*, Mar. 29, 1873, p. 132.
f   This was an offer to sell a $10 million issue in January, 1869, in the London Market. The offer failed.
g   Herbert O. Brayer, William Blackmore, *Early Financing of the Denver & Rio Grande Railway and Ancillary Land Companies*, 1871–1878, Vol. II, 49, 100, (Denver, 1949).
h   *Am. R. R. Journal*, June 24, 1871, p. 683, citing *Louisville Courier-Journal*.
i   *The Road*, May 1, 1875, p. 98, citing president C. W. Cass, Northern Pacific, in a report to the Railroad Commissioners of Minnesota for the year ending June 30, 1874.
j   Henry Villard, *History of Early Transportation in Oregon*, ed. by Oswald Garrison Villard, (University of Oregon, 1944), p. 28. One-half of the issue was sold at 72 and the other half a year later at 75.
k   Huntington to Crocker, Mar. 26, 1872, M. M.
l   *The Road*, June 1, 1875, p. 131. According to William W. Folwell, the bonds were sold at 75. *A History of Minnesota*, (St. Paul: Minnesota Historical Society, 1926), III, 444.
m   *Chron.* Aug. 8, 1874, p. 144.
n   *Ibid.*

defaults of railroad bonds in the middle and late 1870's. The high cost of western railroad capital is well illustrated in Table I.

The examples included in the table are suggestive. They were not selected for the purpose of making a point. The varying rates of return reflect—crudely and approximately, of course—the varying credit risks. The high transportation rates in the late 1860's and early 1870's reflected the high costs of borrowed capital as well as the low volume of business.

Reasonable rates—indeed rates bordering on the high side—were essential to the development of the infant railroad industry. As the traffic volume increased and as transportation costs and rates declined, the problem of capital funds became ever more pressing. With more traffic, new facilities were needed. The leaders of the railroad industry, therefore, were those who were skilled in the raising of capital funds. They were not necessarily efficient railroad operators. The techniques of railroad operation and administration were becoming standardized and the supply of technicians was increasing. They could be secured at reasonable salaries. It is this broad gap between the adequate supply of railroad operators and the inadequate supply of capital that explains much of the railroad history of the last half of the 19th century. In many crises in the lives of railroad properties, capital could not be secured on any terms. Desperate expedients were adopted to raise small sums. Common stock was difficult to sell, even when offered by successful financial leadership. It was rare for any western road, particularly in the pioneer-construction stage, to be able to sell stock for cash. Cooke (for the Northern Pacific), even with the active support of the Pennsylvania Railroad group, raised only some $200 thousand from stock sales. And this money was soon lost. The business leaders whose activities were essential to success were, therefore, the money raisers. They were usually men with imagination, with a sense of bold strategy, with the ability to foresee remote possibilities in the development of the railroad systems. Their first task was to acquire control of the physical routes, the valleys, the mountain passes, and the large cities where traffic was collected and interchanged between the roads coming from and leading into important areas of production and consumption. The number of these natural facilities was limited. The first struggle of the railroad transcontinental leaders was to secure control of these facilities. Such contests involved the building of new lines and the acquisition of existing lines. In almost all cases the raising of capital was essential. Capital was needed to secure an entrenched position along a transcontinental route. This was the grand objective. This was the main purpose for which funds had to be secured; it was the primary objective of business leadership in the transcontinental industry. Attention in the following chapter is accordingly turned to the fight for control of these limited natural facilities and for the command of capital funds.

Notes for Chapter I

[1] *United States Railroad and Mining Register*, May 8, 1869.
[2] Report No. 778, p. 38, Huntington.
[3] Huntington to Stanford, Jan. 4, 1870, M. M.
[4] Report No. 778, p. 38.
[5] Pac. Ry. Commissions, p. 2394, A. A. Cohen.
[6] Huntington to Hopkins, April 13, 1870, M. M.
[7] Huntington to Crocker, July 26, 1870, M. M.

[8]*Ibid.*, April 13, 1870.

[9]*Ibid.*, Aug. 7, 1870.

[10]Evans, I, 238.

[11]Huntington to Crocker, Dec. 28, 1870. M. M.

[12]*Ibid.*

[13]Joy Papers, Taylor to Joy, Aug. 30, 1870.

[14]For an account of the Blair roads, see the *New York Commercial Advertiser*, Mar. 24, 1871

[15]*Bankers Magazine*, Nov. 1874, 399.

[16]*R. R. Gaz,,* Sept. 10, 1870, quoting President William L. Banning, of the Lake Superior and Mississippi.

[17]*Stockholder*, April 27, 1869, 392.

[18]*Philadelphia Press*, cited in the *United States Railroad & Mining Register*, July 1, 1871.

II

Fight for Position

I N THE struggle to secure and maintain control of transcontinental
railroad routes, speed was essential. Considerations of prudence and
financial safety had to be subordinated and frequently submerged. There
was always a race between the strategic necessity of acquiring control of
main routes, mountain passes, important traffic gateways, and terminals,
on the one hand, and of the heavy capital costs on the other. The plans
were laid out by the business strategists in co-operation with engineers.
These plans, however, could not go far unless they were implemented
by an adequate supply of long-term funds. Managerial successes and
managerial failures were accordingly largely associated with the successes
and failures on the financial battlefront.

In the early 1870's, when the competitive transcontinental rivalries
began to develop, the group that appeared to be assured of success was
headed by capitalists associated with the Pennsylvania Railroad. A
monumental expansion program was carried out between 1869 and 1871
under the joint leadership of Scott and Thomson. The scope of the territorial ambition of this group was truly magnificent. It involved not one
but two transcontinental routes.[1]

The Pennsylvania was a profitable line. It had long paid dividends,
and by 1869 had substantially reduced its debt. With the financial
support of the Pennsylvania group, Scott moved in 1869 to develop a
southern transcontinental route. Between 1869 and 1873 he had served in
many managerial roles, successively as president of the Union Pacific,
as the promoter of a transcontinental railroad along the 32nd Parallel,
and as president of the Atlantic and Pacific—the road promoting a
transcontinental route along the 35th Parallel. The Pennsylvania group,

though not in this case under the leadership of Scott, was also the financial supporter of the northern transcontinental route, then being fashioned under the Cooke leadership.

The western end of the completed transcontinental route in 1870, managed under the Huntington leadership and operating through the corporate instrumentalities of the Central Pacific and the Southern Pacific, had by this time succeeded in seizing control of almost all the strategic routes and terminals in California. The financial destiny of the Huntington properties, however, appeared dim indeed. There was little or no market for the Central Pacific stock; the numerous acquisitions by that road had been financed on a dangerously short-term basis; and the Central Pacific was dependent for a flow of funds largely upon the personal activities of Huntington in New York City. The pooled funds of Huntington and his three major associates were insufficient to meet the pressing needs of the expanding transcontinental system. Huntington himself was worn out by his incessant activities in raising funds. He insisted upon selling out. Press reports called attention to his anxiety and to the heavy floating debts. The northern transcontinental route was also in financial difficulties. This project was too speculative to attract the funds of prudent capitalists and active businessmen. Cooke sold bonds largely, though not entirely, in small amounts. A major effort to place a bond issue in Germany was frustrated by the outbreak of the Franco-Prussian War. The eastern end of the completed transcontinental route, controlled by the Union Pacific, appeared in 1870 to be in the weakest financial position of all. Toward the end of the year its securities broke sharply to extremely low levels and the stock sold as low as $9.00 a share.

The strongest financial group therefore appeared to be the one headed by Scott. Yet this was the very one that met with ignominious failure. The Pennsylvania Railroad had found itself financially overexpanded by the fall of 1873. Many of its security holders, particularly those from England, were the passive type, concerned with the desire to secure a stable return on their investment. They were not the active business type, ready to take risks in return for heavier potential gains. When Scott found himself overexpanded, the Pennsylvania Railroad refused to aid him. While Huntington was able to command the pooled funds of his associates, Scott had to appeal for funds from a reluctant group handicapped by heavy financial losses. Huntington and his group, furthermore, controlled an overwhelming percentage of the Central Pacific stock.

That road by 1873—in the panic days—had developed a solid earning power. These funds flowed to New York to be dispensed by Huntington to meet corporate needs. Scott's transcontinental roads on the other hand were pioneer properties with little or no dividend-paying power.

In the transcontinental strategy, Scott made his first major moves in the Old South. As a financial vehicle for his activities he set up a novel device in the form of the Southern Railway Security Company. This was probably the first holding company in American financial history. It was a company created not to build and operate railroads but to buy securities of railroads for control. The Security Company raised funds through sale of its own stock. Additional means to finance the creation of a southern system were provided by the Pennsylvania Railroad itself. That company from time to time purchased both bonds and stocks, originally acquired by the Security Company. Additional funds, substantial in character, were provided from the personal resources of both Scott and Thomson.

On the eastern seaboard the Pennsylvania Railroad in the fall of 1869 terminated at Philadelphia. From Philadelphia to Baltimore, the Philadelphia, Wilmington and Baltimore Railroad served as a connection between the three cities reflected in its corporate name. The company was well operated, well financed, and independent of both its northern and southern trunk-line connections, respectively the Pennsylvania and the Baltimore and Ohio. The pioneer line between Baltimore and Washington was built by the Baltimore and Ohio. The Pennsylvania management had by 1872 finished a connection between these two rapidly growing areas. Below Washington, the next major railroad center was Richmond. The connection between these two cities was made by an independent road. Eventually both the Pennsylvania and the Baltimore and Ohio came to depend permanently upon that line for the carriage of both goods and passengers between these two centers.

South of Richmond the Pennsylvania group in 1869 initiated a number of moves designed to extend the system into the major centers of the Southeast. The stock interest in some of the southeastern roads were owned by state governments. State credit, usually in the form of bonds, had been used to subsidize railroad construction. In view of the losses incurred by the states in these adventures, there was relatively little difficulty in negotiating purchase and sales agreements. In many cases leases were arranged, thereby reducing the amount of capital needed to acquire control. Only infrequently were mergers—100 per cent stock ownership—needed to secure dominance of traffic routes. Substantial amounts of capital, however, were required to acquire majority stock-ownership.

By 1871 the Pennsylvania group managed to acquire control of two major traffic routes to Atlanta and Augusta via the interior route through Richmond and the Piedmont area. Another route from Washington south along the seaboard to Wilmington, North Carolina, was also acquired before the end of 1871. Three major southern routes from Washington were now part of the Scott-sponsored system. (See Map No. 1). These acquisitions were remarkable both for their speed and sweep. Local public opinion reacted strongly against the corporate invader. In Danville, Virginia, for example, a newspaper denounced the "giant corporation which seems to be extending its iron arms all over the United States; and whose purse is as apparently deep as the sea."[2]

Though the Pennsylvania now had access to the major traffic centers in the Southeast, it did not provide a route to the southeastern communities west of the Alleghenies through western Tennessee and down the Mississippi to New Orleans. From Memphis eastward there were a number of roads whose acquisition would afford control of a substantial part of this route.

By the spring of 1872 the Pennsylvania interests had acquired a route between Memphis and the Tennessee-Virginia boundary at Bristol. The line from Bristol north to a connection with the Pennsylvania system below Richmond was made by a road hostile to Scott and the Pennsylvania Railroad—the Atlantic, Mississippi and Ohio, whose leading personality was General William Malone. Threats of the Pennsylvania group to build an intervening line from Bristol east to Danville did not sway Malone. A heavy investment would have been required to build a duplicate road. This construction was never begun.

Scott had plans for a Little Rock–Memphis line. They were never completed.[3] By this time Scott was running short of cash. Capital for the financing of railroad projects was becoming scarce. Scott accordingly traveled to England in the summer of 1873 to enlist foreign capital. Additional amounts of capital were also needed to finance the construction of the western end of his transcontinental enterprise between New Orleans and southern California.

Scott's program in the Southeast, as far-reaching as it was, was indeed not the major part of his activity. He still had time and energy to continue as vice-president of the Pennsylvania Railroad and to conceive and begin the execution of plans for the western arm of the transcontinental route. These efforts must have called for an almost superhuman flow of energy. Huntington once characterized Scott as a man who turned the day into night and the night into day. There were stories that Scott did business throughout the night, catching his sleep between appointments while sitting in an armchair or resting upon a sofa. Prior to 1870 a number of efforts had been made to promote a railroad route along the 32nd Parallel. These efforts were unsuccessful. Promoters as well as the creditors incurred substantial losses. One early project in the southern transcontinental effort was made by General Fremont of Civil War fame. His road, known as the Memphis, El Paso and Pacific, had left behind it a trail of financial reverses for the investing public. Two other corporations had also built some local mileage in Louisiana and Texas. On the Pacific Coast another company had been promoted to build a road east from San Diego. All these companies had almost ceased construction by the early 1870's. They were unable to secure funds to engage in the speculative enterprises of pioneer railroad construction.

Scott with the backing of the same capitalists who supported him in the Security Company fashioned all these odds and ends into an ambitious corporate venture. The first step was to organize, without fanfare of publicity, the California and Texas Construction Company in June, 1870. Substantial sums, contrary to the usual custom, were forthcoming from its stockholders. The authorized and issued stock was $10 million. Initially only 10 per cent was called for, and it was expected, in accordance with previous experiences of construction companies, that the stockholders would not be asked to contribute any more. In this expectation they were mistaken. By the summer of 1873, 75 per cent of the $10 million had been called for.[4] Instead of securing dividends in bonds and stocks of the railroad company, as they had so confidently expected, they were obliged to make substantial cash contributions to finance construction.

This unexpectedly heavy provision of equity capital provided a desirable protection for the bondholders. Their investments were further protected by sums paid in on the stock of the railroad company. By mid-1873 there had been paid in cash 30 per cent on $2 million of issued stock. The road had also issued two classes of bonds, a 6 per cent bond secured by a first mortgage upon the road and by a lien on the federal land grant,

interest and principal payable in gold; and another 7 per cent bond
secured by a land grant, interest and principal payable in legal-tender
currency. The road's securities were issued to the construction company.
The construction company agreed to advance funds to build and equip
125 miles before getting any bond or stocks of the railroad company.[5]

This was a financial device long in use and designed to enable the
speculative type of investor, whose financial aid was so sorely needed to
finance the building of railroads into new areas, to make a profit not
from the operation of the road but from its construction. The construction
company agreed to build the line for a price payable in the railroad's
stocks and bonds whose *par* and *face* values exceeded the cost of construction. The construction company kept the stock and sold the bonds using
the proceeds to finance construction. It was later liquidated and its
railroad stock was distributed to its own stockholders. Expectations of
the success of this construction company were high. The president
observed that even if the bonds of the railroad were sold at a 50 per
cent discount, the construction company would make more money than
the shareholders would "know what to do with."[6]

The railroad instrumentally set up by Scott to build between the
eastern Texas boundary and San Diego was the Texas and Pacific Railway Company. The new road received some federal land grants, and
the state added a grant of $6 million of bonds, though this was changed
two years later to a land grant. In return for these concessions the Texas
and Pacific agreed to build from Shreveport to San Diego. Time limits
were set for completion of the line. Scott was confident the road would be
finished on time. He said there was "no reason why the entire line shall
not be finished within a period of five years"—the time limit set in the
charter.[7]

These heavy land grants, though potentially valuable, brought in no
current funds with which to pay construction costs. The title to the land
could not be obtained until some construction had been completed. It was
therefore essential for Scott to raise money through private sources. An
initial amount of $1.5 million was used up largely in general expenditures
necessary to secure the corporate charter and to pay off various claims.

Scott began to build simultaneously from east and west. The task of
construction was undertaken by General Grenville M. Dodge, who had
recently completed an assignment as chief engineer of the Union Pacific.
The building by the Texas and Pacific elicited widespread praise.

Organs of public opinion expressed admiration for the speed with which the project was undertaken. To the promoters and the investors in this venture the problems became increasingly formidable. Substantial as were the sums that had already been raised, they were nowhere near sufficient to carry out the ambitions of Scott. Individual personal credit had to be used in order to supplement the funds that had been raised through the credit of the railroad and of the construction company. General Dodge himself raised more than $1 million in Texas. Scott strained his personal resources in securing funds to meet pressing obligations. Finally notes of the construction company were endorsed by Scott, Dodge, and a number of other leading capitalists of eastern Pennsylvania.

While Scott was thus engaged in setting up the Texas and Pacific, he was called upon to assume new responsibilities on the eastern wing of the *central* transcontinental route. By the end of 1871 the affairs of the Union Pacific had reached a stage where a receivership seemed imminent. The company had already encountered a number of financial crises. In the spring of 1869 one critical problem had been solved through the loan of the personal credit of some of its leading directors and stockholders. The company had authorized an issue of Land-Grant Bonds secured by a third mortgage on the property and an Income Bond, interest on which was payable only if earned. Leading directors purchased $10 million of first-mortgage bonds and $10 million of Land-Grants at a price of 85 and 55 respectively; and $10 million of 10 per cent income bonds, together with a substantial stock bonus at 80. The purchasers of these securities then borrowed money through the pledge of these securities as collateral. By the end of 1870 prices had declined to a point which eliminated the margin for the loans. One member of the board was suspended and all the others incurred heavy losses.[8] By December the company had no funds to meet the January coupons on its first-mortgage bonds and some directors urged a default. The road had pledged most of its securities for loans. Its only remaining collateral was a bridge bond with a 10 per cent coupon, on which, according to a board member, it was "almost impossible" to raise any funds.[9] Some funds were eventually raised, with the aid of directors, on short-term notes secured by bridge bonds at 50 cents on the dollar.

In an effort to secure additional financial help an approach was made to Scott, Thomson, and Andrew Carnegie, the latter at the time in the iron and bridge business and an important supplier of the Pennsylvania

Railroad. George W. Pullman, also in the railroad equipment industry and a security holder of the Union Pacific, suggested to Carnegie that Thomson, Scott, and he should undertake the management of the Union Pacific. Scott and Thomson decided to share this responsibility. "I had been solicited twice to take the Presidency of that Road." (referring to the Union Pacific), declared Scott before a Congressional Committee. "It was low in credit; its stock was selling at from $8.00 to $12.00 a share; its income bonds were selling at from $30.00 to $40.00; its land-grant bonds at from $35.00 to $55.00; and it wanted a re-organization. . . . After I accepted it, [the Presidency] . . . the company's stock had run up over 250% above the price at which it stood when I took the Road; its income bonds had appreciated to $65.00 and $75.00, and as much as $80.00, and its land-grant bonds had gone up to $80.00 and $82.00 . ."[10]

Under Scott's leadership the affairs of the Union Pacific improved, operating expenses were reduced, and earnings increased. Those investors and traders who followed Scott's leadership in the affairs of the Union Pacific benefited handsomely. It became clear, however, that the activities of Scott in promoting the southern transcontinental route would develop conflicting interests with those of the Union Pacific. For this and other reasons, Scott retired from the presidency after one year's service. In February of 1872 the Union Pacific management changed hands again. This time control was acquired by a New York group under the lead of Horace F. Clark, son-in-law of Cornelius Vanderbilt and president of the Lake Shore and Michigan Southern—the line connecting Chicago with Vanderbilt's system at Buffalo.

Under Clark's administration the Union Pacific's financial affairs did not improve. At the end of 1872 the company had incurred another large floating debt, and again it found relief from advances by directors of between five and six hundred thousand dollars. Furthermore, the $10 million in Income Bonds were due in 1875 and there was only slight prospect of their redemption at maturity. In January of 1873, meanwhile, all the company's available assets, including its investment in some short roads, city bonds, and telegraph stock, had all been hypothecated.[11] The solution to the Union Pacific financial difficulties came from an unexpected source. The trading and speculative genius of Jay Gould proved adequate, and by 1875, in the midst of the general economic depression, the stock was placed on a dividend basis.

In a surprising move, meanwhile, Scott also accepted the presidency of a road then engaged in building a section of another transcontinental route—the Atlantic and Pacific. At the time Scott assumed its presidency the road had been completed to a small town in Indian Territory (Vinita), approximately four hundred miles from its eastern terminus at Pacific, Missouri. The short connection between Pacific and St. Louis was owned by the Pacific Railroad of Missouri.

Scott thus in the summer of 1873 occupied a position of strategic power in western railroad territory. He was in control of two projected major transcontinental routes—routes that had been under discussion for some two decades. The hopes and dreams of thousands of communities long expressed in political and economic channels were now about to be fulfilled. In less than two years, projects that had lain dormant, even though they had been promoted by successive groups of businessmen, were now about to be realized under Scott's inspiring leadership.

Public opinion reflected the growing power of Scott and the Pennsylvania group, expressing both fear and confidence, depending upon the economic interests involved. The success of Scott would bring more business to Philadelphia and less to New York. To the New York area, accordingly, the moves of Scott were looked upon with a critical eye. "The Pennsylvania Napoleon," observed a leading New York daily, "has been ambitious to take possession of the republic under a nine hundred and ninety-nine years' lease."[12] Another New York daily, expressive of the views of that city's commercial interests, referred to the Pennsylvania Railroad as the "Boa Constrictor." If New York, Pennsylvania, Ohio, and states beyond the Mississippi River to California were willing to surrender their railroad to the control of "one railway potentate," then perhaps New York should not object. Furthermore, this paper continued, the "tremendous energy and comprehensive forecast gives him [Scott] triumphs which bid fair to place him and the Pennsylvania Railroad beyond any controlling power."[13]

In Philadelphia, however, the point of view was different. A leading organ of the railroad industry in that area referred to Scott as ". . . the greatest living representative of railroad interests."[14] And a Philadelphia daily quoted with approval an observation of a southern paper which referred to the company of capitalists in which Scott was executive officer and Thomson president as "the most powerful and effective organization of its kind in existence. It seeks, and is rapidly obtaining, control of the entire railroad system of the country. . . ."[15]

Scott himself was optimistic. He assured the public that the board of directors was as one with him in the confident belief that the transcontinental line of the Texas and Pacific would be finished within five years. This consummation would assure the road of valuable land grants. It is true additional funds were needed to pay for these projects, but Scott entertained no doubts of his ability to raise these funds.

Scott's leadership of the group of eastern capitalists was paralleled by an equally able leadership in the Far West, centering in California. There Huntington had, in conjunction with three major associates, Stanford, Hopkins, and Crocker—known collectively as the Big Four— completed by the summer of 1869 the western wing of the Union Pacific– Central Pacific route. By the end of the year the original Ogden-Sacramento line was extended by acquisition and minor construction to San Francisco. Huntington, like Scott, was characterized by a sense of driving and untiring energy. His leadership in his specialized field of raising capital and carrying heavy financial responsibilities was virtually unchallenged. His associates, who owned substantial blocks of the various roads comprising the growing transcontinental route, gave Huntington a blank check to negotiate, borrow, lend, deposit and withdraw collateral, and in general execute the negotiations essential to the raising of an adequate supply of capital.

Huntington, unlike Scott, had a controlling stock interest in the major properties in his growing railroad empire. Together with his three associates, who generally gave him authority to handle financial and corporate matters, he controlled railroad properties almost with no minority interest. Scott, on the other hand, was in no position to control the financial policies of the Pennsylvania Railroad, nor could he spend unlimited funds on the basis of a blank-check authority given him by his financial followers. He could not singly command, as did Huntington, the united support of the constituent properties within his corporate system. Neither could he use the resources of the profitable part of the system for the purpose of aiding the less profitable.

In the dreary days in the fall of 1873 and in the early months of 1874 the financial strength of the Pennsylvania Railroad was denied him. While Huntington's associates continued to support him in these critical months, Scott's followers withdrew their support. The cautious and conservative stockholding interests of the Pennsylvania Railroad were appalled by the heavy responsibilities incurred by management in the Southeast.

They were thunderstruck at the heavy losses, marketwise, in the securities of those same southeastern roads. In many cases, literally no bids appeared for stock which had cost the Pennsylvania group sums in the millions. Scott, personally, incurred heavy losses from his investments in the Security Company. In that property, declared Scott in the mid-1870's, "I am sorry to say, I have over $400,000 today that I would like to sell at 10 cents on the dollar."[16] But in the stock market there were no bids. Heavy losses were also inflicted upon the holders of the Texas and Pacific and of the controlling construction company. The latter had a heavy floating debt which could not be paid at maturity. The stock of the Texas and Pacific, held by the Construction Company, could not be sold. There were no market bids. The endorsers of the paper of the Construction Company, including Scott, were confronted with devastating losses. Scott was saved from bankruptcy by his business associates.

In the early 1870's, in the flush days of the business boom, it seemed, however, that greater financial power rested with Scott rather than with Huntington. Scott was supported by the Pennsylvania Railroad—a property with an earnings and financial record equalled by almost no other road. Huntington had no such solid financial support. His fortune consisted largely of common stock in the Central Pacific. There was in 1869–1870 no market for that stock.[17] The net earnings of the road, however, were substantial and were expanding, but the property had incurred heavy short-term obligations. It had acquired almost every railroad in California, but the monopoly had been achieved at a high cost. Furthermore, there were no powerful banking groups supporting the Huntington empire. A relatively small eastern banking house—Fisk and Hatch— had brought out the Central Pacific bonds. Later a number of California capitalists also made short-term loans. The Pennsylvania on the other hand was financed by Drexel and Company of Philadelphia—a well-established house with a reputation for solidity and integrity. The Pennsylvania also had the support of substantial English investors.

Yet in the transcontinental area, the Pennsylvania group failed and the Huntington group succeeded. The success of the latter flowed from a closely knit personal leadership and a consistent managerial policy. That policy, designed originally to finance the completion of the Central Pacific transcontinental route, was sufficiently flexible to embrace the problems growing out of the acquisition of many local California roads.

By 1870 most of the local California lines had run out of funds. Hunting-ton used cash and corporate credit, as well as his personal credit, to finance their purchase. By early 1871 every property in California, other than a short line in the Los Angeles area and that of the California Pacific, had been added to the Huntington system. The California Pacific controlled the short line with easy grades between Sacramento and Oakland. Early in 1871 a plan for the extension of its property east to Ogden, with the support of a strong group of capitalists was proposed. At Ogden, the road would connect with the Union Pacific, thereby forming a rival transcontinental route. It also laid plans for the building of an extension north to Oregon to secure an opening to the growing Pacific Northwest. Though Huntington believed these plans would not be carried out, it nevertheless seemed advisable to buy control. If this were impossible he "would sink all we have made in our other roads so that we beat them in the end."[18] By July of 1871, through the purchase of stock by Huntington and his associates and by a bit of skillful corporate maneuvering, the California Pacific also fell under the domination of the Huntington system.

During the 1860's when the Central Pacific route was under construc-tion, steps were taken in California to set up a southern transcontinental route. A line beginning at San Francisco was to move south and east to the Colorado River. There it was to meet Scott's Texas and Pacific. This road—the Southern Pacific (in California)—had done some con-struction in the 1860's. By 1870 it had been added to the Huntington system, and Huntington was largely responsible for its acquisition. "I did the dickering," said Huntington many years later, "and paid for it partly in money and partly in credit." In the spring of 1871 the road was consolidated with a number of others into a newly incorporated enter-prise—the Southern Pacific Railroad Company.

Meanwhile, in 1870 the consolidation of the Ogden-Sacramento line with a number of acquired roads led to a new and enlarged Central Pacific. The Huntington group thus consisted largely of two corporate vehicles the control of which meant an almost complete monopoly of railroad through lines, branch lines, and terminal facilities in California. One—the Central Pacific—was publicly controlled by the Huntington group, with Stanford and Huntington as president and vice-president respectively. Care was taken, however, to preserve in the public eye the corporate independence of the Southern Pacific. Although the Big Four controlled its stock, its officers were not—publicly—associated with the Huntington group. Huntington was formulating its policies and raising the funds essential to its growth; he was nevertheless not an executive official. Publicly, he acted only as its financial agent in New York City.

Curious as it may seem to the cursory observer, at the peak of his corporate achievements in the early 1870's, Huntington fell into a mood of deep pessimism. "I know no reason," he wrote in 1871, "why I should wear myself out as I am doing for the sake of getting more money, even if the amount should be untold millions, and have made up my mind to sell if I do not realize above 50% for my stock."[19] Both the Central Pacific and the Southern Pacific acquisitions had required the continual borrowing of large sums. The cash raised from the first-mortgage bonds and the government bonds was insufficient, and the balance was secured through loans from a construction company—the Contract and Finance Company. One loan of the construction company to the Central Pacific was eventually repaid in 1871 with latter's land-grant bonds. And these bonds Huntington sold in New York City. Temporary loans were made there at an annual rate of 10 per cent. Either in 1871 or early in 1872 Huntington borrowed from San Francisco capitalists on call loans—loans payable on demand—to the extent of $2.5 million. A part of this sum was used also to pay interest on Central Pacific bonds. The road in 1870 had incurred heavy floating debts and Huntington had encountered obstacles in his efforts to meet these pressing liabilities.

He was ready to sell out. "The more I think of it," he wrote in August, 1872, "I am inclined to the opinion that we had better close out all our R. R. interest. . . ."[20] By that time long-term capital funds were growing scarce. The scarcity lasted for many months, and long before it became better a financial panic intervened. Like Scott, Huntington found it progressively more difficult to raise sums in the capital market.

Huntington by this time had incurred another financial obligation, ostensibly not connected with the formation of a transcontinental route. In Virginia the Civil War had blocked the efforts of the state to complete a railroad between the seaboard and the Ohio River. Before the war a line had been built from Richmond to Covington. The beginning of an extension from Covington west had also been made. This extension had been paid for by about $3.5 million of public funds. In 1866 the states of Virginia and West Virginia appointed commissioners to interest private capital in the completion of this line. It was proposed to donate the property west of Covington to any group agreeing to complete the road to the Ohio River. The following year the two states passed legislation to join the two companies, one east and the other west of Covington, into a new company under the name of the Chesapeake and Ohio. Efforts were made to raise funds from the cities and counties through which the consolidated road operated. In the fall of 1867 it appeared, at least to one local railroad organ, "as if the work would be completed by capital raised exclusively" in the state of Virginia.[21] Meanwhile valuable concessions were offered to the new road to build the Ohio River line. Efforts to raise funds in this country and abroad failed.

In the spring of 1869 the officials of the Chesapeake and Ohio asked Huntington to take an interest in the property. After six months' consideration Huntington and a group of capitalists assumed the responsibility of raising the funds and of participating in the road's management. That financial plan turned control over to Huntington and his associates, the latter including William H. Aspinwall, long noted for his participation in numerous financial ventures, including the successful Pacific Mail Steamship; Harvey Fisk and A. S. Hatch, partners in the banking house of Fisk and Hatch which had sold the bonds of the Union Pacific and of the Central Pacific railroads; W. B. Hatch, the son of the junior partner of this house; and A. A. Low, a capitalist from New York.

Success thus culminated a three-year effort to raise the necessary capital to fulfill the dream of a generation. The leadership of Huntington was widely acclaimed in the territory to be served by the new line. While Huntington was denounced on the Pacific Coast for his seizure of a monopoly and for his exaction of high rates from local shippers, he was commended in extravagant language for his efforts on the eastern seaboard. "If enterprise, the masterly control of means and force, and a wonderful rapidity of railroad construction entitle a man to wear the crown of railroad king," wrote a newspaper in Richmond, Virginia, "that crown belongs to somebody connected with the Chesapeake and Ohio Railroad; but it belongs to a man remarkable alike for his reticence and modesty. That man is Mr. Huntington. . . ."[22]

Under Huntington's leadership plans were laid out and soon carried into execution to raise $15 million to complete construction. The funds were raised through an issue of first-mortgage 6 per cent bonds. The bonds were offered by Fisk and Hatch, whose partners were on the road's board. The bankers advertised their wares in the confident language characteristic of a period of expansion. The Chesapeake and Ohio was described as "the most important and substantial Railroad enterprise now in progress in this country."[23] The bond offering met a good response. Expressions of opinion in leading eastern organs were optimistic. In June, 1873, shortly before the panic, the road's 6 per cent bonds sold above par.

The Ohio was reached early in 1873. Communication thereby was made between the seaboard and some twelve thousand miles of navigation on the Ohio, Mississippi, and adjoining internal waterways. The Ohio River extension, however, did not make railroad connections with the major producing and marketing centers in the west, such as Cincinnati and Louisville. Louisville by this time had railroad connections with Memphis and St. Louis. A line to Louisville therefore would make Richmond the eastern end of a through route to the west. Local projects with substantial public funds had already made some progress in achieving this objective. Between Louisville and Lexington a railroad known as the Louisville, Cincinnati and Lexington had been built. A further extension had been provided by another small company. That road was built a short piece of mileage from Lexington to Mount Sterling, Kentucky. From that point to the Ohio River, near the western terminus of the newly completed Chesapeake and Ohio, was a gap of 88 miles. Huntington decided to acquire control of both these small roads. By the end of 1871 he had bought enough stock in both to control their corporate policies. The Chesapeake and Ohio advanced $2.6 million, and this amount, together with $950 thousand raised by public subscriptions, was considered sufficient to finance the building of a line to the Ohio.[24]

Thus by the summer of that year, under Huntington's leadership plans had been projected and funds raised to build a through line from Richmond to Cincinnati and Louisville and through those points beyond to the west. Virginia looked forward to competing for western business with Baltimore, Philadelphia, and New York. Though on grounds of the existing channels of trade and commerce it was questionable whether a strong competitive route via Richmond could be set up, there was hope that in the course of time some of the western traffic, particularly cotton from Memphis, would move over the new route.

Though the line to the Ohio River was completed, the finances of the

Chesapeake and Ohio were strained. The panic was followed by a default on this road's bonds and a consequent receivership.

The financial load upon Huntington, so it appeared to him as early as 1870, was more than he could bear. From there on through the panic days in the fall of 1873, Huntington sought rest from business responsibilities. He must sell; his search for buyers was unceasing. He put both Central Pacific and Southern Pacific on the market. But he proposed no bargains. His trading interests left no room for prices sufficiently low to lure the reluctant buyer. In the summer of 1870 Huntington made his first approach. Financially, the strongest link in the transcontinental line from Chicago west appeared to be the Rock Island–Northwestern properties under the leadership of Tracy. Huntington told Tracy he wanted to get out of the railroad business. His terms were stiff—$10 million in cash for an equal par value of Central Pacific stock, plus 7 per cent guaranteed by the consolidated system on an additional $40 million of the stock. As an alternative, he would take bonds of the consolidated line instead of cash. The consolidation would presumably embrace the Rock Island–Northwestern–Union Pacific–Central Pacific, though Huntington looked forward also to a New York–San Francisco line.[25]

Nothing came of this, but Huntington remained watchful. He soon perceived another chance. In January, 1871, it appeared to him that Scott was about to become president of the Union Pacific. If the Pennsylvania guaranteed a return on the Central Pacific stock, he would give Scott $5 million of the stock. Huntington knew nothing of the views of those interested in the Pennsylvania. "But I know *Tom Scott*," he wrote.[26]

Again no success; but Huntington pushed on. By November, he was willing to sell the Central Pacific stock at fifty. "I wish to get out of the pressure of business," he said.[27]

Financial pressure meanwhile continued to mount. By September of 1872, two California capitalists had become interested in the purchase of the Southern Pacific. Huntington still wanted to sell. "I certainly mean business,"[28] he informed Hopkins. Negotiations continued until the spring of 1873. By March they had collapsed. The legal position of the stock remained cloudy; there was fear of a heavy personal liability on the stocks of the Central and Southern Pacific. For this reason, asserted Huntington in April, 1873, the Central Pacific stock "cannot be sold in this market where it is known for 25 cents per barrel."[29] Hope for a sale of his properties now came from a fresh source. Scott early in 1872 had retired from the presidency of the Union Pacific. By late 1872 he was driving forward with his southern transcontinental route. In December Huntington was in high hopes of making a trade with Scott. "It is just possible," he informed Hopkins, "that I may make a sale of S. P. and if so it may be done almost any day. . . ."[30]

By January a trade seemed imminent. Scott said he would pay $16 million and Huntington wrote Hopkins that he would sell at that price.[31] A month later he was still hopeful. "I am doing all I can to close the trade with Scott."[32]

While these negotiations dragged on, prospects for the sale of the Central Pacific brightened. Huntington was anxious to sell. The government's association with the road, he declared, "will always plague us"; a number of recent acquisitions would earn no money for some time; and the Central Pacific rails were wearing out.[33] A buyer for the Central Pacific now appeared certain. Alfred A. Cohen, an attorney closely associated with Huntington in many legal and business transactions, had since 1870 been discussing the purchase of the stock. He was the agent of a number of capitalists. Huntington offered to sell four-fifths of the Central Pacific stock at 80.[34] Discussions continued over the following four months. By June, a leading railroad journal informed its readers that "the sale of the interest of Huntington and Hopkins in the Central Pacific Railroad is . . . nearly consummated. . . ."[35]

Meanwhile, financial problems became more critical. In March, Huntington blanched before the necessity of paying "a fearful amount" of $5.5 million on July 1. Throughout the spring months he grew increasingly desperate. On March 17 he wrote; "Unless I get some sleep soon I shall break in some way"; and two days later he wrote in an even more despairing mood: "If something isn't done soon we shall all go to hell together." And a few days later he learned that Scott was sharing his financial anxieties. Scott, he wrote on March 26th, was "hard up, borrowing heavily."[36]

In these painful months Huntington had an asset denied to Scott. He had a completed railroad system behind him—the Central Pacific. And apparently unknown to him, Huntington also had one of those financial windfalls that so often revolutionize the earning and financial strength of many a business enterprise. Huntington was so involved in his efforts to raise new sums and pay off pressing obligations that he was probably unaware of the traffic movements on the Central Pacific. He repeatedly stressed that traffic problems were not his and that on such matters he respected the views of traffic officers. The growing earnings of the road had been used to expand and improve the property. In the best traditions of financial orthodoxy all the earnings had been used to acquire productive properties, pay for equipment and new terminals, improve the standard of service, and reduce operating costs. In March of 1873 a group of pioneering businessmen, after expending nearly a quarter of a million dollars on mining exploration, finally located a rich outpouring of silver ore. The ore produced a heavy volume of traffic over the Central Pacific—the single trunk line connection with a small railroad that originated near the newly found ore. The traffic, furthermore was carried at high rates. In addition, 1873 produced a heavy increase in the wheat crop.

Accordingly, in the midst of the panic wave in September, 1873, Hopkins wired Huntington the welcome news that the Central Pacific had declared a dividend on its stock.

Huntington and Scott were both in serious financial trouble in the fall of 1873. Huntington's financial load was heavier than Scott's though each was heavy enough to destroy either's personal fortune. Huntington, however, had the advantage of the financial strength and earnings of the Central Pacific. Scott could not control the financial policies of the Pennsylvania as could Huntington those of the Central Pacific. And herein lay the difference between Scott's failure and Huntington's victory.

As the summer months passed, the prospects for the sale of the two roads diminished. Capital funds grew even more scarce. In the summer of 1873 bills of sale were drafted for the Central and the Southern Pacific. The sale of the Southern Pacific to Scott would have given the Texas and Pacific "entry into San Francisco via Yuma and Los Angeles, on the route [later] occupied by the completed Southern Pacific . . . nothing but the failure of Texas Pacific [*sic*] to meet the required payments prevented its passing into their hands," wrote Huntington to a Congressional source early in 1879.[37] Both sales failed. The harrowing experiences in the panic days of the fall put fresh vigor and iron into Huntington's character. His desire to sell dimmed and disappeared. For the next quarter of a century he drove himself and his associates to scale ever greater heights. And the Southern Pacific system remains as a living symbol of these exertions.

At the same time, on the northern transcontinental route the Northern

Pacific, under the Cooke leadership, continued the construction of its line. On the eastern end its Duluth connections was made by the Lake Superior and Mississippi. This road had been built upon the basis of optimistic prospects. It had been expected that a large volume of traffic, particularly wheat, would be shipped by steamer from Duluth to the East. These prospects were destroyed, however, by the competitive rate-cutting between this road and the St. Paul-Chicago lines. Cooke's banking house meanwhile had invested more than $2 million in the Lake Superior and Mississippi project. Presumably in order to relieve the pressure on the Cooke firm, the Northern Pacific in 1872 leased that road, thereby assuming its financial obligations.

Another form of competition led the Northern Pacific into another improvident step. A Minnesota railroad, the St. Paul and Pacific, had completed by 1872 an extension from St. Paul to the Mississippi River; it had also built other lines, including part of a projected line to the Canadian boundary. To finance this extension, a $15 million bond issue was sold, largely to Dutch investors. The promoters of this property asked for additional land grants down the Red River and across the Dakota territory. This was an interesting and successful squeeze play exerted upon Cooke and the Northern Pacific. Cooke was discouraged. "It would never do for that road to have the line down the Red River to Pembina," he asserted.[38] To remove this competition, to secure access to the Twin Cities, and to acquire a strong position in the traffic of Minnesota and Dakota territory, the Northern Pacific bought control of the St. Paul and Pacific. Almost no investigation was made into the merits of the acquisition. The road was heavily bonded. Most of the proceeds had been used on the construction of an uncompleted property still unable to earn its expenses, while part of the remainder, under a most charitable interpretation of the recorded facts, had been imprudently used. Within two years after the purchase, the Northern Pacific poured more than a million dollars into the road. The interest on its bonds was soon passed. An effort was made to sell the stock back to the original buyers in exchange for a million dollars of the road's bonds and its overdue coupons. Negotiations collapsed on details.[39]

On the far western end of the projected transcontinental route in Washington, the Northern Pacific, in another effort to secure a strategic location, purchased three-quarters of the stock of the Oregon Steam Navigation, a company owning steamship lines along the coast and on the Columbia River together with some short railroads in the Columbia River Valley. For this acquisition the Northern Pacific agreed to pay one-half in its bonds at 90, and the other half in cash over a nine-month period.

While the Northern Pacific was assuming these heavy obligations it encountered great difficulty in raising funds. The company had good public relations. Congressional opinion had changed from criticism to commendation. A House of Representatives' committee on Pacific Railroads for example, declared that the road was in sound condition, that it had been built on the basis of competitive bidding, and that no company officer had been pecuniarily interested in construction contracts or in the purchase of materials and supplies. The report credited the president with the observation that the railroad's bonds were "perfect security."[40] The sale of bonds, however, lagged, and from time to time the Cooke firm made heavy advances. These were speculative loans, made by a conservative firm. The funds were obtained from deposits, mostly demand deposits. Such funds, payable on demand, were used to finance an uncompleted property—the kind of loan that normally calls for the use of speculative-risk capital. By the spring of 1873 the sale of bonds had dropped to low levels. Directors of the Northern Pacific also made personal advances. The shortage of long-term capital continued. Cooke faced by this capital shortage resorted, in April, 1873, to a heroic move. He organized a new syndicate to sell an additional $9 million of Northern Pacific bonds at 83, together with a 50 per cent stock bonus. The agents' commissions were also increased. The effort failed. Only a relatively small amount of new funds were raised.

By the summer months of 1873, accordingly, all the transcontinental projects were confronted with pressing financial problems. Neither Cooke, Scott, nor Huntington could raise the sums required to carry out their plans. The Atlantic and Pacific had ceased its building program early in 1872. It had moreover increased its financial burden by a lease of the Pacific Railway of Missouri, thereby supplying an entrance into St. Louis. Scott had gone to Europe with the expectation of raising funds; Cooke was exhausting his last lines of credit by using depositors' money to supply railroad needs; and Huntington was desperately seeking relief from his burdens through a vain effort to sell his property to some willing buyer. The Union Pacific's promoters had lost heavily. The stock traded in large volume at low prices. Default was averted by expensive financing

involving the sale of high-interest-bearing bonds at steep discounts and by
utilizing the personal credit of its directors. The panic in September produced a desperate financial situation for all the leaders and their financial
following. In the crisis the Scott group, the strongest in the transcontinental area, collapsed. Scott himself lingered on through the remaining
years of the 1870's. He finally vanished from the transcontinental stage
in 1879. Cooke disappeared promptly after the panic. The original
backers of the Union Pacific had retreated earlier. Huntington, however,
contrary to public expectations, retained his grip over his properties.
He soon changed his ideas about the sale of his control. From his near
failure to meet his obligations in the panic months of 1873 he seemed to
gather extra energy. Of all the transcontinental railroad men of the early
1870's he alone survived.

Notes for Chapter II

[1]Details on the formation and dissolution of these routes are presented later in this chapter.
[2]*Danville Times*, cited in the *United States Railroad & Mining Register*, Sept. 23, 1871.
[3]For details on these negotiations see The Disposal of the Subsidies Granted Certain Railroad Companies, Miscellaneous Documents, Report No. 176, Part I, House of Representatives,
44th Congress, 1st Session, 1876, pp. 54-55; and *R.R. Gaz.*, September 27, 1873, p. 398.
[4]*R. R. Gaz.*, Aug. 23, 1873, p. 345.
[5]*The Road*, Oct. 1, 1875, p. 257.
[6]*Ibid*, Feb. 15, 1876, p. 26.
[7]*Am. R. R. Journal*, June 7, 1873, p. 712.
[8]*Chron.* Jan. 14, 1871, p. 50; Dec. 31, 1870, p. 849.
[9]*Credit Mobilier*, p. 537.
[10]The Disposal of the Subsidies Granted Certain Railroad Companies, Miscellaneous
Documents, Report No. 176, Part I, House of Representatives, 44th Congress, 1st Session,
1876, p. 48, Scott. Carnegie's connection with this incident is noted in *Ibid*, p. 69.
[11]*Credit Mobilier*, p. 441, Clark.
[12]*New York Herald*, March 11, 1872.
[13]*New York Commercial Advertiser*, Nov. 8, 1871.
[14]*The United States Railroad & Mining Register*, July 20, 1872.
[15]*Memphis Avalanche*, cited in *Philadelphia North American*, Jan. 1, 1872.
[16]The Disposal of the Subsidies Granted Certain Railroad Companies, Miscellaneous
Documents No. 176, Part I, House of Representatives, 44th Congress, 1st Session, 1876, p. 55,
Scott.
[17]Pac. Ry. Commission, p. 2979, William C. Brown, accountant for the Big Four.
[18]Huntington to Hopkins, May 2, 1871, M. M.
[19]*Southern Pacific*, p. 94.
[20]*Ibid.*, p. 94.
[21]*Railroad Record*, Oct. 10, 1867, p. 395.
[22]*Richmond Dispatch*, cited in *Am. R. R. Journal*, Feb. 11, 1871, p. 171.
[23]The bond advertisement appeared in the *New York Commercial Advertiser*, Feb. 17, 1870.

[24]These facts on public and private subscription are based on accounts in the *Am. R. R. Journal*, June 3, 1871, p. 622, and Jan. 20, 1872, p. 73.

[25]Huntington to Stanford, Aug. 30, 1870, M. M.

[26]Huntington to Hopkins, Jan. 20, 1871, M. M.

[27]Huntington to Stanford, Nov. 20, 1871, M. M.

[28]*Southern Pacific*, p. 95.

[29]Huntington to Hopkins, April 16, 1873, M. M.

[30]*Southern Pacific*, p. 95.

[31]Huntington to Hopkins, Jan. 17, 1873, M. M.

[32]*Ibid.*, Feb. 15, 1873.

[33]Huntington to Stanford, Feb. 28, 1873, M. M.

[34]*Ibid.*, Feb. 19, 1873.

[35]*R. R. Gaz.*, June 28, 1873, p. 265.

[36]The three quotations are from *Southern Pacific*, p. 55.

[37]Letter, Huntington to H. W. Blair, House of Representatives, Jan 4., 1879, in *Congressional Record*, 45th Congress, 3rd Session, VIII, Part III, appendix 1879, p. 20.

[38]Larson, p. 337.

[39]Northern Pacific Archives, G. W. Oaks to E. D. Litchfield, June 13, 1873; July 12, 1873.

[40]Miscellaneous Document No. 228, House of Representatives, 42nd Congress, 2nd Session June 3, 1872, p. 14.

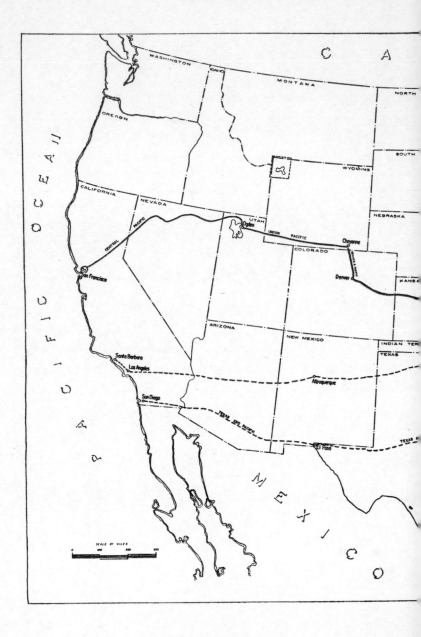

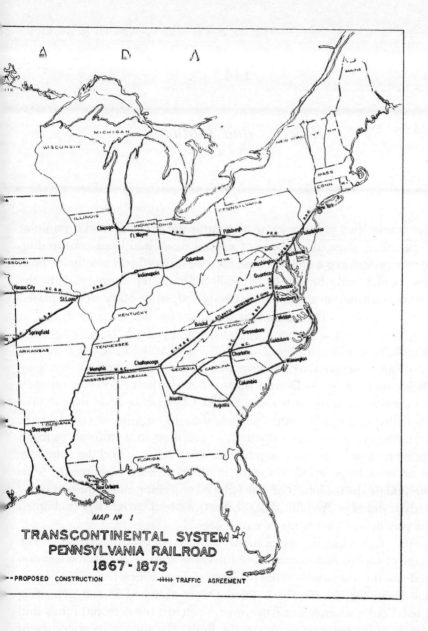

MAP Nº 1

TRANSCONTINENTAL SYSTEM
PENNSYLVANIA RAILROAD
1867-1873

--PROPOSED CONSTRUCTION   ++++ TRAFFIC AGREEMENT

39

III

Reverses and Failures

F OR ALMOST two years prior to the outbreak of the financial panic of September, 1873, the supply of capital funds had been contracting. Funds for capital expansion became increasingly difficult to obtain, both in this country and abroad. In the railroad industry many roads in the process of construction could not be completed, while other contemplated projects languished. The volume of traffic meanwhile expanded, and in some quarters critical equipment shortages appeared. In Chicago, the Burlington general superintendent, informed a harassed shipper that "the Roads from Chicago East are crowded with freight and will not take through cars from us. At Detroit there are more than 1,000 cars on each side of the river waiting for transfer."[1] The Chesapeake and Ohio, to take another illustration, had more business than its equipment could carry. "The traffic . . . is already sufficient," according to a railroad journal, "to bring into use every car, engine and side track . . ., and the company have ordered large reinforcements to their present equipment."[2] To accommodate the business, the road placed orders for more equipment for immediate delivery. An official of the Northwestern late in 1871 exclaimed to the president, "Our want is 'cars—cars.' "[3]

Funds to provide the equipment were, however, inadequate. The shortage of capital to accommodate the rising volume of business characterized all the transcontinental railroads. The difficulties of Cooke in raising funds for the Northern Pacific were sketched in the preceding chapter. Cooke, an inveterate optimist, stretched his personal funds and the funds of his banking house to the limit. His success in government securities blinded him to the dangers arising from his efforts to raise unlimited sums. One of his partners declared that Cooke never believed

40

that his firm could fail for such a "small" sum as $6 million to $8 million. "Mr. Cooke looked upon $8,000,000.00 as a small amount, a mere bagatelle."[4]

The fledgling transcontinental route along the 35th Parallel—the Atlantic and Pacific—had by 1872 already ceased construction. In August, 1873, Scott was elected president. Scott meanwhile was borrowing for capital purposes on a short-term basis—a dangerous procedure. In March he borrowed $1 million from the Drexel banking house: another party offered a three-months' loan of $500 thousand at a monthly 2 per cent interest rate, secured by Pennsylvania Railroad stock.[5] In the summer Scott left for Europe in search of funds. On the Union Pacific the shortage of capital that had handicapped the property since 1867 continued through the succeeding years.

Still another road, later to attain transcontinental status, also encountered financial reverses. Beginning with the summer of 1872 this road, a local enterprise in eastern Kansas, took on a burst of energy. The Atchison was equipped with a charter granting it special privileges in exchange for construction by March, 1873, to the Kansas-Colorado boundary. The line was built rapidly and was completed three months ahead of time. The supply of long-term funds was exhausted. In this crisis, the management was changed, and leadership was taken over by Thomas E. Nickerson. First as vice-president in May of 1873 and next year as president, an office which he held for six additional years, he transformed the Atchison from a local property into a transcontinental line. His first responsibility was to solve the financial crisis. This he accomplished through an arrangement with the bondholders, who were induced to buy a new bond issue to pay off the floating debt.

The most dramatic manifestation of the shortage of capital is, however, furnished by the experiences of Huntington. A record is available of the problems antedating the panic, in the form of extensive correspondence between Huntington, as the financial agent of the Central Pacific in New York, and his California associates. As early as April, 1872, Huntington was already urging his associates to go slow "unless you know where the money is coming from. I certainly do not." In August he declared that the outlook for the sale of bonds of uncompleted railroads was poor and that six roads had defaulted. Nothing could be done, he informed an associate, in selling railroad bonds to German investors. It was therefore essential to reduce expenses and to use earnings to pay interest and bills that could not be postponed, until the Central Pacific stock and the Southern Pacific bonds could be marketed. By November it seemed to Huntington "impossible to borrow," except on governments.[6] The Central Pacific owed the firm of Fisk and Hatch more than $1.8 million. Huntington asked Hopkins to induce Crocker and Stanford to borrow money for the January interest, but cautioned Hopkins not to let them know that the loan was to be used for this purpose. A few weeks later Hopkins informed Huntington of his failure. The funds needed were, however, borrowed in California, for on January 3, 1873, Huntington acknowledged a letter from Hopkins to the effect that the road was then in debt to a California bank to the amount of $1,173,000. Huntington remained gloomy. "I have never seen so blue a time for money," he wrote in March. "Something must be done, and that at once."[7] Yet, he emphasized a few weeks later, the group had no stock-exchange collateral. "How can we expect to borrow on collaterals that would bring next to nothing on a forced sale?"[8]

These facts were not then matters of public knowledge. He was therefore obliged to speak cautiously before congressional committees. He had to use careful language to give the facts without necessarily disclosing the truth. In February, 1873, he was asked by a member of a committee whether the Central Pacific had a floating debt. "We have a little floating debt; and then we have $1,500,000 of California and Oregon bonds, or Central Pacific bonds on that branch," was Huntington's reply.[9]

The bonds listed by Huntington could not be sold. Neither could they be hypothecated. In April, Huntington wrote that money had never been so scarce. "God only knows how the funds could be raised," was a phrase, with numerous variations, that dominated his correspondence in the months of 1872–1873. By this time Huntington had incurred heavy liabilities. He had bought up almost all the California railroads; he had made many terminal improvements; he was engaged in a number of construction programs. His drive to create a California railroad monopoly filled his mind and took up his days and nights. By the fall of 1872 his debts began to overwhelm him. He paid only slight attention to operating and traffic details. His problems were financial—and formidable. As if to intensify his troubles, Huntington in 1871 bought the Crocker interests on terms which called for payment of one-half in two years and the other half in three years.

Huntington relied in part upon earnings of the Central Pacific to meet his debts. And these earnings were growing. Net after interest rose from

$1,507,100 in 1869 to $3,911,300 in 1872.[10] He could call further upon railroad bonds of the small roads he was acquiring and building. Although these had a poor market they might be used as collateral, and in this respect Huntington approached the rank of genius. His ability to borrow was unique. And this ability he utilized almost to the end of his business career. From time to time he made up his mind to pay his debts and be done with borrowing. "I am bound to get out of debt in the next months," he wrote in January, 1873, "if I get out of everything else in doing it. . . ."[11] Huntington repeated this declaration upon numerous occasions. His will was stronger than his deed—and his debts continued to multiply.

To pay the increasing debts Huntington could also utilize the stock of the Central Pacific. This asset appeared indeed to be the very bastion of his fortune, and also that of his associates. And, in the long run it proved to be just that. But in 1872–1873 the stock was not on the market; it had no collateral value. Huntington recognized that the failure to make such a market was a mistake. Carrying $50 million of stock for years, "in such a way that it is of no use to us, I think, is a thing never done before," he wrote early in 1872.[12]

By September, as the debt mounted and the means of payment dwindled, Huntington ordered drastic economies in railroad operations. Wherever possible, he informed Stanford, expenses must be eliminated and earnings used to pay interest and bills that could not be put off—until the road's stock or the Southern Pacific bonds could be marketed.[13]

As the January deadline for the heavy interest payments approached, financial problems grew even more critical. To Fisk and Hatch—the loyal banking associate of the Central Pacific and the Chesapeake and Ohio—there was due a debt of $1.8 million. Fisk and Hatch had in turn borrowed from Brown Brothers another banking firm. In November Huntington tried to borrow from Fisk and Hatch; the latter sought accommodation from Brown. No help was forthcoming. Huntington was desperate, but his ingenuity again rescued him. What he could not do in New York he believed Hopkins could do in California. He therefore asked Hopkins to ask other capitalists—business friends of Huntington—to borrow one, two, or three hundred thousand dollars at a time, allegedly to pay for iron for the Southern Pacific. If Southern Pacific paper was unacceptable, he was to offer them Central Pacific paper. He stressed to Hopkins that the latter had collateral for the California market, even though such collateral could not be used in New York.[14]

The January, 1873, crisis was surmounted. This very success assured an even more severe crisis. The floating debt was higher than ever. Short-term loans were held by capitalists and banks in California, by Fisk and Hatch, by Speyer and Company and by others in New York and elsewhere. "Something must be done at *once*," reiterated Huntington in March.[15] The pressure must have been exceptionally severe: On one occasion that month he complained that he had not slept for seventy-two hours. As one method of raising funds, he accelerated negotiations for the sale of the Central Pacific and Southern Pacific. Cohen was willing to buy the Central Pacific, but he would not agree to take care of some stockholders' suits.[16] Huntington also talked with Scott about the sale of the Southern Pacific. He expected Scott to call at his office in March. Then, said Huntington, "I shall work up the trade with him if I can, if not, what then?"[17] But he declared a few days later, if the Scott trade failed, a trade would have to be made with someone else. On June 1, $1,033,903 became payable, and the call loan due Fisk and Hatch amounted to $1.7 million.[18] Three days thereafter Huntington grew even more desperate. "We must have money or go to protest."[19] The Central Pacific stock had no value for money-raising purposes; it was worth "very little more than blank paper."[20] By April he had become panic-stricken. "What we are all coming to the Lord only knows. As things look now there is no more hope of raising one dollar for the July interest than there is of getting it from the moon."[21]

The floating debt could not be carried much longer, insisted Hopkins. Bank accounts were "all largely overdrawn." To meet other pressing obligations it was necessary to let labor obligations accumulate unpaid. If it were at all possible, Hopkins continued, "we must steal" funds from daily receipts and mail the funds so that "nobody knows we are sending off money."[22]

Huntington's difficulties meanwhile were also gathering on the Chesapeake and Ohio. That road was being built to a connection with the Ohio River. The cost of construction was exceeding original estimates. Again, securities could not be sold and the road accumulated a floating debt.

Financial problems were intensified in September. A shock to public confidence was the immediate outcome of the insolvency of Jay Cooke and Company—a firm with an international reputation. It was both a commercial and an investment banking house. It held the deposits of numerous business enterprises. The closing of the house on September 18, suddenly reduced and in some cases eliminated their cash balances. The firm had invested almost all its cash in unmarketable securities of the Northern Pacific and in advances to that road. On September 18, the managers of three New York banks were invited to the office of Jay Cooke and Company. There the banks "were informed that one million of dollars were necessary by 10 o'clock to save that House from protest. What security do you offer? was asked. A—None; our securities are all used. It is needless to say that the million was not forthcoming. We left. In fifteen minutes Wall Street was in a panic. . . ."[23]

As an aftermath of the panic, the transcontinental plans of the Pennsylvania Railroad and its followers were permanently frustrated. The blow to Scott personally was devastating. The value of his southeastern railroads dwindled to nominal proportions. Many stocks lost all their market value and were later sold at auction. Scott relinquished the presidency of the Atlantic and Pacific, and the road drifted into receivership. In the Texas and Pacific, Scott's affairs assumed a more dramatic form. The railroad owed many thousands of dollars, largely on a short-term basis. Dodge, Scott's chief engineer on the Texas and Pacific, has left a lively account of the shock to the road's investors. A meeting of the representatives of the creditors was held in Scott's headquarters. The meeting lasted all day and nearly all night. "The question was," related Dodge, " 'Shall we save the property or ourselves?' I told them at the outcome of a similar meeting when Ames (of the Union Pacific) said, 'Save the road and let the individuals go to the wall,' and Scott answered that is what we will do, and these men sat down and assumed the entire debt of $10,000,000 or more, putting out their individual notes, known as the five-name paper and the three-name paper."[24]

The three-name and five-name paper mentioned by Dodge grew out of the endorsements by Scott and his associates on the notes of the California and Texas Railway Construction Company. This company had the contract with the Texas and Pacific for building the road. Unlike most other contruction companies, this one raised cash from the sale of stock. It had exhausted this cash, as well as the additional funds realized from the sale of almost $7 million of debt.

The resources of the construction company, consisting largely of the

railroad's securities, had only a slight market value. The endorsers of
the company's paper, nevertheless, including Scott, agreed to pay off its
obligations and 7 per cent interest in twenty-four months.[25] Besides the
financial loss to Scott, there was the impairment in his prestige with his
associates and financial followers. He offered to resign as vice-president
of the Pennsylvania Railroad, but the board refused to accept. A committee of stockholders examined the road's affairs and recommended
that it drop all its commitments west of the Mississippi and south of the
Ohio and Potomac rivers. These suggestions were accepted. Thus came
to an end the transcontinental ambitions of the Pennsylvania Railroad,
and from that day to this it has confined its operations to the area suggested by this investigating committee. Though Scott retained his position in the Pennsylvania's affairs, he also retained the presidency of the
Texas and Pacific.

Scott was unable to secure any further financial support to fulfill his
dream of a transcontinental line. He did not, however, give up hope.
On the contrary, he pressed forward with the task of building a line
between New Orleans and San Diego, but he devoted his attention not
to the task of acquiring long-term private capital but to the effort of
securing the aid of the federal government.

The affairs of the Union Pacific were also revolutionized by the events
of the summer and fall of 1873. The assumption of the presidency of
that road by Clark in 1872 was not followed by any easing of its financial
problems. Here, as on the Central Pacific, the floating debt mounted.
The Union Pacific's destinies were not fashioned, as were those of the
Central Pacific, in the pattern of a consistent, long-term managerial
policy. The company was unable to lay down and execute a program of
acquiring feeders and competitors. It did, however, engage in some expansion, though on a relatively minor scale. In Colorado it financed a
venture—the Colorado Central—to connect its main line with Denver.
By the end of 1872, forty-two miles had been built, and by the following
summer a few additional miles were in operation. And in Utah, two local
enterprises—the Utah Southern and the Utah and Northern—received
financial support from the Union Pacific. These two minor expansions
were responsible for a substantial proportion of the company's 1872 year-
end short-term debt.

The bonds and stocks of these small roads had no market. Neither was
the credit of the Union Pacific itself good enough to sustain the sale of

securities at reasonable prices. In order to secure funds, the road exploited the personal credit of its directors. Such loans were secured by the bonds and stocks of the Colorado and Utah roads, plus some additional securities in the road's treasury.

Risk-taking businessmen in the early 1870's nourished and kept alive *all* the transcontinental roads. They neither requested nor secured public recognition for their services. They risked their personal fortunes to sustain enterprises in which they and their followers had large financial stakes. They were trustees of the private fortunes of others; but as such they performed a public service. The case was well presented by John B. Alley, one of the early supporters of the Union Pacific. "The road stands much better in public estimation from the knowledge of the fact that twenty gentlemen of immense means stand ready to put it through any temporary embarrassment. . . . New roads, that depend solely upon their earnings, must necessarily need a great deal of help, which they receive through the friends of the enterprise."[20]

None of the financial problems had been solved when Clark died in the spring of 1873. His death was followed by the appearance of a newcomer in the transcontinental arena. Gould had been an associate with Clark in a number of financial transactions, and he bought heavily into the Union Pacific. The original promoters, with the exception of Frederick L. Ames, had by this time sold their stock. The most critical problem of the Union Pacific centered about the floating debt and the 1875 maturity of its $10 million in income bonds. These problems remained to be solved by Gould, as indeed they were.

The transcontinental connections between Omaha and Chicago fared much better as a whole than the lines west of the Missouri River. The Rock Island remained in sound financial condition, its debts were low, and it continued to pay dividends. Its president, Tracy, however, was heavily involved financially. He found it impossible to pay the loans incurred to purchase the large block of Northwestern stock. He and W. L. Scott—a financial associate—made speculative commitments in the security markets. Part of these trading activities were financed with the help of a loan endorsed by the Northwestern. The panic was a calamity to both Scott and Tracy. Tracy resigned from the presidencies of both the Rock Island and the Northwestern. The affairs of these two roads were never again operated in common. The Rock Island presidency was assumed by Hugh Riddle, for a number of years the road's general superintendent, a man skilled in railroad operation and conservative in temperament. His conservatism was shared by a majority of the members of the board including Dows, the New York City banker.

The presidency of the Northwestern was assumed by Albert Keep. The Northwestern at the outbreak of the panic was handicapped by the endorsement of the Scott-Tracy paper; it had also incurred heavy fixed charges in the form of leased rentals on its Iowa lines. It paid no dividends and in the language of its financial vice-president, "our finances are low, our business moderate, the fortune not flattering. . . ."[27] By the end of the 1870's Keep had mastered the Northwestern's financial problems. Like Riddle, he was not an expansionist; he was careful about making new commitments and succeeded in so managing the property that by the end of the 1870's he had put the Northwestern on a dividend basis.

The third Chicago-Missouri River connection of the transcontinental Omaha route, the Burlington, also had its share of troubles. In the early 1870's this road embarked on an extensive expansion program. It leased a number of roads on terms involving the guarantee of high-interest-bearing bonds and dividends upon the stock. The road also carried out an ambitious program of branch-line construction and acquisition. These feeder lines were acquired in "self-preservation. They were built mainly by other parties, and those parties hostile to the interests of the Burlington; and if they had continued in the same hands, and the business been diverted on to other roads, the traffic of the main line would have been affected very seriously, and its utility much impaired."[28]

By early 1873 the Burlington was afflicted with the common financial ailment—shortage of cash. In March the treasurer echoed the almost universal complaint. Bills were falling due, he wrote, "and I have no means to pay, and money is very short here now. . . ."[29] A few days later he informed the president of the necessity of raising funds to pay interest, a variety of personal notes and bank loans, and a call loan. "Some way, we must get out of debt, or we shall put down our credit and standings, and our stock." There was a debt due the following day of $60 thousand, and another of $100 thousand to Lee Higginson and Company, a Boston banking firm— "The latter I cannot renew, & the Bank are tired of renewing."[30]

Its finances were thus strained, but not substantially so. Though not in as good financial condition as the Rock Island, it nevertheless was able to pay dividends and its stock sold at a price reflecting a favorable investment appraisal.

In Kansas the rapid expansion of the Atchison had by the end of 1873 accentuated its financial crisis. The floating debt was transformed into 12 per cent income bonds, payable over a two-year period either in cash or in land-mortgage coupons. A 7 per cent bond payable in gold was sold at a 50 per cent discount in legal-tender currency. These high interest rates were a normal feature of the credit market in a period characterized by a capital shortage.

The events of September of 1873 also brought to a frightening climax the financial difficulties of Huntington and the Central Pacific. At the height of the panic, Huntington could borrow nothing. Only by the narrowest of margins was the dishonoring of the paper avoided. One examines with admiration the ingenuity with which funds were raised and the loyalty that Huntington and his associates displayed in the joint effort to keep the Central Pacific afloat. From the correspondence of Huntington it is possible to set up a table of the Central Pacific's floating debt in the panic months, (Table II).

The failure of Cooke brought Huntington's difficulties to a smashing climax. About a week before, Fisk and Hatch had called almost all the loans secured by railroad bonds. "All confidence seems to be lost in R. R. bonds," wrote Huntington on September 11.[31] On the day after the Cooke failure, Fisk and Hatch closed its doors. The fate of the Central Pacific was uppermost in the mind of Huntington. "We must," he wrote, "sustain the C.P. . . ."[32] Three days later a creditor to whom the Central Pacific owed $1 million asked for additional collateral, and Huntington asked Hopkins to send him $4 million face value of Central Pacific stock.[33] The very next day the same creditor insisted that Huntington pay the April, 1873, coupons of the Southern Pacific bonds hypothecated to secure a $1 million loan. If the coupon were paid and additional collateral furnished, the loan would be extended. Huntington again wrote to Hopkins requesting him to send $43,800 to honor this coupon.[34]

Huntington, meanwhile, on the day of the Fisk and Hatch failure had wired Hopkins to send him immediately $500 thousand by telegraph transfer. Hopkins rushed to Stanford's home and got him out of bed at six o'clock in the morning. Stanford was unsuccessful in obtaining the cash. It "can't be done" wired Hopkins.[35] This amount might have saved

Table II

FLOATING DEBT, CENTRAL PACIFIC, SEPTEMBER–NOVEMBER, 1873

Name of Creditor	Amount	Comments
L. von Hoffman	$1,000,000	Secured by $1,460,000 Southern Pacific bonds with April, 1873, coupon. Overdue.
Southern Pacific interest	$43,800	Coupon due April 1, 1873, unpaid, on Southern Pacific bonds hypothecated with L. von Hoffman.
Park Bank	$140,000	Past due.
Eugene Kelly	$67,000	Huntington owed this personally to Kelly, a member of the Park Bank directorate.
Fisk and Hatch	$1,700,000	Secured by $3,373,000 face value collateral.
A Bank	$9,000	Huntington wrote Hopkins, September 24, that this note would likely go to protest. Huntington finally borrowed the $9,000, secured by $15,000 California and Oregon Railroad bonds. The bonds were owned *personally* in equal amounts by Huntington, Stanford, and Hopkins.

Name of Creditor	*Amount*	*Comments*
Central Pacific interest	$42,058	Unpaid Central Pacific interest due July 1, 1873.
Notes	$70,000	Due October 25. Huntington wrote to Stanford on this date that he could not borrow a dollar.
Notes for Iron	$48,150	See page 51 of text for discussion.
Newark Savings Bank	$1,100,000	Overdue on November 4.
Saulsbury Savings Bank	$20,000	Overdue on November 1.
George P. Smith	$50,000	Overdue on November 4.
San Joaquin Valley Railroad Bonds, Interest	$180,000	Due October 1.

Fisk and Hatch from failure. The funds, however, were not forthcoming and the failure followed.

The $1 million creditor demanded payment of $170 thousand due on October 5, insisting that the funds belonged to a London banking house. This obligation was met and the creditor was pleased. Over $1 million had been due this firm from numerous debtors in that particular week, and the debt of the Central Pacific was the only one paid.[36] Meanwhile there were a number of other debts maturing at about the same time. There was only one thing to do, declared Huntington, and that was to "earn money as fast as we can, and stem off payments here, and keep parties from selling our collaterals at a sacrifice."[37]

The financial pressure was maintained throughout October. Toward the end of that month some notes originally issued to purchase iron, amounting to $48,150, became due. The funds for this small amount were not available. "I ran about the streets for two days trying to borrow the money,"[38] said Huntington. Where railroad credit failed his personal credit succeeded. Potential creditors would not lend the railroad; they did lend Huntington. Upon his *personal* credit, he finally was able to make loans in sums of $5 thousand each. These loans were supplemented by the use of $14 thousand of the funds of the Huntington and Hopkins Hardware enterprise on the Pacific Coast. The last note was paid at 4.20 P.M., just in time to avoid a protest. "I would not go through another panic like this for all the railroads in the world,"[39] declared Huntington. He did, nevertheless, go through additional panics. By mid-November the financial problem caused by outstanding short-term paper had been solved. The next major problem was the provision of funds for the payment of the coupon due in January, 1874. If the January interest could be paid, Huntington believed, it would "put our stock where it can be sold at a price that will make us all rich."[40]

The interest coupon was finally paid, though with considerable difficulty. On the last day of the distressing year Huntington was still unable to borrow—general distrust of railroad bonds persisted. Even in January, 1874, after the Central Pacific bond interest had been paid, his mind remained beset by anxiety. He was still anxious to sell his Southern Pacific and Central Pacific stocks. "I want to sell anything that I have on the Pacific Coast,"[41] he wrote. Two months later he was still disstressed. He was giving more for money than it was worth, he insisted in a note to Hopkins.[42]

To add to his financial anxieties, there were the obligations of the Chesapeake and Ohio. The public had benefited handsomely from his association with the enterprise. The 20-year-old dream of a line from the eastern Virginia to the Ohio River had been realized. What state credit had been unable to do had been done by the use of private credit by a group of capitalists under Huntington's leadership. The creditors and stockholders, however, had not fared well. The cost of building the road to the Ohio River had been underestimated; the traffic moving over the new route was not sufficient to provide the revenue to defray the interest. In December, 1873, an agreement was reached that the bondholders forgo the payment of cash for the interest. Here again, as with the Central Pacific, the firm of Fisk and Hatch was a large holder of the floating debt. Huntington had also induced a savings bank in Newark, New Jersey, to invest over $2 million of its funds in the road's junior securities. In 1876, after the Chesapeake and Ohio receivership, these securities would not have brought $300 thousand in the open market.[43] It was believed that Huntington would use his personal credit to avoid a default. His obligations, however, were too heavy and, eventually a receivership was found unavoidable.

Huntington was aided by numerous factors in dealing with all these complex financial problems. First, the Central Pacific in September, 1873, began to pay 6 per cent dividends. Second, he had on hand the bonds of a number of railroads received in part for previous advances. Third, he and his associates owned a block of the Wells Fargo Express stock received in return for an obligation by the Central Pacific to do its express business with that property. Fourth, business in the area served by the Central Pacific continued to expand. Hopkins, writing from California, informed Huntington that in the summer and fall there was not a single business failure. Harvest in grain and gold meanwhile were "abundant."[44] And of course he had the steadfast co-operation of his three associates. Each partner was a man of means and each had good credit standing. They agreed informally, without written obligation or legally enforceable contract, to pool their resources. "Every dollar of mine," wrote Hopkins in 1873, has since 1862 "been *put in and remains in our business.*"[45] Huntington undertook the discharge of the financial responsibilities. When in 1873 he was canvassing all existing resources to insure the payment of the January interest, Crocker informed him that he was collecting all his investments and would soon have $100 thousand for his share of the funds needed to pay interest.[46] Early in November Hopkins delivered to Huntington $275 thousand received as dividends on his Central Pacific stock, while Stanford added to the pool his coupons from the Central Pacific's land-grant bonds.[47]

By early 1874 Huntington was able to think again in terms of creative railroad construction and improvement. He had met his personal obligations and had discharged the heavy floating debt of the Central Pacific. While he had not been able to sustain the solvency of the Chesapeake and Ohio, he did succeed, despite his reverses on this property, in maintaining the confidence of its security holders. In the financial reorganization of the road in 1878 he was again placed in charge of its destinies.

At the eastern end of the two southern transcontinental routes on the 35th and 32nd Parallels, the failure of Scott was all but complete. He lost the financial support of the Pennsylvania Railroad; he lost most of his funds invested in the railroads south of the Ohio and Potomac rivers; he lost the leadership of the Atlantic and Pacific. The Texas and Pacific avoided receivership due to the assumption of heavy financial obligations by the California and Texas Railway Construction Company. The road's stock had been sold for cash at a high price, and that investment was lost.

It is an unrefreshing tribute to the prepossessions, if not the prejudices, of writers and historians that they have so neglected the record of this particular construction company. Inscribed in secondary accounts, in textbooks, and in fiction are the tales of financial successes and misdeeds of the construction companies. Rarely does a word appear about the losses incurred by investors in the stock of this construction company. The paper of the company went to protest. Fortunately for its creditors, the paper had been secured by the personal endorsement of capitalists associated with Scott, and eventually they were paid.

Scott, nevertheless, remained as president of the Texas and Pacific. By the end of 1873 two additional personalties had been introduced into the transcontinental arena. Nickerson proved to be the financial angel of the Atchison and Gould appeared as the man capable of solving, in the midst of the depression, the financial problems of the Union Pacific. And at the eastern end of the central transcontinental route, the Burlington, Rock Island, and the Northwestern continued to build up their financial strength.

The transcontinental railroad problems in the post-depression years centered largely around the personalities and activities of Huntington, Scott, and Gould, and the mangements of the three major Omaha-Chicago connections of the Union Pacific. These managerial problems, conflicts, and adjustments are discussed in succeeding chapters.

Notes for Chapter III

[1] Burlington Archives, Robert Harris to Gaskill Brothers, Feb. 5, 1873.

[2] *Am. R. R. Journal*, July 5, 1873, p. 837.

[3] Northwestern Archives, M. L. Sykes to John F. Tracy, Nov. 15, 1871.

[4] *Financier*, Sept. 26, 1874, p. 223.

[5] Huntington to Hopkins, Mar. 26, 1873, M. M.

[6] *Ibid.*, Nov. 11, 1872, M. M.

[7] *Ibid.*, Mar. 8, 1873.

[8] *Ibid.*, Mar. 26, 1873.

[9] *Credit Mobilier*, 712.

[10] Pacific Railroads, Report No. 440, House of Representatives, 44th Congress, 1st Session, April 25, 1876, p. 240.

[11] *Southern Pacific*, p. 54.

[12] Huntington to Hopkins, May 7, 1872, M. M.

[13] Huntington to Stanford, Sept. 2, 1872, M. M.

[14] Huntington to Hopkins, Nov. 11, 1872, M. M.

[15] *Ibid.*, Mar. 8, 11, 13, 1873.

[16] *Ibid.*, Mar. 8, 1873.

[17] *Ibid.*, Mar. 10, 1873.

[18] *Ibid.*, Mar. 11, 1873.

[19] *Ibid.*, Mar. 14, 1873.

[20] *Ibid.*, Mar. 14, 1873

[21] *Southern Pacific*, p. 55.

[22] Hopkins to Huntington, April 12, 1873, M. M.

[23] These are the remarks of John Thompson, vice-president, Chase National Bank, cited in *Bradstreet's*, Aug. 13, 1881, p. 101.

[24] J. R. Perkins, *Trails, Rails & War* (Indianapolis: Bobbs-Merrill, 1929), p. 258.

[25] The detailed plan of settlement is presented in *R. R. Gaz.*, Dec. 6, 1873, p. 491.

[26] *Credit Mobilier*, p. 29. For data on the Union Pacific's floating debt see pp. 199, 396, 441.

[27] Northwestern Archives, Sykes to Keep, Oct. 28, 1873.

[28] This is the language of Edward Vernon, ed., *American Railroad Manual*, 1874, (New York: American Railroad Manual Company), p. 523.

[29] Burlington Archives, J. N. Denison to A. T. Hall, Mar. 21, 1873.

[30] *Ibid.*, Denison to J. M. Walker, Mar. 27, 1873.

[31] *Southern Pacific*, p. 56.

[32] Huntington to Hopkins, Sept. 19, 1873, M. M.

[33] *Ibid.*, Sept. 22, 1873.

[34] *Ibid.*, Sept. 23, 1873.

[35] Hopkins to Huntington, Sept. 19, 1873, M. M.

[36] Huntington to Stanford, Oct. 4, 1873, M. M.

[37] Huntington to Hopkins, Oct. 1, 1873, M. M.

[38] *Ibid.*, Oct. 29, 1873.

[39] *Ibid.*

[40] Huntington to Crocker, Nov. 8, 1873, M. M.

[41] Huntington to A. N. Towne, Jan. 20, 1874, M. M.

[42] Huntington to Hopkins, Mar. 15, 1874, M. M.

[43] These details are taken from the *New York Tribune*, July 24, 1884. The newspaper account is based upon a suit against the president and managers of the Newark Savings Bank.

[44] Hopkins to Huntington, Nov. 8, 1873, M. M.

[45] *Ibid.*, Feb. 6, 1873.

[46] Crocker to Huntington, Nov. 27, 1873, M. M.

[47] Hopkins to Huntington, Nov. 6, 1873, M. M.

IV

Scott vs. Huntington

THE SHORTAGE of capital of 1872–1873, climaxed by the panic, stopped progress on all the transcontinental routes. Scott in 1873 had been the leader both of the Atlantic and Pacific—the 35th Parallel route, and of the Texas and Pacific—the eastern end of the 32nd Parallel route. Scott promptly abandoned all his interest in the former but retained his holdings and managerial responsibilities in the latter. Only a small section of the Texas and Pacific, from the Louisiana-Texas boundary line toward Fort Worth, had been completed. Under his direction about $10 million had been spent, representing 261 miles of constructed and equipped road. Additional mileage had been graded, bridged, and tied.[1] On the western end of the route Scott had done virtually nothing. Huntington, however, had gone ahead with considerable construction. The Southern Pacific had completed about eighty miles from San Francisco to a small point south of Gilroy, on the western side of the Sierra Nevada Range. There construction ceased in August, 1873. This line had been proposed initially as a part of a major route to Los Angeles and thence, east via the 32nd Parallel. The Central Pacific by August, 1872, had completed more than two hundred miles on the eastern side of the range, terminating in the San Joaquin Valley at Goshen. It was decided to extend the Central Pacific line south from that point through the corporate instrumentality of the Southern Pacific, thereby avoiding the construction of duplicate lines on both sides of the mountains. The construction of the Southern Pacific line in 1873 and early in 1874 was progressing at a leisurely pace. Indeed owing to the financial stringency, Huntington considered the advisability at that time of stopping further construction entirely.

By the summer of 1874, however, Huntington had dropped all his doubts about the future of his railroad program. He abandoned the idea of selling either the Southern or the Central Pacific. The critical test of the payment of the Central Pacific interest was passed. The earnings of the road increased. The grain crop was large: the silver and gold ore and bullion traffic expanded rapidly, and rates in an area free almost entirely of competitive forces were adequate, some running as high as 15 cents per ton-mile.

By the fall of 1874 Huntington had massed his forces for the extension of the Southern Pacific line south to Los Angeles and east to the Colorado River along the 32nd Parallel. The Southern Pacific also had charter rights to build east along the 35th Parallel to a connection with a road building westward to that point. The financial difficulties of the Atlantic and Pacific led Huntington to abandon the construction of a line along that route. He was now convinced of the necessity of protecting the California roads by securing the best passes and valleys. It was also essential to secure a franchise in Arizona and work north in that area, thereby shielding the southern flank of the Central Pacific.[2] Huntington wrote to Crocker to get an Arizona franchise—"We *not* to be known in it. . . ."[3]

On the eastern end of the 32nd Parallel route, construction by 1874 had come to an almost complete halt. Scott had to divide his time between the administration of the Pennsylvania Railroad and the Texas and Pacific. Though the former had its financial troubles, its credit was well maintained. It could not, however, be used to finance the requirements of the Texas and Pacific. Scott, therefore, decided to request aid from the federal government. Late in 1874 he prepared the draft of a bill for submission to Congress early in 1875. Scott solicited the help of Huntington, and sent him a copy of the draft. This provided for the construction by the Texas and Pacific of a road to San Diego. To this Huntington objected; he would, however, throw his support behind the bill provided Scott would stop building west of the Colorado River. This proposal Scott rejected. He would build to San Diego, he declared; whereupon Huntington proclaimed that he would build east of the Colorado River. There was no possibility of a compromise. Neither side would make any concession. "Your suggestions," wrote Scott to Huntington, "are totally inadmissable. . . ."[4] Other letters passed between Huntington, Stanford, and Colton on the same subject.

The battle was now joined. Scott and Huntington became implacable enemies. Scott applied to Congress for a substantial Texas and Pacific subsidy. Huntington opposed him at almost every point. Scott first asked for a subsidy of more than $60 million. This was in addition to the substantial land grant received from Texas and from New Mexico and Arizona Territories. Scott appeared before a congressional committee. The bill in that session did not get beyond the committee. Another bill was offered in the next session. By that time the Scott-Huntington battle had become bitter. Scott mobilized public opinion in communities likely to be benefited by the completion of the transcontinental route. One convention held in St. Louis in November, 1875, attended by more than seven hundred delegates, resolved that the Texas and Pacific had "stronger claims to aid than any extensive scheme of internal improvement that ever sought or obtained governmental assistance."[5]

Another convention was held a few days later at Memphis. There it was resolved to ask Congress to aid in the building of a Shreveport–Pacific Coast line and one from Shreveport to Memphis, Vicksburg, and New Orleans.[6] According to Huntington, Scott as president of the Pennsylvania Railroad, offered free passes on trains leaving Washington to those in a position to influence Congress. Scott had meanwhile reduced his request for congressional aid. He now asked Congress only to endorse 5 per cent bonds secured by a first mortgage. This was later changed to a government guarantee of interest only. A limit of $35 thousand per mile was also placed upon the bonds to be issued, except upon certain costly stretches of construction, where a limit of $40 thousand per mile would prevail.

In his argument before a congressional committee Scott stressed the usefulness of the road as a means of competing with the railroad monopoly. The Central and Southern Pacific, he insisted, were under control of the same group. This group had a virtual monopoly of all California railroads. Federal grants gave this group, argued Scott, an undue advantage, which it used without mercy and without remorse to crush out the possibility of competition.

Huntington was impressed by the strong fight made by Scott. Though he admitted that Scott still had strong political support, he was certain that the bill could not pass. Scott, he declared, was "making a terrible effort. I hear of him everywhere."[7] Scott's attack on the California railroad monopoly was not well received by Huntington. Scott, he said, was "very ugly," and was "making a very dirty fight." Huntington insisted he was sure of success. "You know," he wrote, "I work 365 days in a year when it is necessary."[8] He was willing to spend extensively in order to defeat Scott. An example is afforded by the attempted extension of a Texas and Pacific land grant which lapsed on January 1, 1876. Huntington proposed to spend $20 thousand to fight Scott, with an additional contingent expenditure of $30 thousand. "If we can destroy this grant we can break up Scott."[9] Huntington insisted publicly that Scott was spending in order to secure political influence. He could prove, he declared, that Scott had offered Republican and Democratic national committees $300 thousand to pass resolutions recommending congressional aid in favor of the Texas and Pacific. His roads' rule, he declared, was "never to buy a vote. . . ."[10]

In this battle for the support of public opinion, Huntington adopted still other measures. Impressed by the force of Scott's anti-monopoly argument, he decided to put up a front as the "real" head of the Southern Pacific. For this purpose he selected David D. Colton, a California businessman. Colton was allowed to buy a block of the road's stock at a low price, with the understanding that he would become head of the road. Huntington told Scott—and of course the public, including Congress— that Colton, president of the Southern Pacific, and his friends had a controlling interest in its stock. Persons in control of the Central Pacific had only a small stake in the other road. Colton, Huntington believed, would serve well as a good "front" before congressional committees.[11] Huntington also warned Colton to watch Scott. "You write that you think you have Scott beaten," wrote Huntington to Colton, "but allow me to suggest that you do not go to sleep while he is awake."[12]

While this struggle continued in the public forum and before congressional committees, Huntington prosecuted a rapid railroad construction program in California. It was a program that made a deep impression not only on the railroads and financial communities but also on the general public. It was the country's largest single railroad-building program in the depression years. Begun in the summer of 1874, it was completed by September of 1876. Stanford, as president of the Central Pacific, served as the public mouthpiece. He spoke eloquently of its great advantage to the public. The road, he declared, was "toiling for the greatest prize that this continent affords. The people of California and of San Francisco have no appreciation of the splendid trade opened up for them, nor of the magnificent destiny which awaits that city. . . ." The completion of this program, continued Stanford, "will enrich our merchants, give employment to our mechanics, swell the business of our traders, keep alive our foundries, add to our population, give value to real estate, and make San Francisco in less than ten years a city embracing, with its surroundings, a million of people."[13] Stanford, Huntington repeatedly insisted, was not a good businessman; he was assuredly an acceptable public-relations officer.

Los Angeles by 1876 had an all-rail connection with the East. The line ran north over the Southern Pacific via the San Joaquin Valley line to Goshen and north and east over the Central Pacific to its connection with the Union Pacific at Ogden. It was, it is true, a circuitous line. It did, however, give Los Angeles for the first time a rail connection with the rest of the country. The construction program that made this possible cost approximately $20 million.

It is therefore, important to examine the way this construction program was financed. Most of the strongest railway properties had adopted a policy of caution and retrenchment. They husbanded their financial resources and avoided any extensive new building programs. The Huntington group, however, struck out courageously in a heavy expansion. How were the funds raised? There were no public security offerings. The public was mystified. "Where the money came from nobody but the managers know," wrote a New York correspondent in 1877. "All the public can realize is that the road is built—built of the best materials . . . and that too without any aid from State or Federal Treasury."[14]

The program was carried out through the Western Development Company, a successor to the Contract and Finance Company. Huntington and his three original associates still owned a large block of Central Pacific stock. It had been almost impossible prior to 1874 to sell these shares. By 1874 the company's record during the panic months of 1873 and its good earnings and dividend payments had achieved a respectable record for its stock. In January the stock was placed on the New York stock board. The four associates also owned a considerable amount in bonds, which they had received in exchange for advances made to the Central Pacific. As the construction of the Southern Pacific advanced, its first-mortgage bonds were delivered to Huntington and his group in exchange for cash advances. But what was the source of the cash? The answer was Huntington, as the financial agent of both roads. To aid in establishing the acceptability to investors of the Southern Pacific bonds it was necessary to sustain the prices of the Central Pacific's securities. This Huntington accomplished at critical periods by heavy purchases financed through the creation of short-term liabilities. He insisted upon holding off the market the Southern Pacific bonds until they could be sold at prices reflecting the credit standing of a completed road with an established earning power. When his associates insisted upon selling the bonds in order to pay off the floating debt, Huntington refused. "Never mind the floating debt," he declared; "I will take care of it; that is my part of the business."[15] Late in his life he told a congressional committee that his associates at one time wanted to sell the Southern Pacific bonds at 60. Instead he raised the cash through short-term liabilities; eventually he sold $2 million at 90, and other quantities at higher prices. If the bonds had been sold at 60, it would, in Huntington's estimate, have made a difference of between $12 million and $14 million.[16]

Since the operation of the Southern and Central Pacific were under common control, it was possible to arrange divisions of through rates, and rents for the use of terminal and other facilities in such a way as to increase the earnings of one property and reduce those of the other. Huntington took advantage of these possibilities to increase the earnings of the Southern Pacific and reduce those of the Central Pacific. If there were any doubt, he wrote at one time to Crocker in charge of operations on the Pacific Coast, give the Southern Pacific the benefit. Before putting its securities on the market it was necessary to increase its profits.[17] In preparing them for later sales, Huntington also revealed an appreciation of sound investment-banking principles. To be popular the Southern Pacific bonds he insisted, must be put on the market at a good round price, but one not so high that they would later recede from it. All the bonds must be sold at one price; otherwise, he believed, buyers at lower prices might be disposed to sell at the higher prices and depress the market price.[18] In 1875 there was still no market for the bonds. "This season," wrote Huntington in May, 1875, "I could not sell any Southern Pacific bonds."[19]

While he was thus taking steps to improve the marketability of Southern Pacific securities, he did succeed in selling some of the Central Pacific bonds. In April, 1875, he sold $500 thousand of Central Pacific Land-Grant bonds to Kuhn-Loeb, an investment-banking firm, at 88 with an option to buy $2 million more in ninety days. This firm had connections abroad and the sale facilitated the introduction of the bonds on the

London Stock Exchange and on two or three German bourses.[20] To raise additional funds Huntington returned to his standard device—the floating debt. Floating liabilities for five years prior to 1873 had haunted and hounded him. In the fall of that year failure had been averted by the narrowest of margins. Yet one year later Huntington again resorted to the same device. By November, 1874, the floating debt reached almost $4 million. Huntington expressed great satisfaction with one particular loan. He purchased iron and steel rails from the Cambria Iron Company on terms of one-fourth in cash and three-fourths in notes of Central Pacific due in nine, twelve, and fifteen months. The iron company contracted with the bank to take the Central Pacific's paper at 8 per cent. "I do not think," he wrote, "there is another railroad company in America that could place their paper at so low a rate without collaterals."[21]

By the fall of 1875 Huntington was again in the midst of his accustomed financial difficulties. In September he stressed the need of a large sum of money. In October he instructed Colton to pay all obligations carrying an interest rate of 12 per cent. He had meanwhile succeeded in borrowing $50 thousand for six months at 7 per cent, to pay off other notes with an interest rate of 10 per cent.[22]

Next month the failure of the Atlantic and Pacific complicated his financial problems. Kuhn-Loeb had agreed to take an option on a block of Central Pacific bonds and Huntington had planned to use the funds to pay the January bond interest. The blow to railroad credit arising from this new failure led the investment banker not to exercise the option. Huntington had to use current earnings to pay the interest.[23]

Huntington was far from discouraged over this misadventure. By mid-December he had extracted an offer from another investment banker with international connections to buy $600 thousand of Central Pacific bonds at 90, with an option to buy more at the same price up to July 1, 1876. The total amount would be between $6 million and $7 million. By January, 1876, this buyer completed the purchase of $1 million with an option to buy $3 million more at 93 by May 1. Some of the bonds had been pledged as collateral for short-term loans. Such loans could not be paid. Huntington asked for substitute collateral. Crocker forwarded $1 million of his Land-Grant bonds and Stanford $9 million.[24]

The succession of short-term loans was not easily arranged. The continuous borrowing on the pledge of Central Pacific securities led to queries from prospective lenders. Why, it was asked, if the Central Pacific earnings were improving and the road paying dividends, was it necessary to borrow so extensively? Huntington had his answers: funds were needed to provide steel rails, etc. Huntington was cautious in making too much of these standardized explanations. They would "not do for a large amount," he said. If it were really known, he wrote, that the Central Pacific was building the Southern Pacific with its credit it would hurt the Central Pacific "very much."[25] To prospective lenders Huntington was therefore careful not to say that the Central Pacific was furnishing funds to build the Southern Pacific.[26]

By early 1876 Huntington by these maneuvers had succeeded in the following tasks: to make a market in Europe for Central Pacific bonds; second, to get the Southern Pacific bonds admitted to the New York board, thereby facilitating their sale; third, to make a market for the sale of Central Pacific stock between $70 and $80 per share; fourth, to sell substantial amounts of Central Pacific Land-Grant bonds by private trades; fifth, to negotiate short-term loans at high interest rates. The loans were liquidated later, largely from the sale of the Central Pacific bonds and stocks. It is close to the truth to say that no one else in the Central Pacific–Southern Pacific hierarchy could have accomplished this task, and that without these funds raised by Huntington the Southern Pacific construction program could not have been completed. He was in this sense a public servant and performed a notable public service.

While Huntington was thus consulting, creating, and financing the western end of the transcontinental route, Scott, on the eastern end, was helpless in a business sense. He fought a lone battle heroically; but the battle was with the public press and before congressional committees. There he urged and requested and demanded, but he accomplished nothing. Committee recommendations were ignored. Congress made inquiries and instituted investigations. Early in 1876 a delegation called upon the President of the Senate and the Speaker of the House to present a memorial in favor of government aid for the Texas and Pacific. A few days later a Senate committee listened to arguments presented by Scott. Huntington appeared in opposition.

A few days later a petition was presented from the Pennsylvania Assembly, signed by 1,300 businessmen, in support of a Texas and Pacific subsidy. All this was of no avail. Huntington, on his part, made several attractive offers, climaxed finally by an undertaking that he would build the line to El Paso with no further government aid. He asked only the land grant now held by the Texas and Pacific.

The masterful steps taken by Huntington to finance the construction program of the Southern Pacific could not be matched by Scott on behalf of the Texas and Pacific. His presidency of the Pennsylvania Railroad brought him prestige, but no funds. Scott was the chief executive of a road "whose boast is that it embraces more than 6,500 miles of track," sarcastically observed a Southern Pacific official; ". . . he has large experience in the money markets and ought to be able to call to his assistance all the capital needed."[27] Little money, however, was forthcoming. Scott found it almost impossible to sell railway bonds, either in this country or in Europe, "unless they are those of well-known and dividend-paying corporations."[28] Bonds, Scott continued, could be sold only at discounts of from 10 per cent to 25 per cent or more below their face value.

The rivalry between the Scott and Huntington forces meanwhile grew increasingly personal. The depth of feeling is suggested by a letter from Colton in California. "We must," he wrote, "split Tom Scott wide open if we can and get rid of him . . . he is the head and front at this time of all the devilment against the C. P. & S. P. . . . he is today the most *active* and *practical* enemy, we have in the world."[29]

The decisive struggle was, however, to be settled not in letters nor in the battle of the public opinion, but rather in the railroad-building camps.

While Scott was confessing, in fact insisting, upon his financial inability to proceed with the building of the Texas and Pacific west, Huntington had completed plans for the building of the Southern Pacific line east. Before the end of 1876 he had provided funds to finance an extension to the Colorado River. In order to improve the credit status of the fledgling (financially speaking) Southern Pacific, he leased the property including the projected Colorado River line to the dividend-paying Central Pacific. The lease ran for five years and provided for an annual payment of $3 thousand per mile built and in operation.[30] Scott meanwhile sent his engineers to California to lay out a route for his proposed extension. In December a group of men was organized in Yuma to break ground and to commence grading west of the Colorado River.[31]

These moves, however, were only expectations. The ground was occupied in order to form the basis for a road when funds were available. Huntington, however, waited for no such future. Shortly after the completion of the line to Los Angeles, he moved to extend the Southern Pacific to the Colorado River. The specter of the floating debt emerged again, and again Huntington found it necessary to urge reducing the debt. As early as April he wrote, "We must stop all outlays that we possibly can and reduce our floating debt."[32] Money markets in 1877 were demoralized; the receivership of the Philadelphia and Reading Railroad had brought heavy selling. Security prices dropped below the low level reached in the panic months of 1873.

These financial difficulties did not, however, retard the progress of the new extension. That was finished to the Colorado River early in October, 1877. There was a government Indian Reservation at Yuma, and authority from the War Department was needed to cross the bridge. Scott had foreseen the importance of this strategic point. Permission had been given to the Texas and Pacific to cross the bridge, but this was later revoked. Crocker, on the ground with the Southern Pacific forces, took advantage of some momentary hesitation by the Secretary of War and without official approval erected a bridge and laid a track across the reservation and across the bridge. The Texas and Pacific reacted strongly against this move. Its vice-president wired to the representative of the War Department in Yuma that the Southern Pacific was finishing a bridge across the river and that this was a "great injustice to us. . . . We hope, and believe, you will treat that Company just as you treated ours."[33]

The reservation had been crossed and the bridge built. Yet no official approval of these actions had been obtained. To secure such endorsement was Huntington's responsibility. He consulted the Cabinet and finally called upon the President. After some discussion the President was convinced by the promise of Huntington to build the line east of the Colorado River. According to Huntington, the President asked, "What do you propose to do if we let you run over the bridge?" "Push the road right on through Arizona," Huntington replied. "Will you do that? If you will, that will suit me first-rate," Huntington reported the President as saying.[34] Presidential approval of the action of Crocker and the Southern Pacific was given. The associates were, of course, elated. Colton, in an expression of confidence in the success of the battle of the Yuma bridge, expressed his contempt of Scott. He wrote that Scott could not accomplish any great undertaking; that he talked too much; and that he had no money and could not lay down cash to carry out a scheme. Gould, Colton continued, was the reverse of Scott—"he is a one man power;

consults no one, advises with no one, has no friends, wants none—is bold." Gould, Colton added, could always lay down $200 thousand or $300 thousand.[35]

Huntington had won this last battle with Scott by making a promise to the President. This promise, however, was more than Huntington at that time could fulfill, for the financial strain upon his associates was more than they were willing to accept.

Meanwhile the money market grew tighter. Call loans rose to 1.32 per cent per day in certain cases.[36] Some Central Pacific creditors, furthermore, were growing skeptical. A German banker, for example, informed Huntington in October that he would lend no more funds if the road paid any dividends that fall. Huntington's associates also grew more anxious. They refused to go along with Huntington's extensions, involving further liabilities. In January, 1878, Hopkins refused to sign any more Central Pacific notes: "If the rest of us were determined to go tearing along as we have been, building roads here and there and never counting the result or cost, until they had been built, and then finding out for the first time what they *ought* to have cost was much less than what they *had* cost . . . and if we all wanted to go to the D——l much as he [Huntington] liked us all, he [Hopkins] would not." Colton was in harmony with these views. All the associates finally agreed "*not to build any more roads* or buy any steamships or Property either jointly or individually until we got out of debt and have the money in Bank to pay for what we bought."[37]

Huntington was aware of these conditions and his promise to the President to build east of Yuma was accordingly carefully diluted in its execution. His instructions to Colton with respect to extending the Southern Pacific east was a model of compromising business statesmanship. Do little, he wrote—"just enough to say work, but not enough to feel the cost."[38]

The great project—the connection between Los Angeles and the Colorado River—had been completed; but the cost was high. The floating debt exceeded the peak reached in the fall of 1873. Again and again Huntington's associates insisted in 1877 and early in 1878 that all building must stop. Much of the personal assets of Huntington and his associates were tied up in advances to the Central Pacific. In July, 1878, the floating debt of that road included an advance from Huntington of $2.5 million; from Hopkins, $500 thousand; from Stanford, $600 thousand; and from the firm of Huntington, Hopkins and Company, $300 thousand.

Business conditions in California meanwhile had turned for the worse at the very time that business was about to pick up in the east. Early in 1878 runs on the western banks took place. This posed another problem for Huntington. One bank demanded payment of its loan and Huntington wired Colton that in six days he would need another $250 thousand.[39] Huntington again felt exhausted, as he had so often in the early 1870's. "Our credit has been hurt of late," he wrote in February; and continued, "I am as near used up as I ever was in my life before. I am spending my last winter at Washington."[40] In March the financial emergencies continued. Huntington called on Colton for aid from California. On March 5, Colton, weary from the lack of sleep (since November of the preceding year he had been averaging less than three hours of sleep a night) urged Huntington to "Stand by the wreck to the last—we can at least die game."[41] Four days later, Colton renewed about $700 thousand of loans for twelve months for from 8 to 9 per cent.[42] On March 13, the news from Colton in California was stark and tragic. Accounts in two banks had been overdrawn for three months from $100 thousand to $350 thousand each. "I have picked up every Dollar I could on the outside without showing our hand," wrote Colton. Business, furthermore, was "terribly light."[43] On the twenty-eighth Colton sent Huntington $100 thousand; the next day another $100 thousand was needed; the following day $50 thousand more; and on April 1, still another $50 thousand. All these funds represented borrowings. Colton was desperate. "For Gods [*sic*] sake lets get *out* of debt before we talk about building any more roads."[44]

Meanwhile, on the eastern end, Scott had accomplished little. It seemed at that time that the completion of the 32nd Parallel route would be indefinitely delayed. Scott had been able neither to raise funds privately nor to induce Congress to supply public funds. Huntington and his associates, had, it appeared, exhausted their resources; the Central Pacific had passed its dividends; the future of the southern transcontinental route seemed bleak. But, as is so often the case, pessimistic expectations were belied by the course of events. In the East, a speculative personality with a large following soon emerged to take over the reigns of management from Scott. In a short period Gould succeeded where Scott had failed. And on the western end, Huntington again managed to solve the financial problems of the Central Pacific–Southern Pacific system. Hopkins passed away before the end of the year. Colton proved disloyal and was ousted from the inner group. But Huntington was adamant in his optimism. In conjunction with Crocker he produced results profitable to himself and his associates, and even more profitable to the transportation service of the national economy.

Notes for Chapter IV

[1] These details were presented by Scott to the Senate Committee on Railroads late in 1874, according to the *Am. R. R. Journal*, Jan. 2, 1875, p. 1.

[2] Huntington to Crocker, Nov. 30, 1874, M. M.

[3] *Ibid.*, Dec. 5, 1874.

[4] Scott to Huntington, Dec. 9, 1874, M. M.

[5] *Ry. World*, Nov. 20, 1875, p. 756.

[6] *Ibid.*, Nov. 27, 1875, p. 775.

[7] Huntington to Colton, Oct. 29, 1875, M. M.

[8] Huntington to Colton, Mar. 22, 1876, M. M.

[9] Huntington to Colton, Mar. 30, 1876, M. M.

[10] Huntington to Hopkins, Feb. 19, 1876, M. M.

[11] Huntington to Stanford, Jan. 6, 1875, M. M.

[12] Huntington to Colton, Feb. 2, 1875, M. M.

[13] *Ry. Review*, May 29, 1875, p. 102.

[14] *New York World*, April 20, 1877.

[15] Report No. 778, Huntington, p. 57.

[16] *Ibid.*

[17] Huntington to Crocker, Oct. 1, 1874, M. M.

[18] These views are expressed in *Ibid.*, Dec. 3, 1874.

[19] Huntington to Colton, May 3, 1875, M. M.

[20] Huntington to Hopkins, April 27, 1875, M. M.

[21] Huntington to Colton, May 26, 1875, M. M.

[22] Pac. Ry. Commission, p. 3726.

[23] Huntington to Hopkins, Nov. 8, 1875, M. M.

[24] Huntington to Crocker, Dec. 15, 1875, M. M.

[25] Huntington to Hopkins, Sept. 25, 1875, M. M.

[26] *Ibid.*, Oct. 7, 1875.

[27] Letter J. L. Willicutt, secretary Southern Pacific Railroad Company to the editor, in *R. R. Gaz.*, Feb. 11, 1876, p. 63.

[28] This is the language of Scott in a letter to Stanley Matthews, president of the National Railway Convention, cited in *Ry. World*, Dec. 4, 1875, p. 787.

[29] Colton to Huntington, May 22, 1876, M. M.

[30] Evans, p. 249.

[31] *Ry. World*, Dec. 2, 1876, p. 786; Dec. 30, 1876, p. 849.

[32] Pac. Ry. Commission, Huntington to Colton, p. 3746.

[33] Telegram from Philadelphia—John T. Brown, vice-president, Texas and Pacific, Sept. 23, 1877, M. M.

[34] Huntington to Colton, Oct. 10, 1877, M. M.

[35] Colton to Huntington, Oct. 15, 1877, M. M.

[36] *Bankers Magazine*, Nov. 1877, p. 414.

[37] Colton to Huntington, Jan. 31, 1878, M. M. (This source embraces the two quotations in the paragraph.)

[38] Huntington to Colton, Nov. 22, 1877, M. M.

[39] Huntington to Colton, Jan. 22, 1878, M. M.

[40] Pac. Ry. Commission, p. 3765; Huntington to Colton, Feb. 9, 1878.

[41] Colton to Huntington, Mar. 5, 1878, M. M.
[42] *Ibid.*, Mar. 9, 1878.
[43] *Ibid.*, Mar. 13, 1878.
[44] *Ibid.*, Mar. 28, 1878.

V

Gould vs. Perkins—The Battle at the Omaha Gateway

THE CENTRAL transcontinental route—the national highway—was in 1874 a completed, well-functioning operating unit. The managerial problems of its corporate constituents were unlike those confronting the managers of the routes along the 32nd and 35th Parallels. The financial problems were nowhere near as serious for the managers of the central, as for those of the uncompleted southern lines. The Central Pacific—the western end of the central line—used its credit to finance the construction and expansion programs of Huntington and his associates. The Union Pacific had by the spring of 1874 come under the control of Gould. Clark, the head of a Vanderbilt group that had bought control early in 1872, passed away in the summer of the following year. He had been a heavy speculator and his Union Pacific stock had been pledged as collateral for bank loans. At the time of his death these loans were under-collateraled.[1] The creditors sold the collateral, consisting in part of a large block of Union Pacific stock. Gould bought this stock in the open market and by early 1874 he controlled a sufficient amount to elect himself and his associates to a position of control. Sidney Dillon, an experienced railroad builder, became president and Gould assumed the chairmanship of the executive committee. Gould, however, formulated the policies of the road, and Dillon rarely opposed his views.[2]

The major financial problem upon Gould's election to the Union Pacific board in the spring of 1874 was the payment of the $10 million 10 per cent Income Bond due in 1875. In these negotiations Gould was aided by a number of fortuitous circumstances. The California cereal crop for 1874 was abnormally good. This was supplemented by an increase in the silver ore and bullion traffic originating in Nevada and moving east over the Union Pacific. There was also a substantial rise in passenger traffic. The road's management could therefore say, as it did in the summer of 1874, that while other roads were showing a loss in traffic, the Union Pacific reflected "no falling off whatever."[3] On local traffic, furthermore, the rates were high, reflecting the absence of competition. Early in 1875 rates were increased. On through traffic between the Pacific Coast and the East—to points accessible by water competition —the rate structure had been depressed because of competition with the Pacific Mail Steamship. Gould early in 1875 succeeded in acquiring control. This was followed by an arrangement with the Pacific Mail that enabled the Union Pacific to free itself from steamship competition. In conjunction with the Central Pacific and the Omaha-Chicago roads, the Union Pacific paid a subsidy to the Pacific Mail, and that company in turn agreed to permit the transcontinental roads to fix the rate structure. In March, 1875, rates were raised from 40 to 100 per cent, and a few weeks later, by another 20 to 33 per cent.[1] This rise was so sharp that even Huntington, who himself had been accused of charging high rates in his local territory, was impressed. It was the increase negotiated by Gould in March of 1875 that had "become so notorious of late," as Huntington wrote, early in April.[5]

The increase in the volume of business, combined with the high rate structure, facilitated Gould's successful negotiations in handling the bond maturity. The Union Pacific was thereby relieved of its most pressing financial problem. By the fall of 1875 it was able to declare a dividend. This was a notable achievement, and it was soon registered in the New York stock market. The Union Pacific stock became a leading feature on the Exchange. The impression made abroad was particularly important. In the distressing days of late 1872 and 1873, many thousands of shares were bought by foreign investors. To investors both in this country and abroad Gould now became a speculative hero. This reputation stood him in good stead in numerous negotiations during the middle and late 1870's. What he did for the Union Pacific, it was expected, he would do for other properties.

On the Chicago-Omaha end of the Central route, the financial problems of the three major connections were not acute. The Rock Island was in an enviable financial condition. Its fixed charges were low; it had no floating debt; it paid dividends; and the stock sold in the market at a substantial premium over its par value. The Burlington finances were satisfactory. The company paid dividends and its stock also sold at a premium. The Northwestern's financial problems reached a critical stage in the fall of 1873, due partly to an increase in rents and partly to the assumption of a debt described in the preceding chapter.[6] The road passed its dividend and did not resume until 1879.

Along the middle route between San Francisco and Chicago in the depression years of 1874 to 1878, a policy of defensive caution and conservatism prevailed. There were scattered acquisitions of small roads, almost all of which were in financial difficulties. The Central Pacific acquired a number in California. The Union Pacific picked up the stubs of a number of lines which later grew to be of considerable significance. Only one important piece of construction was effected. That was in 1877, when a connection between Denver and its main line in Wyoming at Cheyenne was completed. In the Omaha-Chicago area there was some local rivalry between the three major roads for the control of a number of strategically located properties. Their owners, just as in California, were unable to raise the funds to pay interest. Control passed to the buyers at prices which left little or nothing for the common stocks.

The managerial problems involving broad decisions of strategy centered largely around the junction points between the Union Pacific and its eastern connections. The government had subsidized the Union-Central Pacific companies with the understanding that they would not discriminate against their connections. It had also subsidized a number of branches with the purpose of stimulating competition between them and the Union Pacific, and also between the branches themselves. The major branch line was the Kansas Pacific. It extended from Kansas City to Denver and, through a controlled subsidiary, the Denver and Pacific, joined the Union Pacific at Cheyenne. Traffic could thus be carried between the East and the Pacific Coast via Omaha and the Union Pacific; or via Kansas City, Denver, and Cheyenne over the Kansas Pacific–Denver Pacific–Union Pacific.

A second branch was the B. & M. Its stock was controlled largely by the major stockholders of the Burlington. It connected with the latter at East Plattsmouth, Nebraska, some miles below Omaha, and extended west to a connection with the Union Pacific at Kearney. Business could flow either over the Union Pacific from Kearney to Omaha or over the B. & M. from Kearney to East Plattsmouth and thence over the Burlington. (See Maps 2 and 3 for clarification of text pages 72-79.)

A third branch was the Sioux City and Pacific. This road connected with the Union Pacific at Fremont, Nebraska, northwest of Omaha. From Fremont the road ran east to a small point in Missouri where it connected with the Northwestern. This line could carry traffic between Fremont and the Northwestern, or it could move it from Fremont east to Omaha over the Union Pacific.

These three branches then—the Kansas Pacific, the B. & M., and the Sioux City—were competitors of the Union Pacific. The Kansas Pacific will be examined in the following chapter. The competition of the other two lines, was, however, only theoretical, unless the rival routes could carry traffic on the basis of a non-discriminatory freight rate. The rate per ton-mile had to be the same by the various routes; otherwise the shipper would prefer the route charging the lower rate. The Union Pacific was in control. On the eastbound traffic, either the Central Pacific or the Union Pacific originated the business, and hence they could control the routing of the business. On westbound traffic destined for points either on the Union Pacific or beyond, west of Ogden, the Union Pacific was also in a dominant position. On both east and westbound traffic it could charge one rate for traffic moving entirely over its own line and another and higher rate for traffic moving in part over its own line and in part over the line of its rivals. The federal legislation requiring non-discriminatory treatment was not clearly drafted; the language was obscure; and the Union Pacific followed its own business interests in setting up a competitive rate structure. It refused, that is, to short-haul itself—to permit competitive roads to carry a part of the business from Kearney to East Plattsmouth or from Fremont to a connection with the Northwestern. It would rather carry the traffic on its own line from these points to Omaha, thereby increasing its earnings.

The other lines demanded a rate per ton-mile approximately similar to that prevailing on the Union Pacific. The approach to the Union Pacific was first made by the B. & M. in October of 1872. That road's line to Kearney had been completed the previous month. Its president wrote to Clark, suggesting a rate structure that would enable the B. & M. to carry traffic via Kearney. The letter was ignored. Appeals were made to some of the large stockholders of the Union Pacific, particularly the Ames brothers. They were business friends of stockholders of the B. & M. and the Burlington. This appeal also brought no results. The B. & M. managers then prepared plans for a solution in the form of congressional legislation. This started a long legal and business war, terminated finally by the elimination of the problem in the 1880's through the formation of new transcontinental routes. The rivalry then changed to one between the Union Pacific–Kansas Pacific merged corporation on the one hand and the extended Burlington-B. & M. line to Denver on the other.

Under the Iowa Pool arrangement the profits of the Iowa roads depended upon the volume of traffic interchanged with the Union Pacific and partly upon the percentage of the through rate received from that road. Early in 1874 the Iowa lines demanded a larger percentage of the rate. The Union Pacific in turn proposed that the percentage be reduced. The Union Pacific then threatened to divert its business to other eastern connections. The major competitors of the Iowa Pool roads were located south of Omaha; they will be referred to hereafter as the southern routes. One of the keys to the southern route was the Council Bluffs Railroad. It extended from Omaha to Kansas City, where it connected with the Missouri Pacific and with the St. Louis, Kansas City and Northern. Both roads ran east to St. Louis. The Kansas City and Northern also connected at some point in Missouri with the Chicago and Alton's line to Chicago. At St. Joseph the Council Bluffs connected with the St. Joseph and Denver City. This road extended west to Hastings, Nebraska, where it connected with the B. & M. Over a 40-mile Hastings-Kearney stretch, the St. Joseph made a connection with the Union Pacific. At a point in Missouri north of St. Joseph, the Council Bluffs by a traffic agreement afforded the Burlington its entrance into Council Bluffs, and from that point, via a bridge connection, the transfer with the Union Pacific was effected. The Union Pacific thus could move traffic south from Council Bluffs over the Council Bluffs road to Kansas City for eastern movement. It could also move the traffic over that same road to St. Joseph and east over the Hannibal and St. Joseph Railroad for a connection with the Wabash at its eastern end at Hannibal. Traffic moving this way competed with the direct routes of the Iowa Pool roads between Omaha and Chicago. The southern routes were circuitous; but there were ample precedents for traffic movements over circuitous routes.

This by no means closed the list of possible competition for the Union Pacific transcontinental business. There was another small property, the Atchison and Nebraska. That line, together with the Council Bluffs road on the east side of the river, were known as the Joy properties. Both had been promoted by Joy; both were operated under his general direction; and the stockholders of both roads entertained confidence in Joy's leadership. The A. & N. operated from Omaha south to Lincoln where a connection was made with the B. & M. From that point the B. & M. could move its traffic east over the Burlington, or by various connections to St. Joseph or Kansas City, and for eastward movement by roads other than the Burlington.

These alternative routes could be used only if a satisfactory rate structure were obtained. If either the Council Bluffs or the A. & N. charged high rates for short hauls, the through rate structure to Chicago and beyond would be higher than over the Iowa roads. The controlling factor in this competition was Joy. By adjusting the rate structures over the A. & N. and the Council Bluffs, he could either obstruct or facilitate the movement of traffic over the southern routes.

Early in February, 1874, shortly after the struggle developed between the Union Pacific and the Iowa lines over the division of the through rate, the Union Pacific aimed its first competitive shot. It asked the Council Bluffs road to make an arrangement for the movement of freight over its line by way of St. Louis. The Council Bluffs had previously endeavored to get some of the Union Pacific business. "All at once," declared the general superintendent of the Council Bluffs, "we were requested to take business that way and as the prospect was that the business would be very considerable and at rates which would pay us very well . . . I at once, and I may say greedily, caught at the opportunity of securing business."[7] The Council Bluffs had been the beneficiary of this new business for about ten days early in February. The Union Pacific promised to give the Council Bluffs "a fair share of the business."[8] To Joy this business was not a pure gain. He had to contend with more than the Council Bluffs. He was aware of the danger that might arise from the rate reduction necessary to accommodate the new flow of Union Pacific traffic. He therefore wired the Council Bluffs superintendent: "Take all business that comes but don't make any arrangement with that Co. [the Union Pacific] and charge full local rates. The quarrel will be short and you can gain nothing permanently by playing into their hands with low rates."[9]

By declining the opportunity to move additional traffic over the Council Bluffs, Joy reduced its earnings. To compensate that road for its loss, Joy made an arrangement with the three Iowa Pool roads by which they agreed to give the Council Bluffs 2/17ths of the pool's earnings on the

Union Pacific business. This satisfied the Council Bluffs, and it accordingly notified the Union Pacific that it would not carry its business at the lower rates but would charge the rates applicable to the local traffic. At these higher rates no business to and from the Union Pacific would move. Traffic would return to the direct line of the Iowa roads.

The Union Pacific by this time was under the leadership of Gould and his associates. Gould moved decisively in the struggle against the Iowa lines. The Union Pacific had tasted defeat in the opening battle to move traffic over the Council Bluffs. Gould thereupon turned his attention to the B. & M. The president of that road was J. W. Brooke, with a long experience in the railroad business and one of the early Joy associates. The vice-president was C. E. Perkins, who was then in his early thirties. Though Brooke was president he spent most of his time in Boston. The man on the field of operations in Nebraska was Perkins. Though there were many stockholders with common holdings in both the Burlington and B. & M., Perkins followed policies designed to further the interest of the B. & M. There was a considerable minority-stockholder interest. That is, there were many stockholders of the B. & M. who had no Burlington stock. Perkins conceived it to be his responsibility to press forward with those policies that aided the B. & M., even though they impaired the Burlington fortunes. When the Union Pacific approached Perkins with its proposal to move traffic via Kearney and the B. & M. beyond, Perkins was overjoyed. The B. & M.'s major connection was the Burlington. The B. & M. could also reach other eastern routes, competitors with the Iowa routes, over the A. & N. Joy moved quickly to close this route to the Union Pacific. He insisted upon charging the higher local rates for traffic interchanged with the B. & M. This decision upset Perkins. He objected to the closing of the B. & M. route. "I am unable to see," he wrote, "why the interests of the B. & M. in Nebraska should be made to suffer in order that the Pool lines may be victorious in the present controversy with the U. P."[10] Perkins was not impressed with the argument of Joy and the Pool roads that the Union Pacific wanted to do business with the B. & M. via Kearney only to force the hand of the Iowa roads. He was convinced that the Union Pacific would not throw his road overboard, once it was able to make an arrangement with the Iowa lines. Perkins for the first time was doing business with Gould. He did not understand Gould's ability in business trading. Events soon proved the soundness of the argument of the Iowa roads. Gould was not interested in working up an alternative route. That route was bound to produce a sub-standard service. He wanted a greater division of the through rate for the Union Pacific, thereby to increase the earnings of that road. Perkins, however, was ready to learn and the lesson he learned in his early experience with Gould stood him in good stead in subsequent negotiations.

There remained still another alternative to enable the B. & M. to participate in the movement of business with the Union Pacific. It was possible that the St. Joseph could arrange with the B. & M. for the movement over the latter's 40-mile line between Kearney and Hastings and beyond over the St. Joseph to the city of St. Joseph. If the St. Joseph offered business on this basis, Perkins thought he could not decline. "How," he insisted "are B. & M. stockholders who do not happen to own C. B. & Q. stock, benefited by my refusing to do it."[11] Furthermore, Perkins insisted that with the A. & N. route closed, and with the B. & M. refusing to do business with the St. Joseph, the Union Pacific would be inclined to aid the St. Joseph to build a line into Kearney.

The conflict between the Iowa Pool roads and the Union Pacific continued for months. Joy changed his mind a number of times, first admitting and then excluding the A. & N. from participation in the movement of the Union Pacific traffic. Various agreements were also made to limit the movement of the business over the B. & M. by the adjustment of the rate structure to St. Louis.

By the summer of 1875 Joy's unity of business interests with the Burlington, an interest that had continued ever since the beginning of the Burlington property, was terminated. Because of a difference in view over some participation in the activities of a number of construction companies, Joy after a proxy contest was ousted from the Burlington's directorate. He remained nevertheless in control of both the A. & N. and the Council Bluffs. In control of these properties, he was not, however, able to follow a consistent policy. He made decisions which forced these two roads to work against each other's interests. The Alton meanwhile was completed to Kansas City. That road was financially strong. It had also a line to Chicago, and from time to time entered into various arrangements to move the traffic by one of the southern routes. The Alton reduced rates in order to force the movement of traffic over its line.

The pressure exerted by the Union Pacific upon the pool lines was designed only in part to force those roads to accept a lower division of the through rates. There was also the motive of separating the interests of the Burlington from those of its two Pool associates. The Burlington interchanged a substantial volume of business with the B. & M. The business of the Union Pacific was divided at Omaha among the three pool roads. The traffic of the B. & M. however, was almost entirely moved to East Plattsmouth for delivery to the Burlington. To facilitate this interchange, the Burlington agreed to give the B. & M. a drawback—a payment in exchange for the eastbound movement over its line of the B. & M.'s business. The Northwestern also had a slight adverse interest in the traffic moving from the Sioux City to its line. As compared with the volume moving over the Burlington and the B. & M., the Northwestern receipts from the Sioux City were nominal. The third member of the Iowa roads, the Rock Island, received no benefit from any trans-Missouri traffic other than that coming from the Union Pacific at Omaha. Though rifts were occasionally introduced between the Burlington and the other two lines, they managed nevertheless to maintain unity of policy against the Union Pacific. The latter's pressure against the Burlington, however, was so strong that that road considered for a time the advisability of joining with the Atchison to build a competitive line to Ogden, to connect there with the Central Pacific. This would have been a damaging blow to the Union Pacific. This intention was reflected in a letter from one of the senior members of the Burlington board to the general superintendent of the Central Pacific. The Union Pacific, he wrote, was "pursuing so autocratic a course that it is in the possibilities that we or our friends may be obliged to aid the Atchison & Topeka to put in the link which would give them a connection with you at Ogden."[12]

Gould by the spring of 1877 had not been successful in his struggles with the Iowa roads. His successive moves to force traffic over the southern route had met with scant success. Perkins had now recognized that Gould was trifling with him. In Nebraska Gould had plunged into successive conflicts with the B. & M. over the construction of local lines. He had solicited public subsidies in aid of new construction. He also moved to acquire control of the Council Bluffs. There was also the fear that Gould would endeavor to acquire control of the Hannibal, thereby completing a southern route under his control. The B. & M., on its part, supported now by the Burlington and the Kansas Pacific, renewed the efforts to secure passage of the so-called pro rata bill. This provided for the establishment of a commission to adjust the rate structure between the Union Pacific and its branches in such a way as to give the latter a fair proportion of the transcontinental business.

The strategic position of Gould in these negotiations was strengthened in the spring of 1877. Stock prices declined to low levels. Furthermore, Tracy and W. L. Scott were unable to honor the terms of a $300 thousand bank loan endorsed by the Northwestern. Their bank loans were called, and the hypothecated Rock Island and Northwestern stocks were sold in the open market. Gould bought enough stock of both of the roads to justify his election to their directorates. The management of the Rock Island, particularly Dows, a prominent member of the New York stock trading fraternity, looked upon Gould with favor. The Northwestern management, however, was dominated by a conservative group under the leadership of President Keep. Some members of the board and many stockholders were suspicious of Gould. In any event, he represented only a minority interest in the directorships. He could exert no significant influence on management unless he enlisted the co-operation of other stockholders.

Shortly after his election to the directorships of the Rock Island and the Northwestern, Gould moved to utilize his improved strategic position. He now believed it possible to mass the joint interests of the Union Pacific, Rock Island, and Northwestern against those of the Burlington—B. & M. combination. He had learned by experience that on some problems the three Iowa roads were united. They would not accept a lower division of the through rate to favor the Union Pacific as against their own lines. Gould had tried unsuccessfully to force a concession on this point. He now moved to force the B. & M. to withdraw its support of the pro rata bill then pending in Congress. The other chief supporter of the bill was the Kansas Pacific. With the B. & M.'s support of the bill withdrawn, it was reasonable to believe that the measure would die.

The B. & M. meanwhile continued to move its growing local traffic in southern Nebraska exclusively over the Burlington. The Union Pacific exchanged its business equally between the three Iowa roads at Omaha. The Union Pacific, however, received no drawback, as did the B. & M. from the Burlington. The Burlington thus received all the interchange business with the B. & M., as well as one-third of the Union Pacific business at Omaha. Gould tried to convince the Rock Island and the Northwestern that this was an inequitable arrangement. He proposed that the Union Pacific turn over all its Omaha-Kearney business at Omaha to these two roads and divide the revenue one-third to the Union Pacific and two-thirds to the Northwestern and Rock Island. The traffic west of Kearney would be divided as heretofore between the three Iowa roads.[13]

A few weeks after Gould's election to the directorships of the Rock Island and the Northwestern, he called a meeting in Boston, attended by representatives of all the interested roads: the Union Pacific, the B. & M., and the three Iowa roads. His proposal to solve the existing problems was comprehensive in character. The solution was in the form of a joint lease of the B. & M. by the Union Pacific and the three Iowa roads. This arrangement was known in subsequent discussions as the Quintuple Contract. A return would be guaranteed to the B. & M. while all its business would be delivered at Omaha for division among the pool roads.

It was obvious that the Burlington under this arrangement would be a loser. It would lose the traffic from the B. & M. at East Plattsmouth and retain only a third of its traffic at Omaha with the Union Pacific. The other two Iowa roads would, of course, gain. They would each receive one-third of the B. & M.'s traffic at Omaha, whereas now they received none. In this way the Gould proposal would, on the face of things, introduce a decisive and, so Gould hoped, a fatal division among the Iowa lines.

It was logical for the Burlington to reject the proposal; and so it did. Discussion and negotiations continued for many weeks. In the Burlington camp there were two parties. One was led by Harris, president of the road. He was genuinely fearful of the Gould pressure. He believed that Gould might succeed in making a preferential arrangement with the Northwestern and Rock Island, to the exclusion of the Burlington. "My own judgment is," declared Harris, "that the C. & N. W. would yield to the pressure that Gould can bring to bear to take the U. P. business in common with C. R. I. & P. and break the pool, and all my action is based upon this idea."[14] This defensive reasoning of Harris led him to conclude that the Union Pacific could turn trade away from the Burlington and over the two other Iowa roads. And he argued that the Burlington could afford better to lose two-thirds of the B. & M.'s business than to lose one-third of the Union Pacific's.

There was, however, another group in the Burlington, led by Perkins. He was now president of the B. & M. He had become dissatisfied with Gould's complicated moves in relation to the B. & M. His enthusiastic acceptance of Gould's proposal to move traffic over his line in his initial encounter early in 1874 was now supplanted by a determined opposition, coupled with an increasing element of personal bitterness. He refused to make any concessions to the Union Pacific. The B. & M. had a contract with the Burlington; that contract had proved profitable to both roads; and that was that.

In the course of these discussions many proposals and counter-proposals were canvassed.[15] There appeared to be some possibility that a joint arrangement between the participating roads would be negotiated. By June, 1877, the Rock Island and the Northwestern had been so convinced of the soundness of some of Gould's proposals that they in turn made a number of their own. One plan would reduce the drawback paid to the B. & M. It was just at this critical time, when Gould appeared to have achieved some co-operation with the Northwestern and Rock Island, that he took another step, misconceived and, as it turned out, fatal to his negotiations. While he was assuring the two Iowa roads of his desire to trade preferentially with them via the Omaha interchange, he began to move business over the southern route, via the Hannibal. Both the Northwestern and the Rock Island were disillusioned. Dows, of the Rock Island, was particularly aggrieved over Gould's double-dealing. The Burlington hurried to complete negotiations for a new interchange contract with the B. & M. By the end of June the contract had been ratified. The proposed Quintuple Contract was dead.

Gould, though defeated, persisted in his campaign to separate the Northwestern and the Rock Island's interests from those of the Burlington.[16] His good faith was brought into question by an abortive move in the summer of 1877 to capture control of the Hannibal. Through the use of a small loan and by some financial methods characteristic of his trading techniques, he almost succeeded in taking control. His failure to do so led him to threaten a substantial diversion of Union Pacific traffic over the southern routes, a move that was probably the major factor in re-establishing a community of interests among the three Iowa roads. They were now closer in the recognition of common business interests than ever before.

The prolonged battle between Gould and Perkins, between the Union Pacific and the Burlington, was not yet resolved. It was, however, clear that Gould had failed in his battle to pry loose the community of interest between the three Iowa roads. Neither the threats to move traffic over the southern routes nor the drives to break up the pool made any pronounced impression. The willingness of Gould to subordinate the interests of the Rock Island and Northwestern to those of the Union Pacific had, furthermore, prejudiced the management of the former two toward Gould. His movement of traffic over the southern routes proved to those managements Gould's inability to represent their real interests. A similar charge of faithlessness to various interests was manifested during the same year in the struggle over the control of the other major branch of the Union Pacific—the Kansas Pacific. That conflict will be examined in the following chapter.

Notes for Chapter V

[1] Huntington to Hopkins, Oct. 1873, M. M.

[2] For details on Gould's acquisition of control of the Union Pacific, see *Gould*, Chapter VII.

[3] *Railway Monitor*, 1874, p. 217.

[4] Details of these increases were presented by Scott to a congressional committee, cited in *Ry. World*, Feb. 12, 1876, p. 92.

[5] Huntington to Colton, April 12, 1875, M. M.

[6] Chapter III, page 48.

[7] Joy papers, J. F. Barnard to Joy, Feb. 10, 1874.

[8] *Ibid.*

[9] *Ibid.*

[10] Burlington Archives, Perkins to Robert Harris, March 20, 1874.

[11] *Ibid.*

[12] *Ibid.*, Griswold to Towne, Oct. 25, 1876.

[13] The approval of the Northwestern and Rock Island to this proposal is noted in Northwestern Archives, Keep to Sykes, vice-president, Northwestern, July 2, 1877.

[14] Burlington Archives, Harris to Griswold, April 7, 1877. This letter was marked "Not sent."

[15] For a detailed examination of these proposals see *Iowa Pool*, pp. 79–84.

[16] One is discussed in Northwestern Archives, Keep to Sykes, July 2, 1877.

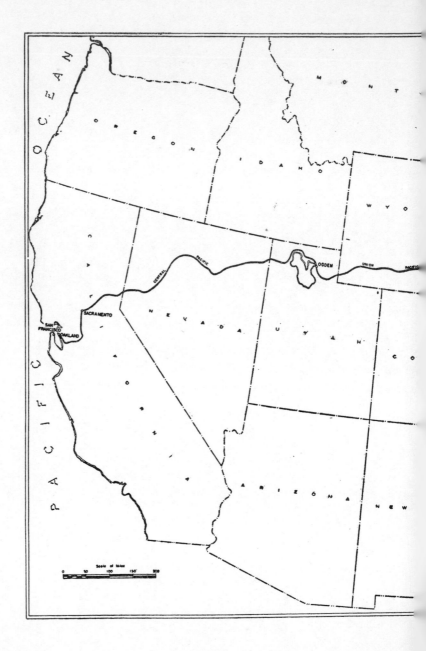

84

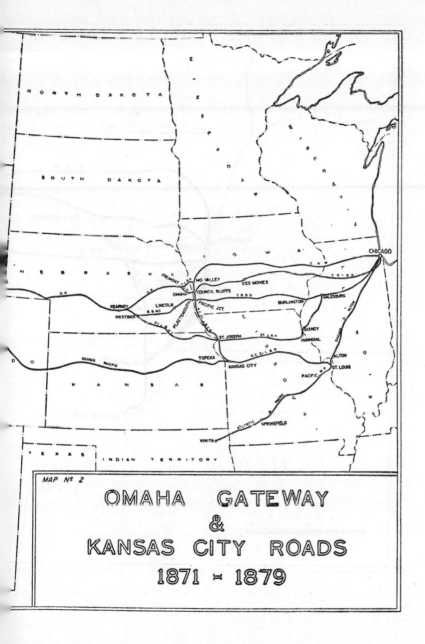

MAP № 2

OMAHA GATEWAY
&
KANSAS CITY ROADS
1871 = 1879

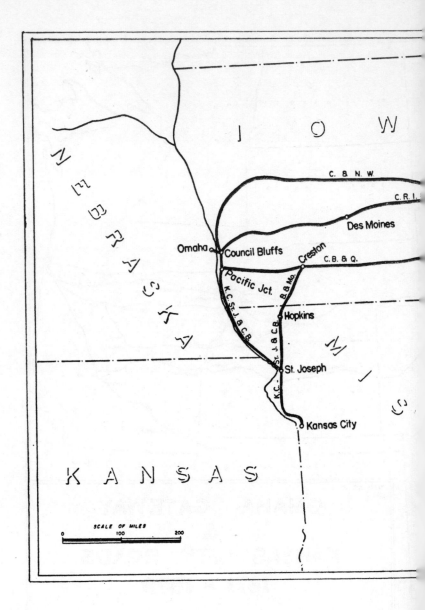

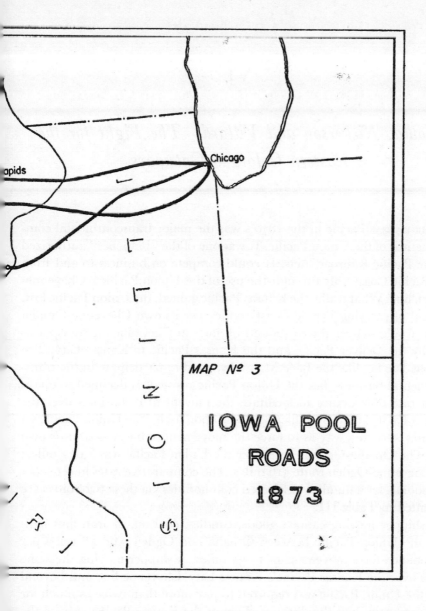

apids

Chicago

MAP Nº 3

IOWA POOL
ROADS
1873

ILLINOIS

VI

Gould, Nickerson and Villard—The Fight for the Eastern Colorado Gateways

THE KANSAS Pacific in the 1870's was the major transcontinental competitor of the Union Pacific. It was one of the "branches" authorized by the Pacific Railroad Acts. It could compete on business to and from the Pacific Coast only through the use of the Union Pacific's Cheyenne-Ogden line. What traffic the Kansas Pacific gained, the Union Pacific lost. Instead of carrying Pacific Coast traffic over its own Cheyenne-Omaha line it would deliver the eastbound business at Cheyenne for transportation by the Denver Pacific and the Kansas Pacific to Kansas City. The Kansas Pacific, like the B. & M., endeavored to participate in the transcontinental business, but the Union Pacific resisted. It declined to establish a rate of structure to facilitate the movement of business over the Kansas Pacific, thereby inflicting a loss upon itself. The Union Pacific set up rates in such a way as to force the movement of business over its own line. The Omaha-Ogden route over the Union Pacific was 1,032 miles; the Cheyenne-Ogden route 516 miles. The comparative rates in cents per 100 pounds for a number of selected commodities via these two routes are presented in Table III.

A shipper moving canned goods, candles, coal oil, or iron and nails over the Union Pacific between Omaha and Ogden paid 78 cents per 100 pounds for a movement of 1,032 miles. A shipper moving the same goods over the Kansas Pacific's Kansas City–Cheyenne line and beyond over the Union Pacific was required to pay more than twice as much for a movement of half the distance. Even if the Kansas Pacific carried the freight between Kansas City and Cheyenne for nothing, it still would be unable to meet the Union Pacific competition.

The Kansas Pacific accordingly instituted suit for damages against

Table III

RATES IN CENTS PER 100 POUNDS,
VIA OMAHA–OGDEN AND CHEYENNE–OGDEN ROUTE[1]

Commodity	Omaha-Ogden	Cheyenne-Ogden
Canned Goods . .	78	219
Candles . . .	78	191
Coal Oil . . .	78	191
Iron and Nails . .	78	163
Stoves . . .	101	219

the Union Pacific, and supported legislation to force the Union Pacific to provide a rate structure to enable it to carry some of the transcontinental traffic. These efforts met with no success.

On the western end of the Kansas Pacific there had been completed in the early 1870's a route extending from Denver south through Pueblo and into southeastern Colorado. That line was built by the Denver and Rio Grande; it was part of a route south to the Rio Grande River and the Republic of Mexico. Traffic from that line would move east over the Kansas Pacific connection at Denver.

Both the Kansas Pacific and the Rio Grande were financed by the Pennsylvania Railroad interests. As early as 1865 Thomson, president, and Scott, vice-president, participated in negotiations leading to the construction of these two lines.[2] In 1870–1871 the orginal subscribers to the Rio Grande included many investors associated with the Pennsylvania Railroad group.

The financial difficulties that swept over the Pennsylvania capitalists in the wake of the 1873 panic made it impossible for the Kansas Pacific and the Rio Grande to get further help from this source. Both roads encountered financial reverses. Late in 1873 the Kansas Pacific found itself unable to pay its interest; this was followed by an arrangement by which the unpaid interest was funded into long-term bonds. The Rio Grande's financial problems were approximately similar, and the road resorted to the same financial mechanism.

8

After his seizure of Union Pacific control, Gould proposed to work out a community of interests between the two roads. He offered to harmonize the corporate differences and for that purpose called upon Scott in Philadelphia. A few weeks thereafter a plan was presented: a new company would be organized, one-half of the stock to be exchanged for the Kansas Pacific stock and the other half to be issued to persons named by the Union Pacific. The Kansas Pacific bondholders would make a sacrifice. They would accept new Kansas Pacific bonds in exchange for their bonds at substantial discounts from their face values. The Union Pacific would withdraw from competition for the local Colorado traffic, while the new company would withdraw from traffic west of Cheyenne.

This scheme never went into effect. Its collapse led to a war of rates between the Kansas Pacific and the Union Pacific. It appears that the Pennsylvania group early in 1875 sold its Kansas Pacific holdings. The negotiations associated with the plan of 1875 led to a rise in the price of Kansas Pacific securities, and it seems that the Pennsylvania security holders sold out on the rise. In the transactions in the following five years, culminating in the Kansas Pacific–Union Pacific merger in 1880, the Pennsylvania group did not participate. The same conclusion must be reached with regard to the Rio Grande's securities. Little is heard of the Pennsylvania interests after 1874.

The friendly relationships based upon the traffic interchange at Denver between the Kansas Pacific and the Rio Grande was disturbed by the entrance of a new competitor early in 1876. The Atchison had encountered financial troubles and the original group sold out to another in 1869. Another financial crisis hit the road in the fall of 1873. Its financial problems were intensified by a costly grasshopper invasion: traffic declined, and wages were cut 20 per cent. A new group of capitalists under the leadership of Nickerson acquired control. Nickerson was a man of means who had made his way in the shipping business. Included in the new group were a number of Boston bankers and businessmen. They included Francis H. Peabody and C. W. Pierce—both of whom soon began a productive association with the Atchison. With this financial support the road undertook an expansion program which carried it by March, 1876, to Pueblo. The road was now a competitor with the Kansas Pacific for the business of the Rio Grande. That road was under the leadership of General William J. Palmer, a graduate of the Pennsylvania Railroad School. He was the promoter and chief executive. Both Palmer and

Nickerson nourished far-reaching corporate ambitions. Meanwhile the competition between the Kansas Pacific and the Atchison for the eastbound traffic of the Rio Grande constituted the immediate problem. The Rio Grande was in a strategic position in the battle between the two eastern connections. The Atchison by this time had completed a line to Kansas City, thereby making it a competitor with the Kansas Pacific for the Colorado–Kansas City traffic. The Rio Grande, by adjusting the rate structure, could divert business either to the one line or to the other. By rate reductions on traffic moving to Denver it could divert over the Kansas Pacific, and by a concession on southbound traffic to Pueblo it could divert over the Atchison. The arrival of the Atchison in Pueblo was followed initially by a showing of corporate friendship. An agreement among the three roads required the Rio Grande to divide its business between the Kansas Pacific and Atchison. This was accompanied by an understanding that the former line would not build to Pueblo and the latter would not build to Denver.

The friendly relations envisioned by this agreement lasted for only a short time. The pool did not function well. Palmer and Nickerson distrusted each other; Nickerson was convinced that Palmer violated the pool contract—Palmer had cheated him, he insisted.[3] A clash between Palmer and Nickerson was followed by a pooling arrangement that diverted the Rio Grande traffic to the Kansas Pacific and reduced the Atchison's to nominal proportions. Nickerson revolted. He would not be "bottled up," he asserted. If Palmer refused the Atchison a reasonable share of the business, the Atchison would be forced to extend its line.[4]

While these traffic struggles continued, the financial problems of the Kansas Pacific took a turn for the worse. In November, 1877, the period of financial relief for the Kansas Pacific expired. The road was forced into receivership. Two receivers were appointed. One, Carlos Greeley, represented the holders of the bonds secured by a first mortgage on the eastern division of the road. Henry Villard, the other receiver, represented largely the holders of the first-mortgage bonds on the western end, known as the Denver Extension bonds. The Kansas Pacific, furthermore, incurred a floating debt. A substantial part of this debt was guaranteed by members of the board. To take care of the debt the creditors accepted a suggestion made by Gould. This was in the form of a funding mortgage bond accompanied by a promise made by Gould, one of his associates, and the Union Pacific itself to relieve the directors of a large portion of the personal liability for the floating debt in the event of a default on the first-mortgage bonds. The funding mortgage was secured by collateral including the Denver Pacific stock. This arrangement placed Gould in a strategic trading position. Upon the default of this mortgage, the Denver Pacific would pass to the Union Pacific. This would eliminate the ability of the Kansas Pacific to compete with the Union Pacific on transcontinental traffic. Gould also made some short-term loans.

By this time, furthermore, Gould had acquired substantial holdings in the Kansas Pacific stock. With these securities Gould planned to acquire control of the road. His major opponent was Villard. A Committee of Nine, representing the Denver Extension bondholders, had been set up in December, 1876. The holders of the junior securities had organized a syndicate to unify their interests under Gould leadership. Gould made various proposals to Villard involving some sacrifice on behalf of the first-mortgage bondholders. Villard declined to make any concession and Gould exerted pressure. At one time he signed a contract with the Iowa Pool lines to move more business via Omaha and less by Kansas City and the Kansas Pacific. According to Villard, this contract was made "preparatory to a desperate raid on our [Kansas Pacific] Colorado business. . . ."[5] Another Gould step was the completion of the unfinished stub of the Colorado Central—a Union Pacific subsidiary—to Cheyenne, for connection with the Union Pacific. The Colorado Central had built a line from Denver to Longmont, a small point in eastern Colorado. For a number of years the Union Pacific held over the Kansas Pacific the threat of the completion of this stub to the Union Pacific main line. Its construction to Cheyenne late in 1877 diverted business from the Kansas Pacific to the Union Pacific. A rate war soon followed.

Heavy losses were incurred by both properties. Still Villard fought on. Gould extended the pressure. By the end of 1877 he had succeeded in inducing the court to dismiss both Villard and Greeley as receivers. Gould intensified the rate war. The Union Pacific, wrote Villard in February of 1878, "seems to be now making war on us in earnest."[6]

Villard, still fighting, continued with plans to foreclose the Denver Extension mortgage. This would eliminate most of Gould's investment in the junior securities. In pursuance of this plan Villard endeavored to enlist leading capitalists behind the Burlington and the Atchison, particularly William Endicott, who soon became a devoted financial follower of Villard and who was destined to invest millions in future Villard enterprises. Funds were needed to acquire control of the primary Kansas Pacific mortgage and to pay off the floating debt and the junior mortgages. Villard proposed that the Kansas Pacific be acquired in joint interest of the Atchison and the Burlington. He even set up in March of 1878 a proposed board of directors of a reorganized Kansas Pacific. Representatives of the Burlington would include Forbes and Perkins— the latter now vice-president of the Burlington—and also George Tyson, president of the B. & M. The Atchison would be represented by Nickerson, C. J. Paine, and Peabody. The other three members of the board would be Villard, Endicott, and Horace White, another Villard follower.[7]

Such an arrangement would give the Burlington an outlet to eastern Colorado and fulfil a project which had long been considered by the Burlington directorate. Tyson urged the Burlington to take an interest in the Kansas Pacific. He believed that control of the road could be acquired for little money and with little risk of loss. Also the co-operation of the Atchison would be secured. If, however, Gould acquired the Kansas Pacific, he would hold "a strong weapon to strike all around."[8] Forbes, the financial leader of the Burlington group, was cool to the idea.

While these negotiations were proceeding, competitive bitterness on a lower official level between the Kansas Pacific and the Atchison continued. A pool for the division of business between the two roads was devised in April of 1877. The arrangement did not work well. Villard claimed that the Atchison was cutting rates. The officials of the latter had other complaints. Its general superintendent opposed the pool; he insisted that the Kansas Pacific was capturing business that belonged to his line.[9] Personal and business relationships grew more bitter.

While Villard was strengthening his grip on the first-mortgage bonds and while the rate wars between the Kansas Pacific and the Atchison continued, Gould joined with another group in a devious effort to acquire control of the Denver Pacific. John Evans, a former governor of Colorado, had organized a road north of Denver known as the Denver, South Park and Pacific. The road had encountered financial difficulties. He had made efforts to obtain financial aid from Villard and Villard had rejected his advances. Evans was personally popular in Denver, and Gould decided to work closely with him in an effort to wrest control of the Denver Pacific from the Kansas Pacific. The Denver Pacific was not earning its interest.

To insure control of that road, the Kansas Pacific provided a fund for the Denver Pacific interest payments. Evans impressed the community of Denver with the wisdom of establishing an independent management of the Denver Pacific; this meant the divorce of that line from its association with the Kansas Pacific. The means used by Gould and Evans to carry out this scheme were strongly resented by Villard. Evans' conduct "in D. P. matters justified the conclusion that it is wise not to have anything to do with him or anything he is interested in," declared Villard.[10] And a close associate of Villard declared strongly that "avaricious and ambition are his [Evan's] ruling passions."[11]

The Kansas Pacific officials reported to Villard that Gould was the instigator of the Denver Pacific's trouble in Denver and that he was using Evans as an instrument. Villard was fearful that the bondholders might decide to work with Evans and thus transfer the Denver Pacific to Union Pacific control. A majority of the bonds were held in Amsterdam, and both Evans and Gould visited that city to consult with the bondholders.

All these Gould pressures against Villard produced no concessions. Villard maintained firmly that the Kansas Pacific road was, as things then stood, the property of the bondholders. Villard continued to press forward in his effort to push through the pro rata bill. Dillon and Gould, on behalf of the Union Pacific, called on Villard to induce him to withdraw his support of this legislation. Villard refused. He was confident of the success of his efforts in Congress. In this campaign Tyson, of the Burlington, declared that Villard "will resist the devil and all his works if not interfered with by others."[12]

By the spring of 1878 Gould concluded that his attack on Villard's position was not producing results. He then approached Villard with a proposal that the interests of the junior and the senior securities be harmonized. To carry out this plan, he first suggested the idea of pooling the junior securities and second, that of Villard's joining the committee administering the pool. After some reluctance, Villard joined the junior pool. The pooled securities were then exchanged for the stock of the pool. Gould then entered into further negotiations to reorganize the property. He now proposed to unite the four properties: Union Pacific, Denver Pacific, Kansas Pacific, and Colorado Central. Together with the Omaha Bridge connecting Omaha and Council Bluffs, the properties would be placed under the direction of the Union Pacific. The revenue from all these roads would be consigned to a common fund. The rate war between the Kansas Pacific and the Union Pacific would be called off; the Kansas Pacific first-mortgage bonds would be exchanged for new securities, and new bonds exchanged for the old first-mortgage bonds would carry a Union Pacific guarantee. The stock of the new company would pay dividends at once. Furthermore, since the Union Pacific would hold a controlling interest in the stock of the new company, it would be to its interest to move California business alternatively either over the Omaha line or over the Cheyenne–Denver–Kansas City Line. Under these arrangements the Union Pacific would get one-half of the new stock of the Kansas Pacific and the other half would go to the security holders of the Kansas Pacific.

Villard was confident that he had reached a satisfactory solution and had successfully defended the interest of the first-mortgage bondholders committed to his care. He was satisfied that Gould was acting in good faith. The sense of satisfaction, however, soon received a heavy shock. Less than one month after this arrangement, a meeting of the pool was held in Lawrence, Kansas. Villard was not present. A resolution was passed with a view of effecting a quick foreclosure under the terms of one of the junior mortgages. It was designed apparently to depress the market price. The purport of the resolution was soon communicated to Villard, who promptly called a meeting of the Committee of Nine representing the first-mortage bondholders.

Gould, in the opinion of Villard, had now violated the pool contract. The break between Villard and Gould was again renewed. Gould, wrote Villard, was "again going back on us. . . . He and the rascally St. Louis people . . . have formed a regular conspiracy in the west to break the contract and cheat the bondholders."[13] A desperate struggle between Villard and Gould now ensued. Villard moved quickly to secure control of a majority of the Denver Extension bond. Through bankers in New York, Germany, England, and France, he succeeded in securing the deposit with his committee of a substantial percentage of the bonds. He then instructed counsel to press for foreclosure.

Villard also secured additional financial support. A syndicate organized to buy the first-mortgage bonds included the firm of Drexel, Morgan and Company and a number of New York brokers, including von Hoffman, who had aided Huntington in 1873. Villard pressed forward in renewed moves to enlist the support of the Burlington and the Atchison. Forbes, though still reluctant to commit the Burlington to the Kansas Pacific acquisition, personally subscribed for $175 thousand of the Denver Extension bonds. Members of the Atchison board also made substantial commitments. Gould, however, was not idle, and he bought Denver Extension bonds in the open market in an effort to prevent the Villard Committee from getting control of a majority. Gould, wrote Villard to Forbes, was "moving heaven and earth and resorting to every possible trick to prevent us from getting a majority."[14] In these efforts Gould was unsuccessful. By the fall of the year the Villard Committee had acquired a substantial majority of the bonds.

Villard was now sure of victory over Gould. The path was clear once he had a majority of the senior bonds under his control. He now conceived the idea of making the Kansas Pacific not only financially but also operatively independent of the Union Pacific. He proposed to accomplish this by building a line to Ogden. There was a chance, he wrote, to make the Kansas Pacific "the most important line on the continent, if its managers will steer clear of Gould and carry out your plan of building to Ogden."[15]

While the negotiations were proceeding between Gould and Villard over the fate of the Kansas Pacific, another business-competition battle was raging in southeastern Colorado. The Atchison's ambition to build west to Salt Lake City involved the construction of a line through a narrow rock canyon about ten yards wide, with room for but one set of rails. This canyon, known as the Royal Gorge, had been surveyed by the Rio Grande. Both roads in the spring of 1878 decided to build a line through the gorge. Beyond the gorge the right of way was clear for the construction of an extension to Leadville, where rich silver-bearing ores had been discovered. Railroad communication was badly needed for the movement of inbound food and supplies for a rapidly growing population and for the outbound movement of the ore. Officers and employees of the Atchison and the Rio Grande clashed in the Royal Gorge. A confused battle of physical force, business rivalry, and judicial proceedings followed. The clash between the rival interests was dramatic and the details provided the newspapers with many interesting, if not entirely accurate, dispatches. Nickerson, in an attempt to solve the problems with the Rio Grande, threw aside financial considerations and induced the Atchison board to approve a lease of the road. It seemed that intercorporate peace would prevail. The trouble, however, continued. Palmer insisted that the Atchison was subordinating the interests of the Rio Grande to those of the South Park; that the Atchison had violated the lease by diverting traffic from the Rio Grande to the other property; and that rates were so manipulated by the Atchison as to force traffic over the latter's line via Pueblo and away from the Kansas Pacific's line at Denver. Resort was again had to judicial proceedings. The lease was cancelled and the property was restored to the custody of the Rio Grande. The Rio Grande, furthermore, was given the right to build the line through the Royal Gorge, to the exclusion of the Atchison. This enabled the Rio Grande to build a line to Leadville, thereby capturing the rich traffic of that rapidly growing area.

On a short-run basis, accordingly, in the battle for the rich Leadville business the Atchison had lost and the Rio Grande had won. The Rio Grande, with a plan to build south, had changed its direction and moved west. The Atchison, on the contrary, which had planned to build west, decided to build south. The low-cost route from eastern Colorado to the Southwest was dominated by the Raton Pass, through which ran the famous Santa Fe trail. This was a route that had been used for years in carrying on the trade between eastern Kansas and the Southwest. The Atchison, under the leadership of William B. Strong, who had recently left the Burlington, seized control of the pass only hours before the forces of the Rio Grande arrived.

The Atchison, by thus pre-empting the pass, won a victory and the Rio Grande suffered a loss. The Atchison soon thereafter built through and beyond the pass and completed within a relatively short time another major transcontinental route.

In these struggles for the control of the eastern Colorado gateways, the fate of both the Rio Grande and the Kansas Pacific had not yet been decided by early 1879. With the cancellation of its lease to the Atchison, the Rio Grande was again an independent property. Its strategic position through its control of the eastbound traffic was reinforced by the prospects of a rapid growth in business. This followed from the completion of its line to Leadville. Control of the line was now sought by the major business rivals, Atchison, Burlington, and Kansas Pacific. The Burlington people had decided in their inner council that eventually the road would be extended to the mountains in Colorado and that a connection between the Burlington and the Rio Grande would be attractive. The Burlington officials at this time had close business relations with the Atchison. Hence co-operation between the two roads in an effort to acquire the Rio Grande was essential.

The Burlington and the Atchison were also desirous of acquiring control of the South Park—the road whose stock control was held by Evans. Gould also had such plans. His ideas remained mysterious. "I do not know," wrote Perkins in May of 1879, "what Gould is up to. ...."[16] Perkins was convinced that Gould would not help Evans. The Union Pacific and the South Park were competitors. Both roads were preparing to reach the rich traffic center of Leadville. With respect to the Rio Grande, there was the personal unfriendliness between Palmer and the Atchison's officials. In the trading for the conquest of the Rio Grande, the Burlington people overlooked some substantial stockholdings. Two members of the Northwestern directorate, C. J. Osborne and W. L. Scott, both important in stock-brokerage circles in New York City, had bought substantial blocks of the Rio Grande stock. They also were large stockholders of the Northwestern. The Northwestern was one of the Iowa roads with a direct line between Chicago and Omaha. It did not have a line to Kansas City. It would, therefore, benefit from the control of the Rio Grande by the Union Pacific instead of by the Atchison. The Northwestern's president accordingly asked Messrs. Scott and Osborne, providing the same terms could be secured from both acquiring candidates, to trade with the Union Pacific rather than with the Atchison. If, wrote Keep to Scott, "you can make as good a trade with the U. P. as with Atchison & Topeka, [*sic*] the interests of our Company and the Rock Island will be better served by having [*sic*] under control of U. P.

"The large and valuable business of Colorado will be competed for by Atchison & Topeka if they secure control of D. & R. R. Road. Our interest in such business is quite large and the only access we have to it is by way of Omaha and in connection with U. P. Line."[17] A letter of similar import, though not couched in identical phraseology, was also sent to Osborne.

In the outcome Gould was successful. In September of 1879 he succeeded in acquiring one-half of the Rio Grande Voting Trust Certificates, payable at his option either in cash, in Kansas Pacific stock at 66, or in its junior bonds at 88.

By this time the securities of the Kansas Pacific had become valuable and were destined within a few months to become even more valuable. Villard in the opening months of 1879 was convinced that Gould's associates, who owned a substantial interest in the road's junior securities, would revolt from Gould's leadership. With the aid of the stock holdings of some of his associates amounting to approximately twenty-five thousand shares, and with the help of the junior securities to be bought from these associates, Villard was certain he could control the new board of directors. "I have been considering," wrote Villard in February, "the possibility of voting the enemy out for some time. . . ."[18]

The negotiations between Villard and his other junior-security holders and between Gould and Villard continued throughout January and February. The holders of the road's junior securities, other than those controlled by Gould, finally advised Villard that they would break away from Gould only if Gould rejected a fair offer from Villard. Villard therefore drew up a plan involving the redemption of the first-mortgage bonds, principal and interest, 100 cents on the dollar. Gould was ready, and in this last trading deal he outmaneuvered Villard. He accepted the Villard plan forthwith, subject only to a slight modification of some detail in relation to the sinking fund. "I had no idea," wrote Villard "that he would allow me to dictate terms, but as it was, I had to submit the scheme to the bondholders."[19] The end of the battle for the Kansas Pacific was now approaching. In a few days Gould bought the holdings of the junior-security holders. The Kansas Pacific bondholders were satisfied. To them Villard was a hero. He had succeeded in recovering the entire bond-holders investment, principal plus accumulated interest. In the battle with Gould, however, Villard, strange as it may seem, was the loser. He saved the bondholders but lost the road. Gould's finances improved throughout 1879. He found little difficulty in financing the payment of the accumulated interest on the Denver Extension bonds. New bonds were issued in exchange for the old bonds on a par-for-par basis. The bondholders accepted a reduction in interest from 7 to 6 per cent. The Denver Extension bonds, which had sold at 35 in the spring of 1877, now advanced to 102. Gould meanwhile realized stock-market profits from the increase in the prices of the securities of Kansas Pacific and of other properties.

By December, 1879, furthermore, Gould had acquired control of the Missouri Pacific, with a line between St. Louis and Kansas City. He also bought a variety of other properties in the Missouri Valley. He now controlled a short line between St. Louis, Kansas City, and Denver. Gould proposed to build a line from Denver to Ogden, thereby creating another transcontinental route—a strong rival of the Union Pacific. To avert this dangerous competition, the Union Pacific proposed to acquire the Kansas Pacific and a number of other roads owned by Gould. The transfer of control was soon completed—but on Gould's terms. The Kansas Pacific stock was exchanged share for share for the Union Pacific stock.[20]

By January of 1880, the Union Pacific controlled the Kansas Pacific, and Gould dominated the management of the Union Pacific. The Atchison controlled the vital pass leading to the Southwest. The competition between the Atchison and the Kansas Pacific was now replaced by the competition between the Atchison and the Union Pacific. The Atchison was threatening to build north from Pueblo to Denver, and the Rio Grande, under the Gould leadership, might renew its bid for construction of a southwestern line in competition with the Atchison. These competitive rivalries were finally adjusted in a comprehensive scheme between the Atchison and Gould, with Gould the major architect of the plan. This restriction of competition, involving the distribution of traffic and territorial understanding, lasted only a short time. In the dynamic railroad industry of the 1880's competition soon reappeared. The Burlington extension to Denver in 1882 was the first, followed by the construction south from Denver of the Denver and New Orleans and, in the late 1880's, by a new alignment of transcontinental competition involving the extension of the Missouri Pacific and the Rock Island to the foot of the Rockies.

Notes for Chapter VI

[1] This table is based upon Appendix A, page 17, in the argument of the Kansas Pacific before the Secretary of the Interior and the Attorney General of the United States by Artemas H. Holmes, 1877.

[2] Details on the early Pennsylvania Railroad interest are noted in *The Road*, May 15, 1875, p. 108.

[3] H. V. P., Villard to Carlos Greeley, April 17, 1877, Box 111.

[4] *Ibid.*, Nickerson to Villard, July 22, 1878.

[5] *Ibid.*, T. F. Oakes to Villard, Nov. 30, 1877, Box 7.

[6] *Ibid.*, Villard to Robert Carr, Feb. 5, 1878, Box 117.

[7] This proposed directorate is found in a letter of Endicott to Villard, Mar. 30, 1878; *Ibid.*, Box 92.

[8] Burlington Archives, Tyson to Perkins, Mar. 18, 1878.

[9] See on this complaint, H. V. P. Oakes to Villard, Dec. 5, 1877. Box 8.

[10] *Ibid.*, Villard to Greeley, Dec. 29, 1877, Box 113.

[11] *Ibid.*, J. P. Usher to Villard, May 13, 1877, Box 111.

[12] Burlington Archives, Tyson to Perkins, Apr. 2, 1878.

[13] H. V. P., Villard to Mrs. Villard, June 25, 1878, Box 7.

[14] *Ibid.*, Villard to Forbes, July 21, 1878, Box 118.
[15] *Ibid.*, Villard to Oakes, Sept. 23, 1878, Box 8.
[16] Burlington Archives, Perkins to Tyson, May 31, 1879.
[17] Northwestern Archives, Keep to Scott, Oct. 30, 1878.
[18] H. V. P., Villard to Oakes, Feb. 12, 1879.
[19] *Ibid.*, Villard to Oakes, Feb. 27, 1879.
[20] For details on the merger of the Union Pacific and Kansas Pacific, see *Gould*, Chapter IX.

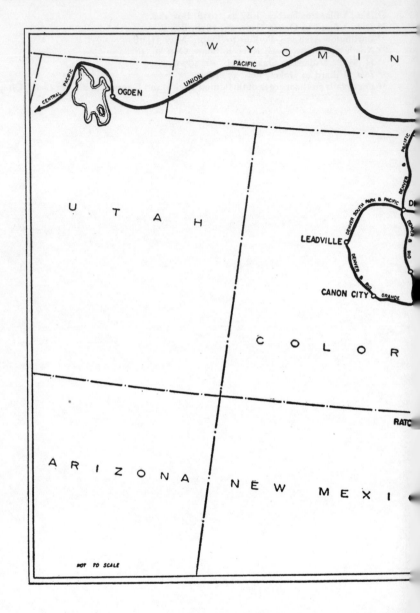

NOT TO SCALE

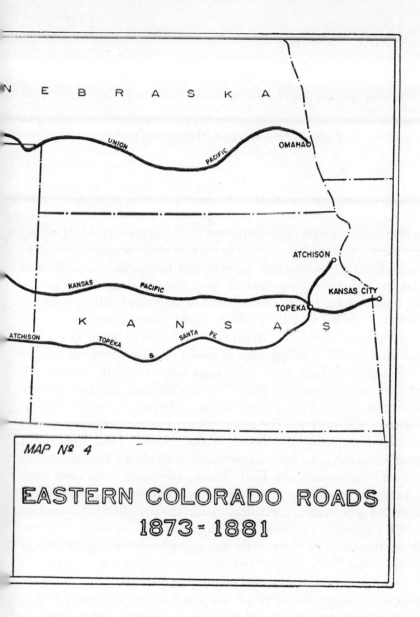

MAP Nº 4

EASTERN COLORADO ROADS
1873 = 1881

VII

Competition and Monopoly

THE STRUGGLES to seize important strategic positions, to control mountain passes, to dominate valleys, to connect major sources of production with important consuming markets, and to establish a position of financial strength were only part of the managerial problems of the railroad businessman. It was also essential to maintain a selling price for transportation service at a level which would insure adequate earning power. Earnings were required to expand and improve the property and to build up a credit standing with investors so as to attract a flow of capital. Satisfactory rates were to a large degree associated with the avoidance of excessive competition. This is a difficult problem to state succinctly and clearly. Competition in the evolution of transcontinental railroads is a relative term. There was always the competition between commodities from different sections of the country. Coal from Iowa competed with coal from Illinois; wheat from Nebraska competed with wheat from Minnesota; corn from Illinois competed with corn from Iowa. A railroad in any one of these states was required by geographical and industrial competition, regardless of costs, to prescribe a rate structure that would move traffic. There were other forms of such competition: the competition between cities, between various ports serving the import and export traffic. There was competition between alternative routes and between sources of production, and consuming markets.

Despite these competitive forces, it still was true that a railroad serving a territory without any railroad competition could charge relatively high rates. To serve a territory with no railroad competition was the ambition of every railroad operator. To control a large area on a monopolistic basis was an ideal for which many sacrifices were made and many complicated adjustments were arranged. Territorial monopolies were, however, vulnerable and temporary.

An exclusively controlled local territory, was a valuable asset, as long as it lasted. A monopoly of this kind was perhaps the most important strategic advantage of a railroad, provided, of course, the monopolized area either originated valuable traffic or served as a market for goods produced in other areas. Territory thus controlled was looked upon as "natural" territory. It belonged to the road that first reached the area. The construction of a line by a competitor was an "invasion." Such a construction, even by a business friend of the "possessing" road, was considered an unfriendly act. The former business friend became an enemy. Many roads created territorial enclaves: mutually monopolistic areas, where each road agreed not to invade the territory of the other. These agreements were usually verbal understandings and were only infrequently reduced to writing. Sometimes they were examined and approved by the directors of the contracting parties, while other arrangements expressed only understandings reached by executive officers. There were agreements between the Burlington and the Rock Island not to extend their lines into each other's territory in Iowa. There were similar understandings between the Rock Island and the Northwestern further north in the same state. There was an agreement between the St. Paul and the Rock Island; the St. Paul agreed not to compete with the Rock Island by building a line to Council Bluffs and the Rock Island agreed not to compete with the St. Paul for the business of the Twin Cities.

There were other devices to restrain competition. The best known was the pool. This was an arrangement between independently owned and operated roads for the purpose of dividing, in accordance with prearranged terms, either the traffic or the earnings realized from the traffic of the participating lines. Since each road was entitled to receive only a fixed division of the business or earnings of all the roads in the pool, there was no incentive to reduce rates. This, of course, was the theory; but in practice the theory seldom worked out in accordance with expectations. The mechanism of the operation of the pool was not standardized. Many diverse schemes were set up to make the pool work successfully. If a road, for example, carried more than its proportion of the allotted traffic, it could pay for the surplus by a percentage of the gross revenue. Another arrangement, which encountered formidable objections from the shipper, authorized a pool officer to divert traffic from the road carrying an excess to the road which carried less than its allotted proportion. In some money pools, where the revenues, instead of the traffic, were divided among the participating roads, the road in excess paid to the road with a deficiency. In other pools the equalization was made by an adjustment in rates. The road with an excessive traffic increased its rates, while the road with the deficiency reduced its rates. Arrangements of this kind were also sturdily opposed by the shipping public.

All these devices did not succeed in avoiding the onrush of the competitive forces so characteristic of a growing economy. The local traffic carried at high rates offered a constant temptation to ambitious businessmen and profit-seeking investors. The direct and short lines between the major producing and consuming centers were eventually in competition with circuitous lines connecting the same areas. The latter could not give the same standard of service as the former. They, therefore, reduced rates as the best means of competing for the available business. Furthermore, pressure from the shipping interests of one town exerted decisive influences in reducing rates to enable it to compete with another. Numerous arrangements were made to restrain this competition. In time these agreements burst wide open; rates were cut; the roads composing the short route followed with similar rate cuts; and at the lower rate levels, restraining agreements were again introduced to stabilize the reduced rates.

Between Omaha and Chicago the Iowa Pool lines succeeded, despite pressure from the Union Pacific on the west and the circuitous alternative roads on the south, in maintaining the rate structure reasonably well. In the summer of 1878, after the pool lines had defeated Gould and the Union Pacific in the battle to reduce rates and increase the division of the through rate to Union Pacific, the pool lines successfully combined to maintain rates on Colorado business. The three pool roads agreed, to use the language of the president of the Northwestern, to charge for the Colorado business "regular, local rates to Council Bluffs."[1]

In the area northwest of Chicago there was in the 1870's virtually no transcontinental traffic. The Northern Pacific's ambition to build from the head of the Lakes to Puget Sound had failed and construction was not substantially renewed until the end of the decade. Traffic between Chicago, Milwaukee, and the Twin Cities was carried on largely by the Northwestern and the St. Paul. In the Mississippi–Missouri Valley area, considerable business came into St. Louis and Chicago through the lower Missouri River cities of St. Joseph, Atchison, Leavenworth, and Kansas City. The traffic originated partly south and west of Kansas City and partly in Nebraska, Colorado, and Kansas. Tonnage from the latter points could move either by Omaha and the Iowa roads or by the lower Missouri Valley cities and a group of other roads. (See Map No. 5.)

West of the Missouri River there were two major lines connecting Kansas and Colorado with the lower Missouri cities: the Kansas Pacific and the Atchison. Another road—the Kansas and Texas—came up from northern Texas and reached Hannibal, for a connection with a Chicago line. It avoided Kansas City and came east through southern and central Missouri.

Competition developed in the 1870's between the Iowa roads and the roads composing the southern routes. If the traffic moved via southern routes, Kansas City would benefit somewhat and St. Louis would benefit even more. Traffic could move from Kansas City north and east over the Burlington and the Rock Island, thereby avoiding St. Louis, or it could move east through St. Louis and thence to Chicago. From Nebraska and most of Colorado to Chicago, the short route was over the Iowa lines. This difference in distance did not deter the southern roads from their efforts to capture a share of the Chicago business. The western lines, furthermore, united with one or another of the eastern connections at Kansas City. The decline in traffic after 1873 intensified competition; and in 1875 a war of rates broke out. Rates and fares were sharply reduced. By the spring of 1876 the railroads involved succeeded in setting up a pool—the Southwestern Railway Association—to divide the traffic between the participating roads. The competitive problems in this area were more difficult than those that confronted the Iowa Pool roads. The stabilizing effects of the territorial agreements in the Iowa Pool area were absent in the southwest. Instead of one westbound connection at Omaha, there were two at Kansas City. There were also the Kansas and Texas coming up from the South, and a number of other local roads feeding the lower Missouri River cities.

Long negotiations throughout the summer months of 1875 preceded the organization of the pool. There were prolonged battles for higher percentages of the traffic in the proposed pool. The fighting was particularly vigorous between the Alton and the Burlington. An agreement was finally reached in September of 1876. The pool remained intact for about 18 months. Early in 1878 it broke down. Two new competitive factors had developed. First, there was an increased movement of grain down the Mississippi River from St. Louis to New Orleans, thereby reducing the traffic over the St. Louis and Chicago railroads. Second, the Wabash, connecting at St. Louis with the Kansas City and Northern, had just been relieved of its receivership status. Soon thereafter it sought to increase its through business with the east via St. Louis by making rate adjustments in co-operation with the Canada Southern.[2]

The outstanding problem in this struggle was the rivalry between the Chicago and the St. Louis roads. The latter insisted upon a larger percentage of the pooled business, which the Chicago roads refused to grant. Another rate war followed, described by a Philadelphia observer, as "one of the fiercest and most energetic railroad fights ever waged."[3]

The breakup of the pool seemed permanent, at least to some of the railroad men involved. A Burlington director believed that the pool would not be renewed—that the roads ended at so many different points that it would be impossible to establish a pool that could be maintained for any reasonable period.[4]

The rate war for the southwestern business continued throughout the spring and summer months. In the fall of 1878 a new pool was effected.

This pool in turn lasted little more than six months. By early in 1879 rates from New York to Southwestern points, in the words of a Burlington traffic official, appeared to have "thoroughly gone to pieces."[5] The major trouble again was the conflict between the Chicago and St. Louis roads. The pressures on the roads came from shippers. The Chicago roads found it difficult, for example, to enforce contracts for the movement of business via Omaha to Chicago. The rate cuts by the lower Missouri Valley lines served as a magnet to attract business from the Nebraska wheatfields away from Omaha. A concrete illustration is afforded by a letter from three traffic executives of the Burlington, Northwestern, and Rock Island to an elevator company in Omaha. "As we have a contract with your companies to ship all your grain to Chicago via the Iowa Pool Lines," reads this communication, "we cannot consistently accept an amendment to that contract to allow you to sell your grain on tracks at Omaha or Co. [Council] Bluffs to parties who will ship to St. Louis and Eastern markets other than Chicago."[6] The reduced rates of the Missouri railroads led to a substantial increase in the volume of business moving via St. Louis. In 1879 a new pool was arranged.

The new agreement lasted even a shorter time than the others. The disturbing factor was the entrance of Gould into the southwestern railroad arena. By December of 1879 Gould had successively acquired control of the Missouri Pacific, the Kansas City and Northern, and the Wabash. He thereby controlled a through line between Kansas City, St. Louis, and Toledo, and within two years, through the Wabash, and by new construction and acquisitions of existing lines, he secured an entrance into Chicago and Detroit. At Chicago connection was made with the Lake Shore, a part of the Vanderbilt System, with connections to Buffalo and New York City. Furthermore, through participation in a financial transaction, it appeared that Gould had entered into an alliance with Vanderbilt. This later proved not to be the case. In December, however, there appeared to be some basis for such a friendly relationship. Gould had some months before purchased the St. Joseph, thereby affording a connection between the city of St. Joseph and the Union Pacific at Kearney, although access to the latter point was reached over a 40-mile stretch of the B. & M. Rivalry between the B. & M. and the St. Joseph followed almost immediately; an official of the former soon complained of the "effective system of encroachment" by the latter.[7]

In December, Gould took advance trading positions to utilize the strategic advantages of his new acquisitions. On behalf of the St. Joseph he insisted that its business would not be pooled. He would thereby, he declared, follow the precedent set for the B. & M., which moved its traffic preferentially over the Burlington and declined to pool it with the Northwestern and the Rock Island at Omaha. If, declared Gould, the B. & M. would pool its business with the Iowa roads, the St. Joseph would pool its traffic with the southwestern lines. Furthermore, insisted Gould, until this problem was settled, the business of the St. Joseph would be delivered to the Hannibal-Wabash route. It would not be pooled with the other roads.[8]

Another rate war followed. Again the rates under Gould's leadership were cut, and again the movement via St. Louis increased. The Iowa roads were again loathe to reduce their rates on the Omaha-Chicago haul. In February, 1880, the Rock Island gave notice of withdrawal from the southwestern pool. The president declared the pool was a farce, that his road had been called upon by the pool to pay substantial sums to equalize the surplus traffic carried by the Rock Island. The Rock Island, insisted its president, had received no benefits; rates had been cut just as badly as if no pool had existed. The Burlington, however, declared that the Rock Island itself was one of the leading rate cutters.[9] But again the pool was saved. Though rate cutting continued under the pool, the alternative without the pool was considered to be even more seriously fraught with evil consequences. By July of 1880 the pool had again been re-established. The traffic allotments among the roads were again changed and new mechanisms were introduced to make the pool foolproof. The competition between the pool members continued as before, though the rates were no longer shaded and the rate structure was strengthened. By the fall of the year a Burlington official was able to say that earnings had been larger than ever before in the history of the road, not because tonnage was larger but because the business had paid tariff rates. "I do not think that any member of the ASSN. [the Southwestern Association] except the Rock Island," he wrote, "are shading rates in the slightest degree and the fact that the latter are doing it will bring upon their heads someday such an explosion as I think will teach them a lesson."[10]

By this time control of the St. Joseph had passed to the Union Pacific. The latter also controlled the Kansas Pacific. Though Gould was still a dominant figure in the enlarged Union Pacific, conservative elements led by Ames, a large Boston stockholder, had succeeded in negotiating outstanding differences between the Union Pacific and its eastern connections. On the eastern side of the Missouri River, however, trouble was still being brewed by the Wabash. That road moved traffic from time to time without making reports to the pool commissioner. All this had been accomplished under Gould's leadership. By acquiring the Missouri Pacific Gould had secured control of the two short lines between St. Louis and Kansas City. Late in 1880 his power over the traffic movements in the lower Missouri Valley was further strengthened. Through a lease contract, he seized managerial dominance of the Kansas and Texas.

In the fall and winter of 1880–1881 extraordinary demands by Gould again broke up the Southwestern Association—*de facto* if not *de jure*. In September, 1880, the managers of the Wabash declared that the road was justified in taking all the freight it could get, east or west, at any price, irrespective of the Southwestern Railway Association.[11] In the early summer of 1881 arbitration of managerial differences was proposed. All the roads except the Wabash agreed.[12] Shortly thereafter the divisive obstacles were overcome and another reorganization of the pool was effected. Though controversies were rarely absent, the pool continued to function throughout the first half of the 1880's. It thus appears clear that despite pools, territorial agreements, and arrangements to maintain rates, competition continued to prevail in the area between the Missouri River and Chicago.

In the decade of the 1870's (subject to but few exceptions) the major roads from the Pacific Coast and from Colorado and New Mexico terminated at the Missouri River. A number of small properties also had Missouri River terminals—the B. & M., the St. Joseph, and the Sioux City. The small roads could either pool their eastbound business or could interchange with roads on a preferential basis. Both the B. & M. and the Sioux City adopted the latter alternative, the former with the Burlington and the latter with the Northwestern. The receiving road east of the river made to the originating road west of the river a payment known in the railroad language of the day as a drawback.

These drawbacks were used by many small, financially weak properties, many of them in the 1870's in receivership. These properties controlled, nevertheless, an important volume of business. Many were strategically located. Some, for example, connected two or more major railroads. This gave them the power to divert business from one road to another. The larger roads, therefore, strove to acquire the traffic of the smaller properties, and the use of the drawback was an important tool. The Northwestern, for example, paid an annual drawback of $100 thousand to the West Wisconsin Railway. The Northwestern in return secured a claim on one-half of the profits of the other property. The West Wisconsin later fell into receivership; the eventual outcome was a foreclosure, and the claim on the other company proved to be of no value to the Northwestern.[13]

The Iowa Pool roads also made payments from time to time to the Council Bluffs. These were designed to induce that road to refrain from moving business on reduced through rates from the Union Pacific for delivery to the lower Missouri Valley lines. Instead of moving to St. Louis the business would then flow over the Iowa lines to Chicago.

The drawback arrangement could succeed only if carried out upon a limited scale. If one road bought most of the business of the Atchison at Kansas City, another would buy all the business of the Kansas Pacific. The connections at Omaha might compete against each other and bid for the Union Pacific business by an increase in drawback payments. The business then would not be increased; it would merely be carried at lower rates. These possibilities precluded any general use of the draw-back system by major transcontinental carriers. The system did, however, continue throughout the 1870's and for some time in the 1880's with respect to the smaller properties. As the latter were acquired by major systems in rapid succession, the drawback system declined.

Another competitive device was the use of special-rate concessions to favored shippers, known as the rebate system. A formidable literature, largely critical, has expounded this phase of railroad activity. Particularly dramatic are the incidents surrounding the growth of the Rockefeller fortune and the rise to power of Standard Oil. Though eventually rebates were widely granted in the free-for-all competitive society, they were early opposed in railroad circles. On the Northwestern, the president instructed a vice-president to inform the governor of Michigan in 1878 "to smother his wish for special rates . . . there is great risk to us in making any special ore rates. Such rates almost invariably come to the knowledge of other parties and would make us infinite trouble."[14] Also in the Burlington pressure for rebates was resisted. In 1868 its superintendent declared that "the practice of giving special rates to particular men is fundamentally bad. I refused it to Alexander [presumably a shipper] the other day, and he will throw his weight against us—but I retained a hundred allies or more."[15]

A number of years later, in 1877, in negotiations with Gould, Forbes requested Harris, at that time president of the Burlington, to decline to listen to any suggestions for rebates.[16]

By 1878 the pressure for rebates was beginning to increase. In one case the shipper had been moving freight from Kansas City via the Alton. He asked for a rebate, to which the traffic manager of the Burlington replied that while he was forced to decline he suggested that he call upon the general freight agent. "I told him," wrote the traffic manager "that we proposed to deal honestly with our neighbors and that we would make no concession whatever . . . . At the same time if Mr. Frazier [the shipper] should turn out to be worth going for you can interview him when he arrives at Cheyenne."[17]

In the 1870's rebates by western roads were not widespread. In the 1880's, however, they increased.

The race between the competitive and monopolistic influences seemed by the end of the 1870's to be in favor of the former. Influences in that direction were the extensive railroad construction and acquisition programs beginning in 1879. (These programs will be examined in succeeding chapters.)

By the spring of 1880 the building-acquisition programs had so far advanced that the emergence of a number of new competitive forces became a possibility. There was the probability that the group in the Burlington board advocating an extension to Denver would be victorious. This would introduce competition to the Union Pacific in Nebraska and Colorado, and, in conjunction with the Rio Grande, also on the transcontinental business to and from the Pacific Coast. On the eastern end of the Union Pacific Gould had secured an interest in Hannibal sufficient to give him *some* control over that road. Early in 1880 he and his associates organized a corporation to build an extension of the Hannibal from Quincy to Chicago. The Burlington retaliated by acquiring control of the Burlington and Southwestern, with an unfinished line from a connection with the Burlington to Kansas City. If the Hannibal built to Chicago the Burlington would then finish this line to Kansas City. Gould, furthermore, had acquired a small road in southern Iowa—the Missouri, Iowa and Nebraska—connecting with the Wabash at Keokuk and extending west for a number of miles into southern Iowa. He now proposed to extend this road to a connection with the Wabash in the western part of the state, thereby forming a new short route between Omaha and the East. This would be an invasion of the Burlington's Iowa territory. In southern Nebraska, furthermore, rate wars between the Union Pacific and the B. & M. were accompanied by competitive construction. In the spring of 1880 both roads hurled threats at each other; both planned to build lines into occupied territories by the other. In the transcontinental area served throughout the 1870's by the Central Pacific, Gould threatened still another invasion. There he moved to extend the Union Pacific from southern Utah into California. Huntington responded by projecting plans for an extension of the Central Pacific from Ogden through the Missouri Valley. Both the Burlington and the Northwestern offered Huntington suitable connections for the completion of through routes.

These threats of war—so called by the roads whose territorial preserves were threatened—did not materialize in 1880. Threatened competition was replaced by competitive restraints. Business war was replaced by business peace. The arguments for peace were well presented by a leading railroad statesman. Forbes urged upon the Union Pacific the necessity of preserving peace. The Union Pacific, he wrote, was a strong property, but it was faced by new competitors. It could well afford to use its power over its eastern connections, the Wabash and elsewhere, to maintain the status quo. "Every year's peace not only gives you & us solid dividends but it enables you," he wrote to Ames, "to complete & consolidate your connections."[18]

The arguments for peace prevailed in 1880. The threatened competitive extensions were not made that year and most of them were postponed for a number of years. Railroad management worked out a number of contracts designed to achieve a territorial equilibrium and a stable rate structure. The first was reached in January of 1880 between the Union Pacific and the Burlington. Gould, Dillon, and Ames, for the Union Pacific, and Perkins, for the Burlington, negotiated the arrangement. It was agreed that the existing Missouri River pools would continue undisturbed; that the Burlington would not build to Denver "for the present"; that "harmonious relations" would prevail in Nebraska; and that the building of the proposed Gould line from Pueblo east into the Atchison territory would "make it much less for the interest" of the Burlington to stop its road east of Denver. The Union Pacific and the Burlington, furthermore, mutually agreed to refrain from building numerous local lines in Nebraska. The contract was subject to cancellation on a thirty-day notice. It was not an iron-clad agreement; there were no sanctions. It amounted merely to a declaration that the peace would be kept. It did, however, protect the Union Pacific from an invasion of its territory in Colorado. It was not entirely satisfactory to the Burlington; but the alternative, as Perkins expressed it, was "an active present war."[19]

Another agreement substituting business peace for business war also involved the Burlington and the Gould railroad systems. This agreement resolved the threatened Gould-inspired Chicago extensions of the Hannibal, and the Burlington's counterthreat of a Kansas City line. Gould, for the Hannibal, agreed neither to build nor to aid in building a road between Quincy and Chicago. The Burlington agreed not to extend the Burlington and Southwestern to Kansas City. Both promised "at all times [to] work in harmony the one with the other, and do all they may lawfully to develop, promote, and protect the business under this agreement." The Burlington reserved the right to make rates on westbound business between competing points, and the Hannibal to make similar rates on eastbound business. The agreement was to continue for two years. (The agreement is dated August 26, 1880, and is in the Burlington

Archives.) The business inspiration behind this contract was well summarized by Perkins in a letter to Gould. "There is probably more money
to be made by not building them [railroads] if we can agree as to the
division of it."[20]

There remained a third area of conflict between the business interests
of the Burlington and those of the Gould circle. The proposed construction by the Wabash's Missouri, Iowa and Nebraska threatened to introduce competition into one of the most profitable of the Burlington areas.
Gould and officials of the Wabash, led by president Solon Humphreys,
insisted that the line was necessary to afford the Wabash a short route for
the movement of its Omaha business. Forbes urged the Union Pacific to
avoid a construction war. Again he communicated with Ames. Again he
emphasized the necessity of maintaining good business relationships
between the two properties. Again, he held out the alluring promise that
the Burlington board could be induced not to build to Denver. If, he
wrote, the Burlington could be protected "from an invasion in Iowa from
the Wabash or any other source within 30 miles of our line running
through to the Mo River—I think our Board can be brought to unite
against going to Denver during the Truce which might be fixed at 2 years
with 18 months notice thereafter and which might last (as the Omaha
pool has against everybody's expectations) for a great many years."[21]

Prolonged discussion followed. An agreement was finally hammered
out in the fall of the year. A line would be built between the western
terminus of the Missouri, Iowa and Nebraska and a point on the Wabash
line in southwestern Iowa. The line would be owned jointly by the
Wabash and the Burlington. The local traffic on the extension would be
pooled; a pool commissioner would divide this traffic, so that the business
would "nearly approximate to the percentage of revenue which each
party is entitled to receive"[22]—a provision sufficiently ambiguous to
facilitate an abundance of competitive misunderstanding.

In eastern Colorado an even more far-reaching agreement ended the
conflict between the Atchison, the Rio Grande, and the Union Pacific.

Gould threatened to extend the Rio Grande (then, in 1880, under his
control) from Pueblo into the Atchison territory. The Atchison in turn
threatened to build from Pueblo to Denver. The building threats were
not carried out. In March of 1880 an arrangement was concluded based
on mutual concessions by all the participating parties. Each road receded
from its original bargaining position. The Atchison promised that for

ten years it would build neither east nor west of Pueblo; the Rio Grande, that it would build neither east of its Denver–El Moro lines nor south of a point 75 miles below Conejos, in the San Luis Valley. The Rio Grande— really Gould—agreed not to build into the Atchison territory parallel to and south of the Kansas Pacific. This territorial agreement was supplemented by another calculated to preserve for the Atchison, Rio Grande, and Union Pacific a close knit territorial monopoly. These roads contracted not to "voluntarily connect with, or take business from or give business to, any railroad which may hereafter be constructed." The business south and west of Denver controlled by the Rio Grande was pooled with the Union Pacific and the Atchison. Each of the three properties agreed not to build competing lines into each others territories within certain defined limits.[23] For the Atchison, the agreement laid the foundation for its transcontinental future. The road was given a clear field in New Mexico and beyond, and it took prompt advantage of the opportunity by building south and west to a connection with the Southern Pacific. The Atchison was also protected from competition in southeastern Colorado and southern Kansas.

This territorial agreement functioned admirably—that is, from the viewpoint of the participating roads. For a number of years it succeeded in precluding any effective railroad competition. Rates were maintained until 1884. By that time the competition between the Burlington and the Union Pacific was substantially strengthened by the completion of the Rio Grande Western route to Ogden. Between 1880 and 1884, however, the agreement helped to stabilize rates and to insure reasonable railroad earnings.

These successive agreements indeed helped to preserve rate and earning stability between the Mississippi River and the foot of the Rockies, between the Kansas City-Denver line on the south and the Chicago-Omaha line on the north, and also between Omaha and eastern Colorado. The through rates between Chicago and Omaha had been stabilized, subject to some exceptions, in the decade of the 1870's. In 1880 that stabilization was still preserved. Some frailties in the Iowa Pool had developed. The local business between the three members of the Iowa Pool—the Burlington, the Rock Island, and the Northwestern—in the face of a number of territorial conflicts and misunderstandings was still carried at rates protected by the territorial agreements.

In the area north and west of Chicago, in Minnesota, and in the Dakota territory, no important rate wars for most of the 1870's had undermined selling prices. Two major roads—the St. Paul and the Northwestern—dominated the through-traffic channels. These roads "except for short intervals of disagreement, kept approximately the same rates."[24] Not until 1878 were there any substantial rate reductions. And not until 1881, upon the sale of the Minneapolis and St. Louis to large Rock Island stockholders, did any intruder appear. Thereafter in rapid succession competitive construction and expansion pressed hard on the rate structure. That, however, is another story.

Yet in 1880 it appeared that each road would continue to serve its own territory, to maintain a reasonable rate structure, and to trade on a friendly basis with connecting roads. A conflict however seemed imminent in the Red River Valley. The Northern Pacific was building west and the newly organized St. Paul, Minneapolis and Manitoba was building north in the Red River Valley. Both roads, under expansion-minded management, projected lines into each other's territory. Top officials of both roads began discussions in the summer of 1881 to forestall this projected warfare. Proposals and counterproposals, threats and counterthreats featured this bargaining. An agreement "by which some of the new east and west lines in process of construction" by the Manitoba "were exchanged for north and south lines" of the Northern Pacific was reached in the fall of 1882.[25] Both sides expressed satisfaction that peace had been achieved. The agreement "will prevent disastrous competition between the respective lines," remarked the Manitoba management; while the other contestant declared that the "permanent settlement" of troubles would "put a definite end to the invasion" of the Northern Pacific territory.[26]

In the Far West, in the Columbia River Valley, another competitive conflict was developing. The Northern Pacific, flushed with financial resources as a result of the sale of $40 million of bonds through the Morgan banking firm, was building its lines west. The Oregon Railway and Navigation Company, under the leadership of Villard, had a local territorial monpoly in the Columbia Valley. The Northern Pacific threatened to build its line into the area served by the Navigation. Both roads negotiated long and anxiously to avoid a war of construction. Here, also, success crowned the work of the negotiators, and in October of 1880 another territorial agreement was reached. The Navigation agreed not to build roads north of the Snake and Columbia rivers and the Northern

Pacific agreed not to build south. The latter also agreed to use the Navigation's line south of Columbia River. It did not, however, agree to abstain from the construction of a parallel line north of the river at some future time.

In southern Kansas still another understanding on competitive restraints was reached between the St. Louis and San Francisco and the Atchison. These roads were partners in a far-reaching program of construction. This partnership was concluded at a time when the Frisco was building in southern Kansas—in the very center of the Atchison's most profitable territory. The Frisco's extension reached Wichita in May, 1880. There building stopped, and both roads agreed to build no further lines in southern Kansas without consulting each other.

In the Southwest the competitive threats of the Union Pacific to build to the Pacific Coast and of the Southern Pacific to build to the Missouri Valley were also settled by negotiation. Here, also, the competitive threat of duplicate construction was avoided. The agreements in this area, however, were not reached until November of 1881.

Over the broad transcontinental area, it seemed in 1880 as though competitive relations had been stabilized. Except for the struggle in the lower Missouri Valley, rates had been well maintained in almost all other areas. In the region served by the Union Pacific, Central Pacific, and Southern Pacific, territorial competition was slight. Except for the rivalry with Burlington in southeastern Nebraska, the Union Pacific in 1880, after its merger with the Kansas Pacific, served central and northern Kansas, eastern Colorado, Wyoming, and eastern Utah with only nominal railroad rivalry. The Central Pacific in central and northern California had gobbled up almost all its competitors. The Southern Pacific in southern California, Arizona, and New Mexico had little competition, although the threats of the Atchison were already looming large. The territorial understandings between so many of the properties tended to preserve the railroad rate structure.

The stabilization, protected by agreements born from concessions and compromises, was not long maintained. In 1879 and 1880 high railroad stock prices reflected the investor belief in the continued maintenance of railroad earnings. This was based to a significant degree upon reasonable rates created in a pattern of competitive equilibrium. The equilibrium, however, was about to be gravely disturbed. The outbreak of railroad construction and corporate acquisition which began in 1879 spread rapidly in the early 1880's. The construction-acquisition-expansion program from 1879 to 1883 fundamentally changed competitive conditions in almost all areas west of the Mississippi River. These programs will be examined in succeeding chapters.

Notes for Chapter VII

[1] Northwestern Archives, Keep to Gould, July 2, 1878.

[2] *New York Tribune*, Feb. 13, 1878.

[3] *Philadelphia North American*, April 15, 1878.

[4] Burlington Archives, Griswold to Harris, Mar. 7, 1878.

[5] *Ibid.*, E. P. Ripley to W. H. McDoel, Mar. 15, 1879.

[6] *Ibid.*, Ripley, Jno. T. Sanford, Henry C. Wicker, to Omaha Elevator Company, April 18, 1879.

[7] *Ibid.*, A. E. Touzalin to Tyson, Aug. 4, 1879.

[8] The views of Gould are presented in *Ibid.*, Perkins to Forbes, Dec. 20, 1879.

[9] The views of the two roads are examined in *Ibid.*, Ripley to George Olds, Feb. 5, 1880.

[10] *Ibid.*, Ripley to J. Q. A. Bean, Sept. 18, 1880.

[11] *New York Tribune*, Sept. 4, 1880.

[12] Burlington Archives, Potter to Perkins, July 13, 1881.

[13] Northwestern Archives, Keep to Sykes, July 30, 1877.

[14] *Ibid.*, Keep to Sykes, Mar. 5, 1878

[15] Burlington Archives, Harris to Perkins, Oct. 26, 1868.

[16] *Ibid.*, Forbes to Harris, Mar. 21, 1877.

[17] *Ibid.*, Ripley to W. R. Crumpton, July 20, 1878.

[18] *Ibid.*, Forbes to Ames, Sept. 25, 1880.

[19] *Ibid.*, Perkins to Forbes, Feb. 4, 1880. The Contract, described as "Memorandum with Union Pac. R. R. Co.," was dated Jan. 30, 1880. The quotations in this paragraph, except for the last one, are from this Memorandum.

[20] *Ibid.*, Perkins to Gould, July 7, 1880.

[21] *Ibid.*, Forbes to Ames, Sept. 22, 1880.

[22] The Memorandum of Agreement between the Wabash and the Burlington Nov. 15, 1880, is found in the Burlington Archives.

[23] Denver and New Orleans Rd., Executive Document No. 186, House of Representatives, 49th Congress, 1st Session, 1886, pp. 13-18. The agreement is examined in Overton, p. 22.

[24] *Bradstreet's*, April 17, 1886, p. 242.

[25] Annual Report, 1883, Manitoba, p. 16.

[26] Annual Report, 1883, Oregon and Transcontinental, pp. 9-10.

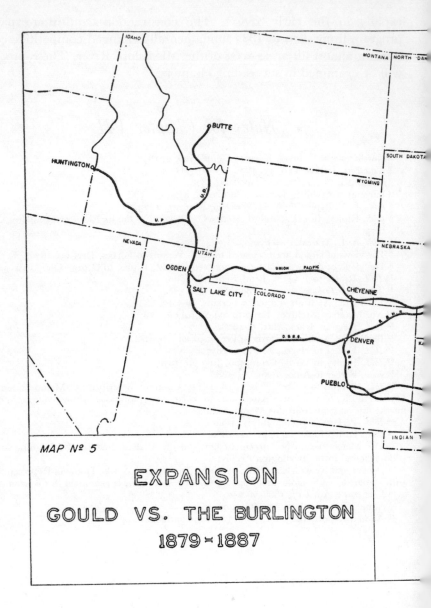

MAP № 5

EXPANSION

GOULD VS. THE BURLINGTON
1879-1887

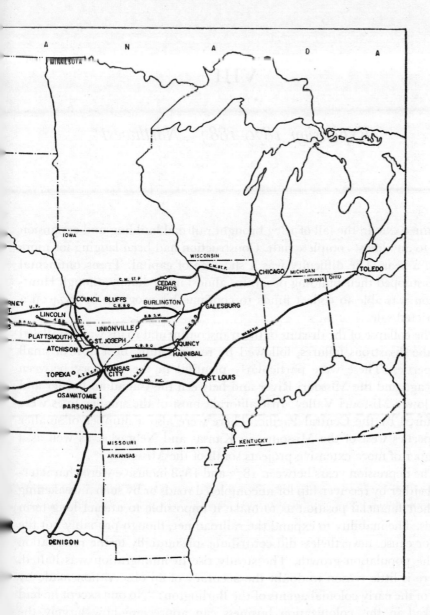

121

VIII

Expansion 1879-1883—Northwest

THE PANIC in the fall of 1873 brought railroad building and expansion to an almost complete halt. Construction had been lagging for more than a year. The difficulty was a shortage of capital. Transcontinental lines stopped their building programs almost immediately, though Huntington was able to collect funds to continue his program in 1874 on a restricted sale.

The collapse of the dreams of the transcontinental roads was paralleled by the disastrous failures, followed by receiverships, of a host of small properties. These were particularly plentiful in the territory between Chicago and the Missouri River and between the Canadian border and the lower Missouri Valley. In California most of the smaller lines were acquired by the Central Pacific. There were also a number of smaller properties west of the Missouri, in Kansas and Nebraska, as well as a number of more extensive projects south of the Missouri.

The depression years between 1873 and 1878 inclusive were characterized either by receivership for uncompleted roads or by such a weakening of their financial position as to make it impossible to attract long-term funds. The inability to expand the railroad net, though probably not the major cause, nevertheless did contribute substantially to the retardation of the population growth. The steady rise in immigration was halted. There is little reason to doubt the accuracy of an observation made by one of the early colonial agents of the Burlington: "No one except he had worked in this colonization business can appreciate how largely the settlement and general interests of a new country depend upon its having equal facilities in freights, passage and accommodations as those offered by other sections."[1] The restriction of population growth in turn reduced the volume of traffic. A closed circuit was set up which impaired the earnings of many of the uncompleted and financially weak roads. The absence of adequate means of transportation left many fertile areas un-inhabited and uncultivated. They grew and prospered only as railroad service became available.

The market prices of the securities of most of these small properties in the 1870's were exceptionally low. In many cases control could be acquired with no value attached to the stock. Bonds could be purchased at low prevailing prices and ownership effected via the foreclosure route. In the depression years of the 1870's, however, relatively few acquisitions of these weak but strategically valuable properties were actually effected. They were acquired in the years of prosperity at the higher prices charac-teristic of those periods.

This is not to say that no consideration was given to the possibility, to say nothing of the necessity, of making acquisitions in the 1870's. There was much discussion; there were many plans; and there were many proposals. Some properties, indeed, were acquired in the years preceding the boom. The Burlington purchased control of two small roads. The Burlington also had opportunities to acquire other roads at low prices. One was the Hannibal, a carrier of valuable local traffic in nothern Missouri and a link in a short Burlington route between Quincy, St. Joseph, and Kansas City. The Burlington management had frequently examined the property in the 1870's; yet in the face of the low prevailing prices it did nothing until competitive forces initiated by Gould forced the Burlington in 1883 to buy at a price more than 300 per cent in excess of that which prevailed in 1875–1877.

Plans were proposed, also, in the 1870's for the corporate unions between the larger properties. In the trans-Missouri area to the Pacific Coast the two dominant personalities in the 1870's were Huntington and Gould. There were numerous clashes between these two. Huntington as early as 1875 envisioned the possibility of a corporate consolidation with the Union Pacific as a solution to these difficulties. Indeed, there is some evidence to suggest that plans for consolidation had already been completed. Failure arose only because of the inability of Gould and Hunt-ington to agree upon terms of an exchange of securities. Such an arrange-ment was contemplated in 1875.[2]

The arrival of the Southern Pacific at the Colorado River and the prospect of further construction east beyond that point led to a Gould threat of competitive construction. As fast as Huntington built east of the Colorado, Gould declared, he would build west from Salt Lake. Huntington was ready for a compromise in order to avert this competitive threat "We want to so fix the S. P.," wrote Huntington, "that the U. P. interest will be just as safe as the C. P." Huntington proposed to give the Union Pacific a one-half interest in the road east of Yuma, or say 10/22nds of the whole road. (This presumably referred to the entire Southern Pacific System.) Huntington thought, however, that the Union Pacific would not pay the Southern Pacific stockholders what the stock had "fairly cost us."[3] A similar offer was made by Huntington in December, 1877.

The proposal of Huntington to unite the interests of the Southern Pacific and the Union Pacific was opposed by his policy-making associates. Colton was particularly violent in his objections. He had rather let the Southern Pacific line south of Los Angeles go "than mix up with Gould and that crowd." He would rather agree with the Union Pacific never to build a road east of the Colorado River than to join with them and with Tom Scott in going on at that time. Huntington was surrounded, Colton wrote him, by "high tone strikers who have become artists. In that way they annoy you more about the danger of Tom Scott and the Texas Pacific than is necessary. Jay Gould could not be true to Christ half an hour. . . ."[4]

At various times after 1874—the date of the Gould assumption of Union Pacific control—both the Huntington group and the Burlington management canvassed the idea of acquiring control of the Union Pacific. Early in 1875, before the Union Pacific stock was placed on a dividend basis, there was a belief that Gould was planning to unload the Union Pacific, to sell out and take his profits. In such event, Huntington planned to buy the Union Pacific stock. He asked Stanford to organize a group, including a number of prominent California capitalists, to buy a majority interest as and when Gould knocked the price down. It would be worthwhile, thought Huntington, to pay $50, a share for the stock, and thereby make possible an agreement with the Pacific Mail so as to enable a unified transcontinental line to charge high rates by avoiding a rate war with the steamship line.[5]

Some years later, early in 1879, there was a general belief that Gould's Waterloo had arrived, that he was about to retire from the railroad business, and that he had sold or was about to sell his Union Pacific stock.

Perkins, now the vice-president of the Burlington, was prepared to take advantage of the anticipated collapse of Gould. "The newspapers talk about Gould's decay & probably early fall," wrote Perkins to Forbes, "& I see that U. P. stock in all this building does not stiffen up much. If Gould shd [should] burst as we all ought to hope, and U. P. stock should take a big tumble it might not be a bad thing to go into." Perkins then expatiated upon the possibility that the Atchison group might also want to take hold. "There might be money in it," declared Perkins.[6]

At various times in the late 1870's both Perkins and Forbes referred also to the prospect of the Burlington acquisition of the Atchison.[7]

Thus, as the depression approached its end in the summer of 1878, the corporate relationship between the major carriers west of Chicago and beyond to the Coast remained substantially unaffected. In the depression years, furthermore, the addition of new lines, with the major exception of the Southern Pacific and to a lesser extent of the Atchison, was only nominal. Between the Missouri River and Chicago, also, little new construction was undertaken. Aside from some small branches built by the Rock Island and an extension of the Alton to Kansas City and of the Kansas City and Northern to Council Bluffs, little in the way of new building was accomplished. The Atchison had completed its line to the Kansas-Colorado boundary by December of 1872 and there it stopped. It had exhausted its financial resources. For a while it was unable even to earn its operating expenses. The construction program was renewed in 1875, and a line was built to Pueblo.

Except for building programs of the Atchison and the Southern Pacific, therefore, transcontinental railroad property remained just about as it was in 1873. This hiatus in railroad building came to an abrupt end even before the outbreak of the business boom in the spring of 1879. The construction boom that began in late 1878 continued until early 1883, though many projects begun earlier were not completed until 1884. It was the largest growth in the railroad industry up to that time. The expansion opened new routes to the Pacific Coast. Most of the transportation monopolies were overthrown. Railroad rate structures were revolutionized. Rates declined. Territorial agreements were violated and replaced in most cases by competition. Immigration was stimulated by policies of public agencies and railroad colonization departments. The railroad construction and expansion boom of the 1879–1883 era was indeed a fruitful step forward in the country's social and economic life.

The boom was initiated almost simultaneously in the Northwest and in the Southwest. In the latter area, major credit for pressing forward with railroad construction goes to the indefatigable genius of Huntington. The completion of the Southern Pacific line to the Colorado River in 1877 was accompanied by an acceleration of financial difficulties. Huntington's associates were exhausted—if not physically, then assuredly psychologically. They were anxious to become solvent, to pay off their debts, and once again become businessmen capable of writing checks against bank deposits. "We want rest," wrote Colton to Huntington. "Stop building all Roads until we can pay our debts, draw a check on the Bank against our own money in place of other People's. . . ."[8] Colton's advice was supported by Crocker. "I am getting very sick of railroad property," he wrote, "and of all other property that the public can manage."[9] And a few weeks later Crocker informed Huntington that "None of our people desire to organize a railroad company in Arizona or New Mexico."[10]

Huntington disagreed. By the fall of 1878, in the face of the opposition by his colleagues, he had decided to push ahead with an extension to El Paso and beyond. The opposition to his ambitious program by his associates continued into early 1879. The purchase by Huntington, without consulting his associates, of twenty thousand tons of steel rails brought another outburst from Crocker. "I assure you, Mr. Huntington, that I really think we ought to get out of debt before we build any more road."[11] The contracts for building through Arizona and New Mexico were nevertheless completed; legislation in both territories for the organization of subsidiaries was secured, contracts with a new construction company were made, labor and materials were assembled, and the construction proceeded.

The beginning of the boom in the Northwest was in many respects even more surprising and exciting than in the Southwest. There the earliest moves were made by the St. Paul. That road at the end of 1877 was relatively small. The property, under the presidency of Alexander Mitchell, was conservatively operated. The guiding hand in the expansion of the property, beginning in 1878, was that of Shelburne S. Merrill, the general manager. In its initial expansion steps the St. Paul did not do much construction. In southern Wisconsin, northern Illinois, southern Minnesota, and eastern and central Iowa were many financially weak properties. Control of most were held by those speculative capitalists whose functions in the national economy are so generally misunderstood and whose contributions to business progress are so frequently interpreted in light of personal profits. This group included such men as Blair, a railroad builder, promoter, and capitalist, operating from Blairtown, New Jersey; Taylor, the aged and wealthy head of National City Bank, with investments of many millions of dollars in railroad bonds bought at high prices in the early 1870's and showing heavy losses based upon the depression prices in the later 1870's; Sage, a heavy investor in railroad securities, with an ability to command cash in periods of low market prices and with courage to use that cash for the purchase of securities; and Porter, long connected with the Northwestern but acting personally as a promoter of various railroad combinations. There were other names involved, but these are sufficient to give an idea of the diversity of business ability engaged in the field of speculative capital. They bought when the conservative groups refused to buy. To paraphrase a cliché, they stepped in where the cautious capitalists feared to tread.

The spark in the expansion program in the Northwest was ignited by the St. Paul. Connecting with the St. Paul in southern Wisconsin, at Racine, was the Western Union Railroad, extending into northwestern Illinois and, by trackage over another line, to Rock Island. The road, in receivership, was acquired through the purchase of the bonds.

In southern Minnesota and northern Iowa other small properties lay orphaned, abandoned by their capitalistic promoters. The control of one (the Hastings and Dakota) was held by Sage through ownership of a large portion of the bonds. This line, approximately 200 miles in length, would give the acquiring road an entrance into the farming areas of the Dakotas. The population in this area was sparse and for a time the line would probably serve as a drag upon the acquiring road's earning power. It was an example of a road built into pioneer territory ahead of settlement. Profit to the owners was based upon the ability of the new road to attract settlers into a sparsely inhabited area. The Northwestern had an opportunity to acquire this property but again the St. Paul outbid the Northwestern and took over its control. Another financially weak property, the Southern Minnesota, extended west from the Wisconsin-Minnesota boundary, opposite La Crosse. The territory served was sparsely populated. This road was also built in advance of settlement and was also in receivership. It owned 212 miles of "indifferently completed" road, and the Northwestern's conservative management rejected the opportunity to buy control. The St. Paul soon thereafter stepped in and took over at a price which covered not only the bonds but also the respectable sum of $625 thousand for $1.25 million par value of its stock.[12]

By this time (May, 1879), early in the railroad expansion boom, the Northwestern, just recovering its financial strength, was already upset by the St. Paul's aggressiveness. The St. Paul, declared the Northwestern's president, seemed "to be building, buying and negotiating for almost every Road in the market."[13]

The St. Paul, however, undaunted by conservative criticism and condemnation, kept pressing ahead with its program. On the eastern Minnesota boundary were a number of roads known as the River Roads. Combined, they controlled a line on the western side of the Mississippi River from Dubuque to a point not far from the Twin Cities. By a short stretch of construction, an acquiring line could thus make a new route between Dubuque and the Twin Cities. The River Roads were in receivership. Negotiations in the depression years for their acquisition involved the Burlington and the Northwestern. The Northwestern management was anxious to acquire ownership. The road's general manager was indeed "very positive in the belief that it would be a misfortune to allow [the River Roads] to pass into the hands of the St. Paul Company, if they can be obtained by us on reasonable terms."[14] The St. Paul again was the successful bidder, however, and by the early 1880's it owned a line between Chicago, northeastern Iowa, and the Twin Cities.

The St. Paul then struck across northern Iowa to the James River, and also across central Iowa with a program to reach Des Moines. It had earlier pushed to Cedar Rapids, again through the purchase of another small road then in receivership. The proposed extension to Des Moines stirred the Northwestern camp. "I do not believe the responsible Directors & Shareholders of the St. Paul Road will engage in any such enterprise. It is simply a raid on the North Western & Rock Island Lines, and would result evidently in such retaliating measures as would make the scheme barren of all interest."[15]

The St. Paul's building and acquisition program exceeded by a substantial degree any of the other programs at that time in the area between Chicago and the Missouri River. In many of the newly invaded areas the population was small and the traffic density substantially below the average of other regional roads. But informed opinion expressed confidence that the new frontier settlements would grow and prosper. The

St. Paul would share in the benefits. By 1883, in the opinion of a leading railroad journal, its prospects were "brilliant."[16] Many communities were the beneficiaries of a low-cost transportation service; but those who supplied the capital to make this possible were destined soon to pass through the fires of adversity.

The expansion of the St. Paul brought it into territory long considered by the Northwestern as its own. That road was headed by Keep, who was characterized by one of the leading eastern financial journals as "an able executive officer, a wise administrator, and a far-sighted manager."[17] Though his conservatism proved misguided in some important matters, his judgments were well balanced; and under his leadership the company expanded without impairing its financial strength. The general manager was Marvin Hughitt and its vice-president of finance M. L. Sykes, Jr. This combination of executive talent had by 1880 lifted the Northwestern from the slough of financial difficulty into the highway of financial success.

Only by a narrow margin was the property able to avoid insolvency in the panic days of 1873. This managerial conservatism was strengthened in the boom years of 1878 and 1879 by its association with William H. Vanderbilt. His counsel to retain earnings for property improvements was generally followed. Its growing financial strength was husbanded; but this very strength was also a competitive weakness.

Not until 1880 did the Northwestern respond actively to the competitive push of its arch competitor. In that year it began to move against the St. Paul. By that time the latter had almost completed a through line from the Mississippi River at La Crosse, Wisconsin, to a point in southeastern Dakota. From there it projected a line north into the James River Valley—an area that was attracting thousands of immigrants. The Northwestern countered by throwing an extension from its main line in north central Iowa (at a point, Tama) a few miles west of Cedar Rapids into southeastern Dakota. There it joined its east-west line from Winona, Minnesota, thereby completing a through route, competitive with the St. Paul's from the Mississippi River via southern Minnesota into Dakota. The Northwestern also extended its line from southeastern Dakota north into the James River Valley, parallel to the St. Paul's. In Dakota the two roads competed vigorously, both along east-west and north-south lines.

Through these acquisition and building programs, the Northwestern and the St. Paul became active competitors over a wide area stretching from Chicago and eastern Wisconsin, on the one hand, through northern

Illinois, northern Iowa, southern Minnesota, and southeastern Dakota, on the other.[18] By 1881 the competition between these two lines led to bitter exchanges. The explosions by the Northwestern management reflected the strength of the feeling that each road had a "natural" territory that every other road should respect. The St. Paul ignored this pretension and "invaded" the territory of its business enemy without prior consultation or efforts to reach an agreement. Indeed, by this time, early in 1881, the St. Paul had decided to move clear across Iowa to a junction with the Union Pacific at Council Bluffs. "Nothing that we may do," regretfully concluded the Northwestern's management, "will prevent the Milwaukee & St. Paul Company from pushing forward to Council Bluffs."[19]

The president of the St. Paul in this period of its rapid growth was Mitchell—long associated with the property and a man respected in the camp of conservative capitalists. The real spark plug, however, was Merrill, the road's general manager. His initiative in the promotion of this bold policy was summarized by the Northwestern's chief executive. The St. Paul's policy, wrote Keep at the height of the expansion program in 1881, was dictated by Merrill in all things "as absolutely as if he were the sole owner of the property."[20] Keep continued, with a note of sadness, that if it had not been for this aggression there would have been no difficulty in adjusting conflicting interests, and both roads could have charged fair rates and each to a considerable extent would have served its own territory. But, he continued, the St. Paul for the previous three years had been aggressive. It built roads wherever it saw fit.[21]

Keep was enunciating the policy of live and let live, which for more than a decade had determined the business relationships of the Northwestern, the Rock Island, and the Burlington. The Northwestern management, even in the midst of its competitive defiance of the St. Paul, still insisted that its "old conservative, but progressive policy, must not be abandoned." Whatever the road needed should be done "regardless of the fever-heat of the St. Paul Co. But forewarned of their purposes to some extent we may need to pre-empt our position by prompter action than we should otherwise take in the regions where their progress means our detriment."[22]

The Northwestern was, however, forced to change its conservative policy. The St. Paul drove the road into an expansion policy, just as Gould drove the Burlington into a similar program. The Northwestern's management reacted bitterly to the St. Paul aggression. "It is a pleasure," declared its general manager, "to notice your fight against the St. Paul Co.'s theft. It cannot be called anything else but a thieving operation."[23]

The policy of competitive expansion of the Northwestern and the St. Paul was not adopted by another major line operating in Iowa and Illinois. This property, lying between the Burlington on the south and the Northwestern on the north, was the Rock Island. It had experienced throughout the 1870's a steady traffic and financial growth. Its earnings expanded, its dividends increased, and its stock sold on an investment basis. Tracy, the expansionist, was replaced in 1873 by Riddle, for a number of years the road's general superintendent. With him was associated, as operating vice-president, Cable, described by an associate in 1871 as "very energetic, able, and very wealthy."[24] Under this joint leadership the road, despite its good financial condition, expanded little during the 1870's. A number of small branches in central Iowa and the lease of the line between Keokuk and Des Moines were its only adventures.[25] In the opening year (1879) of the great expansion the Rock Island engaged in another local territorial contest. This was a struggle with the Northwestern and the Burlington for the control of the Cedar Rapids—a strategically located property extending from Burlington, Iowa, northwest to the southern tip of Minnesota.

After prolonged negotiations, the Rock Island succeeded in acquiring a majority stock though the Burlington retained a substantial minority interest. At about the same time some of the larger stockholders of the Rock Island bought a controlling interest in another enterprise—the Minneapolis and St. Louis. This road joined with the Cedar Rapids in southern Minnesota at Albert Lea. The Rock Island now had a line, rather circuitous, it is true, between Chicago and the Twin Cities. Late in 1882 the Rock Island, the Cedar Rapids, and the Minneapolis and St. Louis negotiated a contract for the creation of the "Albert Lea Route."[26] (See Map No. 6.)

The Rock Island now competed with the St. Paul and the Northwestern for the Chicago–Twin Cities traffic. The Northwestern reached the Twin Cities over the lines of an independent road—the Chicago, St. Paul, Minneapolis and Omaha. This was the successor of the West Wisconsin Railway which the Northwestern in the 1870's had failed to acquire. The Omaha was controlled by Porter. In the 1870's he had been a member of the Northwestern board, and upon its failure to acquire control of the West Wisconsin, Porter with a number of associates bought the property at foreclosure. By the early 1880's the road had expanded in a number of directions; it was now a prosperous property and indispensable to the strategic position of the Northwestern. In control of the Omaha, the Northwestern would be able to control a substantial volume of business between the Northwest and Chicago. Some board members of the Northwestern consistently advocated purchase of control. Late in 1880 its purchase was again considered. Keep renewed his opposition; he "did not feel inclined to take on the responsibility and care of the Omaha property."[27] The St. Paul's expansion, meanwhile, had brought it into the Omaha's territory. Porter was convinced that the St. Paul's "invasion" of his territory must be aggressively resisted, and not only by his road but by the Northwestern and Rock Island as well. "In my judgment," wrote Porter, "some policy will have to be adopted, and that policy a uniform one that each should carry out, to protect it against the St. Paul Company in its own district, for while large disaster will come to them, the result will be disastrous to our interests also."[28]

With respect to the St. Paul, there was obviously a mutuality of interests between the Omaha and the Northwestern. No such harmony appeared in the joint struggle with the Rock Island. The Rock Island's Chicago–Twin Cities line competed not only with the St. Paul but with the Northwestern. To the extent that the competition against the Northwestern succeeded, the Rock Island would divert traffic from the combined Omaha-Northwestern line. It would appear therefore that the Omaha would consider the Rock Island its business enemy. This, however, was not the case. In fact, the Omaha road actually steered traffic toward the Rock Island. The Northwestern obtained "little or none" of the Omaha's wheat traffic from Minneapolis; the business was transferred instead over the combined Minneapolis and St. Louis–Cedar Rapids–Rock Island route to Chicago. Hughitt believed that Porter wanted the Rock Island to control at least one-third of the freight to the Northwest. "There is plenty of evidence to support this conclusion."[29]

Hughitt urged Porter to unite with the Northwestern and, strange as it may appear, also with the St. Paul, to resist the encroachments of the Rock Island "in a parallel where they do not belong."[30] Porter refused. Though he was hostile to the St. Paul, he was not friendly to the Northwestern. The secret to this business duality lay in Porter's desire to sell out the Omaha to the Northwestern at a high price. And in this he soon succeeded. A continued diversion of the Omaha's traffic to the Rock Island would reduce the traffic and earnings of the Northwestern. How much it would hurt the Omaha it was difficult to say. Perhaps the Rock Island offered Porter some other compensating advantages. This is not known. It is, however, clear that because of the growing business brought to the Twin Cities by other northwestern lines, it was essential to acquire control of the Omaha.

The transaction was completed late in 1882. Some of the Omaha's property, to use the language of President Keep in the Northwestern's Annual Report for that year, had become "indispensable." The separation of the Omaha from the Northwestern "would work great injury and loss of revenue to both companies, and millions of capital would be required to replace the facilities which are now enjoyed by each in the harmonious working of the two lines."

The acquisition-expansion program of the Northwestern was supplemented with the purchase of the Sioux City and its controlled Nebraska line in 1884. This property, like the Omaha, could have been bought at a low price in the 1870's. In the early 1880's the owners began to extend the road's Nebraska line, known as the Fremont and Elkhorn Valley. These extensions fed into the Northwestern systems in western Iowa, and the controlling stockholders agreed to the extensions only upon condition that the Northwestern guarantee their bonds. Any earnings from the new lines would go to the stockholders and not to the Northwestern. This was not a comfortable arrangement for the latter. The road's general manager described the dilemma in picturesque language —". . . so long as we provisionally guarantee their bonds, and they [the road's controlling stockholders] can pocket the stock, we are simply nursing a tiger cub until it becomes strong enough to bite off our fingers."[91] The squeeze was successful; the road was sold to the Northwestern at a good price.

Aside from this acquisition of the Sioux City, the competitive expansion plans of the St. Paul, Northwestern, and Rock Island came to an end by 1883. New lines had been built, largely in territories of light traffic volume, in northern Iowa and southern Minnesota. In Dakota the roads were provided almost entirely in advance of the population. Both the Northwestern and the St. Paul assumed major business risks. The Northwestern had surveyed this territory early in 1878, though the St. Paul undertook the first construction steps.

It was believed that the building of new lines in the Dakota area would bring new settlers and increase the traffic, thereby justifying the expectations of the promoters. The outcome did justify the judgment of the pioneer railroad builders. The rapidity of the Dakota settlement, according to the 1883 Annual Report of the St. Paul, was "a marvel of the times." The annual report of the Northwestern referred to the immense increase in immigration and in land cultivation. Thus, operating in an environment of free competition, the public interest was well served. Businessmen and investors accepted risks characteristic of the system of free enterprise; the risk proved to be a good one, and both the public and the risk-taking investors were eventually well compensated. On a short-run basis, the St. Paul stockholders suffered a loss.

The risks assumed in still another section of the Northwest were materially greater than those in Iowa, Minnesota, and Dakota. Though the initial benefits over a short period of about three years were greater, the longer fifteen-year benefits were not realized. Indeed, the confident expectations of capitalists were confounded by substantial losses. The adventure of the Northern Pacific building program between the Great Lakes and the Puget Sound stirred the imagination of the public, stimulated heavy land subsidies from the public domain, heightened the expectations of prospective settlers, farmers, and miners alike, and invited the co-operation of capitalists in this country and abroad. Immense sums were invested under the impetus of a bold and imaginative leadership, confident of exceptionally high profits. If the traffic density in the Iowa, Minnesota, and Dakota areas was light, the density in many of the regions through which the Northern Pacific was built was nominal, in many cases almost nonexistent. The Northern Pacific in 1873 fell into receivership; the bonds were exchanged for stock; and the road, after reorganization, was left with a floating debt in excess of $5 million. During the worst depression year, 1877, directors used their personal credit to purchase rails.[32] On its Far Western end in the Puget Sound–Portland area, the Northern Pacific in 1873 had lost control of the Oregon Steam Navigation Company, which dominated the shipping on the Columbia, Snake, and Williamette Rivers in Washington and Oregon. The purchase of its stock by the Northern Pacific had led to the creation of a bond secured by the stock purchased. Upon default by the debtor, the stock was reacquired by the original owners. Beside the Oregon Steam Navigation, there were three other major transportation companies in the northwestern area. One—the Oregon Steamship—carried on a water business between Portland and San Francisco. Two railroads extending south from Portland completed the transportation net in the middle 1870's. Funds for all three of the ventures had been provided by German investors. Their bonds by this time had passed their interest. Villard, their agent in this country in the Kansas Pacific reorganization, had assumed a similar responsibility for the protection of their interests in the affairs of the steamship and the two railroad companies. By 1877 Villard was serving as president of the two Oregon north and south railroads, as well as of the Oregon Steamship. The three properties were in poor physical condition. The railroads were unfinished. They could carry no through traffic until they were connected with the Central Pacific in California; and, in the 1870's, this was still a long way off. The interest was in default, the earnings were poor, and future favorable prospects could flow only from their completion to the California-Oregon boundary. Villard first endeavored to work out a consolidation of the transportation enterprises under his supervision with the Oregon Steam Navigation.[33] Nothing came of the idea. The financial affairs of that concern had become desperate. Competition with a rival line led to a price war, and a proposal to pool the business met with failure.

By the spring of 1879 the long struggle between Gould and Villard had been resolved. Both—from their own points of view—had been successful. Villard in the eyes of a multitude of investor-followers was a financial hero. Forbes, with a large investor following, had made commitments, at Villard's suggestion, in the Kansas Pacific securities. A number of New York capitalists, notably Charles H. Woerishoffer and some of the partners in the Drexel-Morgan firm, had also made profitable ventures in these securities. Abroad, in England and Germany, Villard had enlisted the support of a number of important financial houses. After the conclusion of his peace with Gould, Villard sold out his Kansas Pacific holdings. He then turned his mind to the speculative possibilities which he saw impending in Oregon. He proposed to Gould that the Union Pacific build a line to Oregon, there to connect with a small railroad net on the south bank of the Columbia River owned by the Oregon Steam Navigation. He also suggested that he and Gould jointly purchase control of that property, thereby completing a through connection over the Union Pacific between Oregon and the East under joint ownership. The capital stock of the proposed company was fixed at $1 million, of which Villard and his friends would subscribe for $500 thousand and Gould and his friends for the other half.

Villard left for the coast and entered into negotiations with the owners of the Oregon Steam Navigation. By this time Villard, with the help of funds secured from his associates, had bought the Oregon Steamship. An arrangement was soon made by which a new company, to be known as the Oregon Railway and Navigation Company, would issue $6 million bonds and $6 million stock, to acquire control of the properties of the two companies and to provide the new company with working capital. For $100 thousand Villard secured an option to buy the stock of the Oregon Steam Navigation at any time up to October 1, 1879. As agreed, Villard offered Gould the half interest. By this time, however, Gould's plans had changed. He was then taking steps to carry forward a consolidation between the Kansas Pacific and the Union Pacific. To accomplish this it was necessary to maintain the friendship of Huntington. In Gould's plan to exert pressure on the Union Pacific to buy the Kansas Pacific was the threat to build a connection between the Kansas Pacific at Denver and Huntington's Central Pacific at Ogden. Huntington opposed the construction of a line to Oregon. Such a new route would divert traffic from the Central Pacific. The Rio Grande purchase and "some other matters," furthermore, required the expenditure of much money.[34] Gould, therefore, rejected the Villard offer of a 50 per cent commitment in the Oregon venture.

Villard accordingly played a lone hand. In ten days he succeeded in raising the cash necessary to carry out the agreement. The Navigation bonds were sold at 90 with a bonus of 70 per cent in stock. By July the transaction was concluded. Villard left for a trip to Europe, and when he returned in November the stock that had been given as a bonus was selling at 95 on the stock exchange. Villard had scored another notable success.

Villard was swept away by the boom psychology. He envisioned dreams of a truly imperialistic character. He looked forward to the creation of a transportation monopoly in the area between Seattle and San Francisco. He would build a railroad from Portland east to a connection with the Northern Pacific in southwestern Washington. He would build another road south and east to join a Union Pacific extension from Salt Lake City. His road would thus serve as the outlet for the Union Pacific and the Northern Pacific to the rapidly growing Northwest. He would make heavy investments in coal, timber, and agricultural resources. He would thereby not only realize profits from their exploitation but also feed his railroad lines with an abundant volume of business. He would also extend the unfinished roads from Portland south to the California boundary. There they would connect with Huntington's Central Pacific.

His confidence in the success of these ventures was unbounded. Even before the completion of the organization of the Navigation Company he wrote to one of his leading financial supporters, "I do not now hesitate to say with absolute confidence that what is recommended in the print [the prospectus] is by far the most promising investment that I have ever known of. It is a large thing now, but the growth of it in the next few years will be positively astounding."[35]

Villard's new ventures were phenomenally successful—that is, in their early stages. By the fall of 1880 he had the command of an enterprise which in some respects was one of the country's greatest transportation accomplishments. His companies controlled the navigable waters of the Columbia, Willamette, and Snake rivers, and a Portland-San Francisco steamship service. Villard was also building railroads designed to drain the products of these three valleys. He invested large sums in real estate for the purpose of securing adequate terminals and railroad repair shops. Furthermore, he organized a company—the Oregon Improvement Company—to exploit the region's natural resources. He moved quickly to acquire property for this new enterprise, with almost no consideration given to prices. What was asked, he paid. He bought some coal lands in western Washington, and from allied interests secured control of a railroad at a price that afforded the promoters an unexpected windfall profit. He bought the stock of the Pacific Coast Steamship Company—controlling the steamship business between Mexico and Alaska—a property which was later described "as a piece of patchwork." The Improvement also bought 150,000 acres of farm land and 10,000 acres of timber from the Northern Pacific. It also acquired competitive steamship lines, not for their earning power but for the purpose of creating a monopoly of the Pacific Coast steamship business.[36]

Villard, meanwhile, began the construction of a through railroad line on the south bank of the Columbia River between Portland and a connection with the Northern Pacific at Wallula. Transportation from Portland up the Columbia at that time required the use of two separate railroads and three separate sets of river steamboats. These were controlled by the Navigation. Villard decided to displace the river lines by railroad

11

tracks, thereby creating an all-rail route between Portland and a connection with the Northern Pacific.

Unfortunately for Villard, the Northern Pacific, under the leadership of an active and forward-looking management, had laid out its own plans. And these plans called for the construction of a line down the Columbia River Valley. Indeed the Northern Pacific charter required the construction of such a road. And the management in its 1880 Annual Report insisted that the road should have an outlet to tidewater, "either over the Cascade Range, or down the river, or by both ways, at the earliest possible moment."[37] These competitive lines spelled trouble for Villard. They would upset his plans for a territorial monopoly. Villard early adopted a program to checkmate his onrushing Northern Pacific rival. He began to occupy for the Navigation "the most strategic positions and the richest agricultural areas" along the nothern approaches to the Columbia Valley.[38] The Northern Pacific, furthermore, under the Cooke regime in the early 1870's had finished a line between a point in southwestern Washington a few miles distant from Portland to Tacoma. The building of the mileage between Portland and this point (Kalama) would create a through route to Portland's great rival in the Puget Sound. With lines to Portland and Tacoma the Northern Pacific would be in a position to compete successfully with the Villard enterprises.

Villard early made approaches to dissuade the Northern Pacific management from carrying out its plan. These negotiations were unsuccessful. They were followed by discussions for the joint use of the Navigation's Columbia Valley road. The Northern Pacific's management resented the occupation by the Navigation of territory on the north side of the Columbia River. Even prior to the occupation of this territory the conviction that one road had a "natural" right to a particular territory continued to characterize business discussions. "Villard's Company," wrote Frederick Billings, president of the Northern Pacific, "has no business really, north of the Snake River."[39] Villard countered that the Northern Pacific had no right to build over the Cascade Range. All problems could be satisfactorily arranged, Villard told Billings, if the Northern Pacific agreed not to build over the range.[40]

The negotiations continued, meanwhile, for the joint use of the Navigation's line south of the Columbia. Numerous drafts of a proposed contract were prepared and discussed. No agreement was reached, and discussions lagged. A contract was finally completed in October of 1880.

(For details, see Chapter VII, p. 117.) This was the first of a number of territorial agreements in the Columbia River–Oregon–Washington area. From this time until 1889 a succession of agreements were proposed; a few of them were authorized; none of them were successful; and the prolonged efforts to divide the territory ended in the early 1890's with a mutual territorial invasion. Thereafter the Northern Pacific and the Union Pacific (then in control of the Navigation) invaded each others "natural" territory.

Villard's expectations that the Northern Pacific would not build through the Columbia Valley received a rude setback early in 1881. It was then announced that the Billings management had sold $40 million of Northern Pacific bonds through the Morgan-Drexel firm. Indeed the subscription was so successful that more than $50 million was actually subscribed.[41] Even before this bond issue, Villard had already determined upon a bold plan. He was unable to checkmate the Northern Pacific; he was certain that the road was determined to build west across the mountains and also down the Columbia Valley. He, therefore, decided to acquire control of that property. As early as November, 1880, he had already conceived a plan "by which I think we can easily obtain control of the N. P."[42] At first he confided his purpose only to two close friends. Later he formed a syndicate to acquire the stock in the open market. His plans originally called for the purchase of a sufficiently substantial interest to assure harmonious relations between the two properties, but later he decided upon actual control. Working control was acquired early in 1881. The sums needed were raised by a move unprecedented in American financial history. (For details on the methods used to raise the funds, see Chapter XI, p. 184-5.)

The Villard Northwestern transportation monopoly was now complete and he decided to unify the control of his extraordinary business empire. He set up a new company—the Oregon and Transcontinental—with a controlling interest in both the Northern Pacific and the Navigation, to build railroads and steamship lines in order to "protect" the interests of the two major roads and to engage in other enterprises to build up the territory served. (See Chapter XI, p. 185 for details on the financing of this company.)

By mid-1883 this holding company controlled more than one-third of the Northern Pacific and slightly more than a majority of the Navigation stocks. With the aid of stock owned by its directors and by the directors of allied companies, the Transcontinental dominated the affairs of the Northern Pacific. And in the 1883 Annual Report of the former, Villard could boast, that that company had undertaken "the general development of a territory representing one-sixth of the area of the entire United States. . . ."[43]

Again Villard expressed his confidence in the outcome of this new enterprise. "I feel absolutely confident," he wrote to one of his followers, "that we shall be able to work results out of this combination of interests that will astonish every participant."[44]

Villard now moved to complete the Northern Pacific system: (1) by building the Oregon and California to the California boundary line— after long negotiations with the bondholders the several corporations owning various parts of the railroads running south of Portland were merged into one company, the Oregon and California and the road was leased to the Transcontinental, with an accompanying contract by the lessee to finish the road to a junction with the Central Pacific at the California boundary; (2) by finishing the Navigation's line between Portland and the Northern Pacific junction; (3) by extending its line southeast to a connection with the Union Pacific; (4) by supplying adequate terminal facilities in Portland and St. Paul; and finally, the climax, by completing the Northern Pacific's main line from Duluth to the connection with the Navigation.

The line to the California boundary and the connection with the Union Pacific were not completed during Villard's administration. The through line between Duluth and Portland was completed in a remarkably short period. In September, 1883, the Northern Pacific was joined with the Navigation. The nation's dream of a generation—a northern transcontinental route between the Great Lakes and the Pacific Coast— was realized. There were, however, no profits to its promoters or to their financial followers. There were, instead, tragic losses. The financial details will be presented in a subsequent chapter. It is sufficient to say here that the confident expectations of 1879 and 1880, so successfully realized in the boom years of 1881 and 1882, were replaced in 1883 by frustration and disaster. The resources of the Transcontinental were strained to the utmost. A succession of security issues and the creation of a heavy floating debt brought it to the verge of bankruptcy, only to be saved from that fate at almost the last possible moment. The Northern Pacific was left with a heavy debt which required some time for its liquidation. Villard himself went down to financial defeat. The losses to his followers were immense, and bitter words were exchanged between him and his financial lieutenants. The public, however, was well served. It had secured the benefits of a new transportation route between the Great Lakes, Chicago, the Twin Cities, and the Pacific Coast. The route was completed far in advance of the time limit projected in 1879, and of course far exceeded expectations entertained during the depression years of the 1870's in any quarter, public or private.

The Villard empire encountered on its eastern end a small group of able businessmen from which there soon emerged a new railroad personality in James J. Hill. Hill emerged as a leader in the western railroad industry on a par with Huntington, Villard, Gould, Perkins, Forbes, Keep, and Mitchell. In a significant sense he differed from the rest. Leadership in these formative days of railroad-creating systems was assumed by financiers—by those with access to sources of capital. They were not experienced in the art of railroading, nor familar with the detailed tactics of railroad construction, tariffs, and rates, and of maintenance and operating problems. There were, of course, presidents who were long schooled in these matters; but they were the hired men. They were not of the promoters and risk-takers who laid out the strategy for the growth of the property and who carried the responsibility for corporate success or failure. Huntington, Villard, Forbes, Gould, Mitchell, Nickerson, Cooke built and put together railroad systems. They either built them or united loose lines into unified through properties. Most systems were created by the use of both methods. Some of these risk-takers tried and lost. They led, they built, they merged, largely because of their ability to raise capital. Usually the tactics of the business were conducted by others. Huntington had Crocker; Villard had Oakes; Forbes had Perkins; Mitchell had Merrill; Gould had Dillon; Nickerson (with his Boston capitalists) had Strong.

Hill, unlike most of these leaders, was an experienced transportation man. When, in the mid-1870's, he appeared as an actor in the railroad industry he had already seen almost two decades in the business of carrying freight and passengers. His center of operations revolved around St. Paul. In the 1860's and early 1870's there was no railroad connection between eastern Canada and the province of Manitoba. Railroad lines reached St. Paul from Chicago. West of St. Paul a line by the late 1860's had been built to St. Cloud. Business from eastern Canada to Manitoba moved by way of Detroit and Chicago to St. Paul. From there the movement was by rail to St. Cloud, by stage to the Red River, and by flatboat down the river to Manitoba. Hill performed a forwarding service; he arranged a through route service between St. Paul and Manitoba for the shipping and travelling public. He also provided a number of ancillary services—his biographer gives him credit for activities in the "warehouse, the river trade, the agency for the Red River buyers, the full contract with the railroad, the fuel business in St. Paul and the storage forwarding and commission business."[45] By the early 1870's, moreover, Hill, in conjunction with a business associate, Norman W. Kittson, had secured a monopoly of the Red River traffic. Though Hill by this time had plenty of experience in the transportation industry, he had only slight contact with capitalists—with men of wealth.

Meanwhile, however, eastern and foreign capital under the leadership of Cooke provided the area with an increasing mileage of railroad facilities. Dutch capital was poured into the St. Paul and Pacific, a road which by 1871 had finished a line from Minneapolis to the Red River at Breckinridge; it had also built an unfinished line projected to the Canadian boundary for a connection with another projected line of the Canadian Pacific. The road, moreover, was in possession of a land grant, contingent upon the completion of the line to the international boundary. It had been extravagantly financed, with a heavy debt; and there was reason to support the belief that to financial improvidence there was added a dose of dishonesty. The financial crisis in the fall of 1873 swept the road into receivership.

Hill meanwhile through his association with Kittson had established close business relationships with the promoters and financial supporters of the Canadian Pacific. The latter needed a railroad outlet to the United States to carry the construction materials for the building of that road. Said the major financial sponsor of the Canadian Pacific, "We certainly did not expect to make much profit out of it, but we did desire, and that very earnestly to have a road into our own North-West country."[46] The man who uttered these remarks was Donald A. Smith, a wealthy capitalist and a member of Parliament with considerable political influence. In association with him was George Stephen, president of the Bank of Montreal, one of the largest and most influential financial institutions in North America.

These four—Hill, Kittson, Smith, and Stephen—joined their interests and their assets in a common undertaking to acquire control of the St. Paul and Pacific. Profits, if any, would be distributed one-fifth to each, with the extra fifth to Stephen, to be used for the purpose of securing additional capital. Smith, meanwhile, used his political influence to good advantage. The Canadian government was building a road to the inter national boundary and by August, 1878, that road was leased for ten years to the St. Paul and Pacific.[47] On the Minnesota side of the boundary the receiver in 1877 endeavored to raise funds to build north to the boundary. The effort failed.[48] The money was not forthcoming.

And that was *the* problem: how to raise funds. Control of the St. Paul and Pacific could be acquired only through the purchase of the bonds— the stock was worthless. Most of the bonds were held in Holland; they were deposited with a committee. There was also a market for the bonds in New York. The four-member American-Canadian team first played for time. Stephen went abroad in an effort to secure an option from the Dutch bondholders. His option offer was rejected. The Dutch bondholders wanted cash. But the buyers did not have enough cash. Neither did the bondholders have the cash to improve and extend the road to Canada and to save the valuable land grant. Out of subsequent negotiations a compromise agreement emerged early in 1878. The four-member team agreed to reorganize the road's financial structure, to build the line to the Canadian boundary in two years, and to arrange for personal bonds with joint and several responsibility, with penalty of $100 thousand as liquidated damages for failure to perform. The sum of $280 thousand would be deposited in the Bank of Montreal, to carry out the contract. The bonds would be bought at prices somewhat higher than the prevailing market, payment to be made in $1,000 6 per cent bonds and $250 of stock of the new company in exchange for $1,000 of bonds of the old company.

The bargain was heavily charged with risks. Bondholders were, it is true, offered securities of a proposed new company with a value in excess of the market value of their bonds of the old company. They might, nevertheless, want to sell their bonds for cash. Funds had to be raised to build the line to the boundary. The funds might not be forthcoming and the line might not be finished in time to save the land grant.

Everything, however, turned out well. The line connecting at the boundary with the Canadian Pacific extension was finished on time. The land grant was saved. Thus, "substantially all the government lands and most of the railroad land near the lines of the railroad in the Red River

Valley were taken. . . ."[49] Northern Pacific competition for the Canadian traffic was eliminated; an agreement between the Canadian Pacific and the St. Paul and Pacific extension left the Northern Pacific without access to Canada.

By May, 1879, early in the business boom, all the formalities were completed. The property of the old company was sold at foreclosure; a new company, the St. Paul, Minneapolis and Manitoba, bought this property and issued bonds and stocks in payment. These securities were then distributed to the bondholders of the old company. Part of the stock of the new company was issued to the Hill–Kittson–Smith–Stephen team, for services rendered and risks assumed. Stephen was elected president and Hill general manager.

The financial windfall which greeted Huntington, Gould, and Villard at this time also showered blessings on this group. Almost simultaneously with the organization of the new company, "the immigration into the Red River Valley and to Manitoba began on a great scale."[50] The wheat crop was heavy; exports, due to the European crop failure, mounted; the price of wheat advanced; and the heavy tonnage, combined with rates only slightly affected by competition, produced an extraordinary increase in revenues. The management rushed construction of branch lines into and through the Red River Valley, thereby intensively exploiting the rapidly settling territory. By prolonged trading, climaxed by the territorial agreement of 1882, it also kept Villard out of the Valley. The finances were, meanwhile, prudently arranged. First-mortgage bonds were limited to $12 thousand per mile; these were distributed to the bondholders of the old company. To pay for improvements and the building of new lines, second-mortgage bonds, also in limited amounts, were issued. The lush profits of 1879–1882 were used entirely for plant requirements. No dividends were paid until 1882.

Notes for Chapter VIII

[1] Burlington Archives, Touzalin to Perkins, May 8, 1871.
[2] Huntington to Hopkins, Jan. 31, 1876, M. M.
[3] Huntington to Colton, Oct. 5, 1877, M. M.
[4] Colton to Huntington, Jan. 31, 1878, M. M.
[5] Huntington to Stanford, Mar. 15, 1875, M. M.
[6] Burlington Archives, Perkins to Forbes, Feb. 1, 1879.
[7] See, for example, *Ibid.*, Nov. 24, 1878.

[8] Colton to Huntington, Oct. 15, 1877, M. M.

[9] Crocker to Huntington, Feb. 12, 1878, M. M.

[10] Crocker to Huntington, Mar. 19, 1878, M. M.

[11] Crocker to Huntington, Jan. 22, 1879, M. M.

[12] Northwestern Archives, Keep to Sykes, May 6, 1879.

[13] *Ibid.*

[14] *Ibid.*, Keep to Sykes, Mar. 1, 1880.

[15] *Ibid.*, Hughitt to the Hon. N. M. Hubbard, Sept. 2, 1879.

[16] *R. R. Gaz.*, April 27, 1889, p. 266.

[17] *Chron.*, June 18, 1887, p. 769.

[18] At a distance of about 50 miles apart, they built duplicate lines; and, in the language of a Boston observer, tried to "circumvent each other." (*Boston Transcript*, Aug. 24, 1880.)

[19] Northwestern Archives, Sykes to Keep, Jan 21, 1881.

[20] *Ibid.*, Keep to John M. Burke of New York City, Aug. 6, 1881.

[21] *Ibid.*

[22] *Ibid.*, Sykes to Keep, Jan. 7, 1881.

[23] *Ibid.*, Hughitt to J. I. Blair, April 24, 1880.

[24] *Ibid.*, J. H. Howe, to A. W. Greenleaf, Aug. 24, 1871.

[25] For details, see *Iowa Pool*, pp. 94–97.

[26] Details of this agreement are found in the *New York World*, Dec. 1, 1882.

[27] Northwestern Archives, Sykes to Keep, Dec. 16, 1880.

[28] *R. R. Gaz.*, Dec. 1, 1882, p. 733.

[29] Northwestern Archives, Hughitt to Sykes, Oct. 21, 1882.

[30] *Ibid.*

[31] *Ibid.*, Jan. 3, 1884.

[32] Hal Bridges, *Iron Millionaire*, (Philadelphia: University of Pennsylvania Press, 1952), p. 107.

[33] H. V. P., Villard to J. C. Ainsworth, May 11, 1878.

[34] *Ibid.*, Artemas H. Holmes to Villard, Sept. 11, 1879, Box 57.

[35] *Ibid.*, Villard to Endicott, June 5, 1879, Box 120, Letter Book 37.

[36] An account of the progress of the Oregon Improvement Company is found in *Bradstreet's*, Feb. 16, 1884. The quotation in the text is taken from p. 100.

[37] Annual Report, Northern Pacific, 1880, p. 33.

[38] Hedges, p. 61.

[39] Northern Pacific Archives, Billings to Joseph D. Potts, Mar. 4, 1880.

[40] *Ibid.*, Billings to Sprague, Feb. 21, 1881.

[41] Northwestern Archives, Sykes to Keep, Jan. 7, 1881.

[42] H. V. P., Villard to Endicott, Nov. 23, 1880, Box 120, Letter Book 39.

[43] Annual Report, Oregon and Transcontinental, 1883, cited in *R. R. Gaz.*, Aug. 3, 1883, p. 511.

[44] H. V. P., Villard to Norris, July 23, 1881, Box 12, Letter Book 40A.

[45] Pyle, Vol. I, p. 90.

[46] Beckles Wilson, *The Life of Lord Strathcona and Mount Royal* II, (Boston: Houghton Mifflin, 1915), p. 61.

[47] *Ibid.*, p. 66.

[48] *Ry. World*, June 23, 1877, p. 588.

[49] *R. R. Gaz.*, Oct. 5, 1883, p. 656.

[50] *Ibid.*, See also *Ry. World*, July 6, 1878, p. 752.

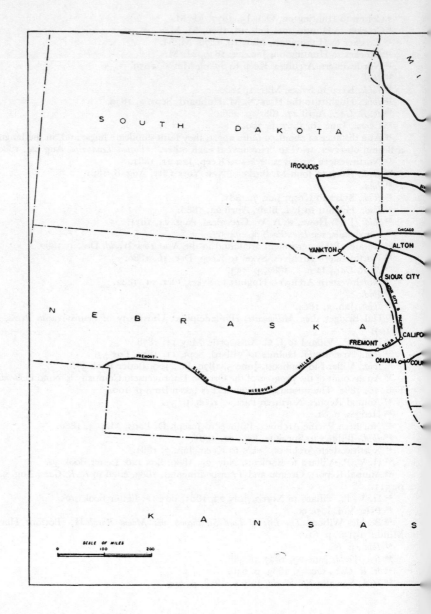

Within the map:

SOUTH   D A K O T A

IROQUOIS

C. &. N.W.

CHICAGO

YANKTON

ALTON

SIOUX CITY

SIOUX CITY & PACIFIC

N E B R A S K A

CALIFO

FREMONT

SCRIB

OMAHA

COU

PREMONT

ELKHORN

MISSOURI

VALLEY

K A N S A S

SCALE OF MILES

0   100   200

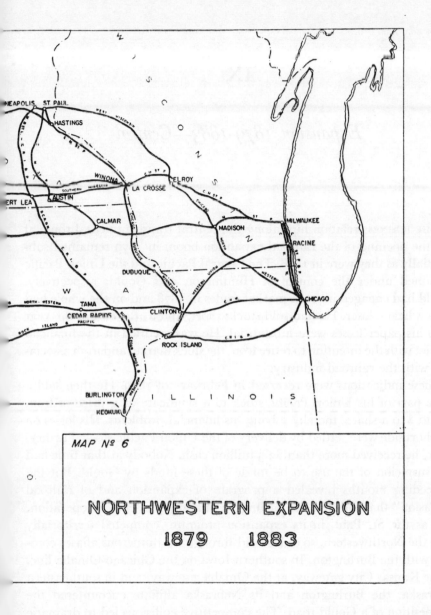

MAP № 6

NORTHWESTERN EXPANSION
1879   1883

147

IX

Expansion 1879-1883—Central

THE BUSINESS relationships along the central transcontinental route at the opening of the railroad expansion boom in 1879 remained substantially as they were in 1878. The Central Pacific and the Union Pacific remained under the control of Huntington and Gould, respectively. Gould had engaged in stock-market trades in 1878 and on the whole had been a heavy loser. He had sold stocks short, and at the end of the year 1878 his paper losses were substantial. He was credited in the financial district with the intention to retire from the stock market and from association with the railroad industry.

These indications were reversed in February of 1879. He then sold a large part of his Union Pacific stock to a syndicate at a price of from $65 to $70 a share, thereby solving his financial problems. His losses on the short side were settled by delivery of the Union Pacific stock. Furthermore, he received more than $3.5 million cash. Nobody at that time had any suspicion of the use to be made of these funds by Gould. But the succeeding months revealed a program of expansion and of railroad "invasion" that affected the Burlington in many phases of its operation. Just as the St. Paul, in its expansion program, competed territorially with the Northwestern, so did Gould through his numerous aliases compete with the Burlington. In southern Iowa on the Chicago-Omaha line, at the Kansas City gateway, at the Omaha gateway, and in southeastern Nebraska, the Burlington and its Nebraska affiliate encountered the competition of a Gould road. The competitive collisions led to dramatic conflicts and to far-reaching changes in the evolution of the American railroad system.

Within two months after the sale of his Union Pacific stock in February,

Gould turned up with the working control, acquired by purchases in the open market, of the Wabash. This road owned a line between Toledo and St. Louis and a connection with the Burlington at Quincy. Within three months thereafter, largely through buying on the stock market, Gould acquired control of the Kansas City and Northern, which owned the line between St. Louis and Kansas City on the north side of the Missouri River. By July he had succeeded in effecting an exchange of the two stocks and consolidating the two companies into the new Wabash, in control of a through line between Kansas City and Toledo. Thereafter he moved quickly to secure a connection with Chicago through the acquisition of an existing weak line and the construction of a short stretch of track. He then bought up, as did the St. Paul at about the same time, a number of bankrupt properties. These he tied together in such a way as to create the possibility of a through line through southern Iowa to Omaha, thereby creating a new short line between Omaha and Chicago. The contest between Gould, the Wabash, and the Burlington, and the "peace" settlement or perhaps more accurately the armistice, that followed has already been described in previous pages. (See Chapter VII, page 114.)

Meanwhile in southeastern Nebraska the war of threats and counter-threats, the building of small branches and the threat to build many more—a war that had begun in 1876—continued. As late as the summer of 1879 the general manager of the Nebraska affiliate of the Burlington denounced the Union Pacific's "recent open acts of aggression in connection with transportation of stock"; and these acts, he continued, were "but trifling as compared with the insidious attacks that are in motion & have been for the last three months."[1] Co-operating with the Union Pacific was the Atchison and Nebraska, a small road built under the leadership of Joy, who had become an opponent of the Burlington. An official of the latter's Nebraska affiliate recommended a program of aggressive construction. The time had come, he wrote, "when offensive operations should be begun by use of the kind which will win, provided, always, of course, that we undertake only such operations as are in themselves wise."[2] Repeatedly he insisted upon securing authority to make war against the Union Pacific. That authority by 1879 had not been granted in such a way as to lead to an extensive program of railroad construction. Those in charge of the executive policies of the Burlington remained cautious. They still hoped to avoid a construction rivalry. The

instructions to this officer were couched in ambiguous terms, characteristic of the expression of an ill-digested and undecided policy. "You may
do as suggested on both lines," read a telegram from an executive officer ,
"provided, however, that you take great care not to commit us, because
we hope for adjustments and must avoid giving just ground for complaint
in the event of not following these lines to completion."[3]

To the veteran business statesman of the Burlington, the Gould onrush
of building threats, on the one hand, and of the acquisition of a succession
of weak roads, on the other, was not particularly impressive. "I doubt,"
wrote Forbes, "if this carnival of bankrupt roads is going to continue."[4]
Forbes was anxious to strengthen the Burlington's Iowa trunk and its
local lines, and to secure a firm hold on the Kansas City gateway. To
achieve the latter purpose there were two possibilities. One was to acquire
a bankrupt road—the Burlington and Southwestern. It owned an unfinished line from Burlington, Iowa, to a small point in northern Missouri
in the direction of Kansas City. The other and more desirable alternative
was the acquisition of the Hannibal. That road connected at Quincy
with the Burlington and afforded it a short connection with Kansas City.
Burlington's hesitation in buying the stock proved costly. By the spring
of 1879 the stock was no longer on the bargain counter. In the summer
the Burlington communicated with William Dowd, president of the
property, for the purpose of making a lease. Dowd was disappointed to
learn that the Burlington people had not purchased enough stock to make
such an arrangement possible. By November, Gould had bought enough
stock to place himself and one of his associates on the Hannibal's directorate. The Burlington had now an insecure hold on a road which was
"practically a part of our line to Kansas City."[5]

Shortly before this defeat the Burlington had encountered another
reversal. In Northern Kansas a small road, financially weak and in receivership—the Central Branch Union Pacific (at that time it had no connection with the Union Pacific Railroad)—owned a line west from Atchison. Early in 1879 it projected a line to Denver. The owners of the property, however, were willing to sell. The Burlington, because of its interest
in a line to Denver, appeared as a buyer. It was also desirous of securing
control in order to develop more friendly business relations with the
Rock Island. That road had no lines west of the Missouri River. Gould
was still insisting that all of the business west of the Missouri River be
pooled. The Rock Island with no business west of the river was thus in-

clined to take sides against the Burlington and in favor of the Gould policy. The Burlington believed that purchase of the Central Branch in behalf of the Rock Island would lead to an alliance between the two Iowa lines with such strength that it "would throw Gould into the shade."[6] Forbes, however, was too much of a conservative Yankee capitalist to think in terms of the fancy prices demanded by the stockholders of the Central Branch. The price that Forbes declined to pay was accepted by Gould. For a stock which was selling at nominal prices early in 1878 Gould paid about $239 per share. Gould then transferred these shares to the Union Pacific at his cost.

The next Gould blow came a few weeks later in early November. This was the purchase of the Missouri Pacific. That road controlled the line south of the Missouri River between Kansas City and St. Louis. Gould was now in control of both the of St. Louis–Kansas City lines, one north and the other south of the Missouri River. Something approaching consternation struck the Burlington camp. "Gould moves so rapidly," explained Perkins, "it is impossible to keep up with him with Boards of Directors."[7]

The Burlington meanwhile was engaged on still another competitive battlefront. From Hannibal south to Denison, Texas, extended the Kansas and Texas. The Burlington traded preferentially with this road. The property during the depression was placed in the hands of a trust company. There was a heavy debt, most of which was held by Dutch investors. They were represented by a committee of Dutch bankers with whom both Gould and the Burlington management were in contact. Patrick Geddes, a large Burlington stockholder and a Kansas and Texas bondholder, urged the purchase of the road upon the Burlington. Forbes was not impressed. "Buying a pig in a poke is a very dangerous experiment when it comes to twenty million."[8] Prolonged negotiations between the Dutch Committee and the Burlington finally led to a willingness on the part of the latter to guarantee a 4 per cent return upon the bonds. Control of the property would then be transferred to the Burlington. The Dutch bondholders insisted upon a 5 per cent guarantee. Gould, strange to say, meanwhile made a heavy investment in the company's common stock. He then installed his own board and induced the stockholders to ratify a lease to the Missouri Pacific. The lease agreed to turn over any surplus earnings to the shareholders of the lessor, the Kansas and Texas. The bondholders were not consulted. To insure permanent control Gould tendered the trust company cash in amount sufficient to pay the interest coupons, thereby removing the default. The property thereafter was returned to the company and Gould's Missouri Pacific retained control through the lease contract.

Probably the most far-reaching blow, however, still remains for consideration. The Burlington and the Union Pacific in 1879 remained locked in a legislative battle over the pro rata bill. That was the effort made both by the B. & M. and the Kansas Pacific to secure such an equivalence in the rate structure as would permit the flow of traffic between these lines and the Union Pacific's Cheyenne to Ogden line. This would enable these two roads to compete with the Union Pacific for transcontinental business. In March of 1879 Gould, in the contest over control of the Kansas Pacific, made his peace with Villard. By buying out the other interests in the Kansas Pacific reorganizing pool, Gould obtained a controlling interest in the stock and junior securities of that road. Gould in September proposed an exchange of Kansas Pacific stock to Union Pacific. The terms were too high and the offer was rejected. Gould then made his successive purchases of the Central Branch, the Missouri Pacific, and of a number of other bankrupt properties. He then announced his determination to build a connection between the Kansas Pacific in eastern Colorado and the Central Pacific at Ogden. He would thereby become an active competitor of the Union Pacific. His threat to reduce rates was certain to impair, if not to destroy, the Union Pacific's earning power. Gould's program was successful, and by early January 1880 it was completed. The Kansas Pacific stock, which about a year and a half before was selling at nominal levels of less than $10 a share, was now exchanged for stock in the newly merged Union Pacific, which was selling at $100 a share.[9]

The long battle for the control of the Kansas Pacific was now over. The Burlington had again lost. The grand strategy of Forbes and the group of Boston capitalists to buy control of the Kansas Pacific at low prices had misfired. The Burlington had lost a friendly Kansas City–Denver connection. Its remaining outlet for this business was the circuitous route of the Atchison, to Pueblo, and the Rio Grande, from Pueblo to Denver. And the Rio Grande line had also fallen into Gould's hands. The extension of the Burlington to Denver had now become more strategically important than ever. One element in the Burlington's board favored immediate construction. The threat to build the line was a major countermove in the Burlington's struggle against Gould. The report of such a decision, in the word of a close railroad observer, was "like shaking a red flag at a mad bull so far as the U. P. [Union Pacific] is concerned."[10] A Denver extension in 1880 was, however, abandoned, as part of a general armistice between the two conflicting forces. A number of treaties providing for respect of each other's territory and for cessation of further construction were negotiated in 1880.

The Burlington began its expansion policy with the acquisition of the Council Bluffs. This company owned a line between Council Bluffs and Kansas City. The Union Pacific business via Omaha could be transferred to the southern competitors of the Iowa lines at such points as St. Joseph and Kansas City only by the use of the Council Bluffs. Gould between 1874 and 1879 had repeatedly diverted traffic from the Iowa lines at Omaha through the exploitation of the strategic position of the Council Bluffs road. The Burlington management now decided that control was essential. One official advised that the Gould seizure of the road would strike the Burlington a severe blow, as it would compete directly for the business for fifty miles south from Council Bluffs and would demoralize rates for fifty miles east.[11] Perkins was also convinced that its acquisition was desirable: ". . . we ought to get it if we can," he wrote. "I think this is pretty important."[12]

The contract for the purchase of the road was negotiated in May of 1880. The price was high, involving not only the assumption of a heavy debt but also a good round price for the common stock. Between 1873 and 1879 the road had almost no earnings. The price which the Burlington paid for control—$125 in its own stock for the stock and income bonds of the other road—was probably the highest price which up to that time the Burlington had ever paid for the control of another property. Burlington was now forced to adopt the policy of so many other roads, *i.e.*, of buying properties not for their earning power but to prevent them from falling into the hands of competitors. Huntington had followed this policy in the late 1860's and early 1870's in California. Gould, on the Union Pacific, did the same in the early 1880's. And the St. Paul and the Northwestern between 1879 and 1882 pursued similar policies. This is an aspect of competitive business that is widespread in the free enterprise system. It was followed then in many lines of business enterprise and it is followed now. It is an effective but expensive method of stabilizing competitive forces; or, according to another interpretation, of eliminating competition and achieving monopoly.

12

In pursuance of this new policy, the Burlington also bought control of the Atchison and Nebraska. Though this road did not have the strategic importance of the Council Bluffs, its control in the hands of Gould and the Missouri Pacific would nevertheless have served as a threat to the Burlington's Nebraska lines. Through the use of the Atchison and Nebraska, the Missouri Pacific could have created a line on the west side of the river between Kansas City and Omaha. The Burlington's acquisition of the two lines on both sides of the Missouri River between Kansas City and Omaha (the Council Bluffs and the Atchison and Nebraska) reduced the competitive strength of the roads between St. Louis and the lower Missouri River cities in their bid for a share of the Union Pacific transcontinental business.

By the end of 1880 Gould's railroad interests had been further expanded, and in a manner destined to affect the future relations between his properties and those of the Burlington. He had moved far into the Southwest. The parent of this new railroad brood was the Missouri Pacific. Gould by January, 1881, had sold out all but a small holding of the Union Pacific.[13] He was, nevertheless, able to dominate its policies. Evidence of this is furnished by the observation of a Burlington vice-president: "Gould could control Dillon [president of the Union Pacific] as he desired and . . . while he had but little interest in the U. P. his influence with the U. P. people was such that he could do about as he pleased with them."[14] Gould was, however, more interested financially in the Missouri Pacific than in the Union Pacific. He would thereby be constrained to favor a policy to promote the welfare of the former road, even at the expense of the other.

The treaty of October, 1880, among other things, stopped the Wabash from further construction in the territory covered by the agreement, thereby handicapping the Union Pacific. It did not hinder the Missouri Pacific. Gould, therefore, in interpreting the agreement, concluded that he could extend the Missouri Pacific from Kansas City to Omaha. Such an extension would serve a number of rich counties in Nebraska, then penetrated exclusively by the Burlington system; it would also connect with the Union Pacific. The Missouri Pacific would then share in the eastbound business of that road. The competitive threat that the Burlington thought it had avoided by acquiring the Council Bluffs and the Atchison and Nebraska would reappear with the construction of a Missouri Pacific line to Omaha. Gould in the spring of 1881 decided to enter the competitive lists against the Burlington in the Kansas City–Omaha territory. Since the Burlington's absorption of these two lines, Gould insisted, the Missouri Pacific's business had "gradually shrunk to small proportions."[15] Gould decided to follow a policy in aid of the Missouri Pacific and against the interest of the Union Pacific. The president of the latter declared that the Missouri Pacific's proposed line had been undertaken against the protest of himself and the Union Pacific board. Efforts were made by the Union Pacific to maintain peace with the Burlington. The Burlington, however, had finally settled upon a policy. The board had made up its collective mind to build a line to Denver. On July 20, 1881, the Burlington's board instructed the vice-president to notify the Union Pacific that the organization of a company including some of its leading directors to build a road in eastern Nebraska was an abrogation of the 1880 agreement with the Burlington. Gould threatened. If the Burlington built west to Denver, the Missouri Pacific would build east to Chicago and west and northwest into Nebraska. "We wish peace," wrote Gould to Perkins, "but we are ready for war if you insist on making it. Carrying out your menace of extending your line to Denver means war."[16]

The Burlington was ready for the war. Its financial position was excellent. Construction was soon begun, and by May of 1882 through trains ran between Chicago and Denver over the Burlington. For the first time the Union Pacific encountered competition between Omaha and Denver.

Gould was thus responsible for the Burlington's Denver line. He was also a participant, though not the major one, in another large building program, that took place along a wide front in Colorado.

The Rio Grande, whose majority stock control Gould had acquired in 1879, had initiated an active construction and expansion program—indeed one of the most ambitious projected by any western road. There was a double lure. The boom in the Colorado mineral industry led to local extension in order to secure access to major sources of traffic. In the fall of 1880, at the height of the building boom, seven separate lines were under construction. The other attraction was the prospect of another transcontinental route. The extension of the Rio Grande to a connection with the Central Pacific at Ogden would, in conjunction with the Burlington's recently completed Denver line, create such a through line between Chicago and the Pacific Coast. The Ogden connection was supplied by a Rio Grande line to the Colorado-Utah boundary, and by a separate company—the Denver and Rio Grande Western—from the boundary to Ogden. Though both roads were organized and operated under the leadership of Palmer, Gould played an important role in the financing of the program. He and two of his associates on the directorate, in co-operation with the road's vice-president, worked out the financial details. Between 1880 and 1883 the Rio Grande–Colorado–Utah system almost quadrupled its mileage.

The cost of this program was heavy. The mineral boom suddenly petered out. The population, which increased rapidly in 1880 and 1881, showed little growth in the following two years. The mileage was built far ahead of the growth in population and production. And as in so many cases, the economy benefited while the security holders lost. The financial pioneers in search of extensive gains incurred extensive losses.

Though Palmer and Gould co-operated in the early phases of this expansion program, they soon parted company. They clashed in the Republic of Mexico. Both were promoting Mexican railroads. Palmer bested Gould in a construction-company venture to build from Laredo to Mexico City. Gould accordingly decided to sell out his interest, and by June of 1881 he had liquidated his Rio Grande holdings at high prices. Thereafter Gould engaged in a number of speculative market forays designed to depress the price of the Rio Grande stock.

When the Burlington finished its line to Denver in the summer of 1882, it accordingly found a business friend. Palmer, at odds with Gould, was willing, indeed anxious, to form a route with the Burlington. In the summer of 1883, thereafter, a new through route, competitive with the Union Pacific between the Missouri Valley and Ogden, was established. The Burlington and Union Pacific now competed over alternative routes between Chicago and Ogden.

The Union Pacific, meanwhile, strengthened itself internally. To the northwest it embarked upon the construction of two major extensions. First was a line to Oregon. In order to carry out the agreement with Villard to build northwest to meet the Navigation's southeastern line at the Oregon-Idaho boundary, the Union Pacific in 1880 incorporated a new venture—the Oregon Short Line. Stockholders of the Union Pacific were given rights to buy the bonds of the new company, with the stock as a bonus. This line was long in building and it was not until December, 1884, that the Oregon Short Line–Navigation Company Route was completed, though by the 1882 year end 238 miles of this extension had been built. The line set up a new competitive through route between the Northwest and the Missouri Valley. The Northern Pacific and the Union Pacific systems now become rivals for this business.

The Union Pacific at about the same time entered upon still another constructive venture. In the middle 1870's a promoter, Colonel Joseph Richardson, had conceived the idea of building a line from the main stem of the Union Pacific north to Butte, Montana, the center of a growing copper industry. This road, the Utah and Northern, was bought up by Gould and his associates. The promoter had exhausted his funds. Gould bought him out in bonds of the acquired road. The road created a bond issue, sold some bonds to raise funds, and transferred a small amount of them to Richardson. Villard tried to block the building of the line. He appealed for help to a United States senator. "Do all you can," Villard wrote, "to defeat the effort of the Utah and Northern to get the right of way in Western Montana."[17] Villard's efforts failed. By the year end of 1881, the 239 miles were finished. The Union Pacific thus secured a monopoly of the region's copper traffic; but not for long. In a little more than a year, the Northern Pacific put through its line, and the two systems were competitors in still another area.

In addition to these two major pieces of construction, the Union Pacific also carried out a program of branch-line extension. Few of these branches were themselves profitable, though indirectly they contributed to the earning power of the main line because of the length of haul.

The sensational moves made by Gould in 1879 and 1880 in the Mississippi and Missouri valleys deeply impressed the rival railroad managements. The Burlington was more particularly concerned. That road in its effort to offset the growing power of Gould considered many alternative policies. There was a substantial affinity of stockholders' interests between the Atchison and the Burlington. Late in 1878 the Atchison's stockholdings by members of the Burlington's directors represented "the largest interest" in that road.[18] Though by 1880 this stock interest was relatively less than in 1878, it was still substantial. Perkins was anxious to acquire the Atchison. It had many connections for transcontinental traffic (to be described in the following chapter) and its construction costs approximated $30 thousand per mile, compared to the Union Pacific's $120 thousand. "I wish we had it," was Perkin's comment in a letter to Forbes.[19] With the Atchison, Perkins believed a strong alliance could be set up either with the Pennsylvania or with Vanderbilt, and perhaps in time with the Rock Island. This combination, he thought, would be strong enough to fight "Gould and Company."

If the Atchison could not be acquired, an alternative would be the acquisition of the Union Pacific. The co-operation of Vanderbilt, who in the summer of 1880 owned about one-sixth of the Union Pacific stock, could be obtained, he thought. Furthermore, since Villard's territory was now being threatened by the Union Pacific it might be possible to secure, also, the help of Villard. A pool thus could be formed to buy enough stock to oust Gould from his position of influence in the Union Pacific. Perkins believed that some large Union Pacific stockholders, like Ames and Sidney Dexter, would rally to the support of the proposed pool. Perkins thought it would be wise for the Burlington, Rock Island, Northwestern, and Alton to acquire the Union Pacific and Atchison. With these properties under a single command, an understanding could be worked out with the Central Pacific, in the west, and with the Vanderbilt properties and the Pennsylvania Railroad, in the east. Then, concluded Perkins, "the solid properties would be stronger than they are now without much understanding & open to Gould & his kind to attack & speculate on."[20]

This proposed program of Perkins died aborning. Vanderbilt, after the determination of the Burlington to extend its line to Denver, lost his interest in both the Union Pacific and the Burlington, and before the expiration of six months he sold out his stockholdings in both roads. The price of the Atchison stock, furthermore, increased and the property expanded. The investment required for its control proved to be far more than the funds at the command of the Burlington and its associates. Perkins also considered the idea of acquiring control of the Rio Grande, thereby bringing under a single management and control the through line between Chicago and Ogden. There was some talk between Perkins and Strong, the newly elected president of the Atchison and a former superintendent of the Burlington. Perkins, however, was suspicious of the underlying value of the Rio Grande stock. The stock, he wrote, was "pretty large"; and on the basis of the current market price would cost over $7 million—a rather excessive price for control. The Burlington's operating vice-president, though in agreement with Perkins over the relatively slight value of the property at existing market prices, believed nevertheless that the Burlington could not "sit still and see all these lines taken away from us. . . . If the U. P. crowd should take it in, they would, it seems to me, be master of the situation in Colorado."[21]

This proposal met the same fate as the proposed pool of railroad interests to fight the Gould properties. While these and other ideas designed to offset the seeming strength of the Gould properties were being considered, Gould suddenly delivered another attack at an important point in the Burlington system. The Hannibal between the summer of 1880 and 1882 was an independent line, controlled completely neither by the Burlington nor by the Gould property. Its strategic position, at least to the Burlington system, was becoming more valuable. In September of 1882 the price of the Hannibal stock suddenly rose to $200 a share. Under the leadership of John Duff, a Boston stockholder, a market corner of the stock was executed, and after the settlement of the short-sale contracts, the market price of the Hannibal stock sharply declined. Duff offered the stock to the Burlington at $50 a share. The latter declined to buy. Shortly thereafter Gould and a number of his associates made the purchase. The Hannibal under the control of Gould raised many of the same problems that had been considered in the summer of 1880. If Gould retained the Hannibal in the interests of his eastern system led by the Wabash, and if the Burlington thereafter built an independent line to Kansas City, Gould might retaliate by extending the Hannibal to Chicago. The Burlington then would be obliged to retaliate by building into and through the Union Pacific's territory in Nebraska. Prolonged negotiations between the Burlington and Gould followed. It eventually developed that Gould would sell, provided he could secure for his Western Union Telegraph a Burlington contract to use the Western Union service on the Hannibal property. By April, 1883, a transaction was arranged. The Hannibal stock was sold to the Burlington and the Hannibal was transferred permanently to the Burlington system.

Some of the competitive bitterness between the Burlington management and Gould was now removed, but not for long. By 1883 the long business friendship between the three original members of the Iowa Pool had become subjected to severe strains. Three new Omaha–Chicago routes had been completed: the St. Paul, the Illinois Central, and the Wabash. One of the three original members of the Pool, the Rock Island, still had no properties west of the Missouri River. Neither did the St. Paul. These two roads were now both under the leadership of two strong expansionists—Cable, of the Rock Island, and Mitchell, in conjunction with Merrill, of the St. Paul. They both agreed with the Union Pacific that since the latter pooled its traffic at Omaha, the Burlington should do the same. This the Burlington declined to do. It continued to forward its business over its own system lines to Chicago. Gould, in charge of the destinies of the Union Pacific, continued his attack on the Iowa Pool, just as he had throughout the 1870's. In December his long-nurtured and persistently pursued ambition was finally realized. On December 1, a 25-year contract between the Union Pacific, the Rock Island, and the St. Paul was announced. The Union Pacific agreed to send its eastbound business over the Rock Island and St. Paul, while the latter agreed to send their westbound business over the Union Pacific.

The Burlington now more than ever was compelled to follow traffic policies calculated to build up the strength of its own system's through line. The Tripartite Pact, meanwhile, failed to carry out the objectives of its architects. Neither the Union Pacific nor the St. Paul and Rock Island realized their anticipated competitive benefits. In fact the reverse occurred. What little traffic the Rock Island and St. Paul captured was more than balanced by the substantial reduction in rates that followed. The solution of these competitive problems by the Rock Island and St. Paul in the 1880's followed different lines. The Rock Island, under the influence of its expansionist, Cable, built lines west of the Missouri for a connection with the Rio Grande on the west and with the Southern Pacific in the southwest. The expansion-minded executives of the St. Paul passed away, however, by the middle 1880's and their place was taken by conservative banking interests representing substantial stockholders both in this country and abroad. They refrained from expansion, and for more than twenty years the St. Paul did not extend its lines west beyond the Missouri River.

Notes for Chapter IX

1 Burlington Archives, Touzalin to Tyson, Aug. 4, 1879.
2 *Ibid.*, Touzalin to Perkins, July 11, 1879.
3 *Ibid.*, Perkins to Touzalin, July 18, 1879.
4 *Ibid.*, Forbes to Perkins, July 12, 1879.
5 *Ibid.*, Perkins to Peter Geddes, Sept. 16, 1882.
6 *Ibid.*, Perkins to Forbes, Nov. 3, 1879.
7 *Ibid.*, Perkins to Forbes, Nov. 19, 1879.
8 *Ibid.*, Forbes to Geddes, Sept. 23, 1879.
9 For further details on this merger see *Gould*, Chap. IX, pp. 175–179.
10 Northwestern Archives, W. L. Scott to Keep, Jan. 20, 1880.
11 Burlington Archives, Potter to Perkins, April 3, 1880.
12 *Ibid.*, Perkins to Forbes, Nov. 19, 1879.
13 H. V. P., Villard to Oakes, Jan. 17, 1881.

14 Burlington Archives, Potter to Perkins, Sept. 25, 1882.
15 *Ibid.*, Gould to Perkins, June 20, 1881.
16 *Ibid.*, Aug. 4, 1881.
17 H. V. P., Villard to J. H. Mitchell, June 23, 1881, Box 123, Letter Book 416.
18 *Ibid.*, C. A. Whittier to Villard, Sept. 18, 1878, Box 7
19 Burlington Archives, Perkins to Forbes, Oct. 18, 1880.
20 *Ibid.*, Perkins to Forbes, Aug. 25, 1881.
21 *Ibid.*, Perkins to T. J. Potter, Sept. 11, 1882; Potter to Perkins, Sept. 8, 1882.

X

Expansion 1879-1883—Southwest

EXPANSION FORCES also dominated the Southwest. In this area, between the Mississippi River and the Pacific Coast and south of a line roughly between St. Louis, Kansas City, and Denver, the major protagonists were Huntington, Gould, and Nickerson, though Nickerson in 1881 was replaced by Strong. Huntington moved his forces east from the Colorado River to carve out a new transcontinental route to New Orleans and beyond to the Ohio River and to Newport News on the seaboard. Nickerson moved south through New Mexico to connect with El Paso and west to the Coast. In conjunction with another road, the Frisco, it also moved west via the 35th Parallel to create still another transcontinental route to the Coast. Gould, acting in part personally and in part through a number of corporate instrumentalities, also moved south and west—south to create a new through route between the Gulf of Mexico, the Republic of Mexico, and St. Louis and Kansas City; and west in an effort to invade the Huntington territorial monopoly in California.

The first moves were made by Huntington. Both Nickerson and Gould were busy for most of the critical year of 1879 in other sections of the western railroad arena. Gould was involved first, in the struggle with Villard over the control of the Kansas Pacific and secondly with the negotiations leading to the merger between the Kansas Pacific and the Union Pacific. Nickerson and the Atchison group were struggling with the problems connected with the battle to acquire control of the Rio Grande. Not until October, with the Gould purchase of the Rio Grande stock, did it become settled that the Atchison's thrust westward over the mountains was blocked.

Huntington's problems in 1878 were largely managerial and financial.

After the extension of the Southern Pacific to the Colorado River at Yuma, in 1877, further movement eastward halted. The financial problems were serious, though at no time did they assume the proportions of disaster. Huntington's associates were not expansion-minded. Hopkins, the close-mouthed keeper of the corporate records, passed away in 1878. Stanford had lost some of his earlier devotion to the business interests of the group. He had converted some of his assets, previously pooled for the welfare of the railroad system, into cash, and had made commitments in such personal ventures as horse racing and real estate speculation. It is, therefore, not surprising that Stanford wanted to call a halt on further railroad construction. Crocker, loyal to the very end of his days to Huntington and his business plans, also agreed with Stanford upon the necessity of a conservative policy of protecting the properties west of the Colorado River and of not extending any further.

The inducements or arguments Huntington made in order to change the minds of his associates are not a matter of record. By November, 1878, however, the decision to build had been made. Construction eastward proceeded rapidly and by the end of 1880 the line to El Paso was completed.

During the same period Huntington moved rapidly on the eastern end of his proposed ocean-to-ocean transcontinental system. Between 1875 and early 1878 the Chesapeake and Ohio was in process of financial reorganization. Despite many obstacles, particularly in the form of a well-organized minority group, Huntington was able to complete a reorganization plan. A mortgage was foreclosed, the property was sold at public auction, the necessary cash was raised for its purchase, and a new Chespeake and Ohio Railway Company was incorporated. It then owned the line between Richmond, at the Ohio River, and Huntington, West Virginia. In the next two years the road built east from Richmond to Newport News, and completed (under the corporate name of two other properties) a continuous line extending the Chesapeake and Ohio from the Ohio River through Lexington and beyond to Elizabethtown, Kentucky. Huntington then bought the Kentucky Central Railway stock, and this road, together with some short construction, gave him a route to Cincinnati. Between Elizabethtown and Louisville and Paducah, on the north and northwest, and Memphis, on the southwest, were a number of railroads then in receivership. In one of them the city of Louisville had made an investment of $2 million. The property prior to Huntington's appearance had already been sold to satisfy the bondholders and $2 million disappeared into thin air. These roads, according to Huntington, had "remained unfinished so many years, without iron being put upon it, that the bridges rotted and fell down. . . ."[1] The bonds of these properties were held abroad. Huntington acquired control through the purchase of the bonds between 18 and 20 cents on the dollar. "I bought the stock almost by the pound; it appeared to be good for nothing," said Huntington.[2] After acquiring control through the purchase of the bonds and the stock, Huntington merged the roads and passed title to a new property, the Chesapeake, Ohio and Southwestern, owning the line between Elizabethtown, Louisville, Paducah, and Memphis. Some additional short construction was needed to connect these various properties. By July, 1882, a through line was opened between Louisville and Memphis.[3]

Even before the completion of this line Huntington had already carried into operation another project to extend the system from Memphis to New Orleans. In conjunction with a number of new business associates, Huntington (under the corporate title of the Louisville, New Orleans and Texas) succeeded by 1884, through the acquisition of existing lines and the construction of a number of connections, in completing a Memphis–New Orleans line. The eastern end of the ocean-to-ocean transcontinental route was thus completed between Newport News and New Orleans. This end of the route was, however, a frail creation. That part of the route west of the Ohio River consisted for the most part of a series of properties that had gone through successive receiverships. They were in poor physical condition. This part of the line, furthermore, was subject to sharp competition from financially sound and efficiently operated enterprises. The Illinois Central and the Louisville and Nashville surrounded, crossed, and recrossed the route at many points. The eastern lines, as part of the transcontinental route, were furthermore, excessively circuitous. Traffic arriving in New Orleans and bound for the north and east could move more cheaply by water. These probably are some of the considerations, together with the heavy financial obligations that by 1884 had again been incurred by the Huntington group, that led Huntington's associates to reject the idea of incorporating the eastern end of the route into the new Southern Pacific Company. The constituent companies of the New Orleans–Atlantic seaboard line soon revealed their weakness. In 1884 an assessment was levied upon the Kentucky Central stock and shortly thereafter the road fell into receivership. Neither the

Chesapeake, Ohio and Southwestern nor the Louisville, New Orleans and Texas demonstrated any real earning power and both were eventually sold to other properties. The Chesapeake and Ohio itself encountered financial difficulties, the interest was defaulted, and a receivership declared in 1887. Soon thereafter Huntington sold his stock to a Drexel-Morgan–led group of capitalists.

The eastern end of Huntington's transcontinental route was thus a failure. This, of course, was not evident by early 1881, after the Southern Pacific completed its line across Arizona and New Mexico and appeared on the Texas boundary at El Paso. While the Southern Pacific was building east in 1880 its two major rivals also expanded. New business problems were created and new business relationships established. A strong clash of corporate interests soon occurred, involving the three major groups, but on different territorial frontiers. The Atchison, by the treaty of January of 1880, had eliminated itself from any territorial extension north or west of Pueblo. Through its Raton Pass line it had control, however, of a strategic route to the Southwest. From that point on the Colorado–New Mexico boundary the Atchison moved quickly. By early 1881 it had completed a line south to Albuquerque and by summer another to El Paso. And by March it had also built a few miles further south to a connection with the Southern Pacific at Deming, a small point. The Atchison had thus completed another transcontinental route between Kansas City and the Southern Pacific via Deming. By an arrangement with the Southern Pacific for the movement of business and the divisions of rates, traffic could thus *physically* move over the new route between the Missouri Valley and the Pacific Coast. From the Deming connections, the Atchison expected "a large business from California and the mining districts of Arizona."[4] The Southern Pacific, however, was no more inclined in 1881 to permit the movement of traffic when it could move alternatively over its own line than the Union Pacific was in the 1870's in favor of the Kansas Pacific and the B. & M. The Southern Pacific merely charged higher rates for traffic interchanged with the Atchison than it did for business moving all the way on its own line. The Atchison, instead of fighting the battle in the courts, continued to fight on the business front. It proposed to reduce rates on traffic moving to California points served by the Huntington lines. The latter could not be expected to collaborate with a policy designed to help a competitor. It refused to make joint rates to San Francisco via the Atchison lower than the one-line rates on the Southern Pacific, thereby enabling the Atchison to divert business from its own lines.[5] The Atchison thereupon decided to break off relations with the Southern Pacific; and within a week after the junction was made with the Southern Pacific it announced it would receive no more shipments for the Pacific Coast.[6]

The Atchison fought on. It decided to strike back. It proposed to invade the Huntington California monopoly. Huntington had encountered competition before, the first of which had appeared in the 1870's. All of the competition had run out of funds and had been bought up either by the Central Pacific or the Southern Pacific. The Atchison was not to easy to eliminate. A group of wealthy Boston capitalists had lined up behind Nickerson. Huntington apparently believed, in the early stages of the Atchison onrush into the Southwest, that the group would not be able to finance their immense expansion. Crocker twitted Huntington on this point. In the spring of 1882 in the midst of an Atchison branch-building program in New Mexico, he wrote ". . . you used to talk the same way several years ago, of what they were going to do." Crocker was referring to Huntington's skepticism over the ability of the Atchison to execute their projects.[7] The Atchison launched its attacks from a number of points. In the Republic of Mexico, through a separate company (the Sonora Railway Company), it built a road from a point on the Gulf of California (Guaymas) north to a connection with the Southern Pacific. This project, begun in the fall of 1879 with the aid of a Mexican government subsidy, was promoted and financed by capitalists independently of the Atchison but in its interests. From the Southern Pacific junction the Atchison planned to build to its own line at Deming. Huntington, in an effort to avoid the building of a parallel line, induced the Atchison to use 174 miles of Southern Pacific tracks. This line was completed early in 1882 and soon thereafter a connection with the Sonora was built. The Atchison had thus completed, between Kansas City and Guaymas in the Republic of Mexico, "the longest continuous line of railway in the world."[8] In 1882, meanwhile, it acquired control of the Sonora by a stock exchange and a bond guarantee. In order to compete with the Huntington lines in California it also established a steamship service north of Guaymas.

Another competitive venture of the Atchison group was the California Southern. This company, incorporated in October, 1880, projected a line from San Diego to a connection with the Atlantic and Pacific to be discussed hereafter. Funds were raised from the stockholders of the Atchison and the St. Louis and San Francisco. The road was built in the face of strong opposition by the Southern Pacific group. By the fall of 1882 it was finished to a point short of its junction with the Atlantic and Pacific at Colton. There construction halted. That junction was not made until 1885; and not until then did the Atchison have a route to California (San Diego) independent of the Southern Pacific.

To understand the strategy of the California Southern, it is necessary to consider still another onslaught aimed at penetrating the Huntington California monopoly. This was a line along the 35th Parallel. The company chartered by Congress to build this road from St. Louis by way of Albuquerque to San Francisco was the Atlantic and Pacific. The road fell victim to the financial panic. Huntington had considered the idea of acquiring the road and thus blocking future competition. "I could get control of the Atlantic and Pacific," wrote Huntington in 1875, "at very small cost, but do we want it as a gift."[9] A few months later Huntington wrote that he did not want the road even at a cheap price.[10] By 1879 the road had been financially reorganized. Two companies succeeded to the original concern. The Frisco took over in Missouri, while the Atlantic and Pacific succeeded to the ownership of the property west of Missouri including the right to build from Albuquerque to the Pacific Coast. The Frisco controlled the other property through ownership of all its stock.

In October, 1879, the Frisco, with the support of German capital, decided to build west to a connection with the Southern Pacific.[11] Shortly thereafter conversations were initiated between the Frisco and the Atchison managements, and by early December a transaction was completed involving the sale of 50 per cent of the Atlantic and Pacific stock to the Atchsion and the consummation of a contract for the joint construction of a Pacific Coast line on the 35th Parallel. The financing would be carried out jointly by the two parent roads. It was agreed that the Frisco would build into St. Louis and complete its line, then in the process of construction, to Wichita, Kansas. The Atchison would make the connection west from Wichita to Albuquerque, while from that point the line to the Pacific Coast would be built by the Atlantic and Pacific. Long-term funds were readily secured and by the spring of 1880 construction began. By the fall of 1881 the Atlantic and Pacific was approaching the Colorado River. The California Southern was moving through San

Diego north and was approaching Colton, a point on the Southern Pacific.

Both the Southern Pacific and the Atchison groups meanwhile were also building lines in the Republic of Mexico. The Atchison had built first, and the Southern Pacific was planning to parallel its line. In California the reverse was true. There the Atchison was threatening to build lines parallel to the Southern Pacific. Nickerson was willing to stop construction at Colton and refrain from invading California north of that point, and to stop the construction of the Atlantic and Pacific on the California boundary line, if the Southern Pacific would agree to use the Atchison line in Mexico.[12] This proposal came to nothing.

Crocker was not willing to compromise. He was all for fighting. He was convinced that Huntington could successfully attack the Atlantic and Pacific in the eastern financial markets. If only Huntington could keep the road from selling its bonds, he was convinced that the property would not get very far into California. He even suggested it might be a good plan to employ some person to keep firing shots at the Atlantic and Pacific in the financial papers. With a little management, suggested Crocker to Huntington, ". . . you could knock their securities a good-deal below par through the newspapers."[13] If the road came to San Diego, asserted Crocker, it would put on a steamship service and compete for the San Francisco business. The best Huntington could do, advised Crocker, was to "try and break them down before they come into California."[14]

The Atlantic and Pacific, however, continued to build west, and Crocker from his post in California grew bitter over this development. "I think," he wrote, "before they earn dividends, they will all be in their grave."[15] Meanwhile, in New York, Huntington was negotiating with the Atlantic and Pacific management to reach an agreement for the use of the Southern Pacific in California and thus to prevent the construction of new roads.[16] In the midst of these negotiations Gould approached Huntington with the idea of acquiring control of the Frisco and thereby securing an influence in the affairs of the Atlantic and Pacific. By this time, early in 1882, Gould and Huntington were at peace. For the moment they had common business interests. Though Gould suggested the idea of the Frisco acquisition, it was Huntington who carried it out. He learned that the investment firm of J. & W. Seligman & Company had a substantial block of the Frisco's stock, and on January 24, Gould and

Huntington together purchased a little less than half of the outstanding stock, each taking a one-half interest. With these shares as additional bargaining power, negotiations were quickened and an agreement was reached early in February. It was settled that the Atlantic and Pacific would build only to the Colorado River. From that point (near Needles) the Southern Pacific would build an extension to a connection with its San Francisco line at Mojave. The line to the river was completed in October, 1883, and thus another through transcontinental route came into being. The route required the co-operation of a number of companies.

This new route, like the one via Deming, also failed to meet the needs of the Atchison. Again the Southern Pacific adjusted its rates and services to stimulate the movement of traffic over its own line and against the traffic of the Atchison. For the Southern Pacific by this time had completed its own transcontinental route via New Orleans. In the summer of 1881, not long after the completion of the line to El Paso, Huntington purchased a number of properties which enabled him to move much closer to his long-sought New Orleans connection. From a local promoter, Thomas W. Pierce, who had been busy organizing the building of roads in Texas for more than a decade, Huntington bought control of an existing line, the Galveston, Harrisburg and San Antonio owning about three hundred miles from San Antonio to Harrisburg. Two other smaller Texas roads were bought, one affording a connection with Houston and the other, the so-called Morgan line to New Orleans. (See Map No. 7.) These lines were bought in the business-boom year of 1881. Huntington paid a high price. For the stock of the Texas and New Orleans, affording a connection with Houston, the price was $85 a share, even though the stock for many years had been "a burden to its owners."[17] The stock of the Galveston, Harrisburg and San Antonio was acquired on a stock-exchange basis—six shares of Southern Pacific for ten of the other property.[18]

Huntington now had a line to Houston, with a connection via the Morgan System to New Orleans. There was a gap, however, between San Antonio and El Paso. In filling this gap Huntington, in conjunction with Pierce, his new associate, met head-on with Gould. By this time, in the summer of 1881, Gould had entered the Southwest, from St. Louis and Kansas City, on a major scale. In November of 1879 he bought control of the Missouri Pacific. From St. Louis and Kansas City south there extended a number of unfinished railroad lines. From Cairo south to Texarkana, on the boundary line between Texas and Arkansas, was the St. Louis, Iron Mountain and Southern. A number of small lines afforded an entrance into St. Louis—lines which were soon acquired by the Missouri Pacific. From Texarkana west to Fort Worth extended Scott's Texas and Pacific. From Longview, a point on this road, extended the International Great Northern, a consolidation of the two companies that had been promoted by a number of capitalists, including Taylor of the National City Bank of New York. The road had been designed as part of a through route to the Rio Grande, connecting on the north with the Texas and Pacific and through the latter with the Iron Mountain, thereby, with the aid of a short line, completing a route to St. Louis.

Another uncompleted route to the Rio Grande River began at Hannibal on the Mississippi River, moved southwest through the state of Missouri, and terminated at Denison, Texas. This was the Kansas and Texas. By the summer of 1881 Gould had succeeded in acquiring control of the Kansas and Texas, the International, and the Texas and Pacific; and by the fall of the year had included within his growing railroad empire the Iron Mountain as well.[19] And by the summer of this year, furthermore, he was in the midst of plans to extend the Texas and Pacific west to El Paso and beyond to the Coast, and to finish the uncompleted line of the Kansas and Texas to the Gulf Coast and the International to the Mexican boundary.

The construction plans of Gould and Huntington clashed. In February, 1881, Gould, through the International, began to build west from its terminus in Palestine, Texas. Pierce and Gould duplicated each other's line for about 25 miles. Since Pierce, in conjunction with Huntington, was building west to El Paso and since the Texas and Pacific was also building west to El Paso from Fort Worth, there appeared to be no reason for Gould's paralleling the Huntington-Pierce line between San Antonio and El Paso. Gould, therefore, diverted the International line to Laredo on the Rio Grande, thereby opening a through route between the Republic of Mexico and St. Louis. At the same time he extended the Kansas and Texas line south from Denison to a small point in southern Texas, for connection with the International.

Thus by the end of 1881 Gould had become a major factor in the Southwest. He had completed a system between St. Louis and Kansas City on the north and the Gulf Coast and the Rio Grande on the south. Huntington had enlarged his transcontinental system with a line to

Houston and Galveston. In somewhat less than two years Huntington and Gould succeeded where a number of groups of promoters with strong financial following had failed. These two businessmen borrowed heavily and incurred speculative risks. Neither Huntington's nor Gould's southwestern roads, ever paid any dividends during their lifetimes. Gould traded in some of his securities—the Texas and Pacific and the Kansas and Texas. On the whole, he lost in these trading activities. Huntington in 1885 exchanged the shares of his southwestern roads for the stock of his newly organized holding company—the Southern Pacific Company. Huntington did not trade these shares nor did he receive any dividends. Gould, meanwhile, in 1881, proceeded with the building of the Texas and Pacific line from Fort Worth to El Paso, taking up where Scott left off. Gould, with the aid of speculative funds, succeeded where Scott had failed.

While Gould was extending the Texas and Pacific west *toward* El Paso, Huntington was building east *from* El Paso. Gould was determined to build from El Paso west. On the north he marshaled the forces of the Union Pacific for an invasion of California. From the end of a small Union Pacific line in Southern Utah he planned to build westward. To facilitate the California invasion, he acquired a small road, the California Central, with the right of way into San Francisco. Huntington moved to retaliate. He instructed Crocker to engage surveyors to examine a route from Ogden east through the Missouri Valley. Huntington was as determined to invade the territory of the Union Pacific as was Gould to invade the territory of the Central Pacific. Gould then proposed a compromise: that a line from Salt Lake to Mojave, California, be built in the joint interests of the two lines. This was unsatisfactory to Crocker, who believed that such a line would give the Union Pacific a long haul and the Huntington lines a short haul on business moving west from Omaha.[20]

Huntington's determination to retaliate by an invasion of the Union Pacific's territory led Gould to hesitate. Instead of proceeding with his plans to invade the Huntington territory, he entered into negotiations with Huntington in New York. Crocker in San Francisco was skeptical over the advisability of these negotiations. Gould had already prepared, insisted Crocker, to stop what little road had already been built in Texas. This was the language Crocker used to characterize some petitions filed on behalf of Gould in the Texas courts to enjoin further construction: "I assure you," he wrote to Huntington, "that I shall never go to sleep on any of their smiles, and I shall go on & organize the companies" to build east.[21] In these discussions Gould, insisted Crocker, meant only mischief. However, Crocker concluded, he was willing to trust his interests to Huntington's hands. Despite his skepticism, he remained loyal to Huntington.

Countermoves taken by Huntington to offset the Gould threat of invasion were successful. The negotiations between Huntington, on one side, and Gould, Dillon, and Sage, on the other, led in November, 1881, to the Gould-Huntington agreement. It was another one of those peace treaties entered into by so many railroads in the 1880's for the purpose of stabilizing competitive forces. For a time, at least, the contract served as an armistice, as a business mechanism for postponing a competitive business war. The agreement required the Texas and Pacific to refrain from building west of El Paso and the Southern Pacific from building north and east of its completed line in Texas. The Southern Pacific's line from El Paso extended approximately ninety miles to a small point in Texas (Sierra Blanca). The Texas and Pacific received trackage rights to use this line. Although not part of the agreement, Gould on behalf of the Union Pacific, surrendered the program for the California invasion. Both Gould and Huntington were business realists, and one can suppose that Gould did not expect to move any great volume of transcontinental traffic via El Paso. Not long after the agreement was consummated, Huntington extended his Texas lines through to New Orleans. Thereafter he moved the bulk of his transcontinental business via New Orleans. The 1884 Annual Report of the Texas and Pacific somewhat curiously confirmed Huntington's traffic diversion. The road informed its stockholders that "portions of the agreement originally made between Messrs. Gould and Huntington affecting the traffic between El Paso and New Orleans, were not complied with on the part of the Huntington system. . . ." But the Texas and Pacific was unrealistically hopeful. Modifications of the contract had been made. These, continued the report were "to the advantage of the company in settling all matters in dispute. . . ."[22]

The access to New Orleans that destroyed the Texas and Pacific ambitions for a share of the California traffic came in 1883 through the acquisition of the Morgan's Louisiana and Texas Railroad and Steamship Company. It owned the road between Houston and New Orleans. Under the leadership of Charles Morgan the property had secured a monopoly of the New Orleans–Texas business. This monopoly was destroyed through the construction, under Gould leadership, by the Texas and Pacific of a Shreveport–New Orleans line. The Morgan system included also a number of local branch lines, as well as a major road—the Houston and Texas Central—with a main line from Houston to Denison and a number of branches, making a total of more than five hundred miles. The Morgan system was purchased for $7.5 million in cash from the Morgan heirs.[23] The transactions also included control of the Morgan Steamship Company, which owned a number of steamers plying a trade between New York and New Orleans. The Huntington ambition for a through line between the Pacific Coast and New Orleans was now realized. A transcontinental route between the Pacific and the Atlantic, by rail to New Orleans and by water to New York, was also completed. It was, on the face of things, superior to the northerly routes of the Northern Pacific and the Union Pacific. The southern route was exempt from snow blockades. It was, furthermore, under one management. The delays associated with the interchange of traffic among separately owned and operated roads were removed.

While Huntington thus completed his 32nd Parallel route and protected his hinterland from invasion by the Gould-led Texas and Pacific and Union Pacific, he was not successful in preventing the invasion of the Atchison. Nickerson resigned from the presidency of the Atchison to assume the leadership of the California Southern, from that vantage point to wage war on the California battle line. He was replaced as president of the Atchison by Strong, the general manager who led the successful battle for the Raton Pass. The Atchison was dissatisfied with the business treatment accorded to the Atlantic and Pacific at the Colorado River. Poor service and unfavorable rate adjustments led to conflicts with the Southern Pacific.[24] The track over which Atlantic and Pacific traffic moved in California was still owned by the Southern Pacific. After long negotiations a contract was concluded in the summer of 1884 for the sale of part of this line to the Atlantic and Pacific. The Atchison System now owned a line to Mojave, California, and from there it used the tracks of the Southern Pacific. This arrangement for the movement of the Atchison's business beyond Mojave was as unsatisfactory as the others, and the Atchison in later years found ways and means to provide its own line to San Francisco.

Thus by the end of 1883 there had been more transcontinental lines created than had been expected either in public or private circles; and they had been built largely without public subsidy. The Atchison-Deming route, the Southern Pacific 32nd Parallel route via El Paso and New Orleans, the Burlington–Rio Grande route, and the Oregon Short Line–Navigation line to Portland were financed without the aid of government credit or land grants. Except for the Oregon Short Line route, which was finished in November, 1884, all these lines were completed by the end of 1883. The Texas Pacific, Northern Pacific, and Atlantic and Pacific were beneficiaries of heavy land grants. Both the Southern Pacific and the Atchison received government aid in the construction of their local lines— the Atchison across Kansas to the Colorado boundary and the Southern Pacific on some of its construction within California. On the Atchison from the Kansas-Colorado boundary to California and on the Southern Pacific from the Colorado River to New Orleans, there were no government grants or credits. The motivating force behind the 1879–1883 construction programs was the competitive play in a search for substantial profits. Fortunes were made and fortunes lost. The financing of these properties will be examined in the following chapter.

These vast expansion programs west of the Mississippi River and between the Canadian and Mexican boundaries were at that time unprecedented. They opened up settlements over many thousand of miles. They involved the investment of hundreds of millions of dollars of capital. They demanded the business leadership of scores of active minds and the assumption of heavy financing risks.

By the end of this expansion in 1883 the railroad industry was overbuilt. The miles of road available were more than were needed to service the economy. There was an over supply of railroads between many communities, which led to lowered prices for railroad service. The competition among many roads soon brought the cost of American railroad service below that of other nations, including those nations whose roads were operated as a public service by their government. Rate competition will be examined in Chapter XIII.

Notes for Chapter X

[1] Report No. 778, p. 132, Huntington.
[2] *Ibid.*
[3] A description of some of the phases of the Chesapeake, Ohio and Southwestern is found in the *Ry. Review*, July 22, 1882, p. 149.

[4] Annual Report, Atchison, 1880, p. 6.

[5] Richard Gray, assistant freight agent, Southern Pacific, in *Boston Transcript*, April 13, 1881.

[6] Waters, p. 127.

[7] Crocker to Huntington, April 27, 1882, M. M.

[8] *Boston Transcript*, March 10, 1882.

[9] Huntington to Colton, Dec. 12, 1875, M. M.

[10] *Ibid.*, Huntington to Hopkins, Feb. 22, 1876.

[11] *R. R. Gaz.*, Oct. 10, 1879, p. 547; Oct. 31, 1879, p. 587.

[12] Crocker to Huntington, Nov. 5, 1881, M. M.

[13] *Ibid.*, Crocker to Huntington, Oct. 4, 1881.

[14] *Ibid.*, Oct. 17, 1881.

[15] *Ibid.*, Jan. 18, 1882.

[16] *New York Tribune*, Jan. 24, 1882. Huntington declared that though no agreement had been reached the chances for a compromise were about even.

[17] *Boston Transcript*, July 9, 1881.

[18] Huntington in the *San Francisco Chronicle*, May 3, 1898.

[19] For details on these acquisitions, see *Gould*, Chapter XIII.

[20] Crocker to Huntington, Oct. 20, 1881, M. M.

[21] *Ibid.*, Oct. 28, 1881.

[22] Annual Report, Texas and Pacific, 1884, p. 17.

[23] Huntington in the *San Francisco Chronicle*, May 3, 1898.

[24] See Waters, p. 130, for a note on the poor service.

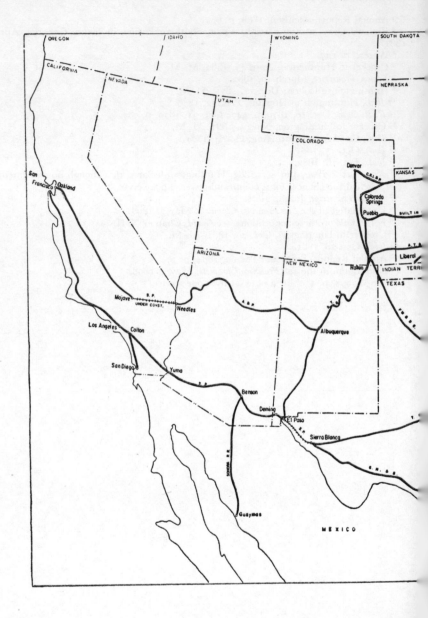

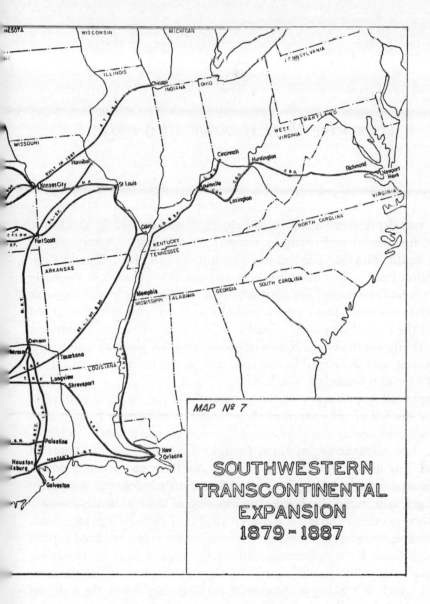

MAP № 7

SOUTHWESTERN
TRANSCONTINENTAL
EXPANSION
1879-1887

XI

Financing the Expansion 1879-1883

As the depression waned in the closing months of 1878, the future of the central and northern transcontinental railways appeared in grave doubt. The only finished line was still the combined Central Pacific–Union Pacific. The other projects, so hopefully initiated in the early 1870's, remained unfinished. All of them, furthermore, were in weak financial condition. There appeared to be little prospect that they could attract the capital necessary to realize their transcontinental ambitions. Similarly the southwestern connections between the Missouri Valley, the Gulf Coast, and the Republic of Mexico were also unfinished, and these roads were also financially weak.

Despite all appearances to the contrary, private business enterprise had by the fall of 1883 supplied the country overabundantly with low-cost transcontinental transportation services. This was a notable achievement. The construction of these facilities involved large amounts of capital. The money was not invested in liquid form, in a manner which permitted the savers to withdraw their funds at their convenience. They could get their money back only by disposing of their securities to other investors, to other risk-takers. Between 1873 and 1878 savings increased. Confidence, however, was lacking to commit those savings to fixed capital although funds for transformation into fixed capital were by that time available. An authoritative source in 1877 referred to a "plethora of capital which is seeking employment and keeping down the rates of interests both here and abroad."[1] Capital was "on strike."

These pools of idle capital had to be mobilized for use by promoters, bankers, and leaders in the fields of investment and speculative capital. There were no government agencies to discharge this heavy responsibility nor government representatives to offer aid. Capital flowed either when there was a prospect of getting a reasonable rate of return or when there were expectations of extraordinary profits to be gained from extraordinary risks. Such capital, called in the first instance, investment funds, or, in the second, speculative (or, more euphemistically, equity) capital, could be attracted by leaders in the financial world, men who were bankers or successful capitalists, men who were trusted by the investors.

This task of attracting the capital was carried out in a variety of ways. There was and is no standardized mechanism for the attraction of capital. A survey of the financing of the western railroad construction program in the 1879–1883 period is fascinating in and of itself. It also discloses some of the unique and mysterious ways in which the flow of capital is channeled from owner to user, from lender to borrower. Broadly speaking there is a distinction between investment and speculative capital. Investment capital is attracted from those who seek a reasonable return on their funds. Reasonableness is judged in light of money rates and the magnitude of the risk involved. Speculative capital flows from those who accept substantially greater risks and look forward to the receipt of correspondingly more munificent rewards. The prime quest is not for interest or dividends or both, paid by the borrowing or issuing corporation, but in an increase in capital values in the market place. There is some disposition to consider this capital gain as parasitic or, at best, a sort of levy on the consuming or shipping public. The profits thus made by the speculative capitalists are considered to have some undesirable moral connotations. Speculative capital, however, is essential to the growth of pioneer industries. Long before conservative investment funds from savings banks, insurance companies, and saving and loan associations, and various funds including those of educational institutions, hospitals, etc. are attracted to an industry, assets must have already been supplied and wealth created. A cushion in wealth and earning power is thereby furnished to protect the integrity of the funds of the conservative investor. A speculative capitalist takes the risk of almost complete loss. Such losses were frequently realized in the years of rapid railroad construction, expansion, and improvement, between 1879 and 1884.

Speculative capital is attracted in larger amounts to the financially weaker than to the financially stronger properties. This situation characterized railroad financing in the period under consideration. Security prices of the weaker roads were selling at low levels in the waning months of 1878: the St. Paul and Pacific, the Northern Pacific, the Kansas Pacific, the Atchison, the Texas and Pacific, the Missouri Pacific, the Frisco, and the Central Pacific. Only the properties between Chicago and the Missouri River could be placed in the financially strong group. These were the roads that had credit to enable them to sell bonds and stocks without schemes designed to attract the speculators. They included the Burlington, Northwestern, St. Paul, and Rock Island.

Leadership in the transcontinental field (excluding the Chicago–Missouri River area where the basis for an investment structure already existed) was assumed by men who pledged their personal fortunes and used their personal credit to raise funds to finance their business ventures. Good fortune accompanied their projects in the early stages. The business boom of 1878–1881 produced a spectacular rise in security prices. Those who sowed their speculative seeds late in 1878 and early in 1879 were blessed with abundant financial crops. Increase in the market value of securities is a source of substantial profits and of capital creation. In the transition from the last stages of a depression to the early stages of a boom the rise in security prices is rapid. The speed of the price movements is a constant source of wonder to many observers and breeds caution and skepticism in the minds of conservative investor-capitalists. The commentator on the outside looks on the heavy capital gain of the risk-taker with a critical eye. Leaders in the transcontinental railway business—Huntington, Gould, Villard, Nickerson, and Hill—were executing their plans as the wave of national prosperity began to roll. All used borrowed funds and in one way or another distributed the stock as bonuses for nominal considerations. Some used the construction company; others did not. Some issued bonds with stock bonuses, and others sold bonds to their shareholders at fancy discounts. Some sold long-term bonds, while others financed by short-term loans.

On the western end of the unfinished section of the 32nd Parallel route, the construction program of the Huntington group had come to a halt near the Colorado River. Huntington and his associates had been and still were under heavy financial pressure. They had lived literally from hand to mouth; they had borrowed almost continuously; and by 1878 they had made up their mind, except for Huntington, to pay off their debts. The business picture in 1878 as it appeared to the promoters of the 32nd Parallel route looked gloomy indeed. The flow of business was declining on both the Central Pacific and the Southern Pacific. The former had passed its dividend. Its short-term debts were heavy, indeed staggering. In the spring of 1878, Colton expressed the opinion of Huntington's associates in favor of "discharging all our construction forces" and of turning "the horses and C [*sic*] money." The group resolved not to "build another mile of r.r. for a few years or at least until we have money we do not know what to do with."[2] Money, meanwhile, was in short supply. Bank accounts in April and May of 1878 were overdrawn. Amounts as small as a hundred thousand dollars were being borrowed at interest rates as high as 9 per cent. Difficulties were encountered in meeting the July coupons; every possible dollar was gathered to provide funds.[3] The extent of the borrowing is well revealed by a Huntington associate. He hoped, he wrote, "that the day will come when we can send you money on hand instead of borrowing," as had been the case for the previous six months.[4]

In the face of opposition by his associates and with the handicap of a heavy floating debt, Huntington pushed ahead. In November, 1878, the decision was made. The construction company that was used to build the Southern Pacific line to the Colorado River—the Western Development—had in 1877 distributed a dividend of $21 million (face value) of bonds and stocks of the Southern Pacific. The market value of these securities was not known. The bonds were used as collateral to secure short-term loans. The Western Development, after the payment of this dividend, maintained its corporate identity. In 1879 it was still a debtor. A note of more than $3 million to the Central Pacific was settled by the delivery of Southern Pacific bonds at 90.[5] This transaction illustrates the indirect way in which the credit of the Central Pacific was used to finance the Huntington construction program.

A new construction company—the Pacific Railway Improvement—contracted to build the line for the Southern Pacific of Arizona in exchange for its bonds and stocks. The bonds were exchanged for the bonds of the Southern Pacific of California. That arrangement did not, however, give Huntington the cash to build the line. The California bonds were secured by a lien on a finished road. They had a better market than the bonds of the new roads in Arizona and New Mexico. These bonds were not known and were not saleable, at least at a reasonable price. Huntington could more successfully use the California bonds to raise funds. But even these could not be sold except at sharp discounts. Accordingly, he continued his depression-period policy of raising funds through short-term loans. By the beginning of 1880, long-term capital markets had opened, stock values had increased, and earnings had expanded. A market had been created for the Central Pacific stock. In January, Huntington was able to sell the stock in large blocks through a banking syndicate. The underwriters included a number of investment houses: Speyer, with which Huntington had long been associated, and Kuhn-Loeb, as well as Gould and Sage. Fifty thousand shares of Central Pacific stock were taken at $75 a share. Stanford, serving as he so often did as the publicity vehicle of the associates, declared that the Central Pacific would "pay six per cent per annum without any trouble."[6] A few months later $10 million 6 per cent bonds were sold. This syndicate was headed by Speyer and included bankers from Germany, Holland, and England. To make these bonds more acceptable, the Southern Pacific of California was leased to the Central Pacific for five years at a rent of $3 thousand per year per mile.[7] The Central Pacific had good earnings; it was then paying dividends; and its stock was selling at a high price. The lease thus improved the quality of the Southern Pacific bonds. The Arizona and New Mexico companies were also leased to the Central Pacific for a five-year term. There still remained in the hands of the Huntington group another $19 million bonds.

These sales were a tribute to Huntington's financial genius. In the critical years of 1872 to 1874, the Central Pacific stock had little market value. By his ability to borrow, thereby meeting the capital needs of the Southern Pacific–Central Pacific system, he was able to withhold the Central Pacific stock from sale until it had a substantial quoted value in the open market. Capital gains thus realized to Huntington and his group were the rewards of long waiting—more than a decade. At various times in the following three years additional blocks of Central Pacific stock were sold: 30,000 shares in October of 1880 at 85; 15,000 exactly one year later at 89; and 20,000 more in May, 1882, also at 89. The substantial sums realized from the sale of stocks and bonds were invested in further railroad expansion. The cash, furthermore, was of crucial significance to Huntington's strategic plans. It enabled him to repeat one of his financial policies of the 1870's—not to sell unseasoned securities. In the 1870's he withheld from sale the shares of the Central Pacific, and in the 1880's he retained the ownership of bonds and stocks of the San Antonio and of the Southern Pacific of New Mexico and Arizona. The cash realized from the sale of Southern Pacific and Central Pacific securities was by 1883 used up in new business ventures. Huntington, therefore, returned to his short-term borrowing techniques, and by 1884 was in the midst of another financial crisis.

On the northern transcontinental route from the Great Lakes to the Pacific Coast there were also heavy borrowings. Here the financial leader was Villard. In his association with a number of properties in the 1870's he had enlisted the support of many capitalists. A major associate was Endicott, "a man of very large wealth and influence in Boston."[8] Another capitalist attracted to the Villard flag was Pullman, a Chicago business-man in charge of the destinies of the Pullman Sleeping Car Company; and another was White, a capitalist well known in eastern banking circles. Abroad he also attracted a large following. The chairman of one of the German Kansas Pacific bondholders' committees wrote that "Mr. Villard has our unqualified confidence."[9] Another large firm from Frankfurt, Germany, J. S. H. Stern, according to Villard one of the strongest houses on the Continent, was also a Villard follower.

In the spring of 1879, shortly after the completion of the settlement of the Kansas Pacific affairs, Villard turned his attention to the Pacific Northwest. The advance in the price of the Navigation stock reflected partly the expansion in the national economy and partly the rise in the stock market. It was also aided by the prospects of earnings based on the road's monopoly. Perhaps the most important cause, however, was the confidence in the company's future. Villard was careful to enlarge the psychological basis underlying the rise in the Navigation stock. In the spring of 1880 he arranged a trip throughout the Navigation's territory by some of its leading financial supporters, including Pullman and Endicott. "They are thoroughly carried away with what they saw in Oregon," wrote Villard in May of 1880, "and you may rest assured that we will be able to raise all the money we need for future building operations by a simple issue of stock."[10]

In addition to the transportation facilities there were valuable natural resources to exploit. The Improvement, incorporated in October of 1880, was another financial success. The sum of $5 million was raised from the sale of $5 million of 6 per cent bonds and a similar amount of stock. Within a few days the stock sold at a 40 per cent premium; and by February, 1881, the investors had almost doubled their capital. The confidence in Villard can be described as almost childlike. "Not a person has asked a question regarding the mortgage, form of the bond or anything else," wrote Villard.[11] In fact the bonds were sold before the mortgage was drafted. Counsel informed Villard that the mortgage had defects. Another tribute to the confidence in Villard's leadership came from the operating executive of the Navigation, later destined to assume the presidency of the Northern Pacific. The Improvement's subscribers, he informed Villard, "took stock because of their faith in you and you may rest assured that they will be only too glad to have you pursue the even tenor of your way, making such investments as your judgment may commend."[12] The Improvement's prospects were so bright that Villard and his chief financial follower, Endicott, subscribed for most of the stock. They owned two-thirds.[13]

Villard, as the controlling factor in the affairs of the Improvement, was thus furnished with vast sums to be used at his discretion. There was no one to question his decisions or to help him weigh his business judgments. He pressed forward in haste to carry out his plans. Haste, as usual, was attended by serious errors, reflected largely in the payment of excessive prices for properties acquired. The sellers recognized the urgency of his needs and they raised their selling prices accordingly. A 30-mile railroad connecting Seattle with some coal mines, for example, cost the promoters $220 thousand, of which $100 thousand was represented by a 12 per cent loan. The majority stockholder could not meet the debt. It appeared at that time that Villard would take control of the road. The promoter, however, passed the loan to a friend, who informed Villard that the money was available to pay. Villard, hungry for the road, bought out the stockholders at a price of between $300 thousand and $350 thousand. The road and the coal company (Villard had early bought this latter property) were then turned over to the Improvement.[14]

The adverse results from these cardinal errors were not, however, evident to the risk-minded investor in 1800 and 1881. The future of the Navigation and the Improvement companies looked bright and the stocks of both companies continued their sensational price advance. When Villard, accordingly, late in 1880 decided to acquire control of the Northern Pacific, he had achieved a reputation as a successful financier. Indeed, his successes were unblemished by a single important loss. Villard bought the Northern Pacific stock on margin. He put up as collateral his Navigation holding and his Kansas Pacific bonds. His buying power was soon exhausted, and he accordingly embarked on a novel project without precedent in American financial history. In February, 1881, he asked **a** number of his friends in New York City to subscribe to an enterprise secret in character but which he would disclose on or before May 15, 1881. By this appeal, he raised $8 million for the "great unknown." The offering was as successful as his previous Navigation and Improvement ventures. He had only a few weeks before announced the intention of the Navigation to build a connection with the Union Pacific. This news was accompanied by a sharp advance in the price of the stock. The effect on the minds of the more conservative businessmen is well reflected in the observation of Billings, president of Northern Pacific, that "the people are getting crazy in speculation."[15] Billings commented a few days later that the Navigation artificially swelled its earnings. Its earnings were low and yet, he observed wistfully, the stock continued to sell at about $200 per share.[16]

The subscribers to Villard's Northern Pacific proposal were able to sell their contracts at a 50 per cent premium. Villard, to use his own language, was "almost drawn to pieces by unsuccessful applicants" for subscriptions.[17] This project led to another wave of Villard confidence—perhaps overconfidence is the better word. "This is the greatest feat of strategy I ever performed," he wrote to Endicott, "and I am being constantly congratulated by the biggest financiers here, upon the achievement."[18]

The Villard financial secret was disclosed in accordance with the promise made. A holding company, the Transcontinental, was organized in June with capital stock of $50 million of which $30 million was issued. Each holder of a receipt from the purchasing syndicate for $10 thousand was offered 122-1/2 shares of the stock of the new holding company, of which 2-1/2 shares represented interest for five months. Each investor was offered an opportunity to buy Transcontinental stock at $83 per share. The new company raised additional cash beyond the original $8 million subscribed early in the year by offering the same subscribers the privilege of buying additional shares of Transcontinental at the same price. Villard and his close associates exchanged most of their Northern Pacific and Navigation stocks for the Transcontinental stock. The new company, therefore, controlled both railroad properties. Upon completion of the Northern Pacific to a connection with the Navigation, the holding company would control a road from the Great Lakes to the Pacific Coast. In addition, Villard soon acquired control of the Oregon and California Railroad, then owing part of an unfinished line from

Portland to the Oregon-California boundary. In the reorganization of this road a 6 per cent mortgage bond was created. Bonds in the sum of $6 million were sold at 88. The old bonds, with accumulated unpaid interest, were exchanged for new preferred and common stock. Villard organized another syndicate to make a market for the bonds. The Improvement guaranteed the bonds.

By the fall of 1881, Villard had thus assumed the leadership of a group of companies engaged in the task of spanning the far Northwest with a network of improved railroad transportation facilities. For this purpose he had on hand large sums of money. There was available more than $35 million in cash realized from the sale of the Northern Pacific bonds. In 1880, before the Villard ascendency in its affairs, the road had sold $40 million bonds to Drexel Morgan and Company. Only a small percentage of these funds had been used. The Improvement had raised between $9 million and $10 million. The Transcontinental had raised through stock issues more cash than was needed to buy control of the Northern Pacific. The Navigation, furthermore, in 1881 and 1882 raised $12 million. On hand, also, were the proceeds of the sale of the Oregon and California bonds, to be used for the extension of the line to the California boundary.

Villard continued to exhibit great confidence in the success of all his enterprises. He was a student neither of railroad traffic nor of operation. His experience was limited largely to financial affairs. In his public remarks he made statements that were unsupported by his personal knowledge. Shortly after the organization of the Transcontinental, for example, he informed a St. Paul audience that $5 million of revenue annually would be contributed by railroads in Oregon and Washington, based on the traffic then carried between the Columbia River and San Francisco. All this traffic, he said, would be diverted upon completion of the Northern Pacific to the lines of that road. An editorial of one of the leading railroad journals called this "an astonishing statement." A traffic analysis concluded that the future of the Northern Pacific would, as with the Central Pacific, depend largely on local traffic.[19] In financial and investment quarters, however, Villard's accomplishment received high praise. "It would not be too much to say," wrote one financial observer, "that in the results accomplished within a short period of time, it [the Navigation] is without an equal among corporate undertakings of its character in the United States."[20]

Nothing succeeds like success, and the followers of Villard continued to reflect in market prices their abiding faith in Villard's financial maneuvers. Villard, himself, was intrigued by his own success. "I begin to believe," he wrote to Endicott early in 1881, "that there is something enchanting in the name of Oregon."[21] Again he bought on margin. He had margin accounts with both foreign and American concerns. In addition to marginal trading, Villard also adopted a number of selling devices calculated to increase his speculative following. He bought securities for some of his friends by advancing his personal funds. In financing the original Navigation venture in 1879 he assumed personal responsibility for subscriptions made for the account of a number of his business associates. For someone in Germany, for example, he agreed to take back on demand $70 thousand of the bonds with the stock bonus between October 1, 1879, and January 1, 1880;[22] while for the account of a close business friend, a loyal follower through all the years of adversity, Villard subscribed $20 thousand of the bonds with the bonus. For this subscription Villard received as collateral $1 thousand in the Kansas Pacific bonds and $3 thousand cash. On the balance of $15 thousand (the subcription price of the bond-stock bundle was 90) there was a 7 per cent interest debit.[23]

Villard thus had attracted millions of dollars to the railroad industry. Supporting him in his quest for funds were some of the leading financial houses in this country and abroad. Drexel Morgan sold securities in England; and Villard sold additional millions on the continent, particularly in Germany.

In comparison with the drama of Villard's rise to fame was the equally sensational but relatively undramatic growth in the fortunes of Hill and the Manitoba. The acquisition of the defunct St. Paul and Pacific was financed by the personal assets and credit of Hill and his associates. Businessmen raised the funds needed by pledging "every particle of property and other security they had in the world."[24] Huntington's use of the credit of his associates and Villard's indiscriminate utilization of all his personal and corporate assets on his sinking corporate ships in 1883 reflected the same kind of business risk-taking. In these speculative ventures, Hill and Huntington were successful, while Villard, after intial successes, went down to inglorious defeat.

The management of the successor company to the St. Paul and Pacific —the Manitoba—combined the financial ability of Stephen, as president, with Hill's knowledge and skill in operating and traffic matters, as general manager and chief executive officer. These two executives and most of the other directors served also on the Canadian Pacific board. The two roads thus worked closely together to their mutual profit.

The economic background at the time of the organization of the new company was favorable, just as it was to other ventures in the western railroad industry. Immigrants poured into an agriculturally rich territory. The crops were good; and due to the needs of Europe, prices were high. There was here another favorable factor—the Canadian Pacific was then being built and a heavy traffic in construction materials moved over the line of the Manitoba for a long haul to Winnipeg.

These advantages were well exploited by the Manitoba management. Hill was essentially an operating man, and his time and attention in these early years were not diverted to financial matters. The lines in the Red River Valley were built at low cost; they were well maintained; and the operating ratio was among the lowest of the northwestern roads. Also, unlike Huntington, Gould, and Villard, the Manitoba leaders in this first expansion period did not build into unsettled frontier areas where the traffic was light nor did it acquire already existing, financially weak lines in such areas. All in all, to use the language of a contemporary journal, "It would hardly have been possible for the circumstances [for the Manitoba] to be more favorable."[25]

The product of these forces was one of the financial marvels of the day. The Manitoba's debt rose from $16.3 million in 1879 to approximately $20 million in 1883. The common stock remained unchanged until that year, when $5 million was sold at par to the stockholders on a privileged-subscription basis. Meanwhile, both the mileage and the passenger revenue doubled; the freight revenue advanced 222 per cent; and the net profit almost tripled. No dividends were paid until 1882, when the stock was placed upon an 8 per cent annual-dividend basis—a rate which was retained until 1884. There were also heavy sinking funds paid out of earnings. Despite debt redemptions and handsome returns paid to the stockholders, there were left substantial earnings for reinvestment in the property.

The sums spent on the property were returned to the stockholders in 1883. The financial mechanism used for this purpose was novel. The company permitted the stockholders to buy $10 million of 50-year 6 per cent bonds at 10 cents on a dollar. In the face of this expansion and the decline in business in 1884—a decline which led to substantial reductions in the earnings of almost all western railroads—the Manitoba after maintaining its 8 per cent dividend managed to report a surplus. The prudent character of the management was further revealed in October, when the quarterly dividend was reduced from 2 to $1\frac{1}{2}$ per cent, in order to build up a reserve fund of approximately $2.5 million. The money would be used to improve the property and to meet emergencies. The decline in year-to-year earnings in 1884—the first registered since the organization of the company—reflected largely the loss of the traffic from the Canadian Pacific. That road by the summer of 1882 had completed its own line to Lake Superior. Business formerly flowing over the Manitoba now moved via the Canadian Pacific. The unity of interests between that road and the Manitoba was dissolved. Hill was "sore" over the traffic diversion—a loss involving "a larger proportion of traffic ... than Hill ... deemed probable."[26] Soon thereafter Hill retired from the Canadian Pacific board; Stephen left the presidency of the Manitoba and in August, 1882, Hill succeeded him. The road thereafter reflected Hill's policies. It became *the* Hill road.

The financing of the southwestern properties under the Gould leadership assumed forms far different from those characterizing the Hill road. Gould, like Villard, was associated with financially weak properties. Almost all of them had either gone through receivership or had escaped by narrow margins. Gould's claim to the confidence of his large speculative following was also supported, like Villard's, by previous successes: in the Kansas Pacific, Union Pacific, and Wabash. His heavy stock-buying program was financed, like Villard's, on a marginal basis. He had, however, no support of investment houses as did Villard. Gould carried on his pyramiding operations with great success.

These personal transactions appear on the face of things to bear little relationship to the means used to attract capital into the expanding railroad industry. First appearances here are, however, deceptive. Gould's stock-trading successes through 1879 and 1880 and on to almost the end of 1881 attracted a large speculative following. Many leading capitalists subscribed to Gould ventures. It was in this indirect way that capital flowed into the Southwest.

The number of capitalists in the Gould ranks at this time constituted an imposing list. It included Sage, a veteran stock-market trader and a loyal follower for many years; Pullman, the railroad sleeping car builder and also a follower of Villard; (William L.) Scott, closely associated with a number of western roads, including the Northwestern; Henry Higginson, a Boston financier; Woerishoffer, an active trader and stock broker, also a follower of Villard; and Cyrus W. Field. Gould also enlisted from time to time the financial support of businessmen who at other times were his business enemies. This list included Huntington, J. P. Morgan, Vanderbilt, and S. H. Kneeland, an active trader, who fought Gould in the struggle over control of the Manhattan Elevated.

Gould, like Huntington, but unlike Villard, used the construction company as a means of securing capital. After an intial attempt in the late 1860's the Huntington group sold little or no construction company stock in the open market. Between 1879 and 1881 Gould used the construction company to secure speculative capital at a time when conservative investment funds were difficult to obtain. Unlike Huntington, he succeeded in making an active market for construction company stocks. He also used the stockholders of railroad companies as a medium for the sale of the construction company stock. The weak roads, financed by Gould's construction companies, had been unable for many years to raise any capital. Construction company stocks were sold for cash. The proceeds were used in large part to buy the railroad stock and bonds. Most of the bonds were sold to the public. Profits to the stockholders of the construction company came, of course, from the increased market value of the railroad stocks. These roads in 1879 and 1880 earned little. They had, however, bright prospects. Future earning power was transferred into present high stock prices. The profits to the construction company speculator rested upon the ability of the construction company officers to sell the railroad securities at the prevailing high prices in 1880 and 1881 or to declare these securities as special-asset dividends during the same period. Gould, on the whole, accomplished this task successfully. These construction companies financed the Gould southwestern building program.[27] Two companies were extraordinarily profitable; the third only moderately so.

The enthusiasm that built up the strong market for the railroad stocks, and therefore for the construction company stocks, also facilitated the sale of railroad bonds. The Texas and Pacific and the Kansas and Texas were able to finance a large part of their requirements through the sale of bonds. The bonds of the Texas and Pacific, due in large part to the close association of that road with T. A. Scott—in 1879, president of the

Pennsylvania Railroad—found a ready market in Philadelphia and eastern Pennsylvania. The bonds of the Kansas and Texas were purchased by some of the outstanding capitalists and financiers. Huntington bought $500 thousand. This was probably an exchange of favors, since Gould early in 1880 had participated in the Central Pacific stock syndicate. Samuel Sloan, formerly president of the International during the difficult days of the 1870's, and in 1880 president of the Delaware, Lackawanna and Western, bought $100 thousand. Pullman bought $75 thousand. Drexel Morgan and Company subscribed to $167 thousand, and J. S. Seligman, through whom Gould and Huntington had bought a large block of the Frisco stock, subscribed to a similar amount. There were many other subscribers well known in the financial and railroad communities: Erastus Corning, Oliver Ames, and Levi Parsons, for many years affiliated with the Kansas and Texas.[28]

Another major southwestern road, the Iron Mountain, which had been for almost ten years in the financial doldrums, was another beneficiary of speculative capital raised by Gould. Acquired by Gould late in 1881, the road served a rapidly growing area in Missouri and Arkansas. No construction had been carried on for many years. The Gould acquisition was followed soon by new construction involving the issue of almost $10 million of new bonds. The program was carried out with the aid of a construction company. This construction program made an excellent impression, one member of the board declaring enthusiastically: "The road has suffered for the want of branch lines and it is now proposed to secure them. This is one of the results of placing live men in the directory. Those western men are able enough, but so very slow."[29]

By midsummer of 1881, accordingly, Huntington, Gould, and Villard, the three major speculatively inclined transcontinental railroad leaders, were riding the top of the speculative boom. Their moves, from late 1878 to this time had been almost continuously successful. They had started their building and financing at the very beginning of the 1879–1881 speculative era. They had been able to acquire properties at low prices. Those who had followed those three speculative leaders had profited. The Union Pacific, Northern Pacific, Central Pacific, Missouri Pacific securities, and those of other roads allied or affiliated with these three leaders, advanced in price. The profits were much more than reasonable—they were spectacular. They exceeded by wide percentages the profits realized from those railroads which had passed through the depression period with banners flying and with a continuous record of dividend payments.

The roads from Chicago west and northwest to the Missouri River were as a whole more profitable than those extending southwest and west from the river. The Burlington, Northwestern, Rock Island, and St. Paul had lower debts in proportion to stocks and per mile of road. They furthermore financed their needs during this period without the use of construction companies. They all reported profits, and the Burlington and Rock Island paid dividends in the depression.

The Rock Island pursued an uneventful, though exceedingly profitable, policy. Between 1879 and 1884 it continued to pay substantial cash dividends. The Burlington was another prosperous road. Its financial policies reflected the views of a group of Boston capitalists led by Forbes, who at various times was board chairman and president. At all times his opinions carried great weight. Except for the Denver extension and a few branches, the Burlington in the 1879–83 era expanded by acquisition of other roads. A risky form of financing was used. The stocks of the Hannibal, the Council Bluffs, and the Burlington and Southwestern were exchanged for Burlington bonds. The acquired roads, however, fitted well into the Burlington system, whose earnings despite heavy debt expansion were well maintained. The Burlington's stock thus retained its long-enjoyed investment prestige.

The Northwestern in the 1870's was financially the weakest of the major Chicago–Missouri River roads. Under guidance of its president and with the strong support of Vanderbilt, who was by 1880 its largest stockholder, it began in 1878 to pay dividends after a long suspension. Vanderbilt took a strong stand against the payment of generous dividends. "The earnings of your company were very large this year," he wrote to the president in 1879, "and there will doubtless be an effort on the part of some of your stockholders to have larger dividends. In my judgment, advantage should be taken of the present business of the Company to place the road in the superior condition in every respect by the large use of steel rails in replacing the iron now in use, in equipment, and furnishing connections suitable, depots, etc. The bonded debt should not be increased, but these improvements should be made from the regular receipts of the road caused by the unusual large crops. The stockholders will get the full benefit of this in the permanent value of the stocks, and if the receipts are of a permanent character, the dividends can be increased when these improvements shall have been made."[30]

Conservative fears were overcome by economic expansion. Heavy crops moving at high prices, bolstered by exports and extensive immigration, increased earnings. Meanwhile the expansion program, pressured by the St. Paul, required financing. Between 1880 and 1884 the debt grew by 125 per cent. The debt structure created in these years set up a pattern that was maintained until the 1930's. The individual mortgages on acquired properties were retained. These mortgage bonds came to be known as divisional bonds. Erected on this foundation was a collateral trust bond created in 1879. A third-story debt in the form of a debenture was also authorized. A debenture bond—i.e., a debt with no mortgage— thus financed the acquisition of the Omaha road. This debt pattern produced a complex structure. In 1884, for example, there were twenty-four small and a number of larger divisional bonds, secured by mortgages on specific sections of property. There was also a so-called consolidated bond issued in 1872. As this bond and the divisional bonds matured they were refunded with new bonds. It was believed that these bonds, outstanding in small amounts and protected by liens on valuable properties, could be sold at higher prices than could be obtained by the sale of bonds secured by a mortgage on the property of the entire railroad. The road's bond policy was successful. The debt on a mileage basis was reasonable, amounting in 1884 to about the same as on the Burlington—about $15 thousand per mile. Earnings covered the interest by comfortable margins and the road became a continuous dividend payer. Its stock entered the charmed field of investment merit—a position which it held securely until the dreary days of the 1930's.

The St. Paul, like the Northwestern, financed its extensive construction program largely through debt. In its expansion between 1878 and 1881 it acquired a succession of small companies. In this program it assumed the bonds of the purchased roads and paid for the stock in its own bonds. The road thus created a hierarchy of bonds; each one was secured by a mortgage on a section of the system. New construction between 1879 and 1882 was also financed by bonds.

Of the major roads, the St. Paul, had the largest debt in proportion to stock. A relatively small change in net earnings was therefore reflected in a large amount per share. Earnings per share were thus highly volatile. The price of the stock, reflecting the rapidly changing *per share* earnings, moved over a wider range. The stock tended to become more speculative.

The rapid growth of the bonded debt did not disturb the St. Paul management. The president, in the 1881 Annual Report, at a time when the debt was almost four times the stock, informed the stockholders that the territory served gives "a promise of future development unequalled by any other railroad system. . . ."[31] It did, however, create some skepticism in the minds of the investor. The "heavy increase in indebtedness," wrote a critic of the St. Paul policy, "and the fact that the increase in earnings of late did not keep pace with the increase in mileage . . ." was a source of concern.[32] The company's earnings were, however, well maintained.

The Atchison, like the Burlington, was backed by a group of capitalists. The road, complained Crocker to Huntington, had "strong backers in Boston, [who] do not seem to want for money."[33] Many of its directory also served on the Burlington board. The Atchison growth's, beginning in 1878, was paralleled by an almost equally rapid transformation of its finances. When in 1878 the drive into the Southwest began, the road's finances were still in a parlous state. Securities could not be sold on an investment basis. What the Union Pacific and Central Pacific did in the early construction stages, the Atchison also accomplished—though on a minor scale. The stock was given away, though not by a construction company. The form was different but the financial substance was the same. Separate corporations were set up to build particular lines. The financial pattern for these and a number of others were uniform. A bundle of bonds and stocks of each company was sold for a price reflecting a discount on the bonds, with the stock as a bonus. The offering of one company, the New Mexico and Southern Pacific, affords an illustration. The Atchison's shareholders were given the opportunity to subscribe to a thousand-dollar (face value) 7 per cent bond, plus nine shares for $900. The bundle of New Mexico and Southern Pacific securities were taken largely by the small group of loyal Boston shareholders. They were bought as a speculation. The outcome, however, was a rousing success. Within eighteen months, the bundle had a market value of $2,380.[34] Similarly profitable returns characterized the offering of two other Atchison affiliates in 1878. Eventually these companies were acquired by the Atchison on a stock-exchange basis.

The sharp rise in business that followed the completion of these lines was "unexpected." The Atchison was then confronted by pressing needs for working capital. The business boom had just begun. Capital was still hard to get. Again the shareholders responded—this time to an offering by the Atchison of 20,000 shares at 100, "to meet pressing wants."[35]

By 1880 the Atchison had attained the distinction of membership in the class of financially strong transcontinental railroads. The company, unlike the Northwestern and St. Paul, followed a policy of increasing its stock instead of its debt.

A major bond issue of the Atchison system was, however, made in connection with the construction of the line to the Colorado River for a connection with the Southern Pacific near Needles. The extension was built by the Atlantic and Pacific, jointly owned by the Atchison and the Frisco. The Atlantic and Pacific issued first-mortgage bonds and income bonds. The stockholders of the two parent roads subscribed to these bonds in amounts of $10 million each to finance the venture. A substantial percentage of the traffic interchanged by the Atlantic and Pacific with the parent roads was set aside to meet the bond interest. This financial mechanism was believed, in some sources at least, to insure the success of this bond. The bonds of the Atlantic and Pacific, declared a critical Boston observer of the Atchison, "will be one of the best railroad bonds ever offered to the investment public."[36]

This was a risky venture, just as risky as the St. Paul's excursions into the unsettled Dakota territory at about the same time. The hopes of the parent roads were not fulfilled. Like so many other western lines the cost of construction was underestimated. Additional funds were needed to build and equip the road, and the two parent properties were soon required to advance additional sums to make possible the completion of the Atlantic and Pacific connection with the Southern Pacific. These unexpected needs were responsible in large part for the issue in 1882 of $5 million Atchison collateral trust bonds. The line from San Diego, built by the California Southern and designed to connect with the Atlantic and Pacific, was also financed independently of the Atchison. The bundle mechanism of 1878 was repeated. The subscribers, consisting largely of Atchison officials, were offered a thousand-dollar bond (face value) and ten shares of the road and one share of the San Diego Land and Town Company, plus, under a certain contingency, two additional shares of the latter.[37] This bundle was also greeted with enthusiasm. Here, as with the Atlantic and Pacific, untoward circumstances plagued the enterprise. Less than two years after the first offering, additional funds were needed, and another bundle was sold to its stockholders. For $800 the subscriber received a thousand-dollar bond (face value), plus eight shares of stock.[38] The financial outcome of these ventures was not happy. The loss was substantial even though the line eventually became an important part of the Atchison system. The Atchison, meanwhile, prospered. The transformation of its finances from poverty to affluence is revealed by the record of dividends. Starting in 1879 at 3 per cent, it rose in 1880 to $8\frac{1}{2}$ per cent and in 1881 and 1882 to 6 per cent on stock enlarged by a 50 per cent stock dividend.

The system, despite its expansion into the frontier—lightly settled areas with only a nominal volume of traffic—disclosed a strong earning power, a phenomenon which confounded the skeptics. The basic strength of the system rested in Kansas. Through that area it built its lines in the low-cost depression years. It also had the benefit of a land grant. The rapid increase in settlement facilitated the sale of a large portion of the land. The proceeds were used to pay off part of the debt. There was, furthermore, little railroad competition in southern Kansas. The 1880 agreement embodied a provision that the Atchison and Frisco would not build in Kansas without consulting each other. As it turned out in the next four years, it was an agreement to limit the expansion of Frisco's lines into the territory of the Atchison. The Frisco's westward expansion into Kansas, in competition with the Atchison, was permanently avoided.

While the Atchison financed so largely by stock, the Union Pacific, except for the sale of $10 million stock in 1881, resorted to bond financing. Its relations with the federal government required the use of a new kind of bond to secure capital funds. The loan of United States government bonds in the late 1860's was protected by a second-mortgage lien on properties then owned and thereafter acquired. There was also a first-mortgage bond outstanding. Thus no additional mortgages on owned property could be created. The Union Pacific accordingly was precluded from securing funds by mortgaging newly built branches and extensions. Instead, the road organized subsidiary companies. The Union Pacific exchanged the funds needed for construction and improvement for their stocks and bonds. It then deposited these securities, accompanied by its guarantee of principal and interest, as collateral for its own bonds.

The Union Pacific in financing the system expansion of some of the major through routes was not obliged to resort to collateral trust bonds. Subsidiary companies were created with sufficient prospective earning power to justify an independent credit status. One was the Oregon Short Line. It was set up to build a connection between the Union Pacific and the Navigation. The sum of $12 million was raised by the sale of that amount of bonds plus 50 per cent of the stock. The other 50 per cent was retained by the Union Pacific. Each holder of a hundred shares of the latter company was offered the opportunity of buying for $2,000 that amount of bonds, plus ten shares of the Oregon Short Line. Another such major subsidiary was the Utah and Northern Railway. This company also sold bonds with a stock bonus; the offering was made to the shareholders of the Union Pacific.

Optimism over the future of the Union Pacific was widespread in the booming years of 1880 and 1881. The merger with the Kansas Pacific seemingly removed competition on the central transcontinental route. The Utah and Northern gave it a hold upon the growing Butte copper traffic. The Oregon Short Line provided another lever to boost future earnings. In the process of creation, competition with corresponding rate reductions was overlooked. Investor reaction to short-term influences was, however, normal. Such overvaluation of current earnings is a phase of every boom economy and of every rising stock market.

In addition to his dominant position in the affairs of the Union Pacific, Gould also played a prominent role in the management of another railroad that soon became a vigorous transcontinental competitor of the Union Pacific—the Rio Grande, whose promoter and chief executive was Palmer. Gould remained affiliated with this road for less than two years. But during that period, the Rio Grande raised most of its capital. The Gould service was short, but it was productive of a large amount of cash.

The Rio Grande management took quick advantage of the exuberant confidence in the future of railroad securities in 1880 and in the optimistic expectations for the continued prosperity of the Rio Grande. In January, with the support of a board including Gould and two of his associates. Palmer began a breath-taking financial program with an issue of $10 million bonds. This was followed in December with a package offer of $4 million each of stock and of 7 per cent bonds. A thousand-dollar bond and stock with a par value of the same amount were sold for $1,650. The subscription was nearly three times the amount offered, and the bundle soon sold at a 16 per cent premium.[39]

This kind of package offering had become a popular investment vehicle in the early 1880's. Its popularity probably was due to the extraordinary profits realized in the Navigation bundle. Thereafter, the Improvement, the New Orleans Pacific, the California and Southern, and the jointly owned Atlantic and Pacific all made such offerings. In every one of these cases the initial offering was successful. The speculative-minded investor could sell the bonds and keep the stock, while the more conservative could keep the bonds and sell the stock.

The Rio Grande's prosperity continued into 1881. In that year the company sold an additional $5 million stock at the relatively high price of 75; and $1 million bonds in London. In that year another bundle offering was made to the shareholders. For $1,100 they received a thousand-dollar bond and $500 in stock.[40] Palmer continued his optimistic declarations with a prediction that the earnings for 1882, upon the enlarged stock base, would approximate 10 per cent.[41] The road also declared a dividend of 6 per cent per annum; it was passed in 1882.

These financial results, combined with the optimistic predictions by Palmer and other officials, did not impress the more sophisticated capitalists. Gould had already sold out his holdings at the high prices of the first half of 1881. In the spring of 1882, moreover, a number of the financial supporters became skeptical. In March a group of stockholders asked Palmer to justify his rosy predictions.[42]

The road by this time had already completed a line from Denver to the Colorado-Utah boundary; and on the Denver end, connection had already been made with an enlarged Burlington. A connection between the Colorado-Utah boundary and Ogden would enable the Rio Grande to interchange traffic with the Central Pacific. In order to build this road Palmer organized the Denver and Rio Grande Western. The Ogden extension was leased to the Rio Grande. Though the Burlington had already been completed to Denver, railroad rates had not yet been reduced. Upon the basis of the prevailing high rates, both lessor and lessee could look forward to a reasonable flow of earnings. Even before the Ogden extension had been completed in May of 1883, however, this situation had changed, and a war of rates broke out between the Union Pacific and the combined Rio Grande–Rio Grande Western–Burlington route. Before the end of 1882, furthermore, the hoary tale of underestimation of construction costs was again dinned into the ears of the unsuspecting investors. "This rapidity of construction," related Palmer to his disappointed shareholders, "although urged by every consideration of advantage to the company has been too great to permit these resources to be utilized in time to avail for payment of the bills."[43]

This survey of the financing of western railroads, though not all-inclusive, embraces a large percentage of the capital funds raised in the 1879–1883 expansion era. The variety of financial methods used reflects in part the temperaments and instincts of businessmen and in part varying fundamental conditions. It is neither by accident nor coincidence that the Chicago–Missouri River roads in these years used neither construction companies nor bundle stock-bond offerings. Their earning power, based on the prosperity of many well-settled communities, created a pattern of financial stability. Securities of these roads attracted the funds of conservative investors. The Union Pacific in these years was also a successful candidate for admission into this exclusive investment fraternity. It sold its stock at par and its bonds—even its collateral trusts—sold at premiums.

In the Southwest, earnings and financial values had not been established. Wide unsettled frontiers still featured the area. Roads had to be pushed into sections with nominal population and traffic. Profits were based on hope and not on past results. People with savings were asked to take a chance on the future. Past records of roads under operation for some time presented tragic tales of financial suffering, of defaults and receiverships. To attract funds from savers appeals were made to hopes for spectacular speculative gains. Hope for such gains outweighed the probability of losses.

It therefore followed that financial devices had to be fashioned to meet this problem. And so, the construction company, abandoned in the Mississippi–Missouri valleys, was used in the Southwest, both by Huntington and Gould. The Atchison made much of its non-use of the construction company. It is thus particularly significant that in its southwestern drive the Atchison *system* found it essential to respond to speculative motives with the financial bundle device. Bond and stock combinations were offered as baits to the speculators. Prices were such as to make the consideration paid for the stock merely nominal. The construction company and the securities bundle accomplished substantially the same results. And as with the construction company, some offerings were profitable and others were not.

Out of the welter of financial details another vital pattern emerges. Savings were released for productive wealth creation in an atmosphere of hope and confidence. Lost in the 1873–1878 years, savings were recovered in the winter of 1878–1879. They bloomed luxuriantly in 1881, only to wither and fade in 1882–1884. Capital funds ran down by 1883 —and so did confidence. The construction boom ceased in 1883. Few new projects were begun. Those railroad managements that began expansion early in the boom obtained the gift of low capital costs. If they came in too late, they paid high costs—that is, if they could get any funds at all. "There is a tide in the affairs of men" applies to the procurement of capital funds the same as it does in other fields.

As the boom dwindled in 1882–1883, and as the supply of savings available for capital expenditure diminished, serious weaknesses in the railroads' financial structures emerged. The rush for expansion built up debts that could not be serviced and created railroads that could not earn their keep. Businessmen were tested by adversity. Some met the test well; others did not. An effort to analyze the results of the bursting of the boom will be made in the following chapter.

Notes for Chapter XI

[1] *Bankers Magazine*, Dec. 1877, p. 493.
[2] Colton to Huntington, May 23, 1878, M. M.
[3] *Ibid.*, May 22, 1878.
[4] *Ibid.*, May 2, 1878.
[5] Pac. Ry. Commission, p. 3001, Crocker; see also p. 2668, Stanford.
[6] *American Manufacturer and Iron World*, Jan. 30, 1880, p. 6.
[7] Advertisement of the bonds in the *Boston Transcript*, March 9, 1880.
[8] Northern Pacific Archives, Billings to Sprague, Feb. 21, 1881.
[9] H. V. P., letter from Ludwig Braunfels, Box 7, Jan. 22, 1877.
[10] *Ibid.*, Villard to C. E. Bretherton, May 5, 1880, Box 120, Letter Book 38.
[11] *Ibid.*, Dec. 14, 1880. Box 121, Letter Book 40.
[12] *Ibid.*, Oakes to Villard, Dec. 19, 1880 Box 55.
[13] *Ibid.*, Villard to Oakes, Dec. 4, 1880 Box 121, Letter Book 41.
[14] *Bradstreet's*, Feb. 16, 1884, p. 100.
[15] Northern Pacific Archives, Billings to Sprague, Feb. 5, 1881.
[16] *Ibid.*, Feb. 28, 1881.
[17] H. V. P., Villard to Pullman, Feb. 12, 1881.
[18] *Ibid.*, Villard to Endicott, Feb. 17, 1881.
[19] *R. R. Gaz.*, July 22, 1881.
[20] *Chron.*, Oct. 28, 1882, p. 472.
[21] H. V. P., Villard to Endicott, Feb. 4, 1881. Box 121, Letter Book 40.
[22] *Ibid.*, Villard to Gebsulzbach, May 27, 1879, Box 115, Letter Book 22.
[23] *Ibid.*, Oakes to Villard, July 7, 1879, Box 55.
[24] Pyle, I, 249.
[25] *R. R. Gaz.*, Sept. 25, 1885, p. 614.
[26] These opinions were credited to Hill by Oakes of the Northern Pacific. Oakes had been talking with Hill with regard to the 1882 settlement of the territorial problems. H. V. P., Oakes to Villard, Oct. 9, 1882.
[27] For details on these companies, see *Gould*, pp. 352–3.

28 The list of these subscribers is found in the Dodge Papers.
29 The *New York Tribune*, Jan. 8, 1881.
30 Northwestern Archives, Vanderbilt to Keep, Sept. 28, 1879.
31 Annual Report, St. Paul, 1881, p. 12.
32 *Chron.*, April 30, 1881, p. 456.
33 Crocker to Huntington, April 27, 1882, M. M.
34 The account of the New Mexico and Southern Pacific is based on *Chron.*, Oct. 19, 1878,
p. 407, and *Boston Transcript*, Feb. 10, 1880.
35 Circular of Atchison, cited in *Chron.*, May 31, 1879, p. 553.
36 *Boston Transcript*, April 22, 1880.
37 *Chron.*, Feb. 26, 1881, p. 231.
38 *Boston Transcript*, Nov. 9, 1882.
39 *Ibid.*, Dec. 22, 1880.
40 *R. R. Gaz.*, May 13, 1881, p. 270.
41 *Chron.*, Feb. 4, 1882, pp. 145–146.
42 *New York Tribune*, Mar. 9, 1882.
43 *Chron.*, Nov. 25, 1882, p. 602.

XII

The Boom Bursts

THE SUMMER of 1881 witnessed the high noon of investor optimism. The business boom began late in 1878 and reached a high in July, 1881. The assassination of President Garfield initiated a downward swing that culminated in the panic of May, 1884. Prosperity was, of course, reflected in the higher prices of railroad stocks. All the western railroad securities participated in the move. Table IV compares the low prices of 1879 and the top prices of 1881–1882. The rise was particularly sharp in the financially weaker companies: in those companies which during the 1870's had gone into receivership or had barely escaped such a fate. Observe for example, the rise in the price of the Frisco from 3 to 55 and of the Rio Grande from 11 to 113. The Navigation stock in 1879 was given as a bonus with bonds. A price of 190 was reached in February, 1881. Observe the rise of the Kansas and Texas stock. Its 1881 high price of 54 was built upon 1881 earnings of five cents per share.

This wide gap between existing earnings and those that could in the future be reasonably expected, on the one hand, and the capitalized value of such earnings in terms of market prices, on the other, is a normal phenomenon of the American security markets. Such differences had prevailed in the past and were destined again and again to occur in the future.

The expansion projects of the railroad leaders were in full swing when the financial markets reached their crest in the summer of 1881. Financial provision, however, had not been made for their completion. The long decline in security prices from the summer of 1881 until the spring of 1884 gradually undermined the confidence of the investing public. As the year 1881 drew to its end the supply of capital became increasingly scarce. By the summer of 1882 few new projects were intitiated.

Table IV

STOCK PRICES, 1879–1882 (FRACTIONS OMITTED)

	Low 1879	High 1881	High 1882
Atchison, Topeka and Santa Fe .	82	N.A.	95
Central Pacific	63	102	97
Chesapeake and Ohio . . .	3	33	27
Chicago and Northwestern . .	49	136	150
Chicago, Burlington and Quincy .	111	182	141
Chicago, Milwaukee and St. Paul ,	34	129	128
Chicago, Rock Island and Pacific .	119	148	140
Denver and Rio Grande . .	11	113	74
Missouri, Kansas and Texas . .	5	54	42
Missouri Pacific	N.A.	114	112
Northern Pacific	16	51	54
Oregon Railway and Navigation .Bonus with bonds		190	163
St. Paul, Minneapolis and Manitoba	67	113	166
St. Louis and San Francisco . .	3	55	46
Texas and Pacific	N.A.	73	55
Union Pacific	57	131	119

The completion of the programs begun in the 1879–1881 period involved the raising of large amounts of capital. Many railroad leaders were unprepared for the financial difficulties that grew out of the increasing scarcity of capital. Resort was had to bank loans, which were believed to be temporary, soon to be replaced by bonds or stocks. By 1883, floating debts began to appear on railroad balance sheets. In each case the expansion required the expenditure of financial resources beyond the means at hand. When Villard secured control of the Northern Pacific in 1881, he appeared to have sufficient cash and credit to carry through his construction plans. By the opening months of 1882 it became clear that the program, so essential to the public interest, could not be financed from the road's own resources. The Northern Pacific, in the language of the company to its stockholders, "was left virtually without any resources." The company obtained personal loans from Villard and from the Transcontinental. Villard declared that these loans were made to the Northern Pacific at "a risk of personal ruin."[1] The most extensive financial aid came from the Transcontinental. By the summer of 1883 the Northern Pacific had spent far more than had been anticipated, and the road was confronted with serious financial problems, involving the possibility of receivership.

Villard, nevertheless, continued to expand. Through the Transcontinental, the bonds of Oregon and California Railroad were guaranteed, thereby assuring, so it was thought, the completion of the line between Portland and the Oregon-California boundary, there to connect with Huntington's Central Pacific. At the far western end of the Northern Pacific, he organized a terminal company financed by a $5 million bond issue. Financial responsibility was shared by the Northern Pacific, the Navigation, and the Oregon and California Railroad. On the eastern end, in the Twin Cities, he organized another terminal company. A $3 million bond guaranteed by the Northern Pacific was sold.

Meanwhile, the loans by Villard and his associated companies were insufficient to defray the heavy capital expenditures. Villard was resourceful, however. He arranged for loans from banks, from investment houses, and from independent brokers, and agents. As early as February, 1883, it had become difficult to renew loans made at a Boston banking house. Villard was informed that, though arrangements had been made for the renewal of all his loans, money was "very close." The loans, furthermore, had not been renewed at as favorable a rate "as we should have liked."

Money rates on Villard's loans were negotiated on an 8 per cent basis.[2] A few months later Villard inquired of a Chicago agency with offices in New York whether a loan for $1 million could be secured.[3] During these critical months Villard also utilized the resources of the Transcontinental to meet pressing obligations. By early 1883 that company had incurred a floating debt of $16 million, of which 75 per cent was due within one year.[4] The lease of the Oregon and California led to additional heavy losses.

The prices of the Villard stocks, meanwhile, began a long decline. Transcontinental, which in December, 1882, sold at 83, dropped by mid-August of 1883 to 56, in late September to less than 52, and a few weeks later to 34½. Navigation declined from 190 early in 1881, to 150 in June, 1883, and to less than 100 in October. The price of Northern Pacific was maintained at a more satisfactory level. Its price declined only from 51 in the summer of 1881 to 49 in August of 1883. From that time on, however, the fall was rapid, and by October it had dropped to 23 1/8.

During these fateful weeks in the summer of 1883 Villard continued to express unrestrained optimism. "I think the depression is only temporary," he wrote to one of his followers.[5] He assured another follower, a Boston banker, that the Northern Pacific would soon be able to take care of itself "easily" out of current earnings. The Transcontinental, he assured his correspondent, would add no new lines. The Oregon and California had all the money it needed. The Improvement similarly had no need for additional capital. "There is no difficulty whatever in our situation," he wrote at this time, "except the large advances which O. & T. has made to the Northern Pacific." Why under these circumstances the price of Northern Pacific should decline, he added, "passes my comprehension."[6]

Villard indeed added to his complications by one of those extraordinary efforts to stave off the inevitable. He used his own funds and those of his companies to sustain the market prices of his stock. This is a highly dangerous practice. Higher prices attract selling, and it soon becomes necessary to buy a very large part or almost all of the outstanding stock. Funds needed for expansion and improvement are devoted to nonproductive uses. A shortage of funds cannot be overcome by this waste of available funds. Early in October he bought heavily of the Navigation stock. He had outstanding loans margined with these shares. If the price fell, his loans might be called. Villard also felt happy that with the supply of shares in the market reduced by his purchases, the short sellers would be in trouble.[7]

He was heavily committed to the market. He had bought thousands of shares, as well as some bonds, on margin. He induced bankers, particularly Endicott, to buy Transcontinental. Endicott was not happy over this experience. He had for some months been disillusioned with Villard. "I cannot quite make up my mind," he had written earlier that summer, "whether it is you, or Barnum . . . that has 'the greatest show on earth.' I suppose that you leave no doubts on that point."[8]

Declines in security prices impaired the safety of Villard's collateral loans, and he accordingly devised a variety of schemes in order to sustain the market price of his holdings. As a trader, Villard was unsuccessful. He did not know how to trim his cargo and cut his losses. He was an inveterate optimist. In the dual capacity of a businessman-stock market speculator, Villard had many forerunners as well as many successors. As a speculator-trader he relied upon the expected rise in prices in consequence of the completion of the main line of the Northern Pacific.

His trading expectations were belied by events. His hope for better times were frustrated, and by the fall of 1883, shortly after the completion of the Northern Pacific main line, the financial affairs of the Northern Pacific reached a climax. It became clear that the cost of the construction had been underestimated. This had occurred so often in railroad affairs that it could almost be considered as normal. The deficiency between the amounts required and the proceeds of the first-mortgage bonds had steadily increased throughout the summer and fall months of 1883. The road was soon faced with bankruptcy. The solution was finally found through a sale to Drexel-Morgan of $20 million of second-mortgage 6 per cent bonds.

The successful completion of this new financial program led to further expressions of Villard optimism. To a Boston supporter he gave renewed assurance, originally expressed in a letter in mid-August, that the Northern Pacific had now "fully weathered the recent storm & that the O. & T. Co. & all our interests will come out all right."[9]

All Villard's schemes and plans—the $20 million financing, the additional sums raised by the Transcontinental and the Navigation—were of no avail. By the end of 1883, the Transcontinental was close to bankruptcy. Only a one-year loan of $8 million saved the company from this tragic fate. It was secured by large blocks of Navigation and Northern

Pacific stocks. The purchasers of the note were given the privilege of buying the pledged stocks for a price considerably lower than that prevailing when the loan was made. If this privilege were exercised, the Transcontinental might lose control of both the Navigation and the Northern Pacific.

After exhausting this loan, the company still remained in trouble. A syndicate of capitalists responded to another appeal for help. Morgan T. Jefferson Coolidge, from Boston, Anthony J. Drexel, from Philadelphia, Gould, and Sage lent the company $1.2 million for six months. The syndicate also bought some Northern Pacific stock from Transcontinental. By this means Transcontinental raised $3.5 millions.[10]

Villard personally was also in serious financial straits. He saved himself by a Drexel-Morgan loan secured by practically all his property, real and personal,[11] and by an Endicott guarantee. Villard retired from the presidency of the Transcontinental and his place was taken by Endicott. He also resigned from the presidency of the Navigation and there his successor was Coolidge, another Villard follower and a member of the Atchison board.

In the first six months of 1884 the price of the Villard securities continued to decline. The break in the Improvement stock from 91½ in 1883 to 10¼ in June, 1884, was a major personal disaster to Villard. Stock to the extent of 11,468 shares had been pledged with Drexel-Morgan as collateral, and the price drop undermargined the loan. This large holding, in Villard's own language, "was one of the causes of my financial ruin."[12]

The effects of Villard's financial misjudgments remained to plague the security holders even after his departure. The Transcontinental, for example, which had early in 1884 converted its maturing debts into a one-year note and a six-month loan, was by the end of that year again confronted with bankruptcy. It appealed to its stockholders for aid but that aid was denied. The stockholders had lost too much. They refused to throw good money after bad. The property was finally saved by a last-minute loan of Drexel-Morgan, the same banking house which earlier that year had averted what appeared to be certain bankruptcy. The response of this private banker to the necessities of a failing corporation epitomizes the services which investment bankers repeatedly performed in the 1870's and 1880's. Some took exceptional risks—risks that sometimes led to failures.

Villard as a financial dealer, from the standpoint of the interests commited to his care by his investor followers, was a failure. Losses were heavy. Those who had made the greatest paper profits, in the 1879–1881 interval were among the heaviest actual losers. Fed with a continuous outpouring of enthusiasm, they held their securities in most cases to the very end, and suffered substantial losses. The non-investing–shipping–consuming public was a beneficiary. Many millions of dollars, raised both in this country and abroad, were attracted to Villard's transportation ventures. Through the use of these funds the long-awaited transcontinental route between the Great Lakes and Portland–Puget Sound was finished. Completed also was the transcontinental route via a connection between the Navigation and the Union Pacific. Terminal facilities were provided, notably in the Twin Cities and Portland. These programs, according to Villard's computations, involved an expenditure of $125 million.[13]

Even more substantial than Villard's projects were those completed under Huntington's leadership. There are numerous resemblances between the financial policies of Huntington and Villard. Both borrowed extensively. Both borrowed on short terms from banks and from individuals. Both were bold. Both possessed vigorous imaginations. And both drove forward with their construction and expansion plans almost heedless of financial consequences. There was, however, one major factor that saved Huntington—he had behind him the established earning power of completed roads. The Central Pacific paid dividends for most of the depression years. There were few roads that could lay claim to such a distinction.

Huntington also had the benefit of $34 million of the bonds of the Southern Pacific of California. These bonds had been husbanded by Huntington and his associates during the depression years. By dint of ingenious short-term borrowings and the use of other means detailed in the preceding chapter, the construction of the Southern Pacific was financed without the public sale of bonds. The increasing earnings of the road during the 1879–1883 period facilitated their private sale. They were sold at an average price of about 90, thereby raising in excess of $30 million.

The 1879–1881 years were for Huntington, as they were for Villard, a time of golden opportunity. Substantial funds for capital purposes were obtained with relative ease. In 1880 and 1881 millions were raised by the sale of Central Pacific stocks and bonds. Additional funds were attracted by methods characteristic of Huntington. None of the companies directly involved in the expansion east of the Colorado River sold securities to the investor. Their securities were exchanged for construction-company contracts. Neither did the construction companies sell any securities. The two of them—the Pacific Improvement and the Southern Development —were in fact aided by the railroads, instead of the reverse. Both, wrote Crocker early in 1882, were "borrowing from the Central Pacific all the time."[14]

Until early 1882 the Huntington system had thus financed its expansion program on a self-sufficient, internal basis. Huntington meanwhile decided to press forward, with the object of completing a through route between the Pacific and Atlantic coasts. This program required fresh capital. There now remained only two associates with whom Huntington had to deal: Crocker and Stanford. Hopkins and Colton had passed away. Stanford was developing personal interests. He was selling his bonds, complained Crocker. They were, he wrote in March of 1883, "not working to one common end."[15] And a few days later Crocker related that Stanford was not placing his dividend and interest accruals to his credit on the books of the construction companies and that he had not done so for more than a year. "I have been putting *all* of mine as usual," wrote Crocker, "and I believe you have done the same, at least so far as I know you have."[16]

Huntington's New Orleans–Memphis line was expensive. The total capital funds involved in its completion exceeded $29 million. This expense was probably the major cause of the financial embarrassment, approaching close to personal failure, that reached a climax in the panic month of May, 1884.

In the opening months of 1882, before embarking upon the New Orleans–Memphis and the Mojave–Needles lines, Huntington was well supplied with cash. According to Crocker, approximately $21 million of the Central Pacific stock had been sold at an average price of 80. At that time the group assets, pooled under Huntington's supervision in New York, approximated $14 million, in cash. This cash was soon put to use. In February, Crocker was insisting that large sums were needed and that some of the group funds be turned over to one of the construction companies. Already the latter were short of the cash needed to complete their programs and were borrowing from the Central Pacific.[17] By early 1883 the cash had become depleted and Huntington returned to his old borrowing habits. The floating debt was recreated. A major expense was now incurred: the purchase of the Morgan Line. Although fulfilling Huntington's dream of a through route between San Francisco and New Orleans, this addition involved an outlay of $7.5 million. Another $2 million was spent for the purchase of additional shares of the Atlantic and Pacific. Huntington by June, 1883, had invested about $6 million in this road.[18] Most of this was later lost. The building of the New Orleans–Memphis line was also in full swing, and the cash needs from that source rapidly increased.

The policy of short-term borrowing was resumed. The demand for capital was outrunning the supply, just as it did in 1872. Railroads, as well as numerous other industries, were confronted with the necessity of completing unfinished projects. Bank-created debt was adopted as a substitute for long-term issues. "At the moment," observed an authoritative financial journal, "floating debts seem to be the bane of railroad corporations."[19] A short-term note of the Southern Development Company, endorsed by the widow of Hopkins (one of the original associates), financed a large part of the $7.5 million purchase price of the Morgan line.[20] The credit of the roads and of the construction companies in the Huntington system were soon fully utilized. In March, Crocker was borrowing to send funds to Huntington. "Our different roads were all overdrawn," he wrote.[21]

Huntington was now in the position in which he found himself in the critical months of 1873, though he had one major advantage denied to him earlier—he and his associates had an open market for their Central Pacific stock. They had disposed of large blocks in 1880 and 1881 through banking syndicates, but a considerable number of shares remained. These from time to time were sold in the open market.[22] Though these proceeds relieved the immediate financial exigency, they of course did not solve the problem. Resort was made on an increasing scale to short-term loans. Some loans were made on the personal credit of Crocker and Huntington; for example, a three-month advance of $500 thousand at $4\frac{1}{2}$ per cent,[23] in June. Others were secured by the bonds of the Southern Pacific of California, illustrated by a four-month loan of $250 thousand at the same rate, in July.[24] Others were made by the Pacific Improvement whose assets consisted in large part of the bonds of the Southern Pacific of Arizona and of New Mexico.[25] From time to time bonds of the Southern Pacific of California were sold to institutions, both in western and in eastern financial centers. By August, 1883, the group was in debt on a short-term basis to an extent of $20 million; yet more money was needed. "I am raising all I can here," wrote Crocker at this time, "& doing all I can to pay it; but I assure you that it will be a long time before this $20,000,000. is paid, unless we can market some of our bonds."[26]

Huntington's mind now conceived of a new fund-raising scheme. The earning power of the Southern Pacific of Arizona and of New Mexico was not sufficient to establish their bonds on an investment basis. No earnings had been published. The bonds were held either by the Pacific Improvement, directly or indirectly, or by the associates individually. Huntington now proposed that the roads be leased to the Central Pacific, with a bond guarantee. To this proposal Crocker raised vigorous objections. The earning power of these two roads, he told Huntington, might be impaired by the competition of the Texas and Pacific and the Atchison. The Atlantic and Pacific, he insisted, would take "a large slice of business from these roads and they may therefore become a tax on the Central Pacific." They would be, he wrote further, "using our position as Trustees of the C. P. R. R., to make valuable $10,000,000. of bonds, which we as individuals hold and own. . . ."[27]

Huntington was not to be so easily frustrated, and he soon made another suggestion. He now proposed that he and Miller resign from the Central Pacific board and that others be elected in their place. The new, presumably independent-minded board would endorse the bonds of the Southern Pacific of Arizona. Crocker did not accept this obvious subterfuge and he, therefore, objected to this latest Huntington proposal. There was, he wrote, "no concealing the fact that we [would] have endorsed those [Arizona] bonds for our own interest and benefit, that I as a Trustee for others, cannot feel justified in doing it." Crocker then gave Huntington some advice, advice of a character which Huntington persisted in rejecting. Stop spending funds in Mexico and on that Mississippi road [referring to some construction projects in Mexico, not covered in this volume, and to the Memphis–New Orleans connection, respectively]. "Let us stop all other new enterprises. It is a fearful amount to carry at this time, and I very much regret that we have got into such a fix. . . ." Furthermore, he continued, he had been "over persuaded" into doing that which his judgment did not approve, referring especially to the Memphis–New Orleans line.[28]

A week later Crocker returned to the attack. The proposal to guarantee the interest on the Arizona bonds with the help of the resignation of Huntington and Miller from the Central Pacific board was, in his opinion, "no more nor less than using our official positions as Trustees for thousands of other stockholders, for our own personal benefit, and without any compensation to the company doing the guaranteeing."[29] Crocker furthermore insisted that, far from guaranteeing the bonds of the Arizona company by burdening the Central Pacific, it might be wiser to alleviate the burden on the latter by reducing the rent to the Arizona company. He further contended that the Southern Pacific of Arizona and of New Mexico should not be permitted to "run in debt, for the sake of furnishing dividends for the Central Pacific."[30]

Before the end of 1883 one of the major sources of financing the needs of Huntington's system had almost been exhausted. By October only $3.5 million of the bonds of the Southern Pacific of California were left. In fact, insisted Crocker, that road had already issued more bonds on completed lines than ought to have been issued.[31] The strain of the floating debt continued to amount. Unsuccessful efforts were made to borrow funds in France.[32] A proposal for a loan from the Mutual Life Insurance Company of New York was another move. It became necessary to renew short-term loans made by Fisk and Hatch. In November, short-term loans were again incurred. The sum of $1 million was borrowed from a Nevada bank at 6 per cent; and Fisk and Hatch were paid a commission of $750 for renewing a $600 thousand note.[33] The Central Pacific was also borrowing, and at the year end it reported a short-term debt of $7 million.

The earnings and financial strength of the Southern and Central Pacific meanwhile continued to weaken. New through routes by competitors led to traffic diversions from the Central Pacific. The earnings of the Chesapeake and Ohio also dropped. The prices of both Central Pacific and Chesapeake and Ohio stocks broke sharply. Though Huntington owned relatively few shares of Central Pacific, he had large holdings in Chesapeake and Ohio. The price of that stock declined from 33-7/8 in 1881 to 5 in 1884.

In the panic months of May and June Huntington was faced with insolvency, just as Gould was at about the same time and just as Villard had been a few months before. Money was so tight, said Crocker publicly, it was "harder than drawing teeth to get any. We cannot get more than 25 cents on Southern Pacific bonds. I am trying hard to borrow some money, and I think I shall be able to get it."[34] Crocker denied stories of financial difficulties, "The Central Pacific is not embarrassed and will probably pay its employees this months as usual."[35] Rumors spread that Huntington was embarrassed. According to a letter published many years later, he wrote that at that time "the money markets crumpled up on me—so that there were times when I was as literally absolutely up against it as the Irish tenant overdue to an absent landlord."[36] At the time, however, he publicly denied stories that he was unable to respond to the calls of his creditors. "There is in my case not the smallest excuse for such a rumor."[37]

Events bore out Huntington's optimistic assertions. Unlike Villard, he was able to solve his financial problems. None of the paper went to protest. His obligations were met under fearful financial strains, just as they had been in the 1873 panic days.

The margin of safety must have been slight. The severe price decline in almost all of the system securities probably undercollateraled all loans —both his and those of the Central Pacific. In the course of litigation in 1885, the statement was made that Huntington, Stanford, and Crocker "were on the brink of insolvency. . . ."[38]

Despite the group's relatively light holdings in the Central Pacific, the fate of the road registered the financial destiny of the western transcontinental system. For the Central Pacific controlled these properties through the lease. And the lease of the roads in California, Arizona, and New Mexico was believed to be profitable. In the summer of 1884, furthermore, Huntington and other Central Pacific officials assured the Central Pacific's English stockholders that the lease relations with the Southern Pacific were satisfactory and would "be continued for a further term of years on substantially the same basis." Indeed, according to Huntington, the lease had "already been extended for a term of ten years."[39] And as late as September, 1883, the stock was still regarded as a good investment. The stockholders, wrote a leading English railway journal, "may congratulate themselves upon the possession of a sound and well conducted property."[40]

Meanwhile, the price of the stock declined while the Company's officials expressed optimism. Gould at this time was duplicating this phenomenon with the Wabash, as was Villard with the Northern Pacific and its allied properties. This paradox of price movement in one direction and official assurances to the contrary is common. It has been and is being widely practiced; it confuses no sophisticated investor. Central

Pacific's official assurances and price declines began in May, 1883. There is "nothing in the business of the Central Pacific which justifies the decline," declared Stanford. "... The ... road has not suffered and will not suffer" from the diversion of business to the Southern Pacific or the Northern Pacific.[41] Crocker informed reporters that, while at one time the dividend appeared dubious, there was now no doubt of its payment. He admitted, however, that he had sold a little of his stock and that his associates had sold a little more.[42]

In the face of these assurances the price of Central Pacific stock continued to fall. The earnings moved correspondingly. They reflected the waning of the capital-expenditure boom and the diversion of business to new transcontinental routes. The dividend was passed in February, 1884. By this time the short-term loans of the group and of the Central Pacific mounted. Details are not available. The Crocker letters, which serve as the basis for the account of most of the Huntington financing in the preceding pages, cease with 1883. Some inferences may be drawn. Huntington was raising funds for railroad ventures in Guatemala and in Mexico; the requirements for the Memphis–New Orleans line were heavy, since no bonds on this line had yet been sold; the Northern Railway—a feeder in Nevada—was under construction; and traffic and earnings on system lines were decreasing.

Huntington's career in the East, the Southwest, and the Far West was paralleled in many respects by his chief competitor and his business associate from time to time. Gould, like Huntington, in the early 1880's expanded rapidly, both in the East and the Southwest. Huntington's Chesapeake and Ohio was matched by Gould's Wabash. In the Southwest, Huntington moved east from Yuma and Gould moved south and west from northern Texas. They clashed in the area between San Antonio and El Paso.

After 1881, however, a broad distinction emerges between the activities of Gould and Huntington. Huntington continued to build new lines and expand his existing system both east and west of New Orleans. Gould, on the other hand, embarked on no system-enlarging expansion programs. He built branches of the Iron Mountain and the Union Pacific. He finished a number of main-line projects, particularly the Oregon Short Line connection with the Navigation. But he did little other building between 1882 and 1885. His personal investment in his railroad system, as the months rolled on into the summer of 1884, was committed largely to the Missouri Pacific. He sold out (at the 1881 high prices) his Wabash and Texas and Pacific holdings; and later on, at lower levels, his Kansas and Texas interest. He held onto his heavy holdings in Missouri Pacific, though he traded heavily in its shares. Huntington, on the other hand, retained intact his holdings in the Southern Pacific system, involving the companies in California, New Mexico, Arizona, Texas, and Louisiana. Huntington and his associates, however, sold out most of their holdings in the Central Pacific, and used the proceeds to finance their ambitious construction and acquisition program.

Gould, as contrasted to Huntington, spent much of his energy and utilized a great part of his financial resources in a security-trading program. This led to some successes, such as the acquisition of the Western Union Telegraph and the Manhattan Elevated, but in other phases this activity brough him heavy losses and a near calamity in May, 1884.

In the Southwest, Gould's greatest failure came with the Texas and Pacific. The compromise with Huntington in November, 1881, brought little business to that road. Huntington, after a short interval, completed his system to New Orleans. Thereafter and as a part of a sound business policy, he shifted his traffic from the Texas and Pacific to his own Southern Pacific. The Texas and Pacific received only a slight transcontinental traffic. Meanwhile the local traffic was light, and local crop failures made things worse. Gould fought an unsuccessful struggle to maintain the Texas and Pacific railroad as a solvent property, and by the summer of 1884 the road defaulted.

A similar disaster a few years later overtook the Kansas and Texas.[43] Neither this road, the Texas and Pacific, nor the International initiated any important building after the summer of 1881. It is difficult to fix definite responsibility for the financial failure of the southwestern properties. The Gould exploitation of these roads to benefit the Missouri Pacific was one contributing factor. The major explanation probably lies in the fact that the southwestern roads, and this includes those also built by Huntington and the Atchison, were built in a new country, sparsely settled and with little traffic. In addition, the Gould roads in the southwest had not the support that Huntington and the Atchison received in the form of substantial earnings from the California and southern Kansas areas, respectively.

Financial failures were the price paid by the pioneering businessmen and investors. In search for high profit they often met with heavy loss.

The poor financial results represent the contribution made to the settlement of the frontier by the risk-taking businessmen and the equally daring investors. The conversion of the frontier in a surprisingly short period into settled villages, towns, and cities was a major contribution of the risk-taker.

The third major southwestern system—the Atchison—traced a financial career somewhat different from that of the Huntington and Gould lines. The earnings in southern Kansas sustained the system's prosperity. Its financial difficulties revolved around its western extensions into California. There three companies were created: the Sonora, the California Southern, and the Atlantic and Pacific. Funds for the latter had been raised in 1880 and 1881. Construction costs were underestimated and additional funds were soon needed. Subscription rights were extended to the stockholders of the two parent roads.[44] Despite repeated calls for funds and continued deficits on the unfinished line, there was no lack of optimism. These views are well reflected in the comments of a journalistic supporter of the Atchison. Local traffic was "reasonably certain" before the Atlantic and Pacific reached the Colorado River, and the moment the road "gets its share" of the California business, earnings on the income bonds "will be assured."[45]

Still more capital was needed, and in 1883 more was obtained. The parent roads had committed themselves for amounts substantially in excess of expectations. They therefore permitted the Atlantic and Pacific to raise cash through the sale of stock, thereby diluting their 100 per cent ownership. Stocks in the amount of 100,000 shares was sold to a syndicate at $15 a share, with an option on an additional 100,000 at $20. The proceeds were used to pay a floating debt to the two parent properties.[46] Huntington was the largest buyer, though control remained with the Atchison and the Frisco.

The Atlantic and Pacific had been designed, in conjunction with the California Southern, to give the parent roads an outlet to California via San Diego. The latter in the early 1880's was building north to connect with the Atlantic and Pacific at some point east of Mojave. The California Southern also encountered financial troubles. A through Atchison–Atlantic Pacific–California Southern route to San Diego would, it was expected, eliminate dependence on the Southern Pacific for access to San Francisco. Business could be moved between San Diego and San Francisco by water. By the summer of 1884 the western hinge of this projected route was in difficulty. Storms had caused heavy damages. Huntington tried to remove this competition by offering to take over the road in exchange for a 3 per cent guarantee on the bonds.[47] The offer was rejected. Instead, Nickerson, the president, asked the shareholders to buy additional stock equal to 10 per cent of the existing par as a "loan . . . to save the property from disaster." To repair the road $250 thousand was needed, but only $114 thousand was raised.[48] The road could not solve its financial problems, and on July 1, it defaulted. To save the western hinge of its transcontinental route, the Atchison was forced to assume a new burden. By the end of the year the California Southern was converted into an Atchison property. The bondholders agreed to accept income bonds for their first-mortgage bonds. The Atchison agreed to build eighty miles to the Atlantic and Pacific and to repair the damage to the existing line. In exchange the Atchison received 50 per cent of the company's stock and new first-mortgage bonds. The Atchison guaranteed the bond interest.[49]

The Sonora, the extension into the Republic of Mexico, was another financial headache, and its burdens were also thrown upon the Atchison. On this road, as on the California Southern, an unexpected event helped to produce disaster. Here the Mexican government refused to honor its agreement to pay a subsidy. The Sonora, in the picturesque language of a Boston critic, had by 1884 been for some years "gnawing at the Atchison's vitals." By 1884 the Atchison had assumed the entire Sonora burden. It placed its guarantee on the road's $4.1 million bonds. The same critic reported that these transactions had "been a quiet scandal in Boston railroad circles. . . ."[50]

The worst financial headache in the summer of 1884, however, was the Atlantic and Pacific. The Colorado River–Mojave route via the Southern Pacific was not working well. From time to time Huntington threw "a sop of a few cars" to the Atlantic and Pacific.[51] It had become clear to the Atchison that little traffic could be expected from the Southern Pacific. When California shippers specified the use of the Atlantic and Pacific route, "service on the Southern Pacific bogged down."[52] This device—a reduction in the standard of service over a multi-line route—was and is customary in order to force business over a one-line route. In this way the latter assures for itself the long haul over its own line. The Atchison did not propose to absorb this business reversal. There were threats and counterthreats. The Atchison proposed to parallel the

Southern Pacific tracks in California, while Huntington threatened to invade Kansas. After prolonged negotiations an agreement was reached. Huntington, as the agent of the Southern Pacific, sold the Colorado River–Mojave line to the Atlantic and Pacific for $7,271,000. Traffic beyond Mojave was carried by the Southern Pacific on the basis of terminal charges and a division of the joint revenue. The parent companies also bought from the Pacific Improvement its Atlantic and Pacific securities at their cost. The purchase of the Mojave line and the acquisition of the Atlantic and Pacific's securities from Huntington involved another financial burden by the Atchison.

The Atchison was severely criticized. The newspaper that for many years had so consistently supported in glowing terms the wisdom of the Atchison management now became an open critic. The purchase of the Mojave line was a surrender of the Atchison's drive to the coast; the terms were excessively favorable to Huntington. The assumption of the debts of the Sonora and the California Southern was also condemned. There was authoritative support for this critical judgment of the California Southern. Crocker once told Huntington that the road was "not worth any more than the material used in its construction."[53]

The losses on its three western extensions were reflected in an increase of the Atchison's bonded debt and in the creation of a contingent liability. The earnings of the road were, however, well maintained and the $6.00 dividend was continued. The good financial condition of the property, so carefully established in the early 1880's, provided sufficient stamina to enable the road to carry its financial burdens.

The Union Pacific, the earliest of the transcontinental lines, had no such reserves in earning power and financial strength. By 1883, its earnings took a turn for the worse. By that time another competitive route had been established. The Huntington system had also completed its New Orleans line. Traffic was thereafter increasingly diverted from the Ogden route to Huntington's southern route. The Northern Pacific had also been completed through Montana, thereby diverting to its line traffic that formerly moved south from Montana by the Union Pacific's Utah and Northern. The Union Pacific in 1883 was still paying the 6 per cent dividend. Despite the postponement of needed repairs and the failure to provide improvements, the road was not earning this dividend. To make a showing of income to cover the dividend, Gould resorted to a manipulation of the branch-line accounting system. It was a device which was later applied on other railroad properties. The Seaboard Air Line and the Van Sweringen roads in the late 1920's and the early 1930's are examples. Income from operations of the Union Pacific main line in 1883 amounted to only 5.6 per cent on the stock. The company reported a profit of $2,066,000 as "interest and dividends received from investments." Including this, the company earned its dividend, and a surplus of more than $1,260,000. The Annual Report for the same year reported "investments in auxiliary companies, payable in bonds and stocks." This account showed an increase between 1882 and 1883 of $2,258,000. The Union Pacific thus lent its subsidiaries funds to enable them to pay their fixed charges and to pay dividends on their stock, all of which was owned by the Union Pacific. Presumably some of the funds raised through the sale of collateral trust bonds was used to pay unearned dividends on the Union Pacific.

Despite expressions of continued confidence in the future of the road earnings continued to decline. By the summer of 1884 the Union Pacific, like the Central Pacific, had passed its dividend and had accumulated a heavy floating debt. Gould, through a number of drastic actions involving understandings with government officials, was ousted from the presidency. His position was taken by Adams, long a firm believer in the future of the Union Pacific, whose advice to buy the stock was accepted by a large number of New Englanders.[54]

Thus by the summer of 1884 leaders of three major western transportation enterprises, Villard, Huntington, and Gould, were in financial trouble. There was in each case a dramatic transformation from financial affluence to financial wreckage, leading in one case to virtual bankruptcy and in the others to a position dangerously close to it. A somewhat similar fate overtook Palmer, another pioneer railroad promoter. His Rio Grande in the first half of the 1880's also moved from wealth to poverty. By the end of 1882 optimism over the company's affairs had vanished, earnings had declined, and dividends passed. The Rio Grande, meanwhile, had leased the Rio Grande Western—the property that had built the extension from the western terminus of the former to Ogden. The contract, advertised as "a mutually advantageous alliance," carried a guarantee of the lessor's bonds up to $7.5 million, with a limit of $16 thousand per mile.[55]

Managerial disputes in the affairs of the Rio Grande soon developed. A new board, elected in January, 1883, included representatives of conservative capitalism—that is men not of the speculative type. In this category were A. J. Cassatt, vice-president of the Pennsylvania Railroad, Peter Geddes, a stockholder in a variety of the western railroads including the Burlington and the St. Paul, and William L. Scott, long associated with the Northwestern.

The change in management brought little relief to the security holders. The same pattern traced by Villard, Huntington, and Gould now marked the career of Palmer and the combined Rio Grande–Rio Grande Western. Earnings sagged, capital requirements could not be secured, and the floating debt increased. Bitter disputes broke out among the board. After what is described as a "violent attack" on him at a director's meeting, Palmer resigned. He did, however, retain his position as head of the Rio Grande Western. A new president of the Rio Grande—Frederick Lovejoy, a former president of the Adams Express Company and representing eastern investors—was elected in the fall of 1883. After a succession of appeals to stockholders and directors, sufficient funds were raised to make the company "almost free of floating debt."[56] The relief was temporary. Bickering broke out between the lessee Rio Grande and the lessor Rio Grande Western. Both roads were now under different management. The Rio Grande's management alleged that the Rio Grande Western's property had been turned over to it incomplete and in poor physical condition; that the Rio Grande had spent over $800 thousand of its own money; and that the Rio Grande Western's management had increased its expenditures by an "exhorbitant" amount.[57]

By July, 1884, the Rio Grande was obliged to default, and a receiver was appointed.

Here again the shipping public was the beneficiary of a new transcontinental route. The combined Rio Grande–Rio Grande Western had increased its mileage from 373 miles in 1878 to 2,047 miles in 1883. The cash investment made by the stockholders was almost a total loss. This loss proved to be permanent, and the investment made by the stockholders, most of them English, turned out in the long run to be a gift to the American shipping and traveling public.

The analysis of the fate of the transcontinental systems in the 1884 panic is thus concluded. The northwestern roads—the three original Iowa Pool roads, the St. Paul, and the Manitoba—did better financially than the transcontinental roads, which extended west beyond the Missouri River to the Pacific Coast and east beyond the Colorado River to

New Orleans and even further east—the latter under Huntington leadership. The Northwestern roads between Lake Michigan, Lake Superior,
and the Missouri River were built through relatively well settled territories not as devoid of traffic as were the areas beyond the Missouri
River and through southern California, New Mexico, Arizona, and
Texas. The northwestern roads, as well as the Atchison, served a number
of territories with a heavy traffic density, particularly in cereals and coal.
Much of this business was carried at rates protected from price cutting,
in many cases by territorial understandings with potential competitors.
The construction and expansion era of the early 1880's undermined and
(by 1884) dissolved almost all of these understandings. This new competition reduced rates and earnings. Despite the increase in mileage, the
earnings of the five major properties declined. The lowered earnings
of the northwestern lines were not, however, sufficient to impair their
financial strength. Dividends in all cases were maintained.

The Rock Island continued throughout the first half of the decade as
the financial citadel of orthodox finance. It continued its policy of conservative expansion—the financing of capital needs from earnings.

The Burlington, an increasingly vigorous competitor of the Rock
Island, also pursued a careful financial policy. In the first half of the
decade it enlarged its capital structure but the expansion of its earnings
was sufficient to maintain a satisfactory coverage for its dividends. In
the summer of 1884, when so many roads were in dire trouble, the Burlington had a substantial cash balance. "We have," wrote Forbes in May,
1884, "ample money in hand for all the outlays we can now see ahead."[58]
The floating debt, the bane of so many other roads at that time, was not a
Burlington problem. In May, 1884, it had funds sufficient to warrant the
consideration of a heavy investment in the Union Pacific. Perkins finally
decided in the negative. "I am very much afraid that Jay Gould and
David Dows will be too much for Ames and Adams," was his conclusion.[59]

Both the Northwestern and the St. Paul, unlike the Rock Island and
the Burlington, expanded largely into areas of relatively slight population.
Both financed largely with debt. The St. Paul's invasions into the lightly
settled territory was more extensive than the Northwestern's. Its bonds,
furthermore, constituted a much larger proportion of its capital structure. It also, unlike the Northwestern, accumulated a floating debt.
In 1882 this debt, in the judgment of some analysts, assumed serious proportions.[60] By the end of 1883, however, most of the debt was liquidated.

Both roads remained solvent and maintained their dividends through 1884.

The Manitoba, the fifth major road in the area, maintained its earnings to a greater extent than the other four major northwestern roads. Both the gross and net swept ahead from 1880 to 1883. A decline in gross in 1884 was accompanied by a slight decline in net. The Manitoba, like the Burlington, conserved its finances well. It avoided the creation of a floating debt. Statistically the Manitoba expanded rapidly, from its organization in 1879 to 1884. Its growth however was confined to the Red River Valley. There both the population and tonnage grew even more swiftly than the mileage. In accordance with the 1882 territorial agreement, the Mantioba during these years did not build west. The road thus enjoyed a monpoly in the Red River area and charged rates accordingly.

Thus is completed the survey made in this and the preceding chapter of the financing of the growth of the western railroads between 1879 and 1884. The growth and decline of earnings and of financial values is a record of great expectations and equally great disappointments; of opportunities realized and of courageous, even foolhardy, expansion and of conservative stabilization. Exciting managerial dramas, as those of Villard, Gould, and Huntington, do not necessarily create satisfactory earnings for investors and high standards of service to the using public.

The compensation received by those who contributed the capital to the building of the transcontinental roads was not substantial. The stockholders of the Southern Pacific and Texas and Pacific received no return whatsoever. Those of the Northern Pacific received but little, while those of the Rio Grande–Western system received only two quarterly dividends. The Union Pacific stockholders received ample dividends between 1880 and 1884, though far more than the dividends received were lost in the price collapse of their stock in 1883–1884 and the passing of the dividend which was not to be resumed for almost twenty years thereafter. To a lesser degree the same results were shared by the Central Pacific stockholders, though here the 6 per cent dividend was paid for a longer period and the dividend, after being passed in 1884, was resumed on a 2 per cent basis in 1885. Of the transcontinental roads, only the Atchison presented a continuous dividend record, with no collapse in 1884.

Investors in the five major northwestern roads included in this survey were, on the other hand, well recompensed and the stock continued during these years to serve as a desirable investment.

It has become almost cliché to assert that what the investors in the securities lost the original promoters gained. The truth, however, is not so clear and obvious. Villard, the promoter of the Northern Pacific and a number of allied enterprises, realized nothing. The reverses in the fall of 1883 wiped him clean financially. He had nothing left. Gould, the promoter and builder of a substantial mileage in the Southwest and of a lesser mileage in the Union Pacific system, prospered between 1879 and 1882. By the summer of 1884 his entire fortune was endangered. The market value of his securities declined to a point where his capital losses were heavy. He managed to save himself from the results of unsuccessful stock speculation by ingenious trading methods. Most of the fortune that he managed to retain to his death in 1892 was invested in the Western Union Telegraph, the Manhattan Elevated, and in a large assortment of railroad bonds.

Huntington, as an aftermath of his vast construction and expansion program, was close to financial failure in the panic months of 1884. He and his associates had sold out their Central Pacific stock at fancy profits. These profits were reinvested in Southern Pacific and Chesapeake and Ohio stocks. The latter's stock in the summer of 1884 sold at almost nominal prices. There was no market for the shares of the Southern Pacific companies nor for the properties in Texas and Louisiana. Palmer, of the Rio Grande, another promoter, after fifteen years of building in Colorado, New Mexico, and the Republic of Mexico, was a financial wreck. The Rio Grande and the Rio Grande Western fell into receivership and his property in Mexico was not much better. Major profits in the 1879–1884 period came to the promoters (and also stockholders) of the Atchison and of the northwestern roads.

The compelling question, however, is not who made little and who made much. The public obtained the transportation service. They got it in quick time and at a reasonable cost in terms of debt per mile of road and of dividends paid upon the investment; and on terms, as will be seen in the following chapter, of steadily declining selling prices for transportation services. The railroads were the creatures of individual leadership. Each road was an institution. It was created through the initiative and leadership of one man or one set of men. A current observer remarked with a considerable degree of truth that ". . . . whatever their [the northwestern roads'] future aid, the Northwestern, the Rock Island, the St. Paul, and the Burlington, & Quincy, will always remain as monuments to the genius, and enterprise of Messrs. Keep and Hughitt, Riddle and Cable, Mitchell and Merrill, and Forbes, Perkins and Potter. . . ."[61] (Potter from 1881 to 1887 was vice-president of the Burlington.) The same can be said of Huntington and the Southern Pacific, of Villard and the Northern Pacific, of Nickerson, Peabody, and Pierce and the Atchison, and of Palmer and the Rio Grande. These leaders planned and built for profit. Sometimes they made profits and sometimes they did not; and sometimes they lost all they had even before they built. It is true, however, that it was their leadership, their enterprise, their ability or genius in their quest for profits, that gave the public an adequate, and in some cases an efficient, transportation system.

Notes for Chapter XII

[1] H. V. P., Villard to Harris, then president of the Northern Pacific, Aug. 18, 1884, Box 24. Though letter was unsigned, it was clearly sent by Villard.

[2] *Ibid.*, statement of Lee Higginson and Company, Feb. 20, 1883, Box 94.

[3] *Ibid.*, Josiah H. Reed to Villard, May 5, 1883.

[4] This analysis is from *Stockholder*, Dec. 26, 1883, p. 182.

[5] H. V. P., Villard to White, July 13, 1883, Letter Book 40A.

[6] *Ibid.*, Villard to Higginson, Aug. 23, 1883, Box 121, Letter Book 40A.

[7] *Ibid.*, Villard to J. N. Dolph, Oct. 8, 1883, Box 121, Letter Book 40A.

[8] *Ibid.*, May 23, 1883, Box 92.

[9] *Ibid.*, Villard to Higginson, Nov. 1, 1883, Box 121.

[10] *Chron.*, Feb. 2, 1884, p. 148.

[11] "Memorandum of Securities sold and monies collected by Drexel Morgan & Co. a/c Henry Villard." Demand Note of Dec. 31, 1883, was found in H. V. P. It presents an idea of the trading and speculative activities of Villard.

[12] *Ibid.*, Villard to Charles Beckwith, Mar. 8, 1884, Box 126.

[13] *R. R. Gaz.*, Sept. 19, 1884, p. 678.

[14] Crocker to Huntington, Feb. 21, 1882, M. M.

[15] *Ibid.*, Crocker to Huntington, Mar. 2 1883.

[16] *Ibid.*, Crocker to Huntington, Mar. 7, 1883.

[17] *Ibid.*, Feb. 21, 1882.

[18] *Boston Transcript*, June 7, 1883.

[19] *Chron.*, Mar. 17, 1883, p. 299.

[20] Crocker to Huntington, April 11, 1883, M. M.

[21] *Ibid.*, Mar. 22, 1883.

[22] This was admitted by Crocker in an interview in the *Stockholder*, May 29, 1883, p. 533.

[23] Crocker to Huntington, June 14, 1883, M. M.

[24] *Ibid.*, July 3, 1883.

[25] *Ibid.*, July 10 and 17, 1883.

[26] *Ibid.*, Crocker to Huntington, Aug. 2, 1883.

[27] *Ibid.*, July 16, 1883.

[28] *Ibid.*, Aug. 7, 1883.

[29] *Ibid.*, Aug. 14, 1883.

[30] *Ibid.*, Aug. 16, 1883.

[31] *Ibid.*, Oct. 24, 1883.

[32] *Ibid.*, Aug. 22, 1883.

[33] *Ibid.*, Nov. 26, 1883.

[34] *New York Tribune*, June 27, 1884.

[35] *Ry. Review*, June 28, 1884, p. 337.

[36] *Wall Street Journal*, May 25, 1937.

[37] *New York Tribune*, June 22, 1884.

[38] This remark was made by Mrs. Ellen M. Colton, widow of David Colton, cited in decision of Judge Jackson Temple in Ellen M. Colton vs. Leland Stanford, Charles Crocker, and others, reproduced in the California *Spirit of the Times and Underwriter's Journal*, Oct. 10, 1885.

[39] These statements were made, according to the chairman of the English Association of American Bond and Shareholders, at a meeting of Central Pacific stockholders, as reported in the *London Railway News*, Dec. 11, 1886, pp. 854–856.

[40] *Herapath's Railway Journal*, Sept. 15, 1883, p. 1100.

[41] *Boston Transcript*, May 21, 1883.

[42] *Stockholder*, May 29, 1883, p. 523.

[43] For details on the failures of these roads and the personal finances of Gould, see *Gould* Chapters XXI, XXIV, XXVII.

[44] For details of the offering see *Chron.*, Jan. 28, 1882, p. 114.

[45] *Boston Transcript*, Sept. 12, 1882.

[46] *Chron.*, June 9, 1883, p. 651.

[47] *Boston Transcript*, Feb. 15, 1884.

[48] *Ibid.*, April 17 and June 18, 1884.

[49] *Chron.*, Nov. 1, 1884, p. 492.

[50] *Boston Transcript*, Mar. 24, 1885.

[51] *Ibid.*, Dec. 21, 1883.

[52] Waters, p. 130.

[53] Crocker to Huntington, July 17, 1883, M. M.

[54] For details see *Gould*, pp. 419–423.

[55] *Bradstreet's* Dec. 19, 1885, p. 398.

[56] Annual Report, Rio Grande, 1883, p. 12.

[57] *R. R. Gaz.*, June 13, 1884, p. 453.

[58] Burlington Archives, Forbes to Perkins, May 27, 1884.

[59] *Ibid.*, Perkins to Forbes, May 24, 1884.

[60] *Chron.*, Mar. 17, 1883, p. 300.

[61] *Ibid.*, June 18, 1887, p. 770.

XIII

The Fight for Traffic

IN THE winter of 1878–1879, on the eve of the extraordinary railroad expansion surveyed in Chapters VIII to X, monopoly was still the general rule west of the Missouri River. In California and east to the Colorado River at Yuma, competition was almost entirely absent. And where the Central and Union Pacific joined at Ogden there was an agreement to maintain rates, "faithfully carried out for a number of years," until the completion of the Union Pacific system's line to Montana in 1880.[1] Railroad rates west of the Missouri River were unusually high. In the midst of the depression of the 1870's the Union Pacific–Central Pacific route took advantage of its monopoly by increasing rates. In Montana and Idaho, according to Stanford, the Central Pacific in the 1870's did "a good deal" of "very profitable business, as we were able to fix our rates free of competition."[2] In the summer of 1882, almost six months after the completion of the Burlington's line to Denver, rates on Colorado business were "so exceptionally high that if we [the Union Pacific and the Burlington] once got into a war and seriously reduced them [railroad rates], it is a question if we could ever get them back again."[3] Hughitt, general manager of the Northwestern, expressed the opinion at about the same time that rates west of the Missouri River were "much higher per mile" than in the territory east of the river.[4] And a year later, shortly before the outbreak of the rate wars, Perkins observed that rates were nearly double west of the river what they were east.[5] The scale of rates in areas untouched by railroad rivalry is illustrated by the price of transportation on the newly built Arizona lines of the Southern Pacific between Yuma and Tucson. The rates on most merchandise in 1882 approximated 15 cents per ton-mile.[6]

While monopoly was the rule west of the Missouri River, competitive forces largely, though not exclusively, dominated the industry further east. Between Chicago and the river the railroad industry can, from the standpoint of this discussion, be divided into three sections. The short route between Chicago and the Missouri River was prior to 1883 controlled by three lines. In this area rates were well maintained by an understanding between the roads for a division of the business. North and west of Chicago rate instability in the early 1870's had also been largely replaced by stabilization based upon understandings between the major roads in that area. The third group participated in the business moving to and from the lower Missouri River cities—mostly Kansas City, Leavenworth, Atchison, and St. Joseph—and interchanging at those points with business from the west and southwest. Of the three short roads between Council Bluffs and Chicago, two also participated in the southwestern business—the Rock Island and Burlington. The Alton also controlled a low-cost line between Chicago and Kansas City.

The rivalry for the southwestern business was intensified by the two short lines between St. Louis and Kansas City. These were the Missouri Pacific, south of the Missouri River, and the Kansas City and Northern, north of the river. Though the Missouri Pacific (as well as the Alton) had no lines between Kansas City and Council Bluffs, they nevertheless were able to compete for business into and out of that point, including the traffic moving over the Union Pacific. The roads could accomplish this by lining up with the Council Bluffs road owning a route between Council Bluffs and Kansas City, east of the Missouri River. West of the river were the rich wheat fields of Nebraska and Kansas. This territory was being rapidly settled in the 1870's, and a profitable volume of business was flowing in both directions. From the west the Atchison carried wheat from southern Kansas to its terminals at Kansas City and Atchison.

The competition for the lower Missouri River business grew in strength after 1873 panic. There was competition between the two roads connecting St. Louis and Kansas City, for convenience referred to as the St. Louis roads, and the Alton, Burlington, and Rock Island, referred to as the Chicago roads. There was also competition *among* the two St. Louis roads and *among* the three Chicago roads. This rivalry led, in 1875, to a war of rates. The rates were so sharply cut that, in the language of a leading railroad journal, it seemed "hard to tell what the rates really were."[7] The war continued with little interruption into the late summer of 1876. The pool—the Southwestern Railway Association—set up to end the rate war, appeared to raise expectations that a "permanent declaration of peace" had been arranged. Rates were immediately raised from a number of points to the lower Missouri River gateways.[8]

Interrailroad competition in the middle and late 1870's was by no means confined to rivalry for the southwestern traffic. The Alton, particularly, made repeated bids to capture a share of the eastbound transcontinental business. Though its line via the Council Bluffs was longer to Chicago than over the direct lines of the Iowa Pool roads, it succeeded, by rate reduction, in carrying some business. The Burlington suggested repeatedly that pooling and a division of traffic would constitute the most profitable arrangement for all the roads concerned in the transcontinental business.[9]

Despite the rivalry of the circuitous routes, the Iowa Pool roads continued to carry an overwhelming proportion of the business. The Pool, at least until 1881, remained intact and succeeded in stabilizing rates. The southwestern pool, between 1876 and 1879, also worked well. This pool, however, soon encountered trouble. Early in April, 1879, it was dissolved. A few weeks thereafter the Chicago roads agreed to form a pool of their own, excluding the St. Louis division from participation. A violent war of rates followed.

Thus, early in 1879, at the very outset of the extensive expansion program, competitive forces were powerful east of the Missouri River. The southwestern lines between Kansas City and Council Bluffs had reduced rates drastically, as severely as in any other part of the country. In the war between April and September of 1879 the average earnings of the Chicago lines were 7-3/4 mills per ton-mile; and of the St. Louis roads, 6 mills per ton-mile[10] This was a rate structure of almost nominal proportions. Along the direct routes between Chicago and the river at Council Bluffs, rates were better maintained. There competition had also begun to cut rates early in 1879. There was considerable acrimony between the Rock Island and the Burlington. There was rate cutting on local traffic in southern Iowa and western Illinois. But the rivalry was not yet serious.

North and west of Chicago, to the Twin Cities and beyond, the St. Paul in 1879 was just beginning its ambitious expansion program. The Northwestern, its major adversary, was not yet fully aware of the scope of its competitor's program. The rates were still maintained in most of these areas. West of the Missouri River the monopoly position of the Union Pacific-Central Pacific route was maintained in almost the entire area.

New forces, however, were in the making. Ambitious railroad managers, under imaginative leadership, looking far ahead for future profits and backed by large funds of speculative and investment capital, were preparing to destroy these centers of monopolistic influence. By the summer of 1882 the railroad expansion programs, both east and west of the Missouri River, had been largely completed. Only a few areas were left without railroad competition. Almost all western communities were now able to ship their goods, both in and out, at rates representing substantial reductions.

There were then still a few important strategic gateways not served by competitive roads. Between Ogden and Salt Lake City, the Union Pacific had a monopoly, though this was terminated by the completion in the spring of 1883 of the Rio Grande system's extension to Ogden. In southern Kansas the Atchison reigned without serious competition, though this was to be changed soon by the entrance of the Missouri Pacific. The Navigation maintained a close control of the business in the Columbia Valley, though this also was to be ended within the next few years. The Central Pacific and the Southern Pacific systems jointly still held most of the local traffic in California without serious rivalry, though this again was soon to be modified by the aggressive incursions of the Atchison's management.

Railroad territorial invasions were not always financially profitable to their promoters and investor followers. Though the rewards of the promoters and investors were checkered, with losses balancing the gains, the benefits to the shipping public were almost universal. A new railroad rival meant a fight for increased traffic and lower freight rates. The entrance of a new railroad into a territory formerly served by one road or by a limited number was followed, in almost every case, by immediate rate reductions. A notable exception was the stabilization of the Colorado rate structure for a year and a half after the completion of the Burlington's Denver extension. If there was an existing pool for the division of the business, the new rival normally thought it best to compete outside the pool. In that way it could demonstrate how much traffic it could acquire in a competitive struggle. Since its rates were lower than those of the members of the pool, it normally secured more than it could reasonably expect as a pool member. In the pool the rates would be higher. The normal effect of the addition of a new road to the list of competitors was a rate reduction.

The expansion programs of the early 1880's involved the traffic and the rates of the three direct Chicago–Missouri River lines. These Iowa Pool roads had in the 1870's succeeded in maintaining largely intact the Chicago–Missouri River rates on traffic interchanged with the Union Pacific. The co-operative spirit between the member roads of the Pool was shaken in 1879 by the growing unfriendliness between the Burlington and the Rock Island. In the fall of 1880 the Burlington general freight agent was directing local traffic officials to assume an aggressive attitude toward the Rock Island. "I wish you would take action . . . and be as aggressive as we have heretofore been conservative. Give a pass to every shipper in Des Moines who would be likely otherwise to pay fare over C. R. I. & P. . . . If you find it impossible to take business, make such rates as will insure the Rock Island carrying it very cheap."[11] Less than two weeks later a Rock Island executive threatened the Burlington that the rate trouble would not be confined to Illinois and Iowa but that soon the Rock Island would "demoralize all our [the Burlington's] business in Nebraska."[12] Outpourings of personal enmity and expressions of strong feelings characterized the correspondence between the Burlington officials. The Burlington accused the Rock Island of "underhandedly reducing rates"; the salesmen of the former were encouraged to encroach on Rock Island territory. The Rock Island was accused of stealing traffic from the Burlington, of never keeping an agreement, and of never telling the truth.[13]

Even more serious than this rivalry was the emergence of two new forces that threatened to unstabilize the rate structure of the Iowa Pool roads. First was the acquisition by Gould of control of the two direct St. Louis–Kansas City roads—the Missouri Pacific and the Wabash (the consolidated successor of the Kansas City and Northern). He also dominated the management of the Union Pacific. Also, that road in January, 1880, merged with the Kansas Pacific. Gould could now move traffic from the Union Pacific south over the Council Bluffs Road, east of the river, or over the Atchison and Nebraska, west of the river. Such a routing would help Gould bolster the traffic of the Wabash and the Missouri Pacific, in which he had large stock interests. Any loss in the Union Pacific business would be of smaller consequence to Gould, since in the early 1880's he owned only a few shares of that road. The Burlington blocked both these routes by acquiring control both of the Council Bluffs and of the Atchison and Nebraska. The Wabash, however, had in October, 1879, provided itself with a shorter line to Council Bluffs, though indeed it was circuitous as compared with the direct line of the Iowa roads.

The other factor adverse to the stability of the Iowa Pool roads' rate structure was the emergence in 1882 of the St. Paul as a competitor for the Chicago–Council Bluffs business. In accordance with custom and precedent it began its career as a rate cutter.

There was still another factor tending to undermine the stability of the Iowa rate structure. The Burlington system, alone of the Iowa Pool roads, competed on a *substantial* scale with the Union Pacific for traffic west of the Missouri River. In southern Nebraska a unit of the Burlington system competed for local traffic—traffic which was moved east not over the Iowa Pool's route between Council Bluffs and Chicago but via a Burlington system line. The traffic moved east via Plattsmouth, Nebraska, a point some miles south of Council Bluffs. The other Pool roads from time to time requested the Burlington to divert some of this traffic to Council Bluffs, so that they could share in the business. The Burlington refused. Clashing business interests led to business estrangement. After the building of the Burlington line to Denver, the Rock Island moved its westbound business almost entirely over the Union Pacific, and the Union Pacific divided its eastbound business between the Rock Island and the Northwestern. The latter, like the Rock Island, interchanged only a nominal amount of business with the Burlington for Colorado movement.

These forces combined by the end of 1883 in precipitating the most damaging war of rates that had as yet occurred west of the Missouri River. In December the preferential traffic relationship between the Union Pacific and the business enemies of the Burlington was transformed into a formal treaty. The Tripartite Pact was tantamount to a declaration of war against the Burlington. Under the pact the Rock Island and St. Paul established rates on westbound traffic and the Union Pacific on eastbound. This pact was followed by a war of rates, which will be discussed below.

The disturbance of the rate structure across Illinois and Iowa was paralleled by a somewhat similar pattern in the territory between Chicago and the Twin Cities. There the St. Paul and the Northwestern, whose extension to the Twin Cities was made by the Omaha road, had an understanding for the maintenance of rates and the division of traffic and earnings.[14] The routes of both roads were reasonably direct. In the spring of 1881 an unsettling factor was introduced. By joining with two other roads, the Rock Island produced a new, though circuitous route, between Chicago and the Twin Cities. The Rock Island refused to join the pool. It followed the usual practice of competing for traffic outside of the pool and at rates below those established by the pool. These differences led in September, 1882, to an open war of rates.

The competitive relationships were further complicated by a common interest by the St. Paul and the Rock Island in the Chicago–Council Bluffs traffic. The Rock Island did a good business between Chicago and Council Bluffs and a slight business between Chicago and the Twin Cities. The St. Paul conversely did an excellent business between Chicago and the Twin Cities and but little between Chicago and Council Bluffs. The Rock Island was the new competitor in the one segment and the St. Paul in the other.

The St. Paul, according to one authority, from the very beginning captured one-fourth of the Chicago–Council Bluffs through freight "and almost ruined the value of the passenger business" in 1883.[15]

Still another competitive factor complicated the already confused business picture. The Northwestern's Twin Cities connection was furnished by the Omaha road, and Porter, the president of that line, became friendly with the Rock Island. In fact Porter, as well as the Manitoba, recognized the legitimacy of the Rock Island's indirect route.[16]

Porter furthermore became incensed over the extension of the St. Paul into territory which he called his "own"—that is to say, territory served by the Omaha. Into this "natural" and "legitimate" area, a small road had in 1882 built about 75 miles of line. In the midst of this rate war the property was sold to the St. Paul. It then turned out that the road had been built by officials of the St. Paul under the name of an ostensibly independent property. This revelation that the road was now part of the St. Paul led Porter to refuse to sign a rate-stabilizing agreement in mid-November of 1882.

Complaints of secret rate cuts had been current for most of 1882. In January, Hughitt expressed the opinion that the Rock Island "is cutting rates and that Mr. Cable knows it."[17] And in October, Hughitt denounced the competition of the Rock Island in northern Minnesota for causing a condition which "could not be made worse on Eastbound business."[18] The competition of the Rock Island and the intransigence of

Porter produced a wide break in rates. Porter, like so many other railroad men at that time, had the territorial-legitimacy complex. The territory served by the Omaha was its legitimate property. He insisted that he would not tolerate the St. Paul invasion and would protect his business at the best obtainable rates. He would, furthermore, decline to pool any business with the St. Paul.[19] Porter forthwith dissolved the understanding for the division of business and the maintenance of rates that had for a number of years prevailed between the Omaha-Northwestern line and the St. Paul. Rates were reduced by approximately 50 per cent. Porter resorted to this "rash action," according to Hughitt, because he wished "to smash everything and thereby reduce the values of all the properties sixty-five to one hundred millions, with the view of organizing a Wall Street party strong enough to purchase the control and dictate the policy of five leading Western Railways. . . ."[20]

The intensification of the rate war stimulated the movement among officials to bring the war to an end. By mid-December, after a number of conferences between railroad officials, a general understanding was reached. It was agreed that no more roads would be built by any of the lines and that rates would be restored for one year; all disputes would be referred to the joint action of the managers of the several roads. The rates were restored, but no agreement was reached on the formation of a pool for the division of the business.[21]

While the war raged between the Chicago–Twin Cities roads, business relations among the properties further north and west were more cordial. There the Northern Pacific had agreed not to build north and the Manitoba not to build west into the area through which the Northern Pacific was then building. The Manitoba exploited this understanding by building branch lines on both sides of the Red River. The roads so thoroughly covered the area as to make it difficult for new competition to develop. This understanding stabilized rates and was one of the major reasons for the increased earnings of the Manitoba. Early in 1883 the picture changed. The Canadian Pacific completed a line competitive with the Manitoba and then reduced rates. The Manitoba followed suit. Security markets reflected their fears in a sharp drop in the price of the Manitoba stock.

Within a few months thereafter, that is by early 1884, the competitive arrangements in the area north and west of Chicago again changed. The Northwestern acquired control of the Omaha road, and the Rock Island now lost the active support of that property. Porter, who in the language of Vanderbilt, had tried, "to wreck all the railroads in the Northwest."[22] was now replaced by officers of the Northwestern.

The rate reductions in the Northwest in 1881 and 1882 were not duplicated in the Southwest. In this area, involving the traffic moving to and from the lower Missouri River points between Kansas City and Council Bluffs, the slashing rate reductions had already taken place in 1879. The St. Louis–Kansas City direct lines had in that year come under Gould control. With these properties and the enlarged Union Pacific under his command, Gould moved to capture the maximum traffic potential. He organized a southwestern pool consisting of the Wabash, the Missouri Pacific, and the Hannibal, and then reduced rates on traffic interchanged between the Wabash and the Union Pacific. By April, 1880, it was, "an understood fact that the Wabash has been doing nearly all the business" from Council Bluffs.[23]

The activities of Gould were checked by countermeasures taken by other roads. The Wabash accordingly agreed that it would "at once make such rates from C. Bluffs on all-through grain, as will be prohibitory and allow the business to again take the natural course via Chicago."[24] The Burlington, furthermore, by acquiring control of the Council Bluffs road blocked the connection between the Missouri Pacific at Kansas City and the Union Pacific at Council Bluffs. Throughout the balance of 1880 rates were well-maintained. Indeed, for the first time since the beginning of the Southwestern Railway Association in the fall of 1876, these roads went through a busy season with no "sharp" rate-cutting practices. The effect the absence of rate wars had upon the rates of the participating roads is shown in Table V.

Table V is based upon articles written by J. W. Midgley, Commissioner of the Southwestern Railway Association. He asserted, further, that the rates maintained by the Southwestern Association also protected the earnings of the Iowa Pool roads, the Burlington's affiliate in Nebraska, and of the Kansas and Texas. The rate protection, declared Midgley further, also protected the local business. He estimated that the total annual saving by the association approximated $10 million.[25]

The relative stability of the rate structure in the lower Missouri River valley points was paralleled, though at a much higher price level, prior to 1882, in the central area west of the Missouri River. The Union Pacific's exemption from competition was reinforced by the stabilization

Table V

TON–MILE RATES OF ROADS
IN THE SOUTHWESTERN RAILWAY ASSOCIATION,
APRIL, 1879, TO SEPTEMBER, 1879,
COMPARED WITH MAY 1, 1880, to DECEMBER, 1880.

Name of Road	*Rates April, 1879,* *to September, 1879* *(Rate War)*	*Rates May* 1, *1880,* *to December, 1880* *(No Rate War)*
Chicago Lines . .	7-¾ mills	N.A.
St. Louis Lines . .	6 mills	1.32 cents
Hannibal . . .	7-½ mills	1.73 cents
Wabash . . .	N.A.	1.15 cents

agreements of 1880. In the east, the Burlington had agreed not to extend its lines to Denver; and on the west the agreement between the Atchison and the Rio Grande similarly precluded the building of competitive lines in eastern Colorado. At Ogden, rates were maintained by agreement between the Union Pacific and the Central Pacific. However, conflict eventually occurred at this latter point, involving the traffic moving to and from southern Montana, centering around the growing copper business at Butte. After the construction of the Union Pacific's Utah and Northern line to that point, traffic was diverted from the Central Pacific. The Union Pacific doubled the Ogden-Butte rates on Montana business interchanged with the Central Pacific at Ogden, setting up a rate structure so that on a Butte–San Francisco shipment it would receive 75 per cent of the through rate for the 400-mile Butte-Ogden haul, while the Central Pacific received the remaining 25 per cent for the 833-mile Ogden–San Francisco haul.[26]

The second invasion of the Union Pacific's "natural" territory followed the breakdown of the stabilization agreement of October, 1880. The Burlington, in May, 1882, extended its Nebraska lines to Denver.[27] Competitive lines followed. Early in 1883 the Rio Grande opened its Salt Lake City line. There was then an understanding with the Union Pacific that rates would be maintained. They were for a time. The Union Pacific issued orders to its agents at Salt Lake City to charge a higher rate on freight arriving at that city over the Rio Grande–Burlington route destined for points beyond than on freight shipped over the Union Pacific.

Rates on traffic between the Pacific Coast, Utah, and the Missouri River soon "went to pieces."[28] A few months later the Northern Pacific completed its transcontinental line; and, even before that, it had reached the copper mines of Montana. This move cut the Union Pacific's business in Butte and in the copper camps "right in two."[29] Again rates declined. To enable its shippers to compete with those moving over the Union Pacific the Northern Pacific made the same rates between St. Paul and Butte that the Union Pacific made between Omaha and Ogden. Sizeable differences in distances were ignored.[30]

The Burlington's extension to Denver, contrary to precedent, was not followed by rate reductions. Prior to the completion of the line the managements of the Burlington and the Rio Grande agreed to trade traffic with no other road until each notified the other. The Burlington also formed a pool with the Union Pacific. It was not permanent and it was not so designed. The pool "was more of an experiment than anything else."[31] The Burlington withdrew from the pool even before its line was finished. It insisted that it receive at least 30 per cent of the Denver traffic. Negotiations for the establishment of a pool and the division of the traffic continued throughout the summer.

The Union Pacific was willing to give the Burlington 25 per cent of the business, and later it increased its offer to 27 per cent. In this move, the Union Pacific was supported by the Northwestern. Hughitt declared that 27 per cent of the Denver traffic was "a very fair" division. The Burlington, he wrote, was not as strong east of the Missouri River in competition for the Colorado traffic as it had been before the completion of the Denver route. "It is true they [the Burlington] proffer to roads terminating at the Missouri River equal facilities *with themselves* in exchange of both East and Westbound Colorado traffic, but I do not know of one Company likely to accept this privilege East of the Missouri River, they are one line in competition with seven (including the Milwaukee & St. Paul Road.)"[32]

The Burlington insisted upon a 30 per cent division, but finally agreed to accept $27\frac{1}{2}$ per cent. Perkins' reflections upon this problem suggest the business realities underlying the establishment of pools in the competitive environments of the 1870's and 1880's. "The fact is," he wrote, "our fair share in the Denver Pool is that proportion of the business which, if rates are maintained, we can do in legitimate and proper manner. In order to determine what this proposition is it is necessary that rates should be maintained and in order that rates may be maintained we must have peace, and in order to have peace we must have a pool I believe—so that at figures anywhere near what we consider to be fair to ourselves I agree . . . it is better to pool than to fight."[33]

An agreement for a pool had been reached in July, but at the last moment the Union Pacific refused to sign. It insisted that the Burlington not interfere with its local business in northern Colorado and not build any more lines in Colorado. The building of such lines would be "an act of hostility. . . ."[34]

Pending the setting up of the pool, the participants agreed, meanwhile, to maintain rates; and indeed, through all these months of negotiation, rates were actually maintained.[35]

On the field of battle there were continuous threats of rate wars. Traffic officials lived from hand to mouth. "I don't see very well how we can much longer hold rates with the U. P.," wrote a Burlington traffic official in August.[36] A pool agreement was finally signed in October, effective November 1, 1882. The business covered an estimated annual gross of $8 million.

An era of peace now descended upon the Colorado–Missouri River area. There was now "no danger of a row west of the Mo. River.," gleefully exclaimed a Burlington officer.[37] For more than a year there were no serious rate disturbances in this area. "In many respects, the year 1883," declared another Burlington official, "was the most successful I have known. Never since my connection with the roads has there been so uniform and steady observance of agreements by our competitors and consequently by ourselves and while we have paid a trifling sum for protection as pool balances, it cannot be doubted that the money has been well invested and that we have been amply paid for the outlay."[38]

There were, however, seeds of trouble. East of the Missouri River between Omaha and Chicago rate cutting had been going on in 1882 and 1883. The St. Paul, according to Burlington sources, had by November, 1883, been cutting rates for six months on two-thirds of their business.[39] The construction of the Denver line had made the Burlington a competitor of its two Pool allies—the Rock Island and the Northwestern. The Burlington insisted upon carrying its traffic between Chicago and

Colorado over its own long haul. The other two roads, therefore, continued to deliver traffic to the Union Pacific, and the latter forwarded its eastbound business to the Burlington's competitors. Between May and November, 1883, for example, it did not give the Burlington a single eastbound carload.[40]

Meanwhile, on the western end of the Union Pacific, competition with the Rio Grande–Burlington route grew sharper. A community of interest between the Rio Grande and the Union Pacific created by the January, 1880, agreement between them and the Atchison was destroyed in 1883.

The three roads had respected this agreement: they had not constructed new lines within the stipulated area: they had refused to interchange traffic with any new property. But a new property, the Denver and New Orleans, now appeared, whose major advantage arose from its support by Denver businessmen. It was therefore expected that the merchants would send traffic over the new road instead of the Rio Grande. The new road built parallel to the Rio Grande between Denver and Pueblo. The ironclad agreement between the Union Pacific, Atchison, and Rio Grande reduced the Denver and New Orleans to a position of traffic and financial impotence. Early in 1883, however, a judge declared that the agreement interdicting the interchange of traffic between the Denver and New Orleans and connecting roads was illegal. Traffic formerly carried by the Rio Grande from Denver to Pueblo and there delivered to the Atchison would instead be carried via the Denver and New Orleans. The Atchison, to compensate for the loss of business, demanded an increased percentage of the pooled traffic from Denver. The Rio Grande and the Burlington refused to make any concession. The Atchison then notified its partners that it would withdraw. The pool agreement was due to expire July 1, 1883. The one-month extension of the pool from July 1 to August 6, 1883, temporarily maintained the rate structure. In mid-July, however, the rates from Denver to Pueblo were reduced from $7.20 to $2.50.[41]

The judicially enforced collapse of their community interest contributed to a sharpening of the competition between the Rio Grande and the Union Pacific. The finances of both roads had been gravely weakened. The Union Pacific was fated soon to pass its dividends and the Rio Grande to fall into receivership. Both were hungry for traffic. In the late summer the Union Pacific announced a 50-cent rate on the Salt Lake

City–Missouri River business, and in November, with the concurrence of the Burlington, the Rio Grande slashed the rate to 25 cents. This was a price that insured losses for the railroads. Both Lovejoy and Perkins took steps to terminate the war. Adams, with a reputation for railroad peace-making efforts, turned a deaf ear to their overtures. To Lovejoy, Adams wrote that it would be useless to enter upon a compromise. It was neces-sary "to fight it out . . ."; and, he continued, a railroad war "which is in no way decisive is just so much waste."[42] To Perkins, he wrote that the Burlington had associated itself with the Rio Grande "in what seems such a thoroughly aggressive way," referring to the 25-cent rate on the Utah-Missouri traffic.[43]

Lovejoy, in a tone of surprise at Adams' uncompromising views, re-plied by observing that if the Union Pacific made "a bitter war, this Com-pany [the Rio Grande] will endeavor to protect its interest and those of its patrons."[44]

The Tripartite Pact, meanwhile, was negotiated. While there were no hopes of the Burlington joining in Pact, there was some ground for be-lieving that the Northwestern would. Hughitt, the road's general mana-ger, was at first opposed to the idea. "If we must wrestle with the illegal and perfidious tri-partite agreement for the neutral traffic of the Union Pacific Ry.," he wrote, "we will do it in a way that will show the bandits that they cannot without opposition walk away with the spoils."[45] After further consideration, the management agreed to join. It believed that the traffic between the Missouri River and Chicago would be carried at stabilized rates and would enable the road to compete for trans-Missouri business. By joining, the Northwestern would "save net money."[46]

The Wabash, with its circuitous line, also joined; and the Omaha, now part of the Northwestern system, also became a member. The par-ticipating roads organized the Western Trunkline Association, to operate what was dubbed the California Fast Freight Line. E. P. Vining, traffic manager of the Union Pacific and a determined foe of the Burlington, was appointed commissioner, with offices in Chicago.

The Burlington was now isolated. It was the Burlington against all the other eastern connections of the Union Pacific. The Burlington's line east of the Missouri River would now get no business from the Union Pacific. It was, therefore, prompted to take steps to supply its eastern lines with business to replace that formerly received from the Union Pacific. Early in January, Perkins therefore instructed his vice-presidents to work up a plan for the building of new lines west of the river.

Forbes, the elder statesman of the Burlington, was determined, if it were at all possible, to avoid a construction war and to negotiate some arrangement to maintain concord between the Burlington and the Union Pacific systems. The negotiations between the officials of the two roads and between the representatives of the stockholders continued almost without interruption throughout the first five months of the year. From the standpoint of the Burlington, the motives of the negotiators are clearly outlined in a voluminous correspondence recorded in the Burlington Archives. Rich material on the art of business trading is there revealed. Offers and counteroffers, rejections and partial acceptances of offers, compromises and counterpromises, definitive arrangements designed to be permanent but broken in the course of a few weeks or even a few days, the difficulties of the enforcement of agreements—all these and more are revealed in this correspondence.

Perkins early in these negotiations endeavored to effect an arrangement based on what he considered a shrewd analysis of the character of Adams. Perkins had a number of schemes to convey to Adams, who continued to serve as representative of the Union Pacific. He believed, however, that Adams would not approve the ideas unless Adams was made to feel that they were his own. "You can do this if anybody can," wrote Perkins to Forbes.[47] The Union Pacific, suggested Perkins, desired only a fair basis for a division of the through rate, guaranteed for five years; it also wanted peace. Peace, however, could not be achieved if the Burlington were left out as a connection at Omaha, because then the Burlington would build into the Union Pacific's territory. Adams, therefore, should suggest that the Tripartite be abrogated and that all the roads, including the Burlington, guarantee the Union Pacific a fair division of the rate for five years; that the Union Pacific's traffic be divided equally among the Iowa lines, and that the Burlington, as well as the Northwestern, should have the full benefit of money spent on their own lines west of the river.[48]

Forbes rejected Perkins' ideas. He insisted upon negotiating through committees. Forbes' mind was beset now, as it had been for many years, by fears of competitive overexpansion. Excessive railroad building could lead only to slashed rates and the destruction of railroad earnings.

Committees representing the Burlington and the Union Pacific on the level of the operating officers were appointed early in February. In these discussions, the Union Pacific offered proposals that were rejected by the Burlington. "I should stultify myself if I recommended such percentages," assured an official of that road. The Union Pacific official insisted there were only two alternatives: to fight or to arbitrate. All roads would arbitrate, he thought, except the Rock Island. Cable, all accounts agreed, was the main force in the Tripartite, and in the refusal to accept any compromises.[49]

These preliminary negotiations ended in failure. Rate cutting meanwhile broke out in the Chicago-Colorado area. By mid-March Perkins, with the Atchison support, was ready to "knock the bottom" out of Colorado rates.[50] The relationships between the major contestants soon became embittered. Perkins accused the railroads in the Western Trunkline Association of competitive irresponsibility. They "seemed determined upon so aggressive and outrageous policy." He also denounced the Union Pacific's traffic executive for proposing to cut into the Burlington's Nebraska business, not to benefit the Union Pacific itself but to injure the Burlington.[51]

In the Western Trunkline Association, meanwhile, a rift opened between the Northwestern and the Rock Island. In mid-March, the former complained that the Rock Island was determined that it (the Northwestern) should not "enjoy business relations" with the Union Pacific in conflict with the terms of the original Tripartite Pact "unless we submit to their terms. . . . I have not, and do not now see the way clear to submit to such exactions," wrote Hughitt.[52]

Forbes during these early months of 1884 persisted with his policy of negotiations. Since the operating officers had failed to reach a solution, his mind turned to another tactic. He concluded that discussions between the large stockholders and their representatives might lead to peace. A meeting was therefore arranged in Boston between Forbes and Ames, of the Union Pacific. A number of others attended the meeting, but the tenor of the negotiations and their final results emphasized the personalities and activities of these two. On March 21, Ames and Forbes, after an informal discussion, exchanged a memo which read as follows: "It is understood that pending the present discussions or until otherwise notified, Messrs. Ames and Forbes personally agree to use all efforts to cause rates in Nebraska both east and west, to be honestly maintained and each will notify the other of his inability to do so, this being the sense of the Conference Committee unanimously." Forbes did not entertain much confidence in the success of this agreement, writing that "we do not see any great probability of a result. . . ."[53]

While the negotiations proceeded for the settlement of the rate problems in Nebraska and eastern Colorado, efforts were also made to maintain the rate structure on Utah business. From the very opening of the Rio Grande Western to Ogden, in the spring of 1883, "ruinous rates" had prevailed on the Utah business.[54] The slash in rates in November, 1883, was used by Adams as a partial justification of the alliance with the Rock Island and St. Paul. An arrangement to maintain Utah rates was negotiated late in January, 1884, between Clark and Lovejoy for the Union Pacific and the Rio Grande, respectively. It was a personal understanding between the two officials. The roads agreed to divide the traffic and maintain the rates.[55]

Within a few days after the signing of the agreement the Union Pacific's allies east of the Missouri River challenged its validity. They insisted that under the Tripartite, they, and not the Union Pacific, had the right to determine westbound rates. Accordingly they refused to recognize the terms of the Utah peace and declined to approve the settlement unless the Burlington agreed also to make a satisfactory division of its Nebraska business.[56] By the end of February the war on Utah traffic was again renewed. The Western Trunkline Association ordered a cut in rates. The cut applied to traffic moving from both Utah and Colorado.

The rough treatment of the Clark-Lovejoy agreement was duplicated in the Forbes-Ames agreement on Nebraska rates. Vining, the Union Pacific traffic head, characterized the Forbes-Ames armistice in frank and even brutal language. An agreement made in Boston between the directors, who had no knowledge of contracts signed between general managers of the respective roads, "is worse than useless," he declared.[57] Each road accused the other of having made time contracts with Nebraska businessmen at special rates. Many of the Burlington contracts could not be cancelled, Vining insisted, before May 1, and the Burlington, he declared further, had made no effort to cancel them. The Union Pacific had over the course of years made scores of agreements with the Burlington to maintain rates, but the Burlington had always had special time contracts. He did not see the wisdom, declared Vining, of agreeing to maintain rates with those who had not the slightest intention of abiding by the agreement and who entered them only to obtain an advantage of gaining freedom to cut rates.[58]

The Burlington accused the Union Pacific of the same crime. It contended that the Union Pacific itself had outstanding contracts that could not be terminated.[59] The Burlington officials, meanwhile and on the very day the Forbes-Ames truce was negotiated, ordered its traffic officials to maintain rates absolutely and to make no deviation from regular rates. "This order is imperative and absolute," was the directive of the Burlington's vice-president.[60] Charges and countercharges of rate reductions disturbed the relations between the two roads. In short, the Forbes-Ames agreement to maintain rates in the area was not observed. These disturbances were not overlooked by the directors and large stockholders of the two roads. The committees met again in late March, shortly after the Forbes-Ames agreement had been concluded. The negotiations produced some nice distinctions. The Union Pacific suggested that it would agree to accept the Burlington's business at Omaha on the same terms accorded to the Union Pacific's allies provided the Burlington's Nebraska line agreed to take business from the Union Pacific's allies on the same basis accorded to the Burlington. No, said the Burlington, that cannot be done. The Missouri River was the middle of the Burlington's line but it was the eastern terminus of the Union Pacific's. Hence there was "nothing fair or reasonable in the proposition that we [the Burlington] should treat the other Iowa lines just as we expect the U. P. to treat us." The Union Pacific replied that the Missouri River was not the eastern end of its road; that its road terminated in Chicago. This was an argument that the Union Pacific had long used, and it was one to which Perkins had most strenuously rejected. Perkins called this argument the "fiat concept." The Union Pacific, that is to say, had by a mere agreement, so Perkins contended, extended its line from Omaha to Chicago. If this argument were sound, insisted Perkins, the Burlington had made a serious mistake in investing funds to build its Denver line.[61]

A conference between the Union Pacific and the Burlington committees on March 28, produced no results. Charges and countercharges, involving complaints of reduced rates, continued.

Another meeting of the committees was held on April 4. A reasonable truce was reached, or so it was thought. The understanding of March 21, for rate maintenance was reaffirmed. It was agreed, further, to pool the traffic of competing points west of the Mississippi River. The Union Pacific was not to aid its Iowa allies to attack the Burlington's local business. The meeting was then adjourned to April 12.

Trouble broke out almost immediately. Specific complaints of cut rates reached the executives of both roads. Thereupon Forbes, the chief peacemaker of the Burlington, assumed the initiative. He wired Ames, who held a somewhat similar position in the Union Pacific, that unless Ames could arrange the pool as agreed only a few days before the truce could not be continued. The truce, declared Forbes, seems "to be held firmly by us. . . ." Ames's answer by wire was a pleasant invitation to Forbes to do his worst. They were overrun with wires from the west, declared Ames, adding that the Burlington was not keeping the agreement, and that if the Burlington suffered from the truce "perhaps you would prefer to terminate it. . . ."[62]

This exchange of views disclosed a bargaining impasse. Four days later the committees met again. Discussions continued all day long. An agreement was reached the following day, the thirteenth. The new peace treaty revealed again the objective of the Iowa allies in negotiating the Tripartite, for this agreement stated, first, that these roads wanted "to get for themselves the whole of the U. P. share of competitive traffic, leaving to the C. B. & Q. the B. & M. share of such traffic, and no more." (The B. & M. refers to the Burlington's lines west of the Missouri River.) The second article read as follows: "If the C. B. & Q. will give up any claim to any share of the U. P. competitive, the U. P. and B. & M. will pool west of the River and the Iowa lines will pool east of the River, and the C. B. & Q. will get 1st, all the business controlled by its own lines, and 2nd a fair share of all U. P. business, except such as the C. B. & Q. competes for by its own lines."

The success of the treaty depended obviously upon the definition of the term "competitive" traffic. Clark, for the Union Pacific, and Potter, for the Burlington, were appointed to agree "as to what is competitive territory."[63]

Under the arrangement the Burlington would get at Omaha a fair share of the Union Pacific local traffic. The traffic for which there was competition between the Union Pacific and the Burlington system west of the Missouri would be delivered to the Union Pacific's Iowa allies. There were, however, no standards by which to differentiate the competitive from the non-competitive traffic. Within two days after the truce agreement Perkins had already prepared a memorandum expressing his views on the meaning of competitive traffic. In accordance with his character, he exploited to the full the strategic advantages of the Burlington. At Ogden, for example, traffic from the Central Pacific was delivered in part to the Union Pacific and in part to the Rio Grande. Some of this was carried east to Denver for delivery to the Burlington. Perkins contended that, of the traffic received by the Union Pacific at Ogden from the Central Pacific, a part should be redelivered to the Burlington at Omaha. The Burlington thus claimed a share of the Central Pacific's business at two points: at Denver from the Rio Grande, and at Omaha from the Union Pacific. If the Union Pacific denied the Burlington claim to a share of the latter-mentioned Utah business the Burlington, according to Perkins, would deliver all its westbound Utah business at Denver to the Rio Grande and would give the Union Pacific none. No agreement on this point was reached on the days following the conclusion of the armistice of April 13. Instead there was a failure to agree upon the exact meeting of the Forbes-Ames truce. Again rates were cut. Again claims and counterclaims were made about the source of the rate disturbances and over the responsibility of the rival carriers. Again Perkins, aided by his able vice-president Potter, expressed vindictive feelings against his business opponent. There was some misunderstanding of the meaning of the truce of April 13, especially by Clark of the Union Pacific. The contention by Clark, Perkins denounced as "a piece of brazen effrontery."[64] And to Forbes, he wrote, "Shall we allow ourselves to be trifled with any longer?" Potter expressed even stronger feelings. "I feel now" he declared, "as though we ought to cut the thing wide open."[65]

Again the battle revealed Perkins and Cable as the two leaders of opposite camps. Cable insisted upon the letter of the Tripartite—that the Iowa allies were entitled to fix rates on westbound business. A meeting at Chicago between the representatives of the Rock Island, St. Paul, Union Pacific, and Burlington broke up in confusion. Cable, according to Potter, who attended the meeting for the Burlington, lost his temper and declared that he would see the time when the Burlington would ultimately recognize the Tripartite.

Shortly after the Chicago meeting broke up in confusion, it appeared that an open war of rates would soon break out. The Union Pacific insisted that it had done all it could to maintain the truce. No agreement was reached and Potter declared that the Union Pacific could be hurt worst in Colorado, and "that is where I propose to let them [the Union Pacific] have it."[66]

By evening of the same day, however, Potter wired Perkins that he had arranged for a continuation of the truce. The Union Pacific had agreed to withdraw its special rates in Nebraska and to maintain rates—pending negotiations for a further settlement.

There was, however, no pool nor any other agreement to implement the truce. There was just an understanding that both major contestants as well as the Iowa allies, would maintain existing rates. Again the truce lasted only a few days. Within a week thereafter both sides complained that the special rates had not been cancelled. Vining epitomized his experience by admitting that an agreement to maintain rates did "not amount to anything," unless backed by a pool.[67] The Burlington insisted, as it had after previous truces, that the Union Pacific was not maintaining rates.

Repeating the pattern prevailing since the Tripartite, the war on the western front proceeded simultaneously with the eastern negotiations between the stockholders-directors. Ames referred optimistically to these conversations; he saw no obstacles likely to occur to prevent their consummation.[68]

By this time, May, the financial affairs of the Union Pacific had reached a critical stage. The panic was on and railroad stock prices had declined—that of the Union Pacific's even more than the rest. There was, furthermore, strong pressure in the Senate to impose fines on the Union Pacific for alleged failure to comply with certain federal laws.[69] Adams, soon to become president, was convinced then, as he had been for some time, that the Burlington was trying to ruin the Union Pacific.

Despite all these conferences, negotiations, discussions, peace treaties, and truces, no definitive settlement had been reached. In Nebraska, Colorado, and Utah rates were maintained by short-lived agreements. The approaching end of Gould's control over the Union Pacific lent hopes for securing a peaceful arrangement. Late in May, Perkins wrote Adams that the interest of the Burlington was "to live in peace and harmony with the Union Pacific. Together, we occupy a vast and rich region of the country from which both can make a fair profit out of the business of transportation."

This approach led to no concrete results. Indeed, after Adams' elevation to the presidency in mid-June, rate troubles in Colorado took a turn for the worse. While the Atchison played no role in the traffic picture in Nebraska, its influence in Colorado could not be overlooked. With its line to Pueblo and its interchange there with the Rio Grande, it could by rate reductions divert business at Denver and other Colorado points from the Union Pacific and the Burlington. The Tripartite agreement, with its aim of diverting the Union Pacific's eastbound business to its allies, injured the Atchison as well as the Burlington. The Atchison connected both at Kansas City and at the city of Atchison with the Rock Island, and at the former point also with the Wabash, also a member of the Pact. Under the Pact these roads were entitled to the eastbound business of the Union Pacific, and they also fixed the rates on westbound business. Therefore, any reduction in rates over their lines between Chicago and the Missouri River applied to traffic moving west beyond the river. The Wabash and the Rock Island, therefore, by cutting rates on their own lines also cut on the Union Pacific, thereby damaging the Atchison. That road retaliated by cutting Colorado rates. It refused to enter into any negotiations with the Union Pacific; that road, it declared, was a business captive of its eastern allies; it would discuss a Colorado rate agreement only if the Union Pacific became independent of the Tripartite. By July, according to a Burlington official, the rates on Colorado business could not be much worse; they were demoralized.[70]

Shortly after his elevation to the presidency, Adams made an effort to end the Colorado rate war. He had reached an understanding with Perkins for a conference to be held in Denver. His approach to the Atchison was met by a stern rebuff. "We do not need nor do we offer peace," wired Strong, of the Atchison, to Adams, "but we must protect ourselves as best we can when attacked."[71] The wire irritated Adams. "I am young in railroad business," he wrote in a complaining note to Perkins, "and perhaps may get accustomed to it in time. I am not yet accustomed to being sat upon in this style. . . . I don't like to be talked to like a small boy. . . . It's [Strong's telegram] the 'God-Almighty to a black beetle' style."[72] Communications of the kind illustrated by Strong's wire illuminate the criticism of businessmen and business relationships displayed in Adams' autobiography. Perkins moved fast to soothe Adams' feelings. The usual explanation of misinterpretation was advanced. The telegraph, it was declared, had blotched Strong's message, and Perkins prepared a "true copy." It should have read, "We do not intend war, we are for peace." Whether this play on words satisfied Adams is not revealed. In any event the conference was held in late July. Adams again presented his long-issued mechanism for corporate peace. The idea of personal negotiations between top executives, so often used in relations between the Burlington and Union Pacific, was again presented. It was suggested that he, Perkins, and Strong agree *personally* to hold things firm west of the river, subject to five days' notice. It would, theoretically, be a firm and permanent agreement, subject, however, to cancellation.

After two days of discussion an agreement in the pattern of Adams' suggestion was finally reached. Rates on Colorado business were to be maintained until December 31, subject to five days' notice of cancellation. By July, accordingly, rates over the Union Pacific between the Missouri River and Ogden were maintained on a short-term basis without any formal agreement. The truce was temporary and could be cancelled on short notice by either party.

Hardly had this truce gone into effect than a new disturbing factor was injected. The Northwestern in joining the Tripartite, had agreed to divide the revenue interchanged with both the Union Pacific and the Sioux City and Pacific. In the spring of 1884 the Northwestern acquired control of the Sioux City; and in August it informed the Association that it would no longer report its traffic to the Association. It would do exactly as the Burlington did with its Nebraska traffic. The Sioux City traffic, insisted the Northwestern, was local business and therefore would not be pooled. It was system business that belonged to the Northwestern. This action eliminated the Northwestern from membership in the Western Trunk Line Association.

The same mixture of business rivalry and personal bitterness that characterized the relationships between the Union Pacific with its Iowa allies and the Burlington now spread to the Northwestern. Keep, the Northwestern's president, inclined to use restraint in his expressions, declared testily that the road would have been at the mercy of the Union Pacific, Rock Island, and St. Paul if it had not shown it could secure a fair share of the cattle traffic "without getting down on our knees to those corporations."[73] Cable observed cynically that the Northwestern and the Burlington had "never been distinguished for exceeding forbearance in actions which affected the interest of competing lines."[74] Since the Northwestern was now out of the Tripartite, it could look for no favors from the Union Pacific; it could, for example, expect no eastbound traffic from that road. To get a share of the growing traffic (particularly the cattle business) in Nebraska and Wyoming, the Northwestern would be forced to extend its lines.

Negotiations meanwhile proceeded for the purpose of arranging a pool west of the Missouri River. The Burlington now acted with the Northwestern. Both had Nebraska traffic of their own to protect. Both were ready to make concessions to the Iowa allies of the Union Pacific. They hoped that by making concessions they could prevent the Rock Island and the St. Paul from building west of the river. An agreement was reached in September. Three pools were set up for the Colorado and Utah traffic. The agreement would continue until December 31, 1884, and the percentages of business allotted to each road would be determined by arbitration. A separate understanding for a pool covering the Nebraska business between the Union Pacific and the Burlington was concluded in December.

The pattern of temporary rate agreements that thus characterized railroad relationships in the Missouri River–Utah area also prevailed in the Northwest. There, an agreement concluded late in 1882 lasted for more than a year. Between Chicago and the Twin Cities, including also the area east to the Great Lakes and west into the Dakotas, rate harmony had prevailed. The Rock Island then emerged as a dissatisfied party. It declared that it could get more traffic by withdrawing from the Northwestern Traffic Association. It could then charge rates which would meet the competition of the direct lines of the Northwestern and the St. Paul. Early in February, 1884, it gave the thirty days' notice of withdrawal from the Association. Hughitt took the lead in the effort to prevent a rate war. He placed responsibility for the rate difficulties upon Cable. "From the first," he wrote, "the representatives of the Rock Island Company have been determined not to negotiate in the spirit of fair dealing, & with an intention to arrive at an agreement fair to all interests."[75] Perkins expressed a similar dissatisfaction. "I do not suppose," he stated, "we shall ever have a very satisfactory time in the West so long as Cable runs that institution [referring to the Rock Island]."[76]

After some discussion a pool was negotiated. A new organization, with the same name as the old—the Northwestern Traffic Association—was set up. The pool was given a term of two years and the percentages were to be fixed by arbitration.

A new competitive problem had now to be considered. Most of the Chicago–St. Paul traffic was then interchanged at Chicago with the eastern lines. This business could also be carried by a rail-lake haul to Duluth and Washburn. Connection between Duluth and St. Paul was made over the St. Paul and Duluth, successor to the Lake Superior and

Mississippi. The Washburn connection was made by the Omaha, now controlled by the Northwestern. The St. Paul–Washburn distance was 190 miles, as contrasted with the 409-mile St. Paul and Chicago haul. The St. Paul and Duluth road refused to join the new pool. The Omaha, as part of the Northwestern, was a member of the pool, and as an inducement to maintain rates it was given an extra 10 per cent of the traffic. If the St. Paul and Duluth road cut rates between these two cities, then, in conjunction with the lower water rates, it could divert business from the St. Paul–Chicago movement. This is what actually happened. The Omaha, even though it was in the pool, reduced rates in order to meet the competition of the St. Paul and Duluth. The St. Paul, with no line to Lake Superior, then reduced its rates to Chicago. These rate troubles were temporarily settled in the summer of 1884 and they caused little difficulty for most of the year.

The chief business leader in the field of lower rail-lake rates had not, however, yet appeared. Hill was still busy exploiting the Red River Valley territory and furthering his relationships with the Canadian Pacific.

In the far Northwest, meanwhile, another competitive factor was asserting its effect in reducing freight rates. The Union Pacific and the Central Pacific had been "interested in common . . . in having all the business of Oregon go by way of California. And it all did prior to the construction of the Northern Pacific" in 1883.[77] As soon as the Oregon Short Line route was opened late in 1884 the Union Pacific diverted the Oregon business from the Central Pacific. Prior to the construction of this new line the Central Pacific did "a good deal" of business in Montana and Idaho. The business, furthermore, was "very profitable," and the Central Pacific was "able to fix our own rates, free of competition."[78] Most of the Oregon and Washington business had, of course, gone over the combined lines of the Navigation and the Northern Pacific. The business was now divided between the Northern Pacific and the Union Pacific. The Navigation, divorced as it was in 1884 from the interests of the Northern Pacific, preferred to trade with the Union Pacific. It thereby secured a 404-mile haul instead of one of 214 miles via the Northern Pacific. The Northern Pacific thus lost some business to the Union Pacific. The loss of the Oregon, Montana, and Idaho business by the Central Pacific was, however, almost complete. The Union Pacific, again in accord with established practice, charged the Central Pacific a "very high" local rate. That was enough to divert the movement to the Union

Pacific.[79] The new Short Line route did not, however, disturb the regional monopoly of the Navigation. Indeed this was one of the few territorial monopolies that the construction and extension program of the early 1880's did not overthrow.

The inauguration of this new route did not, however, introduce any destructive rate slashing. The Union Pacific (through the Oregon Short Line) and the Northern Pacific had made an arrangement in February, 1883, to divide the through traffic among themselves.[80]

The peace agreements in the form of truces, armistices, informal gentlemen's agreements, and the more formal pools so laboriously negotiated throughout the winter and spring months of 1884 were on the whole faithfully carried out through the following fall and winter. These hard-won agreements began to weaken early in 1885. Late in February the St. Paul stopped reporting its Colorado, Utah, and Pacific Coast business to the pool. The Burlington then threatened to withdraw from the Northwestern Traffic Association.[81]

A more significant disturbing factor was the refusal of the Northwestern to report the traffic received from its Sioux City and Pacific to the old Iowa Pool. Its sister roads in the Pool insisted that the Northwestern include this traffic; but the Northwestern followed the same policy upon which the Burlington had so long insisted with reference to the latter's Nebraska traffic. The Northwestern refused formally to withdraw from the Association. It maintained the curious situation of maintaining its membership and the same time refusing to pay any attention to the urgent request of the other members of the pool. It was neither in nor out of the pool.

Another novel problem now arose to create a further competitive perplexity. The St. Paul decided not to allow its "milling-in-transit" business to be reported to the Northwestern Traffic Association. This phrase referred to grain taken from the St. Paul's local points, delivered to other points, there made into flour and forwarded to further destinations. The St. Paul contended that this was local business. The other pool members insisted that it was through business and therefore should be reported to the pool. The Northwestern and the Rock Island argued the point strongly. An attack by the Rock Island upon the St. Paul–Twin Cities' traffic could be met by a counterattack by the St. Paul on the Rock Island's Iowa traffic. The Northwestern carried a large volume on both routes.

An interregional war, thus possible as a theory, was carried into practice in April, 1885. In the Northwest "there is war," declared a leading business journal.[82] There was war at the same time in the Chicago-Omaha area. It also spread west of the Missouri. There the Rock Island and St. Paul reduced rates to Lincoln to less than one-half the regular rates.[83] In this area the Union Pacific and the Burlington, in accordance with the pool of December, 1884, endeavored to maintain rates.

Relations between the two roads, however, suddenly took a turn for the worse. The Burlington discovered evidence that the Union Pacific and the Rock Island had been cutting rates on this business in violation of the pool of the previous December. These documents, according to the Burlington's chief traffic official, were offered as "positive evidence of bad faith on the part of the Union Pacific, and shows what I have always suspected, namely, that Kimball and the man Shelby cannot live up to a contract."[84] This officer expressed his conviction that the Burlington should take effective warlike measures. "It looks to me now as though we had got to force the fighting and give the Union Pacific such a dose on Colorado and Utah as will sufficiently make them up for all time to come."[85]

This indeed was a rate war on all fronts. The rate concessions were too drastic to last. They imposed heavy losses on the contestants. A meeting of the Western Trunk Line Association, combining the Iowa Trunk Lines Association (the successors to the old Iowa Pool), the Colorado Traffic Association, and the Nebraska Pool, was held in Chicago. The meeting lasted five days, and at its end (May, 1885) the rates between Omaha and Chicago were restored to their former levels. The name of the Association was changed to the Western Freight Association. As a part of the settlement, the rates between Chicago and Omaha and Chicago and Kansas City were equalized.[86]

Out of the discussions in the Chicago meeting there emerged a comprehensive settlement aimed at stabilizing the relations of all the roads between eastern Colorado and Chicago. The traffic between Omaha and Julesburg, a junction point on the Union Pacific to Denver, was divided between local and through traffic. On the former, the Union Pacific agreed to deliver 13 per cent each to the Burlington and the Northwestern and the balance of 74 per cent to the Rock Island, the Wabash, and the St. Paul. On the competitive Burlington–Union Pacific traffic, the latter agreed to deliver 13 per cent to the Northwestern and 87 per cent to the

Rock Island, the St. Paul, and the Wabash. The Burlington would get nothing. On that traffic for which the Northwestern competed with the Union Pacific, the latter would give the Burlington east of Omaha 13 per cent, and 87 per cent would go to the Rock Island, the St. Paul, and the Wabash. The Northwestern would get nothing of this traffic. On the Union Pacific's business west of Julesburg, 20 per cent each would go to the Burlington and the Northwestern, and the remaining 60 per cent to the other three roads. The Council Bluffs, the Missouri Pacific, and the Omaha, though they were not admitted to the pool, agreed to maintain rates.

In the Chicago–Twin Cities area, the St. Paul won its contention for $72\frac{1}{2}$ per cent of the milling-in-transit business, after a deduction for local consumption.[87]

Perkins was enthusiastic over the outcome. Referring to the settlement, he declared, "It looks, therefore, as if rates were in a fair way to be reasonably well maintained west of Chicago for some time to come, and on the whole the adjustment of matters with regard to the Union Pacific traffic seemed to me to be a pretty good one for us."[88] Perkins reasoned that if the Union Pacific had exercised no discrimination against the Burlington there would have been five roads participating in the Union Pacific eastbound traffic. The Burlington, as one of the five, would have received 20 per cent of the business; under the agreement it received only 13 per cent. This business, according to Perkins' estimate, was worth approximately $300 thousand, per year. Hence by surrendering 7 per cent, or $21 thousand, the Burlington received reasonable assurances that the Rock Island and the St. Paul would probably not build new lines west of the river.[89]

The Tripartite Pact was now eliminated as a serious factor in the railroad business. The Rock Island and St. Paul had failed in their efforts, so persistently maintained for so many months, to capture all the Union Pacific's eastbound business. The Northwestern had become a much more powerful factor than it had been in 1883 when the Tripartite agreement was consummated. Through its affiliated trans-Missouri River lines it was now an important force in the eastbound cattle business from Wyoming and Nebraska. Any effort on the part of the Union Pacific to divert business from the Northwestern could be met by retaliatory action. The latter line could, if necessary, cut rates on the cattle traffic and inflict damage on the Union Pacific. The agreement of May, 1885, furthermore, allowed both the Northwestern and the Burlington, as they thought necessary, to continue the construction of new lines west of the Missouri River. The Tripartite was now a shell, and as a factor of business significance its existence could well be ignored.

The May settlement in the Northwest favored the aggressor roads just as it did along the Central route. The demand by the St. Paul that the milling-in-transit business be recognized as local traffic, and thereby exempt from the jurisdiction of the pool, was practically conceded.

The agreement in the Northwest ran for one year from April 1, 1885, and in the Omaha-Colorado area, for a similar term from December 31, 1885.[90]

The expectations of business peace generated by this comprehensive settlement, were soon confounded by events. Both in the Northwest and in the Missouri Valley competition again took its toll. In the former region, competition between the Omaha and the St. Paul and Duluth roads continued to produce trouble. The St. Paul and Duluth declined to enter into any pool. It was, therefore, free to determine its rates in accordance with its own idea of sound business strategy. The Northwestern, in control of the Omaha, insisted that the latter's traffic via the Washburn route should also be free of the pool unless the St. Paul and Duluth joined. The Northwestern believed that the St. Paul and Duluth, operating outside the pool, as against the Omaha, operating inside, would get the bulk of the Lake Superior traffic. The problem was made more complicated by the entrance in the spring of 1884 of a new competitor for the Lake Superior business. This was the Wisconsin Central, which opened a new route from St. Paul via Green Bay, Wisconsin. This company, like the St. Paul and Duluth, declined to join the pool. The Northwestern, at least according to newspaper reports, insisted that the St. Paul was supporting the St. Paul and Duluth in its refusal to become a pool member. The latter road by quoting lower rates would justify the St. Paul in quoting lower rates over its own Chicago line. The pool, the Northwestern Traffic Association, was finally driven by force of competition to permit the Omaha road to make rates via Washburn equal to those established by the St. Paul and Duluth.[91]

Shortly after the conclusion of the May agreement competitive trouble also broke out along the Central route. There the St. Paul made a long-term contract to carry dressed beef at a low rate between Omaha and Chicago. Soon thereafter it withdrew from the Missouri Valley pool.

The Burlington followed. "It seems," wrote a vice-president, "as though the St. Paul road was bound to wreck itself and everybody else if it can."[92]

A few weeks thereafter the St. Paul expressed its dissatisfaction with the percentage of the business allotted to it for the Colorado-Utah traffic. It announced that it would resign from the Association. The arbitrators later met and increased the percentage accorded to the St. Paul. Whereupon the Rock Island, whose percentage was reduced, announced its dissatisfaction, coupled with further notice that it would withdraw. By November of 1885, not only the Rock Island but also the Burlington and the Alton had expressed their intentions by giving the necessary cancellation notice.[93]

As the year 1885 drew to a close rates were being maintained on a tenuous basis in both the St. Paul-Chicago and the Omaha-Chicago areas. Similarly, the rates between points east of the Missouri River and Nebraska, Colorado, and Utah were also maintained on a fragile basis by pools and understandings. Rates on competitive traffic, meanwhile, had over the previous few years been substantially reduced. The fight for traffic, accompanied by rate concessions, reduced earnings of most of the western roads.

A conclusion on the effect of rate competition awaits an examination of competition in the transcontinental area, between the Pacific coast and points east of the Missouri River and beyond to the Atlantic seaboard. This competition will be dealt with in the following chapter.

Notes for Chapter XIII

[1] Pac. Ry. Commission, p. 2122, Peter B. Shelby, assistant traffic manager, Union Pacific.

[2] *Ibid.*, p. 2849, Stanford.

[3] Burlington Archives, Perkins to Geddes, Aug. 3, 1882.

[4] Northwestern Archives, Hughitt to S. H. H. Clark, July 11, 1882. Clark was general manager of the Union Pacific.

[5] Burlington Archives, Perkins to Potter, July 2, 1883.

[6] Crocker to Huntington, Jan. 23, 1882, M. M.

[7] *R. R. Gaz.*, Aug. 14, 1875, p. 340.

[8] *Ibid.*, Sept. 9, 1876, p. 589.

[9] A typical suggestion is noted in a letter in the Burlington Archives, Strong to J. C. McMullin, vice-president, Alton, May 4, 1877.

[10] These rates were presented by J. W. Midgely, Commissioner of the Southwestern Railway Association, in *R. R. Gaz.*, Dec. 17, 1880, p. 669.

[11] Burlington Archives, E. P. Ripley to J. C. Manley, Sept. 18, 1880.

[12] *Ibid.*, Ripley to E. P. Vining, Sept. 28, 1880.

[13] *Ibid.*, Ripley to Thomas Miller, Sept. 18, 1880.

[14] This arrangement is referred to in Northwestern Archives, Hughitt to H. B. Ledyard, general manager, Michigan Central, May 19, 1882; also Hughitt to Sykes, Oct. 21, 1882.

[15] *R. R. Gaz.*, Feb. 22, 1884, p. 149.

[16] The Manitoba's support of the route is noted in Northwestern Archives, Hughitt to Ledyard, May 19, 1882.

[17] *Ibid.*, Hughitt to Merrill, Jan. 24, 1882.

[18] *Ibid.*, Hughitt to Sykes, Oct. 21, 1882.

[19] For the views of Porter, see *R. R. Gaz.*, Dec. 8, 1882, p. 760.

[20] Northwestern Archives, Hughitt to Sykes, Oct. 21, 1882.

[21] *R. R. Gaz.*, Dec. 15, 1882, p. 779.

[22] *Boston Transcript*, April 24, 1884.

[23] Burlington Archives, Ripley to George Olds, April 2, 1880.

[24] *Ibid.*

[25] *R. R. Gaz.*, Dec. 17, 1880, p. 669.

[26] Pac. Ry. Commission, p. 3361, Stubbs, traffic manager, Central Pacific.

[27] For details see *Gould*, Chap. XII, pp. 244–249.

[28] Pac. Ry. Commission, p. 2122, Shelby, assistant traffic manager, Union Pacific.

[29] *Ibid.*, p. 103, Adams.

[30] *Ibid.*, p. 2177, Shelby.

[31] Burlington Archives, Potter to Perkins, April 17, 1882.

[32] Northwestern Archives, Hughitt to Clark, July 11, 1882.

[33] Burlington Archives, Perkins to Potter, July 11, 1882.

[34] *Ibid.*, Potter to Perkins, July 16, 1882.

[35] On these discussions, see *Ibid.*, Perkins to Potter, Aug. 2, 1882.

[36] *Ibid.*, Potter to Perkins, Aug. 29, 1882.

[37] *Ibid.*, Potter to Elijah Smith, Oct. 16, 1882.

[38] *Ibid.*, Ripley to Potter, Mar. 21, 1884.

[39] *Ibid.*, Potter to Perkins, Nov. 19, 1883.

[40] *Ibid.*, Potter to Perkins, Nov. 16, 1883.

[41] *R. R. Gaz.*, July 20, 1883, p. 486.

[42] Burlington Archives, Adams to Lovejoy, Dec. 4, 1883.

[43] *Ibid.*, Adams to Perkins, Dec. 17, 1883.

[44] *Ibid.*, Lovejoy to Adams, Dec. 7, 1883.

[45] Northwestern Archives, Hughitt to Sykes, Dec. 15, 1883.

[46] *Ibid.*, Hughitt to Sykes, Jan. 3, 1884.

[47] Burlington Archives, Perkins to Forbes, Jan. 18, 1884.

[48] *Ibid.*

[49] *Ibid.*, E. P. Ripley to Potter, Feb. 29, 1884.

[50] *Ibid.*, Perkins to Forbes, Mar. 17, 1884.

[51] *Ibid.*, Perkins to Forbes, Mar. 17, 1884.

[52] Northwestern Archives, Hughitt to Sykes, Mar. 14, 1884.

[53] Burlington Archives, Forbes to Perkins, Mar. 21, 1884. This is also the source for the text of the memorandum.

[54] This language is used by the Rio Grande in its 1883 Annual Report, p. 8.

[55] Burlington Archives, Perkins to Potter, Feb. 3, 1884.

[56] *R. R. Gaz.*, Feb. 8, 1884, p. 118.

[57] Burlington Archives, Vining to T. L. Kimball, Mar. 22, 1884.

[58] *Ibid.*

[59] *Ibid.*, Wire, Potter to Perkins, Mar. 28, 1884.

[60] *Ibid.*, Potter to Holdrege, Mar. 21, 1884.

[61] *Ibid.*, Perkins to Potter, March 29, 1884.

[62] *Ibid.*, Wires, Forbes to Ames and Ames to Forbes, April 8, 1884.

[63] Copy of the agreement, signed by C. E. P., in Burlington Archives.

[64] *Ibid.*, Perkins to Potter, April 23, 1884.

65 *Ibid.*, Perkins to Forbes, April 23, 1884, and Potter to Perkins, April 25, 1884, respectively, for the above two quotations.

66 *Ibid.*, Potter to Perkins, April 26, 1884.

67 *Ibid.*, Vining to Ripley, June 11, 1884.

68 *Ibid.*, W. J. Ladd to Forbes, May 26, 1884.

69 For details, see *Gould*, pp. 419–420.

70 Burlington Archives, Potter to Perkins, July 24, 1884.

71 *Ibid.*, Strong to Adams, July 17, 1884.

72 *Ibid.*, Adams to Perkins, July 18, 1884.

73 Northwestern Archives, Keep to Sykes, Sept. 14, 1885.

74 Burlington Archives, Cable to Vining, Aug. 11, 1884.

75 Northwestern Archives, Hughitt to Sykes, March 14, 1884.

76 Burlington Archives, Perkins to Potter, Oct. 3, 1884.

77 Pac. Ry. Commission, p. 2812, Stanford.

78 *Ibid.*, p. 2489.

79 *Ibid.*, p. 2823, Stanford.

80 Some details on the negotiations between the Union Pacific and the Northern Pacific for the division of the Navigation Company's traffic are found in Northern Pacific Archives, Harris to Adams, Oct. 11, 1884.

81 Burlington Archives, Perkins to Potter, Feb. 28, 1885.

82 *Bradstreet's* April 25, 1885, p. 282.

83 Burlington Archives, Potter to S. R. Callaway, April 19, 1885.

84 *Ibid.*, Potter to Perkins, April 2, 1885; Kimball and Shelby were traffic officials of the Union Pacific.

85 *Ibid.*

86 *R. R. Gaz.*, May 22, 1885, p. 335.

87 *Bradstreet's*, May 16, 1885, p. 332. Text of the contract is in the *Chicago Tribune*, May 20, 1885.

88 Burlington Archives, Perkins to Ladd, May 11, 1885.

89 *Ibid.*

90 *Bradstreet's*, May 16, 1885, p. 332.

91 *Chicago Tribune*, July 21, 1885.

92 Burlington Archives, Potter to Perkins, May 28, 1885.

93 *R. R. Gaz.*, Aug. 28, 1885, p. 557; *Chicago Tribune*, Aug. 29, 1885.

XIV

The Fight for Traffic—Transcontinental

BY THE fall of 1883 railroad competition prevailed all over the transcontinental territory for the first time. Routes were created at breathtaking speed in a period of about four years. Between them there was stiff competition. The rivalry rose in 1883 to commanding importance upon the establishment of the Sunset Route. This embraced the low-cost water service between New Orleans and New York. Non-Huntington lines fought the Sunset Route largely by rate reductions. Prior to 1883, when the Central Pacific was the sole California connection, this technique was not particularly useful. The competitive problems were not complicated, and the transcontinental lines decided to pool their business, and so avoid the necessity of rate cuts.

The first pool, dated 1881, continued until the year end. The Union Pacific was given 66 2/3 per cent of the traffic and the Atchison the balance. In 1882 the Texas and Pacific completed its transcontinental line through a connection with the Southern Pacific at a point ninety miles east of El Paso. By quoting lower rates it diverted some business from the Union Pacific. A second pool was organized. The Union Pacific proportion was reduced to 60 per cent and the Atchison and Texas and Pacific were allotted 20 per cent each.

By early 1883 these percentages proved to be unsatisfactory. The Sunset Route could now cut rates and divert traffic to its newly established line. To avoid this contingency, another pool was set up on February 1, 1883. The Union Pacific reduced its division to 56 per cent, the Atchison to 16 per cent, the Texas and Pacific to 14 per cent. The San Antonio was also given 14 per cent.[1] Under Huntington's leadership, the Sunset Route cut rates, and succeeded within a few months in capturing some-

where between two-thirds and three-quarters of the business between
the Pacific Coast and a wide area extending from New York inland. The
northern and central routes, represented respectively by the Northern
Pacific and the Union Pacific complained of this rate competition. By
price cuts, it was contended, the Sunset had within a few months diverted
a substantial volume from the others. The Huntington system in turn
complained of competition by its rivals. "The Guerrilla chiefs" who
managed the Texas roads, wrote the Central Pacific superintendent,
"encroach on our territory and otherwise threaten our revenue." Furthermore, eastbound Nevada traffic was endangered by the Union Pacific
and the Rio Grande, while the "tariff-wreckers" of the Northern Pacific
threatened also to take possession of British Columbia, Washington
Territory, and Oregon, and to divide the Asiatic and California business.[2]
This businessman who complained so bitterly over competitive losses had
for a number of years lived in an aura of protective monopoly. He soon
learned some lessons of the rigors of competitive life. To begin with, the
Atchison did not get along well with the Southern Pacific. The through-
traffic relationships at Deming and at the Colorado River connection
proved to be a paper arrangement. The Southern Pacific declined to
surrender part of its haul in order to cement more friendly relations with
the Atchison. By doing so it would lose profits. On business moving east
on the Union Pacific at Ogden in 1883, for example, the Central Pacific
received 46 per cent of the through rate, while over the Atchison–Atlantic
and Pacific route its division was only $29\frac{1}{3}$ per cent. "We would therefore
be cutting our own heads off," wrote Crocker to Huntington, "to enter
into such an arrangement." Crocker was referring to a proposed contract
for the movement of business over the Atchison.[3] There was, furthermore,
no counterbalancing westbound traffic from the Atlantic and Pacific. Its
local business between Albuquerque and Needles promised to be "very
light for a long time;"[4] while in 1883, according to Crocker, the traffic
west of the Colorado River between Needles and Mojave, the connection
with the Southern Pacific main line to San Francisco, was not enough
to fill one train weekly.[5] Crocker at the same time seized the opportunity
of again pressing his opposition to the steadily widening expansion program of Huntington. "Really it seems to me," he wrote, "as though our
revenues were melting away under the great number of roads we are
building...."[6]

A further complication developed, meanwhile, in the Atchison's

eastern terminal. There, along the Missouri River, the Atchison's relations with its long-time business associate, the Burlington, became unfriendly. The Atchison insisted that it was entitled to the same division
of the through rate on transcontinental business via Kansas City that the
Union Pacific received via Omaha. This the Burlington refused to accept.

Another problem grew out of the competition between the northern
and southern transcontinental routes. Shippers east of the Mississippi
River could move traffic to San Francisco via the Northern Pacific to
Portland and via steamship beyond; or east via rail to the Atlantic seaboard and thence via steamship and a rail haul over the Sunset Route.
The latter could move business by rail to San Francisco and by water to
Portland. Both the Northern Pacific haul to San Francisco and the
Southern Pacific's to Portland were uneconomic. They were probably
unprofitable to both roads. The rate structure on this traffic was weakening, thereby depressing rates on all the routes. In an effort to avoid a war
the roads concerned in the business met at San Francisco in September,
1883. There were present representatives of all the participating roads.
An attempt was made to arrange a pool and divide the traffic, and so
remove the inducement to cut rates. It was found impossible to agree
upon the division of the business. Each road wanted a percentage based
upon highly optimistic expectations of future traffic volume. The amount
of allotted business expected by each property, reported Crocker, would
be such as "would require 250% to go around among the different
claimants."[7]

An agreement was finally reached; but not for a pool and a division
of the business. "All lines here represented solemnly agree to maintain
the rates, now in force, or which may hereafter be agreed upon" for a
period of fifteen months. An understanding for the equalization of rates
between the southern transcontinental routes and the Northern Pacific
route was also effected. It was agreed that rates would be the same to
San Francisco and to Portland only by the direct routes. An extra charge
would be made for steamer transportation moving between one port and
another—that is to say, for freight moving between San Francisco and
Portland. There would thus be no "useless" steamer transfer service
between these two ports. A shipper moving traffic over the Northern
Pacific to San Francisco would pay the railroad rate to Portland and
the steamship charge from that point to San Francisco; and a shipper
moving freight over the Huntington lines to Portland would pay the

railroad rate to San Francisco and the rate for steamship service from San Francisco to Portland. This was a stabilization arrangement dear to the hearts of business monopolists. It was a lovely transaction and it represented the efforts of private business planning worked out along "scientific" lines. It was also provided that any differences regarding the meaning of the agreement would be arbitrated.[8]

The agreement almost immediately encountered a new competitive problem. Shortly after the organization of the Transcontinental Association came the Tripartite Pact between the Union Pacific and its two Iowa allies. An underlying philosophy of this contract was the insistence by the Union Pacific that its terminus be fixed not at the Missouri River but at Chicago. The Union Pacific accordingly suggested that its Iowa allies be invited to participate in the proceedings of the Association. The Burlington announced its opposition, whereupon the Union Pacific replied that it would refuse to discuss regulations until the settlement of the territorial question. The defeat of the Union Pacific's move was followed by notice of its withdrawal from the Association.[9] The other roads remained, and the Association was kept alive.

The first elaborate effort at maintaining rates and restraining competition was therefore not a resounding success. Competition was left undisturbed for a number of months, but rates were well maintained. The Southern Pacific, at the lower rates competitively determined before the organization of the Association, still moved almost 70 per cent of the transcontinental business. Competitors could not approve such a traffic diversion. Accordingly in May of 1884 another meeting was held in order to settle the question of the percentages of the pooled business. After a number of days of discussion, adjournments, and more discussion, an understanding was apparently reached for the transformation of the Association from a rate agreement to a money pool. The Atchison nullified the decision. The bugbear was again the Tripartite. It would not join the money pool as long as the Union Pacific's allies had the power to fix westbound rates. The Association accordingly voted to continue the pool as it stood, and referred the percentage of business problem to a committee.[10]

These results did not satisfy the Atchison. Rate reductions east of the Missouri River by the Iowa roads could still be extended to the territory west of the river. The Tripartite remained in existence; the Iowa roads refused to surrender their control over westbound rates; and so the Atchison withdrew from the Association, which perished almost before it was born.[11] Within a few days the Burlington gave its notice. Though the withdrawal dates were later extended and its life formally maintained, the Association was a shell without any substance. By August, 1884, transcontinental freight rates were reduced between 15 and 20 per cent.[12]

By this time a number of new forces had made their appearance. The Northwestern had acquired control of the Sioux City, and, though still retaining its nominal membership in the Tripartite, refused to pool the business of its new acquisition with the other Iowa roads. The Northwestern, like the Burlington, decided to retain the long haul of its lines west of the Missouri River for movement over its own line east of the river. The other development was the receivership of the Wabash. The Wabash was no longer under the full control of Gould. It could expect little traffic from the Union Pacific. It seemed probable that the Atchison would arrange either with the Wabash or the Alton, or with both, for the interchange of business at Kansas City. A third factor was introduced by the refusal of the Frisco to join a pool under any conditions. In this move it had the approval of the Atchison. In the Northwest the Northern Pacific demanded a subsidy for agreeing not to compete with the Oriental and Occidental steamship affiliate of the Central Pacific. The Central Pacific was willing to pay, provided the other roads shared in the payment.

In order to solve these perplexing problems, a series of meetings of general managers were held in September. From these discussions, a new line of thinking soon emerged. It was proposed to form separate pools, one to cover business west of the Missouri River and one for traffic to the east. It was thought that in this way the Atchison's objections to a pool would be minimized, if not removed. Eventually two pools were set up. The one east of the river was called the Pacific Coast Association and the one west, the Transcontinental Association. An understanding was reached in Omaha on October 1, 1884, to set up a money pool from that date to December 31. Percentages again were to be settled by arbitration. Rates on California traffic were ordered restored. The Central and Southern Pacific agreed to pay 6 per cent of their gross to the Northern Pacific, and the latter agreed not to compete for California business.

The higher rates were not supported by a pool. The allotment of traffic to each of the participating roads was a condition precedent to the formation of the pool, and that condition was not fulfilled. The arbitrator held long meetings and not until mid-December did he reach a decision. The divisions were not accepted by the Central Pacific and Southern Pacific. These two roads together were awarded slightly less than 40 per cent of the total. They did not propose to surrender any substantial proportion of their business. They insisted that this award was too low.

Another novel factor now appeared. The eastern roads between Chicago and the seaboard saw no reason why, in view of the decreasing volume of railroad overland traffic, they should carry business at the new relatively low rates ordered by the Association. They therefore proposed that all the California traffic be pooled, including that moving by water between the Atlantic seaboard, Galveston, and New Orleans. They pointed out that by rate cuts the Sunset Route had secured about two-thirds of the California traffic. No solution was reached. Shortly after the arbitrator's award, the Central Pacific gave notice of its withdrawal from the Association.

The meeting of the Association at which these problems were discussed lasted for four days in December and adjourned to meet again on January 12, 1885. An agreement for a rate truce until January 31 was also reached.

At the January meeting some progress was made in setting up a division to remove the incentive for rate cutting. Two pools were set up, an eastern and a western. Objections to the decisions of this meeting were soon raised. The Northern Pacific announced that it would not sign unless it received a higher subsidy than the one allotted to it for non-interference with the San Francisco traffic. The Texas and Pacific objected because the Frisco was not a member.

When the rate truce expired on January 31, rate cutting was resumed. The eastern roads decided that the transcontinental traffic was so unprofitable that the little traffic that was carried should be charged reasonable rates. Through its Trunk Line Commissioner, they issued a circular that the through rates between the Atlantic seaboard and the Pacific Coast would be withdrawn. The new rate would be the local New York–Chicago rate plus the Chicago–Pacific Coast rate. Thus any reduction by the roads west of Chicago would be confined to that area. Eastern roads would charge their local rates for shipments between New York and Chicago, even though the business moved thereafter west to the Pacific. Rate wars by the roads west of Chicago would not be extended east to Chicago.

Meanwhile, a similar move was made by the Central Pacific, controlling the western end of the central transcontinental rail route. The two new transcontinental pools had reduced rates from Chicago west. The Central Pacific, however, declined to accept these rates, and informed the Union Pacific that if it did quote the reduced rates, the Union Pacific would bear the full amount of the reduction. The Central Pacific would not share in any rate reduction between Chicago and Ogden. For its haul it would charge its local rate; it would not accept its share of the reduced through rate. By this move the Central Pacific, as a part of the Sunset Route, would secure more business from the Southern Pacific and less from the Union Pacific. Since the Central Pacific secured a longer haul on the former, it would gain some profit for its own lines.[13] The Union Pacific then threatened to route all its business via the Oregon Short Line-Navigation route to Portland and by steamship to San Francisco.

The move of the Central Pacific in refusing to participate in rate reductions made by its connecting roads was unprecedented. This action incited deep and bitter resentment. The manager of a major Chicago road, for example, denounced the Central Pacific. "This is simply a game of bluff on the part of the Central Pacific. This road thinks it can bulldoze us. . . . What the Central Pacific wants is to make the rates via Chicago so high as to enable its Sunset Route via New Orleans and the Southern Pacific to continue to take the bulk of the business."[14]

It seemed now that the transcontinental pool was ready for dissolution. The penalty for its dissolution, however, was too great for the roads to make an abject surrender. Efforts were therefore made to continue the association. The executive committee met late in February, and it was resolved to continue the Association until April 30. A little more than three weeks later, at another meeting in Denver, the roads unanimously agreed to end the war and to restore rates to the November, 1884, level. A new idea was now introduced. It was resolved "that the power to make rates other than those authorized by this association shall (if heretofore confirmed) be taken absolutely out of the hands of all agents, and such authority shall rest exclusively with the chief of the freight department of each road."[15]

Some weeks later the arbitrators appointed at an earlier meeting announced their awards on various matters. Dissatisfaction was immediate. The Central Pacific declined to abide by the decision and the Atchison gave notice of its withdrawal. Another meeting of the Association, held shortly after the awards, instructed the committee to prepare a plan for the division of the business. The committee reported on the following day that it had failed to agree, and it then suggested that responsibility be passed to the railroad presidents. Nothing fruitful followed this suggestion. Adams asked Perkins to use his influence with the Atchison to induce it to modify its position. Perkins entertained "no doubt that Mr. Strong and the Atchison people, as reasonable men will agree that the pool ought not to go to pieces, and that, if they are dissatisfied with the percentage which has been awarded to them, their true course is to call for a new arbitration to award percentages to date from July 1st, letting the pool run on."[16]

Further efforts were made to preserve the pool. A committee to fix percentages failed to agree; it proposed that the task be discharged by the railroad presidents. This proposal was not accepted. At a meeting in June a compromise was reached. Awards were to be made on all business carried from January 1 to June 30. The business to be carried during July, August, and September would be based on the actual earnings for April, May, and June. After September, it was proposed that a new arrangement be made.[17]

This resolution seemed to solve all the problems. In fact, it solved none. The Association met again in September for the purpose of making those more permanent arrangements called for by the June meeting. By a majority vote, over the objections of the Central and Southern Pacific, the Association adopted a resolution requesting each line to make out a statement of claims against the Southern Pacific for the first six months of 1885. Each road was asked to draw a draft against the Southern Pacific for the amount due it because of the carriage by the Southern Pacific of traffic in excess of the amount allotted to it by the June compromise. The Southern Pacific declared that if such drafts were drawn they would not be honored. The feeling of the majority of the roads against the Huntington lines is well reflected by a statement of a Burlington vice-president. His road, he said, had paid large amounts to various roads and "he took his medicine like a man." The Southern Pacific, he concluded, must settle old accounts before he would agree to a reorganization of the Transcontinental Association.[18] The Rio Grande took the Association's resolution seriously and sent one draft to the Southern Pacific for the amount due. The Southern Pacific returned the draft unhonored, whereupon the Rio Grande and the Burlington announced their withdrawal

19

from the Association. The pool was helpless. It had no power to enforce its mandates. Its resolutions, even though passed by heavy majorities, were as futile as many of those issued by the League of Nations in the 1930's and the United Nations in the 1950's. The Southern Pacific and the Central Pacific held strategic positions on the western end of the transcontinental lines south of Portland. The pool could be kept alive only by submitting to their desires—to their dictation, it might be better to say. Such a policy was not to be expected from such vigorous personalities as Strong and Perkins.

In rates and in service standards the Central Pacific took full advantage of its strategic location. The Union Pacific and its Iowa allies had organized a through California service known as the California Fast Freight Line. On various pretexts the Central Pacific at Ogden refused to receive its cars. These cars, declared the Central Pacific, were of improper length or were not in suitable condition. Such delays made the shippers more inclined to send their business via the Sunset Route, thereby giving the Central and Southern Pacific a longer haul.[19] This friction continued for months. In October, the Central Pacific withdrew from the Freight Line and announced that it would not pay its share of the expenses nor contribute its percentage of cars.[20]

Competitive rivalries, despite all efforts made both in and out of the Association, became more and more embittered. Rates in the last three months of 1885 were cut as much as 40 per cent.[21] Efforts were made to reorganize the pool. They were of no avail. Even Huntington, that uncompromising advocate of his own railroad interests, became disturbed. In November he wrote to Adams suggesting that the owners and the managers of the properties meet to work out some amicable arrangements and to "lay a broader foundation for the conduct of this Trans-Continental business in the future. . . ."[22] Huntington was proposing the revival of personal relationships among owners and stockholders as a remedy. He was repeating in the fall of 1885 the kind of negotiations carried on between the stockholders of the Burlington and the Union Pacific in 1884. Both were equally unsuccessful. Adams gratefully responded to Huntington's initiative and entered into discussions with Perkins. Perkins was doubtful about the success of this new approach. "I don't see how Pools," he wrote "can exist if the ground taken by the Central Pacific is proper & I do not see how we can compromise—but we can meet Huntington & talk."[23]

Adams was more optimistic. He believed, as did Forbes, that discussions among executives and leading stockholders would bring about results. Adams was rather naive. "I'm well satisfied," he wrote, "after one year's experience of this sort of thing, that the fact that presidents are so afraid of each other, and will not come together, cultivating personal relations, has cost the railroad properties of this country many tens of millions of dollars. They get to fighting simply because they will not meet. . . . I think it would be well worth the while of all the leading railroads to give their presidents houses, say on Fifth Avenue or Commonwealth Avenue, or where not, in some block;—a sort of President's Road. Then they would walk down to their offices together in the morning, and I would be willing, I think, to wager my head that there would not be one quarrel then where there are five quarrels now." He did not, however, have complete faith in that childish optimism in regard to personal discussions.

"I simply am a go-between," he concluded, "carrying out my high mission among the railroads of the country. Here again I am simply acting as the friend of peace Probably, before we get through, both parties will unite in pitching into me. Nevertheless, so it was of old."[24] And so it soon proved to be anew.

There is no record available of the nature or of the results of these discussions. The efforts to reorganize the pool and restore the rates continued. The Atchison assumed an even more belligerent attitude. It now insisted that its claim as a transcontinental road be more fully recognized by an increase in the percentage of the pool's business and by the admission of the California Southern as a member of the pool. Nothing was accomplished. The pool was discontinued at the 1885 year end. Further efforts at reorganization continued but the parties could not agree, and in February the Association was formally dissolved and another slashing rate war followed.

The overexpansion of railroad facilities between the Mississippi River and the Pacific Coast and between the Canadian and Mexican boundaries culminated in a classical competitive price war. The public was now served with adequate facilities. The investors had committed many hundreds of millions of dollars over a short period in a search for a return on their investments. Some funds had been placed in bonds in the hope of securing a reasonable rate of return—reasonable, that is to say, in the light of interest rates. Others had committed their funds in exchange for stocks, in the hope of securing a higher return than that obtainable on bonds. The investors assumed greater risks, and those risks were realized in the form of heavy losses, both in the reduction or elimination of returns on investment funds and in a fall in stock prices.

Strong competition in a period of overexpansion produced little profit for the investor. The expansion of plant facilities to a point which led to price pressure was characteristic of a free enterprise economy. In the face of declines in selling prices, impairment of profit margins, reduction of dividends, and, in some cases, passing of interest, the forces of expansion led to renewed railroad building and overbuilding in the latter years of the decade. The degree of overexpansion was thereby intensified and an even more drastic succession of rate reductions followed. Repeated overexpansion is characteristic of a competitive economy. In the railroad industry, as in others, the forces leading to price stability and the emergence of a flow of reasonable returns come only after repeated price wars and the impairment of profits. The attainment of such a status was postponed in the railroad industry until the early part of the twentieth century. The extraordinary extension of railroad facilities in the late 1880's, in the face of repeated warnings by industry leaders and others of the dangers involved, are examined in the next two chapters.

Notes for Chapter XIV

[1] Report No. 46, Part 2, U. S. Senate, 49th Congress, 1st Session, Thomas L. Kimball, general traffic manager, Union Pacific, 1886, p. 1236.
[2] Towne to Crocker, Feb. 27, 1883, M. M.
[3] Crocker to Huntington June 28, 1883, M. M.
[4] *Ibid.*, June 29, 1883.
[5] *Ibid.*, Sept. 24, 1883.
[6] *Ibid.*, June 28, 1883.
[7] *Ibid.*, Sept. 28, 1883.
[8] The text on the agreement is given in Pac. Ry. Commission, p. 4260.
[9] *R. R. Gaz.*, Jan. 18, 1884, pp. 37, 54, for details on these negotiations.
[10] *Ibid.*, May 30, 1884, p. 419.
[11] *Ibid.*, June 6, 1884, p. 436.
[12] *Boston Transcript*, Aug. 27, 1884.
[13] *Chron.*, March 21, 1885, pp. 348–349.
[14] *Chicago Tribune*, March 15, 1885.
[15] *R. R. Gaz.*, April 3, 1885, p. 222.
[16] Burlington Archives, Perkins to Adams, June 16, 1885.
[17] *R. R. Gaz.*, June 26, 1885, p. 415.
[18] *Chicago Tribune*, Oct. 29, 1885.

[19] For statement of the obstacles thrown up by the Central Pacific, see *Boston Transcript*, Aug. 29, 1885.

[20] *R. R. Gaz.*, Oct. 23, 1885, p. 605.

[21] Estimate of Stubbs, traffic manager, Central Pacific in Pac. Ry. Commission, p. 3330.

[22] Burlington Archives, Huntington to Adams, Nov. 5, 1885.

[23] *Ibid.*, Perkins to Adams, Nov. 9, 1885.

[24] *Ibid.*, Adams to Perkins, Nov. 9, 1885.

XV

Expansion Program Renewed, 1886-1887
Central West

THE EXPANSION program initiated early in 1879 came to a halt by the end of 1882. It produced a heavy drain on the supply of savings. The difficulty of raising capital was one of the factors that impaired the economy and brought about the financial panic in 1884. Competition between the old and new routes reduced railroad rates, earnings, and dividends. It also catapulted a number of the weaker lines into receivership.

This turn of events inflicted heavy losses upon many leading railroad businessmen. Gould's imposing railroad empire crumbled.[1] Disaster also befell Huntington. In the Northwest the dramatic career of Villard was by 1883 brought to an unexpected termination. The Northern Pacific–Great Lakes–Pacific Coast route was finished, and so was Villard. The failure of Villard did, however, lead to an important expansion of the Northern Pacific. Its access to the Pacific Coast under Villard depended upon the Navigation. The Northern Pacific's new management was not so involved in the affairs of the Navigation. An important group, led by Charles Wright, a capitalist-promoter from Philadelphia, had made heavy real estate investments in Tacoma. This was an important factor, aside from the genuine merits of the action, in inducing the Northern Pacific to build the so-called Cascades division to Tacoma. This gave the Northern Pacific an outlet to the Pacific Coast, independent of the Navigation.

The relatively prosperous western railroads were no more inclined than their financially weak sisters to engage in new construction programs in the mid-1880's. The competitive status quo of many, perhaps most, of the western lines seemed, on the surface at least, to be insured by a number of contractual understandings. It was accordingly not surprising that in 1883–1885 there was agreement that the building of additional railroads would be a waste of capital. Even more significant was the almost universal chorus of condemnation by responsible commentators and railroad officials. Hughitt, general manager and soon to become president of the Northwestern, characterized the proposed building of a line on the eastern bank of the Mississippi River (soon to be carried out by the Burlington system) as "a needless paralleling [sic] of existing systems."[2] Cable of the Rock Island declared there were "already more roads than were needed both east and west of the Missouri River, and to build additional roads meant ruin to all the existing lines."[3] Potter, of the Burlington, declared in 1886, after the construction program had begun, "I am not a full believer by any means, in the great boom that seems to have struck the country. Perhaps I am on the wrong side but still I cannot see what upon earth there is to make our business any better than it has been or even as good. . . . I do not want you to understand by this that I am opposed to building new lines, but I think the business should be weighed well with the question of the construction of new lines."[4]

Forbes, in one of his characteristic diatribes, expressed a similar view. "The tribe of Hinckleys, Cranes, Graves, Villards, and other cranks and thieves led by Hopkins and Gould, have built and will build Roads wherever fools with money will follow, and where three roads stimulated by contracts, are thus built to do the work of one, it, in the very near future, leads right up to a necessity for the nearest solvent Railroad to buy the other useless ones."[5]

A western railroad journal observed that "the sentiment against unrestricted railway construction is growing stronger and stronger throughout the country," while the completion of new railroads to divert traffic from an existing road was a "needless destruction of capital."[6] A financial journal, reflecting the views of the investment community, joined this chorus of denunciation.[7]

Informed opinion could not, however, restrain the onrushing force of competitive realities, and these counsels of wisdom were lost in the scramble for position. The most active construction years in the history of the railroad industry were 1886 and 1887. Another period of overexpansion was added to the overexpansion of 1879–1883. The losses to investors were heavy; the destruction of capital, at least over the short run, confirmed the predictions of experts both in and outside the industry. The public, however, was well served. Rates were slashed and this induced a reduction of operating costs that kept rates at a low level for many years to come.

The race to capture the traffic of new areas was the dynamic force. The building by one road of even a relatively unimportant branch into the territory of another road was enough to elicit a challenging construction threat from the latter. The earnings likely to flow from the competition of the new line was not usually the controlling consideration. If an invasion was not countered it was feared that the building of one branch would be followed by the construction of others. The best defense in this case, as in military matters, was a strong offense, and the offense took the form of retaliatory building of roads into areas served by the invading road. Overbuilding might be dangerous, but, as Perkins once expressed it, "We could better afford to take the risk of having some property on our hands which would not pay very much *directly*, than to take the chance of having the country occupied by our enemies."[8] Business, furthermore, could be carried either by one railroad from origin to destination or by a combination of roads. A road which controlled the traffic from origin to destination under one full ownership competed with a multi-line route consisting of two or more roads under separate ownerships. The relationships between the members of a multi-line route were complicated. Such problems as the division of the through rate among the participating roads; the character of the equipment used in the multi-line service; the time required to transfer cars between one line and another; the nature of the time schedules; the character of the service rendered on one line as compared with another, both of which were parts of the through-route—these were only some of the problems that required continuous adjustment. If the participating lines served separate areas, if they did not compete with each other in any part of the systems, then they were considered as friendly connections. If, however, a connecting road carrying through traffic for an originating line competed with that line, then the connections were competitive and unfriendly. There was, therefore, a competitive urge to create one-line hauls wherever possible, to replace multi-line hauls that included the lines of a competitor.

This desire to control the movement of through traffic over a single-ownership or single-control system was supplemented by the need to control a large volume of local traffic. It is difficult to draw hard and fast distinctions between the competition for local and for through traffic.

Invasion of the local preserves of one road might be countered by a retaliatory invasion of the aggressor's local territory. Or, under other conditions, it might be met with construction into new areas designed to serve through traffic. Such, for example, was the countermove by the Burlington in retaliation for the construction by the Missouri Pacific of a relatively short line into southeastern Nebraska. The Burlington contended that the Missouri Pacific line was an invasion of its territory, in violation of a signed contract. The Burlington countered by construction of its Denver line.[9] In some cases no retaliation followed invasions, but threats and counterthreats kept the relations between the rival roads in a state of ferment.

There were still other causes for the second expansion boom of the decade. One was the abundant supply of funds and the accompanying low interest rates. Savings, combined with a low demand for capital, had by 1886 reduced interest rates on high grade corporate bonds to a $2\frac{1}{2}$ per cent basis—not much higher than the return on United States government bonds.[10] The demand for railroad bonds was described in a financial journal as "genuine" and "of large volume."[11] Also, prices of railroad construction supplies were low and there was the general belief that they would soon advance. "With money plenty and a possible boom in prices ahead of us," declared Perkins, "I have felt, on the whole, as if delay in such matter [railroad building] might be dangerous."[12] Whether prices would advance was not certain; it was certain that prices then were low. Roads could be built at little more than $500 a mile in interest, "painfully close" to others which required $1,000 to $1,200.[13]

These general considerations take life and form in an analysis of the competitive forces actually prevailing in the territory west of the Missouri in the middle 1880's. The competitive problems were acute in an area between the Canadian boundary and the Rockies on the north, the Twin Cities-Chicago-Lake Superior region on the northwest, and a line on the south from Kansas City west through southern Kansas to Colorado. The region between the Missouri River and Colorado-Wyoming-Montana districts is also included. Here, between 1883 and 1885, every important center was connected by railroad, and in most cases by a number of roads. There were three competitors for the Twin Cities-Chicago business. The Burlington had an Omaha line, but none to the Twin Cities. It did, however, have a relatively short route to Kansas City.

West of the Missouri the Union Pacific and the Burlington operated lines. From Denver to Ogden the Union Pacific competed with the Rio Grande. The Union Pacific and the Burlington had long been at logger-heads over their relative competitive positions.

East of the Missouri River, the St. Paul, Rock Island, and North-western, among others, competed with the Burlington for Omaha–Chicago business. Both the Union Pacific and its connections, other than the Burlington, were dissatisfied with the competitive dispensation at the Omaha junction. The Tripartite Pact of 1883 was an unsuccessful attempt to solve this problem. Negotiations followed, with the view of adjusting these relations on a basis of business peace.

In these discussions Gould and Dillon, the latter still president of the Union Pacific, were ignored. The road's emissaries were Adams, elected to the board in 1883, and Ames, a large stockholder who also represented a number of other substantial holders. The Burlington refused to make any substantial concessions to the Union Pacific. Both roads made plans to build into each other's territory, and on both sides strong feelings were entertained over the motives of the other. Adams believed that he was being "waylaid by pirates"; while a Burlington official believed that the alliance of the Union Pacific with the St. Paul and the Rock Island in the Tripartite had in its inception "an inimical and piratical intent."[14] While these conversations continued, the financial strength of the Union Pacific waned and the market price of its stock declined. Dividends were passed in June, and its management changed. Adams, who was appointed president, felt "quite strongly" that the Burlington was planning to take advantage of the Union Pacific's unfortunate condition with a view of driving the road "to the Wall."[15]

In this battle of fears and threats, of suspicions and countersuspicions, the Union Pacific had a dangerous weapon in the form of two controlled roads: the Central Branch Union Pacific and the St. Joseph and Western (a successor to the St. Joseph). The first was owned by the Union Pacific but leased on a temporary basis to the Missouri Pacific. The road, accord-to Perkins, occupied a rich region in Kansas and was a "very valuable" property for the Missouri Pacific. It could be used as the basis for another line to Denver. Gould was anxious to buy the property. The other road, the St. Joseph and Western, connected with the Union Pacific in southern Nebraska and joined the Burlington at St. Joseph, Mis-souri. Cable offered to buy and the Union Pacific was ready to make the sale. As it turned out, a difference in price blocked the transaction.

The threat of selling the roads to the Missouri Pacific and the Rock Island made a deep impression upon the minds of the Burlington officials The repeated postponement of the Burlington's extension plans north and west through Nebraska and Wyoming were due in part, at least, to the reports that the Union Pacific had not yet sold either one or both of these properties to the Burlington's competitors. Perkins asserted that the St. Joseph and Western road was "no part of their [Union Pacific] system but is part of ours."[16]

Still another competitive factor in the middle 1880's characterized the Nebraska area. The Northwestern had expanded rapidly in Wisconsin and Iowa, and to some extent in Minnesota and Dakota. It had not, however, penetrated Nebraska or Kansas. By the purchase of the Sioux City and Pacific and its allied lines, it acquired some mileage in northeastern Nebraska, but none south of the Platte River. There was at that time a substantial movement of lumber from Wisconsin to the treeless prairies of southern Nebraska. Keep complained that the Burlington was not giving Northwestern "a fair show on the lumber" to that territory, though the Burlington denied the charge.[17] The Northwestern as early as 1883 had threatened to invade southern Nebraska, and in 1885 it built a line to Lincoln.

Further southwest in Kansas another competitive factor developed. The Atchison, with little competition, had served southern Kansas throughout the 1870's and early 1880's. Late in 1882, it decided, as did so many others, to build no more lines. It did not, however, reckon with Gould. Acting indirectly and unobtrusively, Gould began a move into southern Kansas. There he observed the growth of a small road—the St. Louis, Fort Scott and Wichita. This company, organized to build between Fort Scott and Wichita, opened for business in July, 1881. In 1882 Gould acquired a majority of its stock. In the spring of 1883 the Wichita began to build west into the center of the Atchison territory. The Atchison management began to review its decision to build no more roads. In the language of a New England journal that closely followed the property's affairs, it appeared "that to maintain the prosperity peace must be abandoned."[18] It was not to be expected that the Atchison would permit its territory to be invaded without taking retaliatory measures. And such measures included the building of lines both in its own territory in southern Kansas and into the territory of the invaders. The Atchison did not act hastily, although, according to a Boston paper, it was "furtively watching" every movement of the Wichita.[19]

Thus in a vast territory all the roads, against their own will, against their repeated desires to avoid the building of new roads, found themselves forced into major building programs. The Burlington was determined to build to the Twin Cities and so to share in the growing business of the Northwest; the St. Paul and Northwestern promised to retaliate by building to Kansas City; the St. Paul and Rock Island, dissatisfied with their inability to command much of the traffic of the trans-Missouri Valley area, were determined to build into that region. If the Atchison's friendly eastern connections built west of the Missouri River, thus invading the Atchison's territory, it was likely that the Atchison would retaliate by building east from Kansas City. This is what it actually did.

The same line of reasoning led the Burlington officials to suggest that, though no new roads were needed west of the Missouri, if the Rock Island and the St. Paul did build there "they would expect retaliation on the part of the Burlington and the Chicago & Northwestern wherever the latter Companies should find an opportunity for it."[20] Both the St. Paul and the Rock Island finally concluded that the Tripartite, as a means of securing a "fair and equitable share" of the trans-Missouri business, was unsuccessful. As the months rolled on in 1884 and 1885 the prospects of a war of construction, with the possibility of widespread rate concessions, grew increasingly certain. Despite the competition between the Northwestern, Burlington, and Union Pacific west of the Missouri, they had a common interest in protecting the territory against the St. Paul and Rock Island. Perkins, Adams, and Hughitt, representing respectively the Burlington, Union Pacific, and Northwestern, therefore entered into discussions in order to arrange a common front against the potential invaders. Perkins suggested to Adams, that the three roads agree about division of the territory, the agreement to be "kept quiet and out of sight, because of public feeling." To such an agreement the Northwestern, in the opinion of Perkins, would give its assent "because if there was to be a trial of strength and swiftness out there, the C. B. & Q. would probably go north of the Platte, into the region which the Northwestern wants to occupy, and the U. P. might do the same." Perkins, approaching the Northwestern official through Potter, directed the latter to ascertain whether Hughitt was willing to disclose his intentions about the North Platte country. It would not be expedient for the Burlington to sit still "and see the Northwestern gobble the whole North Platte country." Potter was therefore asked to ascertain Hughitt's views. What the three roads—Burlington, Union Pacific, and Northwestern—wanted, wrote Perkins, was "an arrangement of some kind by which the country West of the Missouri River can be held by them while the Rock Island and the St. Paul are held at the River. If we can maintain that situation for five years longer, we can so thoroughly occupy that country that the temptation will be very slight to anybody else to build over there."[21] The "haves" wanted to exclude the "have nots."

While the Burlington was thus trying to achieve a peaceful relationship in Nebraska, it was preparing an invasion of the Twin Cities–Chicago area. To the three routes in this region two more had been added by 1885. The Twin Cities business was well worth fighting for. The population of St. Paul between 1880 and 1885 had increased from 41,000 to almost 112,000, and that of Minneapolis from 47,000 to 129,000.[22] Further evidence of the increasing volume of traffic over this route is disclosed by the tonnage data of the Rock Island. Between 1881 and 1885 its flour business increased from approximately 88 million pounds to 379 million, and wheat from 124 million pounds to 247 million.[23] Flour and wheat traffic was the kind of business that moved largely from the Twin Cities to Chicago. Another important traffic was lumber. "In no part of the United States," wrote Forbes, "are the chances of a rapid and healthy growth so promising as in the region of the Northwest beyond Minneapolis and St. Paul, which by themselves represent 200,000 people, with active capital, and the abundant energy of a thrifty, hardy, northern population."[24]

The possibility of such an extension was first called to the Burlington's attention in 1883; and between that time and the summer of 1885 the Burlington had spent approximately $800 thousand in surveying the area and taking steps necessary to occupy the ground in advance of construction.[25]

Public announcement of financial support of a Twin Cities–Chicago line was made in July, 1885.[26] It seemed, both to its competitors and to the public, that the Burlington had adopted an aggressive policy and that it had invaded an area thickly occupied by other roads. "Public necessity," declared a leading financial journal, did not call for this extension. "The section through which it runs is already over supplied with roads. It is not demanded by any interest of the Company, for it is clearly outside of the territory which the Burlington can legitimately call its own. . . . It cannot but provoke hostility and strife, and lower rates and profits as a result. . . . In a word it is entirely outside the pale of conservative action, unnecessary and uncalled for, and so far from being justifiable, borders close on to recklessness."[27]

To the competitors of the Burlington this extension appeared to be rank aggression. Hughitt, according to Potter, said many things about this line "that it is not worth while for me to repeat."[28] Keep declared the line was being built in accordance with an understanding with Hill of the Manitoba, and that the business controlled by his road would be given to the new extension. Hill denied such an understanding, but Keep was suspicious. "We have no faith in Mr. Hill's statement. We have no doubt he is interested in the new line."[29]

To the St. Paul, this Burlington extension was equally distasteful. Philip Armour, the meat packer of Chicago and one of the St. Paul's largest stockholders, condemned the action. His complaint carried little weight with Perkins. It "reminds one of Satan reproving sin," was his rejoinder.[30] The Burlington–St. Paul dispute was a classic case of retaliation. The former asserted that the Twin Cities line was only a retaliation for the St. Paul's Council Bluffs line. The St. Paul had first (in 1882) invaded the Burlington territory. Now the Burlington was invading the enclave of the St. Paul. The St. Paul's answer was the further invasion of the Burlington country. Soon after the announcement of the proposed Burlington-supported extension, the St. Paul organized surveys to prepare for the construction of a Kansas City line.

This move, like the Burlington's Twin Cities action, was also condemned. An authoritative railroad periodical thought that a little interchanging with each other would give them what they needed without their having to build new roads. But the major western roads seemed to believe that "each must have a line to every place where any competitor has a line."[31]

The Northwestern was somewhat slower in reacting than the St. Paul. That road moved in two directions: south of the Platte River to Lincoln, and west by its Sioux City line into the range-cattle country of northern Nebraska and Wyoming. Keep told Adams that he was determined to build south because the Burlington had invaded its territory. He was sorry to cross the Union Pacific "or to do anything against its interest, but replied, in very strong language, that they must punish the C. B. & Q., even if, in doing so they also punished the Union Pacific."[32]

The Rock Island's move west of the Missouri River was delayed even longer than that of the Northwestern. The extension involved such a change of policy as to produce a strong opposition in the board of directors. The opposition was led by Riddle. The pro-expansion leader was Cable. Potter, though recognizing his ability, had little love for Cable. Cable, said Potter on one occasion, was "a bulldozer and wants something that belongs to someone else."[33] Cable probably returned this compliment, though no records are available to prove this inference. The first move of the Rock Island was apparently a compromise between the viewpoints of the expansionists and the anti-expansionists. Cable sent out a corps of engineers to examine the country between the Union Pacific and the Northwestern—this was the idea of exerting pressure on the Union Pacific to sell the St. Joseph and Western.[34] After further examination, Cable offered $7 million payable in Rock Island bonds. Adams declined to sell at this price. He could do better, he said, with another road. Cable would not pay more, and if the Union Pacific did not sell he would parallel that road for 150 miles.[35]

While the St. Paul, Northwestern, and Rock Island were thus reacting to the Burlington's moves along the Twin Cities–Chicago route, the Burlington and the Atchison were reacting to the moves made by Gould in Kansas. After months of trading the Union Pacific leased the Central Branch to the Missouri Pacific for twenty-eight years. Gould promised not to extend the line to Denver, and this seemed to be the reason for Adams' decision. Gould, via the Missouri Pacific, was thus introduced into an area from which he could make extensions into the Burlington territory.

Forbes now surrendered his long-maintained conviction of the necessity of peaceable relationships with the Union Pacific: "It seems to me wise to organize and be prepared for war." He was, however, not yet prepared to declare open warfare. "I surely would not begin building, or take any steps which will even informally commit us to building the important line from Grand Island northwest, which makes the absolute break with Adams." He had, however, lost his respect for Adams as a shrewd business negotiator. Adams' dealings with Gould showed his "utter incapacity to wrestle with that unscrupulous enemy. . . ." Though he was certain that war with the Union Pacific was justified, he still hesitated. Would

it not be advisable, he suggested, to "rest content with our Burlington &
Northern [Twin Cities extension] and after giving warning to Adams of
our views of the effect of his ill-advised alliance with Gould, do nothing
more this fall which we are not free to do without formally breaking up
our understanding with him?"[36]

Perkins, on the other hand, was determined to move ahead almost
immediately. He described his building plans and explained their potential value. The territory through which the road would be built was fast
filling up with people, and in Wyoming and western Nebraska there
were growing cattle and mining areas. The Burlington's extension would
stir up Adams and the Union Pacific, admitted Perkins, but that should
be ignored. "If, with an agreement not to do that which affects the
interest of the other without notice and consultation," Perkins argued,
"Adams feels free to sell the Central Branch to Gould, and expressly
agrees that he may build to Nebraska City—where Adams has no interest,
—and to Lincoln, where he has little, and in both of which towns we
have a large interest, what protection do we get from the relations of
peace and friendship we have been trying to cultivate?"[37]

The views of Forbes as usual triumphed. The Burlington again postponed its long-delayed plans to build north of the Platte. Perkins then
entered into further negotiations with Adams. The conversations led to
nothing, and the Burlington board in December finally approved a building program into the North Platte country. Adams charged that in trying
to protect its own interests the Burlington was doing what it can "to
destroy the property of the Union Pacific." The new lines into the North
Platte country "would inflict great injury, presumably designed." Because of the Missouri Pacific's lease of the Central Branch and the threatened invasion of the South Platte country by the Rock Island and the
Northwestern, the Burlington finally decided that it must complete its
system in northern Nebraska without delay.[38]

In southern Kansas the Gould moves involved primarily the Atchison.
Gould's Missouri Pacific and the Atchison had an understanding not to
invade each other's territory. The Missouri Pacific agreed with the letter
of the contract but not with its spirit. Or rather it might be said more
accurately that while the Missouri Pacific observed the agreement, Gould
personally violated its spirit. By early 1884 an official of the Gould railroad family was appointed president of the Wichita, thereby making it
clear that the road was under the Missouri Pacific's influence; and by the

fall of 1885 the Wichita had been extended to a point near the major gateway to the Oklahoma cattle traffic of the Atchison.

The Atchison, except for completing some unfinished projects, had done little new building since the fall of 1883. It now changed its policy. Gould's moves set the stage for the Atchison's expansion plans. It was in Kansas that the Atchison, recognizing the weakness of its defensive policy, lashed out in a battle against Gould. In early 1886, through a subsidiary, it announced plans for the building of 450 miles in Kansas, while the Missouri Pacific projected an even more ambitious program.

By early 1886 the plans were all set for the extraordinary railroad building that followed in 1886 and 1887. This new boom was unlike the 1879-1883 expansion. The latter consisted largely of the building of new through lines between areas not then served by railroad facilities. The later boom, however, was different. Lines were built through areas already adequately, and in most cases more than adequately, served by existing lines. The new through lines projected in 1885 and early in 1886 for the most part paralleled existing lines. Once the programs were initiated, as they were largely by the spring of 1886, they fed upon themselves. Each new addition seemed to make even further additions more attractive.

By the end of 1887 the Missouri Pacific had completed a line from eastern Kansas to Pueblo. There it made a contract with the Rio Grande which led it into the Colorado mountain country. In order that it might accommodate the prospective increase in traffic expected to arise from this affiliation, the Rio Grande agreed to build a third rail on its narrow-gauge road. By the time the Missouri Pacific's extension was completed the third rail was finished. The Missouri Pacific now had a through line from the Missouri Valley to an independent connection with the Huntington system at Ogden. The Atchison recognizing the implications of this new development abandoned its trackage agreement with the Rio Grande. It was offered another agreement by the Denver and New Orleans. This Strong refused. His experience with the Rio Grande had been unsatisfactory.[39] Strong's refusal led the Denver and New Orleans, with the "tacit acquiescence" of the Union Pacific, to proceed with its plans for further construction to complete the Panhandle Route. Strong retaliated quickly with the building of a parallel Pueblo–Denver line.[40]

By the spring of 1886, furthermore, the plans of the Rock Island for the extension of its lines west of the Missouri River had already been publicly formulated. In April it announced a proposal for the issue of $10 million bonds to finance the program. The Rock Island, after threatening to build north and thereby to compete with the Burlington and the Union Pacific, decided to move south, thereby to compete more largely with the Atchison. From St. Joseph it built southwest across Kansas, reaching Liberal in the southern corner early in 1888. It also extended due west across Kansas, and with the aid of a trackage agreement with the Union Pacific reached Denver and Colorado Springs later in the same year.

The Rock Island invasion of the trans-Missouri River area led the Atchison finally to adopt long-considered retaliatory steps. The Atchison's lines terminated at Kansas City. The road had served Chicago and the Middle West by a variety of traffic agreements. It was the history of such contracts, observed the Atchison in its 1886 Annual Report, that they were effective only so long as it was to the interest of the parties to make them so, and broken as soon as they became burdensome to either party. An official of the road insisted that there was no desire to build east of the Missouri River—it had satisfactory outlets over other roads; but those roads had now invaded the territory served by the Atchison. The other lines had ample facilities for reaching the sections traversed by the Atchison system. An invasion of the trans-Missouri area by the eastern lines must be met by a corresponding invasion of the East by the western lines. "If," declared this official, "we were to keep out of their Eastern territory, they could cut our rates at will and we would have to meet them in the best paying country we traverse without being able to strike them at any vulnerable point. But by building to Chicago we shall be on an equal footing, and can say to them if they demoralize our Kansas business we will hurt them equally as bad in Missouri, Iowa and Illinois. . . . We don't want a war, but peace, and the only way to secure and keep it is by being in a position to defend our interests at every point."[41]

The Atchison therefore decided early in 1886 to construct its own Kansas City–Chicago line. The Atchison and the Burlington had long been friendly connections and the latter had delivered a good volume of traffic to the former at Kansas City. Furthermore, there were large common stock-holdings in both roads. The Burlington accordingly made approaches to the Atchison in an effort to dissuade it from building a Chicago extension. Perkins in June wrote to Strong that he understood that while the Atchison seriously considered the idea of such a line it had not "positively & definitely" decided to build. The Burlington had also considered the idea of invading the Atchison territory by the construction of a Kansas line. Therefore, continued Perkins, "it seemed to me to be for the interest of both of us, that before it goes further you and I would try to reach an understanding & to prevent if possible the building of unnecessary railroads." The Burlington-owned roads could carry all the business likely to be offered between Kansas City and Chicago for many years to come, at lower rates than any new road could carry it. Perkins also assured Strong that the Atchison could provide for all the business which a Burlington extension could develop in Kansas and to better advantage than could the Burlington. Perkins accordingly reached the rational conclusion "that by acting together we can probably make for our combined constituency two dollars against one dollar if we act independently & in antagonism—in the one case we can make a dollar a piece & in the other fifty cents."[42]

The arguments of Perkins were sound, but they fell on deaf ears. By the fall of the year the Atchison announced its plan of issuing $20 million of bonds to finance the Chicago extensions. Forbes now took over. Perhaps Strong might be dissuaded from building the extension by an arrangement to make rates between Kansas City and points east for a term of years. This move also failed. In response to the suggestion of Potter and Perkins of "getting a Backfire," Forbes thought it might be well to tell the Burlington's stockholders of the "threatened mischief" which would follow from the building of the Atchison's Chicago line. Such a move, thought Forbes, would "indirectly set those stockholders who are also owners of Atchison on the right track as to its effect on them in both stocks."[43] Forbes now conceived an even more advanced and really Machiavellian idea. The Burlington had expensive unmortgaged lines west of the Missouri River. Why not inquire from the bankers upon what terms these lines could be mortgaged to secure a $10 million 40-year, 4 per cent bond issue. If the Burlington were to ask for this sum when the Atchison was in the market for $20 million, "it will be apparent enough that trouble is on hand and may embarrass the Atchison."[44] None of these moves succeeded, and it became clear by the fall of 1886 that the Atchison would build the Chicago line. The extensions, actual and proposed, of the Atchison, Rock Island, and Northwestern led the Burlington in December, 1885, to proceed with its long-delayed construc-

tion program north of the Platte River. This constituted an invasion of
Union Pacific territory. Adams described this move as "a declaration of
war," and, as was his custom from time to time, used some bitter language.
He suggested that the Burlington wanted him to turn over the Union
Pacific to that company.[45] The Burlington's building program north of
Platte toward Wyoming amounted to an invasion of the territory of the
Union Pacific, and it meant a construction war with the Northwestern.
It did not, however, constitute retaliation against the Chicago extension
of the Atchison. The latter's profitable traffic strength lay in southern
Kansas. In the summer of 1886, accordingly, the Burlington, convinced
that the extension of the Atchison to Chicago was a reasonable certainty,
laid plans to extend its line from northern Kansas, at Concordia, southwest into the center of the Atchison's territory. In mid-June a party was
sent into the field for the purpose of locating a line. Such a line, furthermore, would share in the Kansas traffic as a competitor of the proposed
Rock Island line. The report of the field trip was ready by early September. Potter recommended that if the Atchison began its Chicago extension
the Burlington should build its Kansas line. Furthermore, declared
Potter, "if we expect to get a strong line of road through Kansas we
cannot put it off much longer."[46]

After long consideration Perkins decided that there was no urgency
in the building of this mileage. It might be better, he thought, to wait another year than to "push in there now and enter on a race with the Rock
Island, the Santa Fe and other companies for the occupation of particular
places." After a lengthy analysis of construction problems in Kansas and
Nebraska, Perkins concluded with the broad, statesman-like judgment
that the Burlington could not build everywhere at once, "and it becomes
necessary to judge, therefore, where it is most important to do so."[47]

The delay of a year, as things turned out, proved fatal to the Kansas
extension. By that time other events to be examined in subsequent chapters precluded the possibility of raising funds to finance any ambitious
extensions. The Nebraska building program, however, did not lag long.
By August of 1886 the Burlington began to build in Nebraska, both south
and north of the Platte River. By the end of the year the program was in
full flower.

By early 1887, accordingly, the railroad-building strategy between
the Twin Cities–Chicago line on the north and the Kansas–Nebraska–
eastern Colorado line on the south was clearly determined. The Atchison

was moving east beyond the river to Chicago. The Northwestern, for the first time moved into Nebraska south of the Platte River and invaded the Burlington's area. The Burlington for the first time moved north of the Platte River and competed there with the Northwestern and the Union Pacific. The Northwestern moved west through Nebraska into Wyoming, and made plans for an extension to the Pacific Coast.[48] The Rock Island for the first time moved west of the Missouri River, with intentions, according to published reports, to extend to El Paso and beyond. The Rock Island, as well as the Missouri Pacific, also moved west to eastern Colorado and from there, by trackage and traffic alliances, secured through routes via the Rio Grande and the Rio Grande Western, to Ogden.

Competition was now stimulated along new lines. It was brought about not by new or financially weak companies but by well-established corporations with good credit standings. They had little difficulty in raising the sums necessary to finance these new programs. They did not have to resort to construction companies nor to speculative bond-stock offerings. Even Gould, the leader in the field of speculative capital, found it no longer necessary to use the construction company. The Missouri Pacific financed its construction program by the sale of its own stocks and bonds.

While the competitive forces thus expressed themselves, conservative opinion still was not certain about the ultimate success of this new building rage. The Union Pacific, under the leadership of Adams, spent its time and energy in fortifying its financial position. It did relatively little building. Though Adams planned, he did not act, even though the expansion by rival lines damaged the Union Pacific's business. Prior to the building of the Northwestern's line into Wyoming about a hundred miles north of Cheyenne, for example, the Union Pacific did 75 per cent of the cattle business. By the fall of 1886 the same percentage was being carried by the Northwestern.[49] Not until the fall of 1886 did the Union Pacific begin to consider the adoption of a policy of competitive construction designed to develop new traffic to replace that lost to its competitors. It then became obvious to Adams "that the Union Pacific has arrived . . . at a point where it must enter upon the stage of active development. We cannot longer continue our present waiting policy." Adams believed that competitive efforts should be directed primarily in the area west of Cheyenne. He wanted to build on the west side of the continental divide in the valleys of western Colorado, with a view of reaching the coal and coke fields in the rapidly developing area of Aspen. He would also "develop vigorously" in western Idaho and in southeastern Oregon. East of Cheyenne and Denver, in the area through which so many new lines were under construction, he would build "only as much as was necessary to protect existing business." To aid the board to reach a conclusion, Adams asked Dodge to survey the entire system and make recommendations.[50]

Forbes, like Adams, also preserved a strong sense of caution. Though, as chairman of the board, he had approved the Burlington's building program, he insisted that it be limited to those lines which could promise some profit. As to the wisdom of the whole building program there was, of course, "room for doubt. We are always liable to catch the infection of such an atmosphere of R. R. building as is now prevailing, and of course always liable to make mistakes."[51] The banner construction year of 1887 was also featured by more competition along the St. Paul–Minneapolis–Chicago through route. A new competitor emerged in the form of the so-called Stickney Road. G. B. Stickney in 1886 was president of a small line from St. Paul to a point in Iowa. This road through a traffic arrangement afforded the Illinois Central access to St. Paul. By the fall of 1887, however, Stickney, with the help largely of British capital, succeeded in financing a consolidation of other properties with his road. Title to these and some newly built lines, was passed to a new corporation, the Chicago, St. Paul and Kansas City. A new through line was thereby created between St. Paul and Chicago and between St. Paul and Kansas City.

Another entrant into the Chicago–St. Paul traffic race was the Wisconsin Central. That road by the end of 1887 had completed its Chicago connection. Though financially and physically weak, it served nevertheless to exert additional pressure upon the rate structure. This road was financed by a new group of capitalists including John D. Rockefeller, who, according to press reports, owned a "large portion" of the stock.[52]

The construction program in the Midwest, including the St. Paul–Chicago area, though it was the major one, was by no means the only one in western railroad territory. Another program, gaining its main impetus from Hill's colorful personality, was underway in the territory west of the Twin Cities. In the southwest the building programs were somewhat smaller. These construction and expansion programs will be surveyed in the following chapter.

Notes for Chapter XV

[1] For details see *Gould*, Chap. XXI, pp. 411–425.
[2] Joy Papers, Hughitt to Joy, Aug. 20, 1885.
[3] *Ry. Review*, Aug. 16, 1884, p. 428.
[4] Burlington Archives, Potter to Perkins, Jan. 2, 1886.
[5] *Ibid.*, Forbes to Perkins, Aug. 25, 1885.
[6] *Ry. Review*, Oct. 3, 1885, pp. 472, 477.
[7] *Chron.*, Aug. 29, 1885, p. 231.
[8] Burlington Archives, Perkins to Potter, Jan. 5, 1886.
[9] For details on this construction and retaliatory action, see *Gould*, Chap. XII, pp. 244–249.
[10] *Chron.*, June 26, 1886, p. 766.
[11] *Bankers Magazine*, July 1886, p. 78.
[12] Burlington Archives, Perkins to Potter, Jan. 5, 1886.
[13] *R. R. Gaz.*, July 2, 1886, p. 458.
[14] Burlington Archives, Holdrege to Perkins, May 22, 1884.
[15] *Ibid.*, May 17, 1884.
[16] *Ibid.*, Perkins to Forbes, Jan. 30, 1884.
[17] *Ibid.*, Potter to Perkins, Dec. 3, 1885.
[18] *Boston Transcript*, July 25, 1883.
[19] *Ibid.*, April 9, 1884.
[20] Burlington Archives, Aug. 20, 1884, Boston Memorandum, unsigned, but from its text clearly the work of Perkins.
[21] *Ibid.*, Perkins to Potter, Mar. 27, 1885.
[22] *Boston Transcript*, Aug. 25, 1885.
[23] *Chron.*, June 12, 1886, p. 708.
[24] Burlington Archives, Forbes to an unnamed correspondent, Aug. 1885.
[25] Annual Report, Burlington, 1888, p. 22.
[26] Details of the financial arrangments between the Burlington and the company building the line in *Chron.*, Aug. 8, 1885, p. 160.
[27] *Ibid.*, Aug. 29, 1885, p. 233.
[28] Burlington Archives, Potter to Perkins, Jan. 6, 1886.
[29] Northwestern Archives, Keep to Sykes, Aug. 18, 1885.
[30] Burlington Archives, Perkins to Potter, Sept. 4, 1885.
[31] *R. R. Gaz.*, Oct. 2, 1885, p. 631.
[32] Burlington Archives; Perkins in a letter to Potter, Jan. 6, 1886, credits Keep with these remarks in a letter written by Keep to Adams, seen by Perkins.
[33] *Ibid.*, Potter to Perkins, June 23, 1886.
[34] *Ibid.*, Potter to Perkins, Nov. 27, 1885.
[35] *Ibid.*, Potter to Perkins, May 22, 1886.
[36] *Ibid.*, Forbes to Perkins, Oct. 30, 1885.
[37] *Ibid.*, Perkins to Forbes, Oct. 25, 1885.
[38] *Ibid.*, Perkins to Adams, Dec. 31, 1885.
[39] Overton, p. 147.
[40] *Ibid.*, p. 150.
[41] *Ry. Review*, June 5, 1886, p. 286.
[42] Burlington Archives, Perkins to Strong, June 5, 1886.
[43] *Ibid.*, Forbes to Perkins, Oct. 24, 1886.

[44] *Ibid.*, Ladd to Griswold, Oct. 27, 1886.

[45] These are the remarks attributed to Adams by Perkins in the letter of Perkins to Adams, Dec. 28, 1885, in the Burlington Archives.

[46] *Ibid.*, Potter to Perkins, Sept. 2, 1886.

[47] *Ibid.*, Perkins to Potter, Jan. 4, 1887.

[48] See on this point Robert J. Casey and W. A. S. Douglas, *Pioneer Railroad*, (New York: McGraw-Hill, 1948), p. 139.

[49] *Chicago Tribune*, Oct. 6, 1886. Testimony by shippers in the area on the diversion of business from the Union Pacific to the Northwestern is found in Pac. Ry. Commission, pp. 2069, 2101.

[50] Dodge Papers, Adams to General G. M. Dodge, Sept. 2, 1886.

[51] Burlington Archives, Forbes to N. M. Beckwith, April 14, 1887.

[52] *Chicago Tribune*, Nov. 16, 1887.

XVI

Expansion Program Renewed, 1886-1887
Northwest and Southwest

THE LEADERS during the railroad-expansion decade of the 1880's present an instructive study in contrasts. Some, like Mitchell, Gould, and Huntington, were strong-minded expansionists. They moved earliest in the winter of 1878–1879, when depression influences still motivated business policies. They acted boldly in the face of heavy risks, thereby securing the inestimable advantage of low construction costs, and they also risked the possibility that the lightly populated frontier areas would not grow quickly enough to justify the heavy investments. Just as important was the danger involved in buying stock control of roads with heavy interest charges arising partly out of past financial errors and more largely out of high prices in previous construction eras, particularly in the late 1860's and the early 1870's.

Other businessmen were conservative to the point of refusing to expand except under the utmost competitive pressure. Riddle and Adams were such men. There were men of still other temperaments. Though conservative, they were open-minded and realistic, ever ready to examine new and changing conditions, to expand and to build if need be. Keep and Forbes were men of this latter type.

Keep was essentially conservative, though his mind was not closed to the necessity of risk-incurring expansion when and as circumstances required. The Northwestern board, under the leadership of Vanderbilt until his death in December, 1885, was even more conservative. Keep, for example, was ready to retaliate against the Burlington–St. Paul line with a line to Kansas City. Uppermost in his mind was the excessive cost of such a venture. Nevertheless, he asserted that if his board stood "square-ly and positively with us" he would, despite the cost, favor the building

of the line.[1] Keep had been at the helm for many years, and was destined
to pass away shortly after the beginning of the construction boom. He
was replaced by Hughitt, his able general manager from the very beginning of his administration in 1873. Hughitt was Keep's commanding
officer on the construction battle front. He made the surveys on the
steadily receding American frontier in Minnesota, Dakota, Iowa, Nebraska, and Wyoming. These surveys were usually, though not always,
followed by the building of railroad mileage. Keep and Hughitt were
the twin leaders in the camp of the Northwestern. Hughitt, as president
after 1887, was even more conservative than Keep. Hughitt did not build
on a major scale.

The Burlington's expansion was carried out under the co-operative
leadership of Forbes, Perkins, and Potter, respectively chairman, president, and vice-president. Forbes, was the veteran Nestor of the western
railway world. During his long business career he had substantial stock
ownership in almost all the western roads. His position of leadership was
respected, and he did not hesitate to assert it. He was sarcastic and
savage in his criticism both of his business foes and associates. Under his
leadership the Burlington built up a substantial financial reserve in 1883
and 1884; but even with this financially solid background, he refused to
support a program of expansion in the panic days of 1884. Perkins was a
younger man than Forbes. He had neither the personal fortune of Forbes
nor his capitalist following. He did, however, possess a lively imagination.
Intimately acquainted with the strategy of western railroads, he developed the road's construction programs years before they were put into
practice. His actions were, of course, subject to the approval of the board.
And the board, frequently in line with the views of Forbes, delayed their
fulfillment. Potter was the field man of Perkins, as Hughitt was of Keep.
Frequently he carried out Perkins' suggestions, but upon many occasions
he developed plans on his own initiative. Potter was forever soliciting
the view of the Burlington competitors and in this way contributed much
to the development of a sound policy based on business realities.

The Rock Island's business strategy, after Riddle's retirement from
the presidency in 1882, was worked out by Cable—a dramatic and colorful figure. Like Forbes he was a man of considerable private means. He
had long been associated with the road as general manager and vice-
president. Under Riddle's guidance the Rock Island in the 1870's had
increased its financial strength and maintained a generous dividend. Out-

side of some local sparring in Iowa and in northwest Illinois, it engaged in no expansion plans. Riddle steadfastly adhered to this policy even in the 1879–1882 boom. Cable, as general manager, had already shown his ability as a business fighter in the struggle for traffic.

The transformation of the St. Paul from a local road into a major railroad system was the product of another business team. Mitchell, as president, and Merrill, as general manager, were the dynamic personalities in the 1879–1883 growth of that road. The punch and drive that characterized the management early in 1879 was largely the work of Merrill, though Mitchell uniformly supported his program. The last major expansion move of Mitchell was the Kansas City extension. By that time the weakening of the road's finances led to control by banking interests. A conservative corporate policy followed, not to be disturbed until the middle of the first decade of the twentieth century.

Adams, as leader of the Union Pacific, was a newcomer in the western railroad field. His previous experience had been confined largely to the literary and public regulatory phase of the business. In his *Essays on Erie*, he denounced the tactics of Gould in relationship to the Erie. Thereafter he was a member of the Massachusetts regulatory commission and an arbitrator in various disputes. In the early 1870's he acted as a sort of investment counsellor, and not a successful one. His recommendations for the purchase of railroad bonds did not turn out well. He was a citizen with a strong sense of public interest and his reputation as a man of sterling integrity brought him a considerable following, particularly in New England. In the early 1880's he was intrigued with the financial possibilities of the Union Pacific, and recommended purchase of the stock. By 1884 the control of the road passed into the hands of New England investors. Gould was expelled from control of the property in 1884 and Adams was appointed in his place.[2] Adams was a good administrator. He reduced expenses and rebuilt the physical property that had been so neglected under the Gould leadership. He was not, however, an able executive. He could not respond quickly to changing business conditions. Neither could he act decisively in framing and executing a difficult policy in the presence of conflicting forces. He observed carefully; he talked a great deal; but he was unable to act decisively. In the construction boom of 1886–1887 he permitted himself to be surrounded and outmaneuvered. Late in 1886 he recognized his errors. In order to formulate a policy he engaged the services of General Dodge and also those of Potter, who resigned from the vice-presidency of the Burlington. Unfortunately, Potter soon passed away. Dodge performed notable services for the Union Pacific, and it is probable that his counsel led to the expansion of the road in the 1880's—that is, the lease of the Navigation and the acquisition of the Panhandle Route.

Such were the leaders who fashioned the railroad routes in the Midwest in the decade of the 1880's. To these should be added Gould, who was, however, more active in the southwest. In the northwest, west of the Twin Cities and Lake Superior, additional construction programs exploded. The chief actor there was Hill. The Manitoba had in the first boom in the early 1880's created a sensational success both in railroad and financial circles. Hill's early leadership in these accomplishments was not clearly recognized. The road was directed and officered by a group of Canadians interested primarily in the Canadian Pacific. By 1883 the rivalry between the Canadian Pacific and the Manitoba led to the resignation of the Canadians from the Manitoba board and to the emergence of Hill as president. Hill over the following four years continued the policy of nurturing the Red River Valley area. He built branches into productive areas, already rich in grain. He created no lines in frontier areas devoid of population. He did not, *at that time*, cross the frontier into lightly populated areas—as did the Northwestern and St. Paul. The road, as Perkins expressed it in 1885 was "a snug property, with very little, if any, waste mileages."[3]

The Northern Pacific under Villard, meanwhile adopted a diametrically opposite policy. In the effort to build a transcontinental line between Lake Superior and the Pacific Coast the management boldly invaded the frontier and threw lines across an inhospitable country, part of which was almost devoid of population. While Hill was building carefully and checking his costs minutely Villard built in ignorance of costs. Indeed, he knew little about expenses, but depended upon estimates made by others. A grave underestimation of costs was a major factor in the road's debacle in 1883. Under the succeeding administration of Harris the road continued to expand and build. The new management decided, in 1888, despite some internal dissension, to build an independent line to the Pacific Coast—independent, that is, of the Navigation's Portland line. This extension, the so-called Cascade Division, was completed to Tacoma in July, 1887.

While this line was under construction, Hill suddenly announced a change in business policy—a change that led to the most serious competitive invasion of Northern Pacific territory. The 1883 agreement between the Hill and Villard forces, by which each party agreed not to penetrate the territory of the other, had been respected for the following three years. The Manitoba did, however, expand in an easterly direction. Through the personal holdings of Hill it bought an interest in a small road which afforded access to Duluth. At a junction in Minnesota the Manitoba connected with the St. Paul and Duluth Railroad, the successor in financial reorganization to the Lake Superior and Mississippi. The Manitoba forwarded its Duluth-bound business over that road. The Hill–Villard truce, adapted to the furtherance of business stability, was broken in the summer of 1886. A new and powerful factor was thus introduced in the transcontinental railroad industry.

Hill soon disclosed his new policies. He moved west from the Red River Valley across North Dakota to Great Falls, Montana, and south over the lines of another company, the Montana Central, to the heart of the copper territory centering around Butte. Hill had previously on personal account bought up the rights of way, etc., organized the company, and then turned over control, at his cost, to the Manitoba. This policy of expansion was new, and so was the business personality of Hill. He had always been a hard trader. In 1877 and 1878 he had painted to the Dutch bondholders in dark and dreary hues the future prospects of the St. Paul and Pacific. And in the negotiations leading to the territorial agreement of 1883, Villard's agent learned something of Hill's trading tactics. Hill is "most dangerous . . . when he wears his most winning smile," was the characterization of one of his officials.[4] Hill who had hitherto respected the agreement over territory and had maintained rates, now suddenly violated the former and reversed the latter policy. He accompanied every territorial invasion with rate cuts. He refused to respect pools, associations, and other devices to stabilize rates. Like Carnegie in iron and steel and Gould in the central and southwestern areas, he became a leading rate cutter in the Northwest. "Mr. Hill is a law unto himself. He attends no meetings, keeps aloof from such and is therefore dangerous."[5] This was the opinion of one who, as a director of the Burlington and the St. Paul roads, had had a long experience in western railroad affairs. Hill pressed forward with rate reductions on every front from the Lake Superior rail-water routes in the late 1880's to the eastbound lumber movement rates from the Pacific in 1893.

The first forward push of the Manitoba brought it into conflict with both the Northern Pacific and the Union Pacific. The management of these two roads in the summer of 1886 was dominated by two cautious personalities. The competitive rivalries of the Burlington and of the Northwestern had built up powerful competition with the Union Pacific. In Montana a similar pattern was developing. Hill's push into Montana invaded a source of traffic rich to both the Northern Pacific and the Union Pacific. Harris was, like Adams, a careful manager, but with little aggressive imagination. In charge of the Burlington in the 1870's his policy of concession led to an open break with the aggressive Perkins, at that time the executive of the Burlington's Nebraska affiliate. Relations between Harris and Adams were friendly.

Neither Adams nor Harris were in 1887 prepared with any forward-looking plans of their own to counter the invasion of their territory. Harris retaliated feebly by building a number of short lines by which the Northern Pacific "got very much in the way of the Montana Central."[6] This move did not seriously retard the Manitoba. Adams did nothing. Hill moved quickly. The decision to build west from Minot, North Dakota, to Great Falls, and from there to Butte, was made early in 1887. There was some delay caused by negotiations with the Northern Pacific. The latter road declined, except at unusually high rates, to carry steel rails and supplies to the western end of the proposed line at Great Falls. Hill, therefore, decided to move simultaneously from the east and west. The line was completed ahead of schedule. The new road was described in authoritative business circles in praiseworthy language. An eastern railroad journal referred to "the magnificent organization of the work,"[7] while a steel trade periodical described the work as one "without a parallel in point of rapidity, and the work has been well done, too."[8]

Hill's ability as a railroad operator was by this time widely recognized. His lines were built at low cost, first at the depression-induced low prices in 1878–1879 and then in 1887 at the then relatively low prices—low in relation to the high construction costs of the Northern Pacific incurred in 1869–1873 and again in 1880–1883; and low also in relation to the costs of the Butte extension of the Union Pacific in 1880–1881. Moreover, unlike the executives of these two major competitors, Hill was an operating man, skilled and trained in the art of physical operations—an accomplishment which neither Gould, Villard, nor Adams could emulate and which Harris only slightly approached. Hill's road, in short, established the distinction of the low-cost railroad of the West. Hill's influence as a low cost rate-cutting factor was felt also on the eastern end of his growing system. From the Twin Cities south and west, by acquisition of existing lines and additional building, he penetrated the territory of the St. Paul, Northwestern, and additional country of the Northern Pacific. In these areas population had increased and rail tonnage mounted.

This traffic moved largely to Chicago. The haul afforded the St. Paul and the Northwestern was long and profitable. The Manitoba had no Chicago system lines. Hill accordingly arranged to send the business east to the Lake Superior ports. To accomplish this he took two major steps. First, he eliminated his system's dependence on the St. Paul and Duluth for access to these ports. That line in 1886 had made ambitious plans for the raising of new funds to improve its property. Hill was on the board. Apparently the St. Paul and Duluth's management was not informed of Hill's decision to build his own line to Lake Superior, parallel to the St. Paul and Duluth. Moving quickly, Hill abandoned his traffic contract with the St. Paul and Duluth and through a subsidiary built an extension from the junction point with the St. Paul and Duluth to Lake Superior. The St. Paul and Duluth was badly hurt.

The Manitoba thus helped to destroy the earning power of a small road. Its second major move on the eastern end of its system created much greater competitive havoc. For a number of years through rail-lake routes had been made by a number of lake transportation companies with the railroads terminating at Lake Superior. The Lake carriers were small and were unable to raise sufficient funds to provide modern equipment and render a high standard of transportation service. Hill revolutionized this situation. He built a fleet of modern steamships and then organized the Northern Steamship Line, to carry freight between Duluth and the Great Lakes. The Manitoba could now compete for through hauls via Duluth from the Twin Cities and the hinterland to the east with the lines running from the same sources to Chicago. The Manitoba, with a haul of less than two hundred miles from St. Paul to Duluth, now competed with the St. Paul railroads, with lines from St. Paul to Chicago of more than four hundred miles.

The Manitoba thus competed on a favorable basis with the St. Paul, as well as with the Northern Pacific and the Northwestern. This new competition was characterized by sharp rate reductions. Strange to say, neither the St. Paul nor the Northwestern took any strong countermeasures. Hill had used good timing in his extension moves. Only two years prior to the beginning of his expansion policy both of these roads, together with the Northern Pacific, had engaged in a competitive struggle for territorial advantage in northern Dakota. It appeared likely that a construction war of major properties might develop. The St. Paul acquired a line in the Red River Valley. The Northern Pacific meanwhile, under the administration of Harris and a conservative board, had decided to enlarge its branch-line construction. This decision was presented in the road's Annual Report for the year ended June 30, 1887. "The area of the district between the boundary line on the North, Snake River and the Clearwater on the south, the Bitter Root Mountains on the East and the Columbia River on the West is 32,700 square miles. By the construction of a judicious system of Branch Roads, the business of this large and productive district can be made permanently tributary to the Northern Pacific. This is the only way for the Company to get full advantage from what has been done. If this company neglects to secure the control of this business other Companies will hasten to take advantage of the neglect. The directors therefore recommend that the policy that has been pursued in promoting Branch Roads be continued."[9]

This statement reflected a traditional railroad philosophy. A road, in order to lay a base for its future prosperity, was compelled to pre-empt territory that showed any sign of promising growth. It was necessary to take risks: the territory might not grow as rapidly as anticipated; crop failures might reduce railroad tonnage; rates might be cut by forces outside the control of management; construction costs might be so high as to preclude the possibility of earning enough to pay the fixed charges on the newly created debt. All these risks were assumed by railroad management. This Northern Pacific program, carried out over the next six years, proved to be profitable in the first half of the period but a source of serious losses in the later years. Branches were built in Minnesota, Dakota, Montana, Idaho, and Washington. Some were built under an arrangement with outside contractors, by which they graded, tied, and bridged the roads, and accepted payment for one-half the cost in branch-line bonds, the other one-half in freight. The bonds were guaranteed by the Northern Pacific. It was hoped that in this way businessmen would support the interests of the Northern Pacific.[10] By 1889, in the midst of prosperity, the branch-line policy paid off well. The road's earnings in Montana in the previous two or three years had probably tripled, while the population of Puget Sound had doubled a number of times.[11] The success of the first phase of the branch-line construction was followed by a program along less conservative lines in the following three years. In 1889 Harris was replaced by more expansion-minded management, led by Villard.

The Northern Pacific's branch-line program was not aimed at the Manitoba. Another one, however, was definitely a battle of construction. This was the struggle between Villard and Hill in the Red River Valley area. In 1887, shortly after the reappearance of Villard, the Northern Pacific leased a small road in the Red River Valley extending from a point on its main line east of Fargo to the international boundary. The road ran parallel to the Manitoba. The latter at the boundary connected with the Canadian Pacific with a line to Winnipeg. The Manitoba–Canadian Pacific route had a monopoly of the Red River Valley traffic between Dakota and Minnesota and Winnipeg. Businessmen of Winnipeg and the province complained of high rates. To introduce competition and reduce rates, the province of Manitoba built a line competitive with the Canadian Pacific. Upon its completion it was to be leased or sold to private enterprise. Both the Northern Pacific and the Manitoba made bids for the acquisition of the property.

The rivalry between these two roads for the control of the line was hot and heavy. The Manitoba made what appeared to be a liberal offer —more liberal than that proposed by the Northern Pacific. It agreed to keep the road open to all others, including the Northern Pacific. The contract proposed by the latter excluded other roads from the use of the provincial line. The Manitoba, however, was tarred with the monopoly brush of the Canadian Pacific. The provincial line, therefore, was sold to the Northern Pacific, and it in turn agreed to finish construction to Winnipeg and to build branches northwest from that point. And, finally, it guaranteed "very low rates" from Manitoba to Duluth.[12] The Manitoba–Canadian Pacific monopoly of the business to and from the province of Manitoba was destroyed.

The clash in the building program of the Northwest thus centered largely around the leaderships of Hill and Villard. In the Southwest, in the area west of the Mississippi and south of the St. Louis–Kansas City line and the southern Kansas border and on to the Pacific Coast, the rivalry revolved around other personalities. Here the industry was dominated by Gould, Huntington, and Strong. Huntington and Gould dis-

21

played the ability to trade quickly, and both paid prices for railroads that were higher than could be justified on the basis of past and present earnings. A high percentage of risk accompanied the buying of existing lines and the building of new roads, and in both cases the financial results were for many years unsatisfactory. Stockholders received few dividends. Gould's southwestern roads were thrown into receivership. Those of Huntington, however, were incorporated into the Southern Pacific System. The unprofitable sections were carried by the more profitable ones; and, though the Southern Pacific Company paid no dividends during Huntington's lifetime, there were no defaults (except for the comparatively minor, though dramatic, incident of the Houston and Texas Central). Gould and Huntington over the years had numerous business relationships. They were successively friends and foes. At the very beginning of their relationship Huntington realized the caliber of his business opponent. Gould, he declared in 1875, was "the most difficult man to do anything with I ever knew."[13] From time to time Huntington made similar allusions to the difficulties of trading with Gould, but he carefully avoided any direct clashes until the stormy days of 1881. What Gould thought of Huntington is not a matter of record, but we know that Gould's lifelong transcontinental ambitions were blocked by the stubborn opposition of Huntington. Both Gould and Huntington knew how to strike bargains by personal negotiations.

Huntington, unlike Gould, was not a trader in the public security market. He did not buy and sell miscellaneous securities, nor did he have a large following of stock traders. He did, however, realize heavy gains from the sale of railroad properties. He took pride in displaying to regulatory bodies the profits realized from the sale of eastern railroads such as the Kentucky Central, the Chesapeake and Ohio, and others. Indeed, he performed a public service by investing these personal gains in extensions of and improvements to his western roads.

Gould's southwest system was built on the parent stem of the Missouri Pacific, whose property extended for the most part between St. Louis and Kansas City. Two major lines of the system extended into the Southwest. The eastern hinged directly upon St. Louis. The western, represented by the Kansas and Texas, extended from Hannibal on the Mississippi River, southwest across Missouri and beyond into Texas via Denison to a connection with the International at a small point in southern Texas. In the winter of 1885–1886, on the eve of the railroad construction program of the late 1880's, Gould's southwestern system was beset with financial difficulties. The Missouri Pacific, the parent system road, was, however, in good financial condition. Its stock was paying dividends and its credit standing was satisfactory.

The Huntington system had by 1885 been unified under control of a holding company, the Southern Pacific Company. Huntington proposed to unite all his properties, from California to Newport News, into a single corporate vehicle. He had "the vision of a railway line that should stretch straight way across the continent," wrote Huntington; but he "found security investors laggard; they just could not grasp what I personally saw was natural."[14] Both Crocker and Stanford, however, renewed their objections to the assumptions of the financial burdens of the lines east of New Orleans. They had, after all, in 1884 barely escaped disaster.

Huntington did not immediately surrender the idea of relinquishing the eastern wing of his transcontinental system. He organized a new holding company (the Newport News and Mississippi Valley) to unite the various parts of the lines east of New Orleans. His efforts were unsuccessful. The Chesapeake and Ohio soon passed into receivership. Huntington began to liquidate: he sold the Chesapeake and Ohio and Kentucky Central stocks at a profit, and in 1892, with the sale of the Louisville, New Orleans and Texas (the Memphis–New Orleans line), he completed the task. This was fortunate for Huntington; for he had a difficult task of surmounting the crises in the summer of 1893. The burden of the eastern lines might have tumbled him into a financial abyss.

The lines west of New Orleans, however, were united under a single leadership. The stock of all the Huntington system roads were exchanged for the new enterprise—the Southern Pacific Company. The roads were also leased to the holding company. Upon the Central Pacific stock a 2 per cent dividend was guaranteed as part consideration of the lease contract. All these transactions were completed in 1885.

The other business leader in the southwestern railroad triumvirate—Strong, head of the fighting institution known as the Atchison—was in many respects unlike both Huntington and Gould. He was neither ready nor able to assume the leadership in taking heavy financial risks, to borrow personally in such heavy amounts as to endanger his own personal solvency. He was not a promoter; he did not personally attract the funds of capitalists. He did not through his individual business ability carve out a railroad system. He was, in brief, not a capitalist in his own name and he had no large following among men of wealth. He was an able railroad operator. He was bold and skilful in the acquisition of operating properties. Like Perkins, he was uncompromising in his support of policies to aid his road. Decisive in his actions, he rarely hesitated once he made up his mind. Elected to the presidency in 1881, he carried into effect the ambitions of Boston capitalists to convert the property into a transcontinental system.

Strong, like Perkins, Harris, and Adams, carried out his plans in close co-operation with his directorate. This represented what might be termed professional management. As the executive, he was clothed with the necessary authority to carry out policies laid down at the directorate level. It is probably correct to assert that properties so managed were laid out better and were more efficiently operated than those administered by the promoter business type—by such men as Villard, Gould, and Huntington. It is, however, equally sound to say that many railroads built quickly through lightly populated areas, far in advance of the growth of population, might not have been built but for the activities of these promoters. Perhaps it might be more accurate to suggest that the lines would not have been built until many years later. Such a policy of delayed building would have prevented the loss of millions contributed by wealthy capitalists and by their less wealthy followers. The public welfare, however, was well served. For years it was given a transportation service at low costs, even though it was not always maintained on a particularly high standard; indeed, not infrequently, selling prices were considerably below unit costs.

These three systems dominated the Southwest. Only a few scattered competitors challenged them in this vast domain. One was the Frisco, with an indirect line between St. Louis and Kansas City and another through southern Kansas to Wichita. While there was rivalry in Kansas between the Atchison and the Frisco, there remained nevertheless a close co-operative relationship, arising out of their joint Atlantic and Pacific Railroad venture. There was also the understanding of 1880 not to build lines in Kansas without notifying each other.

The construction programs in the Southwest in 1886–1887 were not on the same major scale that characterized those in the Midwest and Northwest. The systems built under the leadership of Huntington, Gould, and Strong in the first half of the decade had not been profitable. There was no such large volume of local business here as there was in many parts of the Northwest and the Midwest. To the risk-taking capitalists of 1879–1883, profit and prosperity frequently appeared in the promised glow of transcontinental traffic. The volume of such business by 1886 was not heavy; yet the expectation of increases represented a perennial hope, even though it was so continuously deferred.

Most of the transcontinental business via the Southwest moved over the Southern Pacific. The rates, however, were low and the profits small. Of the three southwestern systems only the Southern Pacific controlled through transcontinental routes over its own lines. Gould's system in this respect was the weakest of all. On the Missouri–Mississippi Valley–Gulf Coast routes, however, in the first half of the decade the Gould System controlled the through lines of traffic.

A strong competitor on the western end was the Gulf, a pioneer road in Galveston. It was, wrote Crocker, "a valuable road, as I believe it runs through a portion of the best part of Texas. . . ." Crocker, indeed, recommended its purchase.[15] It did a profitable local business and, what is equally important, it was conservatively financed. The Gulf connected with the Gould lines at Fort Worth, thus giving it an outlet to the thriving communities in the north and east. From time to time the Gould lines clashed with the Gulf. Early in 1882 competitive tactics led to a rate war. In May, as a means of settling these disturbances, a traffic pool was established. Peace did not continue long, for the Gulf insisted upon a larger percentage of the business. It demanded 75 per cent of the Galveston business, pool or no pool.[16] The Gulf also competed with the Huntington roads, particularly the Houston and Texas Central.

The owners of the Gulf decided sometime in 1883 or 1884 to rid itself of its dependence on the Gould system for its through business north and east. It endeavored to sell its property to the Alton and the Burlington. Such a sale would give a northern road a through route to the Gulf and give the Gulf a through line to the North and East. Neither road was interested. In the summer of 1886, however, an arrangement was negotiated with the Atchison. That road acquired the Gulf stock in exchange for its own. The Gulf terminated at Fort Worth, and the Atchison in southern Kansas. The gap was filled by construction by both roads. The Atchison built south and the Gulf north. They met at Purcell, in the Indian territory. The Gould system for the first time was now confronted by a strong competitor for the Gulf Coast–Mississippi and Missouri Valley business.

The entrance of the Atchison into the Indian territory was followed by a building program to exploit the rapidly growing farm and cattle country in that area and in the neighboring section of northwestern Texas. The Atchison built a branch west to the Texas–Indian territory boundary and beyond to Panhandle City. These lines, finished by the end of 1887, put the Atchison System into an area in which the population was rapidly increasing.

On the Pacific Coast the Atchison had by 1886 completed its connection between the Atlantic and Pacific Railroad and the California Southern, thereby furnishing a system line to San Diego. It would no longer, declared a contemporary journal, "be at the mercy of the Southern Pacific."[17] By the spring of 1887, moreover, the Atchison succeeded, through the purchase of a number of small roads and the building of a short connection, in securing an entrance into Los Angeles.[18]

The Gould line most adversely affected by the Atchison program in the southwest was the Kansas and Texas. The Gulf's business moving north from Fort Worth was diverted to the Atchison. The Kansas and Texas was also hit almost at the same time by the long-postponed construction of a Frisco line paralleling the Kansas and Texas on the west. Ever since 1881 the Frisco had planned the construction of a connection with either one or the other of the non-Gould lines in northern Texas.[19] Gould defeated these plans. In 1886, concurrently with the Atchison's expansion program into the Indian Territory, the Frisco began the construction of a line between Fort Smith, Arkansas, and Paris, Texas, making connections at the latter point with both the Texas and Pacific and the Gulf. The Frisco, in conjunction with other roads, thus opened still another through route between the Gulf Coast and the Missouri and Mississippi Valleys.

The Kansas and Texas was now surrounded by competitors, both on the east and west. The road had in 1881 been leased to the Missouri Pacific. The lease obliged the lessee to assume no financial obligations. The latter was required only to return to the lessor any net earnings. In 1887 the road fell into receivership. Despite Gould's efforts to retain control, the property passed from the Gould system and was thereafter operated as an independent, non-Gould enterprise.[20]

Another major construction program, from Fort Worth north and west through the Panhandle country, was conducted in the 1880's by a number of pioneer roads. Their combined new track may be called the

Panhandle route, for convenience.[21] The leaders in this building program were Dodge and Governor John Evans. Both had long been operating in the field of railroad building.

In the expansion of the Gould lines in the early 1880's Dodge was in direct charge of most of the building. Though Dodge also served as an intimate adviser to Adams, he was nevertheless a loyal Gould follower and an enthusiastic admirer.

Evans, though a businessman of lesser stature than Dodge, had by 1889 made his mark in eastern Colorado. He was neither an able financier nor a passably good railroad operator. He served for a number of years as president of the pioneer Denver Pacific. Later in the 1870's and in the face of financial difficulties, he persisted in the construction of the South Park, a line that penetrated the prosperous Leadville mining area. In 1880, at the very height of the boom, Evans sold out to Gould, who then transferred the property, at his cost, to the Union Pacific.[22] "His real talent, and consequently his zeal," according to a careful student of Evans, "lay in formulating large schemes, selling them to the community, and watching them, if they succeeded, quicken the pulse of trade and contribute to the general development of society."[23]

After the sale of the South Park, Evans conceived the idea of affording eastern Colorado a new competitive route to the seaboard. In the face of declining rates elsewhere businessmen in eastern Colorado were handicapped by higher rates. Evans sketched the possibility of a railroad route southeast to Fort Worth, there connecting with other lines to Galveston and New Orleans. This was the genesis of the so-called Gulf to the Rockies route.

Interest in the possibilities of a railroad connecting Denver with the Gulf Coast emerged in the early 1870's. The project was repeatedly postponed. In 1881 the idea was revived, both at the proposed northern and southern termini, but by different parties. Evans organized the Denver and New Orleans, to build from Denver south; and a group under the leadership of Dodge, initiated a project to build north from Fort Worth. This project was a pioneer enterprise. It was not, that is to say, sponsored by a railroad with an established earning power. In order to attract speculative capital the bankers of both parts adopted the construction company device. Difficulty was encountered in raising funds. Evans solicited the aid of Gould, as a foremost leader of speculative capital. Gould approved the project "and promptly referred Evans to Dodge, saying that any 'trade' made with the General would be satisfactory to him."[24]

This approach to Gould proved successful. Shortly thereafter an agreement was reached between the Denver and New Orleans and the Fort Worth to build a line from different directions to join at the Canadian River. Construction followed and by the spring of 1882 the Denver and New Orleans was completed to Pueblo, while the line from Fort Worth was built north only about fifty miles. Soon thereafter, Evans again encountered financial difficulties: he underestimated the cost of construction. To secure additional funds he negotiated a short-term loan burdened with the restrictions normally inserted in emergency financing. The 10 per cent loan, due in 1883, was secured by a mortgage on "the pooled assets of his [Evans] construction company, including his own stock and bonds."[25] The loan was not paid at maturity, and the default involved the possibility of loss of control. Evans, however, raised sufficient funds to buy in the mortgaged collateral at the auction sale.

For more than three years thereafter no progress was made on building beyond Pueblo. The poverty of the Denver and New Orleans was due in part to the 1880 contract by which the connecting roads "refused to interchange freights and passengers with the D. & N. O. . . ."[26] In 1883 a court decision invalidated the contract as "a conspiracy to grasp commerce and suppress the building of railroads in two great States."[27] There followed a three-road pool (excluding the Denver and New Orleans) and an accompanying reduction of rates. After two years of this warfare, the Evans road fell into receivership. In 1886 Evans organized a successor property, the Denver, Texas and Gulf.

Between 1882 and 1886 the southern end of the route was built to a point in Texas (Quannah), 481 miles from Pueblo. In February, 1887, an agreement was negotiated between Evans and Dodge for the construction of a line to close the gap. A new company was organized to build this line. By the summer of 1888, through a stock exchange, all the roads were brought under a single control under the corporate parenthood of the Denver, Texas and Fort Worth.

A new competitive route between Colorado, Texas, and the Gulf Coast was created. The route competed on a basis of reduced rates via a rail and water haul to the eastern seaboard. The all-rail routes were obliged either to meet the reduced rates or lose the business.

While new through lines were being carved out by the Panhandle

Route, and by the Atchison and the Gould Systems to the Gulf Coast and Colorado, the Huntington System confined its attention largely to strengthening its control on local traffic in California. One major through line was, however, completed in the boom of the middle 1880's—the filling of the gap between Portland and the Oregon–California boundary. Despite large capital expenditures Villard was unable to build the connection. After his failure in 1883 he endeavored to induce Huntington to lease the Oregon and California Railroad on a relatively high basis of $2,200 per mile.[28] Huntington was too realistic a trader to consider such a proposal seriously. After the elimination of Villard from control, Smith, president of the Transcontinental, offered the property to the Union Pacific. Adams was still in his non-expansion frame of mind. He therefore refused to accept a responsibility which had resulted in such serious losses to former owners. "At least," he wrote in November, 1885, "I want to know what the thing might cost; also, whether securing it would keep the California people out of Oregon. There would be no great object in buying it and then having the Southern Pacific crowd build parallel to it from one end to the other, utterly destroying its value."[29]

This was the property that Huntington bought and subsequently leased to the Central Pacific. Huntington took pleasure in describing the success with which this line, in process of construction for so many years, was completed under his leadership. "The magnitude of that work [the building of the line from the California–Oregon boundary to Portland] was the main cause of breaking Ben Holliday and his associates in the early days, and the Oregon Transcontinental and the associated Villard interest at a later date."[30] Where these had failed Huntington succeeded. Construction was carried out by the Pacific Improvement Company, in exchange for Central Pacific bonds and stocks. This was the last Huntington construction company.

This survey of the western railroad building boom in 1886 and 1887 is not complete in all details. It does, however, cover a large percentage of the mileage involved. The program was not carefully planned. There were too many lines in some areas. The roads were built under the spur of intense competition, many by reason of the interplay of complex personalities. It was clear to thoughtful observers that many lines would not be profitably employed for years to come. But it is equally true that had many of these roads awaited the actual development of traffic, they probably would never have been built. Perhaps there would have been a substantial saving of capital. Perhaps the capital could have been better invested in other more productive facilities. These are theoretical considerations to which there can be no definite answer. It is clear that the western country did get the benefit of more than adequate transportation facilities; and, as will be disclosed in the following chapter, these facilities were accompanied by a reasonable rate structure.

Though it was well established by the end of the record building year of 1887 that the country was well supplied with railroad facilities there still remained many potential building projects. Businessmen were planning to build even more lines. In the Northwest the invasion by the Burlington and Northern brought retaliatory construction threats from the Northwestern and the St. Paul. Roswell Miller, president of the St. Paul, asserted that his road would build in the West and Southwest to retaliate for the Burlington's affiliate in the Chicago–St. Paul area.[31]

Further south, after the Rock Island completed a construction program across Kansas to eastern Colorado and southwest to the Kansas–Oklahoma boundary line, Cable insisted that the road would be extended to the Gulf of Mexico, but "only as the business justifies it."[32] Indeed, an organ of financial opinion observed early in 1888 that the Rock Island was planning a line to the Pacific Coast.[33] The Northwestern was also planning to build to a junction with the Central Pacific at Ogden;[34] while the Missouri Pacific, according to one railroad commentator, was planning to build to Los Angeles and Salt Lake City. The Burlington was discussing a line from Denver to a junction with the Central Pacific. By 1888, however, effects of overexpansion had expressed themselves in financial terms. Rate cutting produced declines in earnings and dividends. It was difficult to raise capital. Major companies successively announced their refusal to build new lines.

Even though financial conditions made construction of additional lines impossible, the building program of 1886–1887 eliminated most of the territorial monopolies that remained after the completion of the earlier boom. The Union Pacific's control north of the Platte River was overthrown by the Northwestern and the Burlington; the Northern Pacific's hold in Dakota, Montana, and the cattle country in Wyoming was weakened by the competition of the Manitoba, the Northwestern, and the Burlington; the Manitoba's traffic between St. Paul and the province of Manitoba was shared with the Northern Pacific; the exclusive Gould control of the Kansas City–St. Louis–Gulf Coast route was eliminated by the Atchison–Gulf Line to Galveston. The Atchison, furthermore, shared business in southern Kansas with the Rock Island and Missouri Pacific. The Navigation's control of the lower Columbia River Valley business was impaired by the Northern Pacific's extension to Tacoma. Few location monopolies were left in western territory. Among the most notable was that of the Huntington lines in central and northern California.

The competition engendered by the building boom led to the most widespread rate reductions in western railroad history. The public benefited, as it normally does, from heavy investment in plant and equipment. And the investors, at least over the short run, lost, as they so frequently do.

Notes for Chapter XVI

[1] Northwestern Archives, Keep to Sykes, August 11, 1885.

[2] For details, see *Gould*, Chap. XXI, pp. 419–423.

[3] Burlington Archives, Perkins to H. D. Minot. No precise date, but written in the summer of 1885.

[4] H. V. P., Oakes to Villard, Oct. 2, 1882, Oakes quoted Allen Manvel, a Manitoba official.

[5] Burlington Archives, Geddes to Perkins, March 18, 1890.

[6] Northern Pacific Archives, Harris to Adams, Dec. 6, 1886.

[7] *R. R. Gaz.*, Dec. 9, 1887, p. 791.

[8] *Iron Age*, Nov. 3, 1887, p. 13.

[9] Annual Report, Northern Pacific, 1887, p. 17.

[10] *Chron.*, Feb. 4, 1888, p. 147.

[11] J. M. Hannaford, traffic manager, Northern Pacific, *The United States and Canada*, Report No. 847, U. S. Senate, 51st Congress, 1st Session, 1889, p. 567. Hannaford probably referred to 1883 in his remark about the doubling of the population since the road was completed.

[12] This account is based upon *The New York Times*, Jan. 28, Aug. 29, Aug. 30, Aug. 31, and Sept. 9, 1888.

[13] Huntington to Colton, April 12, 1875, M. M.

[14] *Wall Street Journal*, May 25, 1927.

[15] Crocker to Huntington, Nov. 5, 1881, M. M.

[16] *R. R. Gaz.*, May 26, 1882, p. 321.

[17] *Bradstreet's*, Nov. 14, 1885, p. 314.

[18] For details of this move into Los Angeles, see Glenn S. Dumke, *Boom of the Eighties in Southern California*, (San Marino, California, 1944), pp. 22–23.

[19] The earliest notice of such a project is in *Ry. Review*, Jan. 22, 1881, p. 32.

[20] For details, see *Gould*, Chap. XXVII, pp. 538–546.

[21] A detailed and interesting survey of the formation and progress of this venture is presented in Overton.

[22] For details, see *Gould*, Chap. XVII, pp. 343–344.

[23] Overton, p. 46.

[24] *Ibid.*, p. 57.

[25] *Ibid.*, p. 84.

[26] *Ibid.*, p. 142.

[27] Denver and New Orleans Railroad, Executive Document, No. 186, House of Representatives, 49th Congress, 1st Session, 1886, p. 18.

[28] H. V. P., Villard to Huntington, Aug. 19, 1884.

[29] Hedges, p. 138.

[30] Report No. 778, p. 198, Huntington.

[31] Burlington Archives, Perkins to Geddes, Feb. 11, 1888.

[32] *Chicago Tribune*, Feb. 17, 1888.

[33] *Chron.*, Jan. 7, 1888, p. 40.

[34] *San Francisco Bulletin*, cited in *Ry. Review*, Mar. 31, 1888, p. 176.

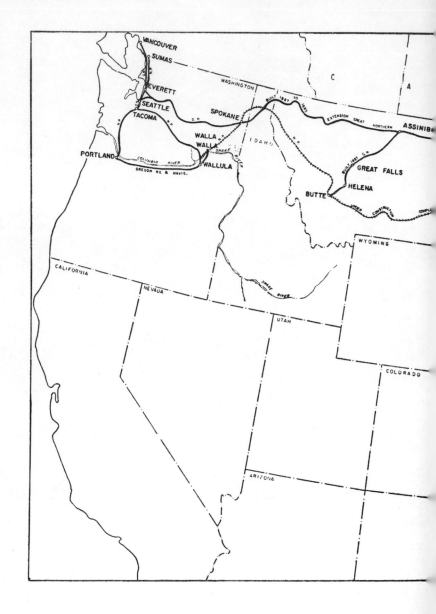

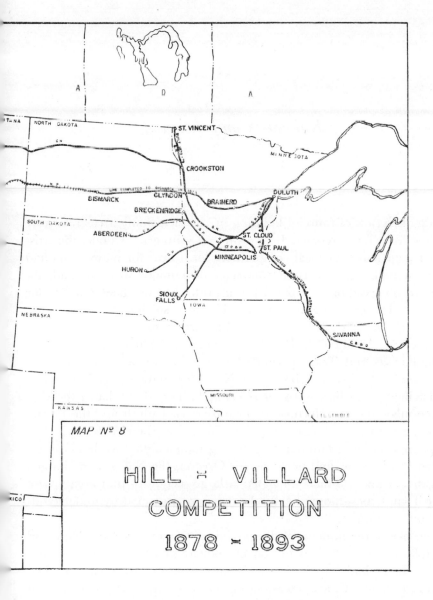

MAP № 8

HILL - VILLARD
COMPETITION
1878 - 1893

XVII

Ruinous Competition

THE CESSATION of railroad building in 1883 left many areas relatively free from rate pressure. In central and southern Missouri the Missouri Pacific had little local competition; local rates for many years had not been reduced. The traffic manager of a major western road, for example, observed in 1887 that Missouri rates had not been reduced for ten years.[1] In southern Kansas reasonable rates, shielded by the absence of railroad competition, was an important force in preserving the earning power of the Atchison. In eastern Oklahoma the monopolistic position of the Kansas and Texas permitted it to maintain a reasonable rate structure. In California, Arizona, and New Mexico the rates of the Southern Pacific System lines were relatively high. The Manitoba in the Red River Valley and the Northern Pacific between Duluth and the Pacific Coast maintained rates fairly well. The farmers in the Red River Valley complained of the Manitoba's "grinding monopoly";[2] while in southeastern Washington and northeastern Oregon, the Navigation charged rates that seemed to have alienated a large section of that area.[3] West of the Twin Cities, moreover, local rates were protected by understandings and agreements.

Even before the impetus of the expansion program of the middle and late 1880's had exerted its full effect upon railroad selling prices competitive forces had impaired the vitality of many agreements reached in previous years. Chicago was one of the most strategic points around which competition revolved. The Lake Superior rail-water route diverted traffic from the St. Paul–Chicago–Lake Michigan route. The position of the Manitoba was particularly significant. It brought to Minneapolis more grain than all the other roads put together. This road could become, in the language of an official of a road involved in this traffic, "either the strongest ally or the most dangerous enemy of Chicago trade and Chicago lines."[4] The Manitoba had no interest in any Lake Michigan port. The Northwestern had a direct line between St. Paul and Chicago, while the St. Paul, with no access to the Lake Superior ports, also had a direct Chicago line. The newly established St. Paul–Chicago lines in the middle 1880's controlled no outlet to Lake Superior. The expansion of the Manitoba promised to increase the strength of Lake Superior routes in their rivalry with the Chicago routes. And, of course, this is what happened between 1887 and 1893, and on a major scale.

The rates made by the Chicago lines to compete with the Lake Superior routes influenced the rate structure on the trans-Missouri traffic, altogether there seemed at first glance no direct relationship between the factors governing the St. Paul–Chicago rates and those affecting the Chicago–Iowa–trans-Missouri River business. The newly established commissions in such states as Iowa and Nebraska did not overlook an indirect relationship, and they repeatedly made a Chicago–Iowa–trans-Missouri rate in response to a low Chicago–St. Paul rate. These decisions of the state commissions were re-enforced by the policies of the St. Paul–Chicago roads in extending the Chicago rates to points as far down as St. Louis. This was done on the theory that the points south and southwest of Chicago were subject to the competition of Lake Superior ports. Still another influence drove in the direction of upsetting the Chicago–trans-Missouri rate structure. Building of competitive lines to the Twin Cities, Council Bluffs, and Kansas City strengthened the rivalries between the Burlington, Rock Island, St. Paul, and Northwestern. The Kansas City–Chicago extension of the Atchison introduced another complicating factor. The Alton, previously a preferred connection for the Atchison eastbound business, now became a competitor. With no lines west of the Missouri River, the Alton lined up with the Missouri Pacific, thereby competing, in part at least, for business over that line between Kansas City and Omaha. Gould, in order to carry some of the westbound business of the Alton for the Missouri Pacific, gave some of the latter's eastbound business to the Alton, at the expense of the Wabash. The Wabash for the last half of the decade of the 1880's was in receivership. Accordingly, at least on a short-run basis, Gould did not owe much responsibility to the fortunes of the Wabash.

In the trans-Missouri Valley the eastbound traffic prior to 1887 flowed largely over the Burlington and the Union Pacific. The extension of a line with a direct route to a Lake Superior port promised to divert some of this business. Either the Northern Pacific or the Manitoba could effect such a diversion. More wheat moved over those roads to Duluth and less to Chicago over the Burlington, Union Pacific, and the latter's eastern connections.

Chicago was also an important focal point for business to and from the lower Missouri River gateways between Omaha and Kansas City. The rate disturbances that had proved so costly in 1879 and 1880 were by 1881 largely eliminated. This happy outcome flowed largely from the absence of new railroad competition. By 1887 competition had changed in such a way as to impair the friendly relationships among the lower Missouri Valley lines. The Union Pacific, by the construction of a line between its Omaha and Kansas divisions, permitted both the St. Paul and the Northwestern to gain access to this area, thereby diverting traffic from the Burlington's Council Bluffs–Kansas City line. In 1887 the St. Paul's extension to Kansas City increased the competitive complexities; while the Atchison's line east from Kansas City made it extremely difficult to work out equitable proportions of traffic for the purpose of organizing a satisfactory pool.

While Chicago continued to play a role in the transcontinental traffic, competitive forces had weakened the importance of its early relationship. Between 1869 and 1881 Chicago exercised a dominant influence. In the following five years new transcontinental routes were established in rapid succession, and these were based to an increasing degree upon the flow of business through centers other than Chicago. In the summer of 1886 still another transcontinental candidate entered the field. This was the Canadian Pacific. With the help of a steamship line between Vancouver and San Francisco it afforded strong competition to transcontinental lines operating solely in the United States.

Both the old and the new competitive forces began to operate on a vast scale early in 1886. Even while new roads were being projected, the prospects of rate stability were already being undermined. In 1885, while some rate stability had been established west of the Mississippi and Missouri Rivers, widespread rate wars were eroding the earning power of eastern roads. An executive of a smaller line in this area caught well the spirit of the times: "I tell you," he declared, "a war of rates is about as catching a disease as ever was seen. You gentlemen may think that you can make a barrier of the Mississippi and think that you can cut the rates there, but I tell you that it will creep beyond the Mississippi and will then go to the Rocky Mountains. . . ."[5] This prophecy was well timed.

Rate wars broke out simultaneously in the West, Northwest, and over the transcontinental routes. Between Chicago and the Twin Cities, the Rock Island insisted upon participation in the passenger traffic via its circuitous route. It proposed that the time schedule between St. Paul and Chicago should be changed only with the unanimous agreement of the general superintendents of all the participating lines. This proposal was rejected by the Rock Island competitors. The Rock Island management contended that in exchange for its agreeing to charge the same fares, the short lines should allow it to make as good time as they made. Far from agreeing to these demands, the direct lines put on faster trains. The Rock Island followed by a cut in fares. The St. Paul retaliated by price cuts between Chicago and Omaha. Thus the circle of retaliation was completed. Cable, by thus insisting on the necessity of putting a short and a circuitous line upon the same competitive level, was introducing a new line of thinking. If this reasoning were to be carried to its logical conclusion, it would mean either price cuts by the longer lines, to gain business in competition with the shorter ones, or the surrender of the geographical advantages of the short line to help bolster the business of the long line. To the mind of Perkins, the acceptance of Cable's line of thinking was unacceptable. "If everybody who can patch up a roundabout line of railroad communication between two points is justified in cutting the rates because he has a roundabout line, it must end, it seems to me, in great injury to all the roads."[6]

This dispute was soon followed by a more serious affair involving the rate structure between Chicago, the Twin Cities, the Lake Superior Ports, and Omaha and Nebraska points. The Burlington contended that a number of northwestern roads had secured contracts at exceptionally low rates. It accordingly reduced first-class rates between Chicago and St. Paul. A pool covering this traffic had expired earlier in the year and a temporary agreement had been reached to continue the pool until April 1. Meanwhile a struggle had developed over the maintenance of rates on the Nebraska business. Hughitt asked Potter to increase rates on St. Paul–Chicago traffic. Potter refused. He in turn asked the other roads to make concessions on the Nebraska business; the managers of those roads also refused. Hughitt endeavored to act as a mediator, but his failure was complete.

Trouble meanwhile broke out over the Chicago–Twin Cities traffic. Traffic via Duluth was increasing, largely at the expense of the Chicago lines. An effort was made to set up a pool for the division of the Lake Superior traffic and thus remove the incentive to cut rates. It failed.

It was clear that no arrangement could be made to stabilize the rate structure, either by a pool or by a rate agreement. When the Chicago–Twin Cities agreement ended on the first of April, nothing in the way of rate stabilization had occurred. The managers of the participating roads decided to hold another meeting a week later. The gesture was futile. Within twenty-four hours rates began to tumble. A week later the scheduled meeting was held. Rates were increased, but even the increased figures were less than a fourth of the rate twenty years before. But this higher rate was doomed. Both the Illinois Central and Rock Island, with the two circuitous Chicago–Twin Cities lines, continued to quote the lower rates. Soon thereafter the other roads followed.[7]

Such low rates were obviously below costs and could be maintained only at the price of general bankruptcy. Before the end of the month these rate cuts were stopped by agreement, and rates restored to their pre-April level.[8]

Negotiations meanwhile continued in the effort to organize a new pool. By the fall of the year (1886), however, new competitive problems appeared. Another candidate for the Chicago–St. Paul business, the Wisconsin Central, emerged. It entered Chicago under the charter of a terminal road—the Chicago and Great Western—that had long been in receivership.[9] Still another problem arose from the Northwestern's new line to the cattle country, formerly served exclusively by the Northern Pacific and Union Pacific. Differences arose over the apportionment of the cattle business. In early October the Northwestern agreed to solve the problem by ignoring most of it. It accepted an idea of Cable's to set up a pool and maintain rates, and at the same time agreed to waive the problems which had produced the disturbances. The milling-in-transit privileges and the division of the range-cattle business were not included in the pool. Furthermore, the grain traffic, which represented approximately 90 per cent of the business, was excluded from the settlement. The one-year pool, dated October 15, 1886, under the title of Northwestern Freight Association, left for later settlement those problems which would "just as likely . . . furnish the pretext for the next outburst whenever one is desired."[10]

During the spring and summer months, while these rate wars were ravaging railroad earnings, disturbances also broke out between Chicago and the trans-Missouri River area. The Iowa Pool, covering the business between Chicago and Omaha, had by May, 1885, been replaced by the Western Freight Association. Shortly thereafter the St. Paul made a long term agreement—the so-called Hammond contract—for the movement of dressed beef from Omaha at rates lower than the published tariff. The refusal of the St. Paul to report the revenues from this contract to the Association was responsible in part for the Burlington's intransigence over the rate structure in the Chicago–St. Paul area. Meanwhile the rapid expansion of the Northwestern lines into northern Nebraska created another complicating factor. This new road produced more eastbound traffic for the Northwestern than the percentage of the pooled business to which it was entitled. By June the Association was an empty shell. By the end of the month the rate between Chicago and Omaha was reduced by 50 per cent. The war embraced the traffic between Chicago and St. Louis, as well as that in Nebraska reached by the Burlington and Union Pacific. The fight, in the language of a current observer, "involved all the lines, west of Chicago."[11]

By July the railroad managers were ready for some kind of settlement. Cable proposed that a gross pool be formed to cover the competitive business between Chicago, St. Louis, Peoria, and points north and west thereof, and also that in the Missouri Valley. The three major pools in these areas—the Northwestern, the Western Freight, and the Southwestern—would be replaced by one. The majority of the railroad managers approved; since, however, unanimity was required, the proposal was lost.[12] At this meeting another of those temporary truces that had now become so common in the western railroad industry was adopted. Agreement was reached by all the lines to restore rates pending negotiations for a definitive settlement. A committee recommended that a new pool be formed to consist of the same members that were part of the old pool; that the rates in effect on April 1, 1886, be re-established; and that the same percentages that prevailed in the old pool be continued. Furthermore, all existing contracts with shippers would be revised so that the contract rates should be the same as those provided for in the pool contract. The resolution designed to implement the recommendations of the committee referred to the desire to "put into full effect" the terms of the derelict Western Freight Association.[13]

The managers met again in mid-September and reached what appeared to be a permanent agreement. A five-year pool was set up to cover the traffic between Chicago, St. Louis, Council Bluffs, Omaha, and other Nebraska common points. Provisions were made for the settlement of outstanding debit balances under the old Association. Rates were reestablished as recommended by the committee in July, but it was not possible to reach any agreement on the division of the range-cattle business. This business was growing, and the Northwestern, owing to its new system lines in Nebraska, was getting a larger share. The Northwestern declined to surrender any part of it. The name of the new pool was changed to the Western Traffic Association.[14] Meanwhile, on the transcontinental routes, the early months of 1886 were featured by a wide break. The Transcontinental Association, the pool set up in the fall of 1883, had been maintained by compromises and concessions. This pool was supplemented by another, the Pacific Coast Association, covering the business between Chicago and St. Louis and the Pacific Coast. This traffic was divided among seven railroads. The Sunset Route, however, continued to carry an increasingly large share of the transcontinental business.[15] Under the pool's terms a number of the roads competitive with the Sunset Route endeavored to collect balances due them. At a five-day meeting held in December, 1885, the negotiators "did practically nothing."[16] The Burlington and the Rio Grande then declared that unless the balances were paid the notices of withdrawal from the Association already made some weeks before would not be cancelled, and in such a case the Association would probably be dissolved.

The do-nothing meeting of December postponed the decision to another meeting to be held in New York in February. At that meeting another formidable obstacle developed. The Atchison expressed its dissatisfaction with the existing traffic division.[17]

According to an official of a Huntington road, the Huntington representatives did all they could "to keep peace, and even agreed to give the Atchison some of our earnings for the sake of peace, but it wanted more than it had earned or could earn. . . . We have done all we propose to do and I guess the Atchison will get tired of it before we are through."[18] The Sunset Route meanwhile continued to move between 70 and 75 per cent of the traffic.

Another obstruction to transcontinental peace was presented by the completion of the Canadian Pacific line to Port Moody, British Columbia. There the Canadian Pacific decided to take advantage of its newly constructed line by making an impossible demand on the Transcontinental Association. It would join only if it secured 50 per cent of the Pacific Coast business. In view of the firm position taken by the Atchison and the Sunset Route, this demand was unrealistic and the Canadian Pacific probably was aware of that fact. The conflict of interests was too powerful to permit any solution based upon mutual concession. Strong and Huntington were uncompromising realists. There was some hope that Adams could effect a settlement. Probably with a bit of humor, Palmer, of the Rio Grande, engaged Adams at the February meeting of the transcontinental roads with the suggestion that "he was the Moses we were all waiting for to lift us out of the quandary."[19]

The meeting accomplished nothing. In the language of a leading railroad periodical, the transcontinental roads "for the first time in their history are engaged in open warfare."[20] There followed almost immediately "a complete demoralization" of transcontinental rates.[21] For a number of weeks after the dissolution of the Association, rates to California fluctuated from day to day, indeed almost from hour to hour. By late March the cutting of passenger rates reduced the business to an economic absurdity. On March 30, the Union Pacific sold tickets from Council Bluffs to San Francisco for $30, with a rebate payable at San Francisco of $25. The fare between the two points was thus reduced to $5.00.[22]

In view of the extensive rate cuts and the disappearance of the pool, there was no point in continuing the subsidy to the Pacific Mail Steamship. The subsidy was cancelled. The Pacific Mail did not choose to remain quiescent, a mere spectator in this business battle. The management decided to participate in the intercoastal transportation business by cutting rates. A board member announced that the management would "teach those roads a lesson."[23] Huntington was equally uncompromising. "Nobody," he declared, "shall carry freight between New York and San Francisco any better or cheaper than we do. . . . We do not look upon that as a war; we call that looking after our interests."[24] In order to fight the Pacific Mail more effectively Huntington ordered four additional steamships between San Francisco and New Orleans and reduced rates on coffee and tea more than 50 per cent. The Pacific Mail countered by asserting its willingness to take freight at any rates on the route from Japan and China direct to New York City, thereby avoiding the use of the railroad facilities.[25]

By the end of April, though no agreement was reached, there was an increase in rates to Pacific Coast points. And in early June, Perkins believed that a settlement awaited only the determination of the price the Pacific Mail would accept as compensation for not cutting the rates. The Atchison and the Union Pacific, according to Perkins, considered that the problem was in the hands of Huntington.[26]

Unfortunately, the trend of events upset the favorable expectation of the negotiators. While the Pacific Mail hesitated and Huntington delayed, another event upset calculations. The Canadian Pacific line was opened for through traffic in June. It had little local traffic from Winnipeg to Vancouver. To stimulate through business it cut rates and made alliances with a number of western roads, particularly the Manitoba. This gave the Canadian Pacific an entrance to the Twin Cities. And from that point to Chicago it negotiated an understanding with the newly established route of the Wisconsin Central. Neither of these two American lines were members of the Transcontinental or the Pacific Coast Association. The Canadian Pacific policy was described by a government official as "a bulldozing policy in regard to freights with the object plainly in view of wresting from the American Lines a larger share of the through traffic."[27]

While the transcontinental rate trouble thus continued the business peace, negotiated after so much difficulty in the Northwest, was weakened by a number of new developments. The one-year pool of the Northwestern Traffic Association went into effect in October, 1886. Shortly thereafter the Burlington and Northern, with the financial and traffic support of the Burlington, opened its St. Paul–Chicago line. The line was designed primarily for low-cost movement of through traffic. It commanded only a small amount of local business.

About a month after the opening of this Chicago line, another one—the so-called Washburn road—named after its chief promoter and president, was opened from Minneapolis to a Lake Superior port. The organization of the line reflected the determination of the Minneapolis flour-milling interests to protect their traffic against the growing threat arising from the movement of grain to the Lake Superior ports. Later in the year still another St. Paul–Chicago road, under the Stickney leadership, appeared.

The Northwestern pool, it should be noted, covered only about 10 per cent of the eastbound traffic from the Twin Cities. Ninety per cent of the business consisted of grain traffic, and this was excluded from the pool's jurisdiction. The westbound traffic, however, was more profitable, and it was not covered. This traffic, largely merchandise, carried higher rates than the war-ridden eastbound grain business.

None of the new lines in the St. Paul–Chicago and in the St. Paul–Lake Superior routes were anxious to extend the pool to include the grain business. As pool members, they would have to limit themselves to the amount of the allotted traffic. Neither could they advertise rate concessions in order to court the patronage of the shipper. By remaining outside the pool they were at liberty to reduce rates and to grant other concessions to shippers. They could make their new routes known and engage in open-rate competition to capture as much business as such a policy could stimulate.

There was some expectation in railroad circles that the Burlington, led by a conservative management, would attempt to check the rate-cutting tactics of the Burlington and Northern. By agreement, the traffic of that road moved over the Burlington. The latter, further-more, had its important rate structure on its Chicago–Missouri Valley line to protect. The Burlington, however, did not control the destinies of the other line. Some of the larger Burlington stockholders also held substantial blocks of the other's stock; in fact, some had larger interests in the Burlington and Northern than in the Burlington. In February a rate war broke out in the Chicago–St. Paul flour business. Rates were cut to $7\frac{1}{2}$ cents. The Burlington and Northern's general manager was un-certain what policy to follow. He asked the Burlington's president "to decide whether we should accept the situation and the consequent loss in the general interests or to stand out for some basis of rates suited to our necessities."[28] By late April the road finally decided upon a rate policy calculated to serve its own interests, regardless of the effects upon the Burlington. The earlier agreement had, in the opinion of its president, led to a tariff that was "absolutely prohibitory." He therefore gave the sixty-day withdrawal notice from the Northwestern Freight Association. His line, said the president, would be operated in such a way that the cities of St. Paul and Minneapolis would "be made the distributing center for the North West."[29]

While these rate wars progressed in the Northwest and Central West, the revenue of the roads in these areas suffered further from rate reductions on transcontinental business. The Sunset Route did not relinquish its drive to increase its percentage of the trade. The consequent reduction in the traffic moving over the all-rail hauls diminished the importance of the Pacific Coast Association. The traffic was so little and the rates so low that the members decided late in 1886 to refuse the payment of funds necessary to maintain the pool structure. By January 1, 1887, the Pacific Coast Association collapsed. What little all-rail traffic remained was carried largely over the Canadian Pacific and its business allies in the United States.

While these rate disturbances continued in the Northwest and Central West and along the transcontinental routes, a new set of problems suddenly appeared. They arose from the passage of the Interstate Commerce Act early in 1887. The law prohibited pools, and thus removed a rate-stabilizing incentive. No longer could roads agree to divide traffic or earnings in such a way as to make it unprofitable to reduce rates. The law also prohibited the roads from charging higher rates "under substantially similar circumstances" for a shorter distance than for a longer distance on traffic moving in the same direction. In the case of dissimilar circumstances, however, the commission could exempt a road from the necessity of complying with this provision. A road competing for long-distance through traffic on the basis of low rates was now compelled to charge the same low rates for traffic moving to intermediate points, even though at such intermediate points there was no competition. To carry competitive traffic at low rates on through business would compel a road to charge low rates on local business. More through business could be acquired only at the expense of reducing the revenue on the local business. The effect on such a road as the Union Pacific, with a large volume of local business, was explained by Adams in a request to the Commission to exempt that line from the operation of this provision—the famous long and short haul clause. The Union Pacific, according to Adams, by not reducing its through and local rates, had lost 90 per cent of its through business. On the other hand, if both through and local rates were reduced to the level needed in order to secure the through traffic, the earnings of the road would not equal its fixed charges.[30]

This clause increased the competitive strength of the Canadian Pacific. That line had relatively little local traffic. Even if it had been substantial it was not bound by the Interstate Commerce Act. The road could thus reduce its through rates without a corresponding reduction of its local rates. Soon after the passage of the law the Canadian Pacific reduced rates from San Francisco to Chicago to a point considerably lower than those charged by the Southern Pacific.[31]

The long and short haul clause of the act also affected business in the Northwest and Central West. Shortly after the Burlington and Northern notified the Northwestern pool of its decision to withdraw it entered upon another rate-cutting policy. The grain rates which had increased in March were lowered in May. Since the *new* Chicago–St. Paul lines had little local traffic, their competitive power on through traffic was strengthened by the long and short haul clause. They were at greater liberty to reduce the through rates. They were thus able to secure more business without sacrificing much local business. The initiative in rate cutting among the new lines was taken by the Stickney road. In the summer of 1887 it reduced the St. Paul–Chicago rate about 33 per cent below that prevailing on the older lines. It also made agreements with shippers by various "private cuts and favors." By these means it secured pledges to move traffic over its line. By the end of the year it was doing about 50 per cent of the Chicago–Twin Cities business. The Burlington and Northern management was undecided upon a policy to meet this competition. In August, shortly after the traffic began to flow so heavily over the new line, one of its officials proposed to reduce rates openly. Another official disagreed. He insisted that the very fact that some lines were not in the Association should bind the members more closely. If the road withdrew the Burlington could charge it full local rates, and it would then be "bottled up." The present relations were "most unfortunate."[32]

By the end of the year the views of both roads changed. The official who had insisted upon the continuance of the rate structure now favored a new policy. He now proposed that the road's general manager accept "the responsibility of making rates necessary to secure a fair share of the business, . . . letting him understand that our wishes are against private arrangements in direct violation of law, . . . but that having to contend with the Minnesota & Northwestern, [the Stickney line] which is carrying on a guerrilla warfare, we recognize that in making this fight, we must leave this considerably to his discretion. In other words, while we would prefer an open fight, if he finds himself in a dark room, he will have to use such weapons as the others do."[33] The road, that is, would use secret rate reductions, underbilling, violation of the rules, weight classifications, and other such measures. A Burlington official disagreed with these views. The competition of the Stickney line, in his opinion, could be blocked either by following similar tactics or by an open reduction of rates. The first alternative was "not to be thought of by any road, having a reputation to sustain or expecting to be in operation next year and the year after." If, however, the other line persisted in its policies, rates should be reduced, "regardless of the consequences."[34]

The combined Burlington–Burlington and Northern management still hesitated. An announcement was made publicly that the latter would withdraw from the Northwestern Freight Association. Some of the bitterness in railroad officialdom over the actions of the Stickney road is disclosed in the following picturesque language of a Burlington officer. That road could "paddle its own canoe, refuse to act with other roads and be a rover and a general pirate, just so long as it pays the older and stronger lines better to wink at their transgressions than to thrash them."[35]

A businessman representing the financial community, a member of both the St. Paul and the Burlington boards and for many years an intimate observer of railroad affairs, was seriously disturbed over this kind of competition. "If two or three wild cat roads west and northwest of Chicago can make rates for that whole region," he wrote, "what are we coming to? . . . Can they be boycotted, starved into submission, and compelled to do business on business principles?"[36] This is a typical protest of conservative businessmen in well-established enterprises against the invasions by new competitors. If the new businessmen succeed by reducing prices they may conceivably perform a public service. From the business standpoint, however, they are "pirates." They steal profits by doing business at lower than existing prices. Some of the leading price cutters in business history were the most hated men and frequently the least understood. Gould and Hill, in railroads, and Carnegie, in steel, are good illustrations of competitive price cutters.

Further west the building and expansion program had also disturbed the rate structure in Colorado and Utah. The closely knit 1880 understanding between the Atchison, the Burlington, and the Rio Grande had withstood numerous divisive influences. The most threatening factor was the aggressive competition offered by Evans. The Denver and New Orleans, whatever its primary aim might have been, could succeed only at the cost of destroying the relatively high rate structure in eastern

Colorado. In accordance with the 1880 understanding the roads declined to interchange freight with the Evans road, and a prolonged law suit was necessary in order to enable the line to deliver and receive freight from these major connections on a basis which would enable it to survive.

Still another competitive threat developed in the fall of 1885. Another railroad pioneer, James J. Hagerman, promoted the construction of a new line from Colorado Springs into the growing mining area around Aspen, Colorado. Like so many other small builders and promoters, Hagerman offered to sell the property to Gould. The offer was not accepted. Hagerman then succeeded in raising a substantial sum in New York City. In his efforts to arrange satisfactory relations with the Colorado trunk lines he encountered, as did Evans, the organized opposition of the members of the 1880 agreement. Three of the four members were also included in a Missouri River pool. The Burlington, the Atchison, and the Union Pacific refused to reduce rates between the Missouri River and Denver. Negotiations with the executives of these roads was characterized by a sense of futility and frustration. "It seems folly," wrote Hagerman, "to put any dependence in Jackson & Adams doing anything fair."[37]

By 1886 competition had broken up the 1880 agreement. Furthermore the act of 1887 required the railroads to interchange traffic with each other on a nondiscriminatory basis. By 1888 the rates on Colorado–Utah traffic were in "bad condition."[38] In November all the roads in a newly established Colorado Association agreed to restore rates, with some slight exceptions, by December 8. The Rock Island, the most recent candidate for the Colorado traffic (whose Denver line had just been finished), refused to join. The distribution of the traffic by a pool was now illegal. It was proposed to accomplish results indirectly. In order to maintain rates it was proposed that a commissioner or board be authorized to divert business from one line to another by differential rates. In this way each road would be given a fair share of the business. It was recognized that an agreement so arranged would be "largely an experiment." The condition of Colorado rates was so bad that it was recognized "that something must be done."[39]

While negotiations were going on, the Rock Island reduced rates on bullion from Denver and Pueblo to the Missouri River.[40] Early in 1889, furthermore, at least according to charges made by the Burlington, both the Rock Island and the Union Pacific were paying commission on some

Montana business, though doubt was expressed whether any road other than the Rock Island was following this practice to any considerable extent. "I have no confidence" in the Rock Island, bluntly observed a Burlington executive. Rates, nevertheless, were "very well maintained." The company was making more money, declared this same official, even with the "stealing" by the Rock Island than if it had ventured on reprisals.[41]

A far more serious threat to the rate structure during the same period occurred further south. The completion of the Panhandle Route between Denver, Fort Worth, and Galveston affected the traffic between Colorado and the Atlantic Coast. The Panhandle Route offered a circuitous rail-water route between Colorado and the eastern seaboard. It was obvious that this line, with a slower service than the overland rail haul, could secure through traffic only by offering lower rates. Its intermediate traffic was relatively slight. If, therefore, in accordance with the law, it quoted rates as low on through traffic as it did on local traffic, it would lose little. On the other hand, the overland railroad lines had much to lose. Their local traffic was large and relatively profitable. The Union Pacific, for example, in order to compete with the new route and to enable it to observe the long and short haul clause, would be obliged to reduce its rates to the level of the lower through rates. In the summer of 1889 an agent of the road estimated that reductions "already made" in the efforts to meet the Panhandle competition would reduce earnings in that year by $2 million.[42] Between 1888 and 1890 the Union Pacific, according to its own officers, was seriously hurt by the Panhandle Route. The latter secured traffic only by virtue of its differential, thereby demoralizing through rates.

This loss to the Union Pacific was of no concern to the Panhandle. The spirited leader of the Denver–Pueblo section of that route declared emphatically that the major lines between Colorado and the Missouri River had been charging his line "three times as much per ton mile for all their traffic as they charged across Iowa to Chicago." He was determined "to get around Gould and Strong and Perkins and Adams."[43]

The rate war on the business between Colorado and the seaboard began in 1888, soon after the completion of the route. The rate on lumber between Colorado points and Texas and the Gulf ports was reduced. This forced the Union Pacific to reduce its rates from Portland. The Panhandle then dropped rates even further. The Colorado Association endeavored to induce the Panhandle to advance rates; the latter agreed only to make rates between Galveston and Denver the same as between St. Louis and Denver, and from New Orleans the same as from Chicago. The Union Pacific did not immediately meet these rates; it feared adverse effects because of the necessity to reduce rates on intermediate traffic to the level of the low through rates. The Missouri Pacific and the Atchison, however, quoted rates a few cents lower than those set by the Panhandle. The New York agents of the major Colorado roads were authorized to meet from day to day the competition of the new route. Early in May the representatives of all the lines met in Chicago and set up a committee of three, with authority to decide the problems growing out of competition with the new route. It seemed for a while that a satisfactory settlement could be negotiated. These expectations were not borne out and the intensity of the competition increased.[44]

The construction program of the late 1880's that thus disrupted the relatively stabilized rate structure in eastern Colorado also impaired the success of another one in the Northwest and Rocky Mountain area. The 1880 agreement between the Manitoba and the Northern Pacific had permitted these two lines to follow stable rate policies in the Red River Valley and in Dakota and Montana. The Manitoba's extension through Dakota into Montana and the Northern Pacific's into the Red River Valley and the province of Manitoba were accompanied by rate reductions. The Manitoba reached Helena in November, 1887. This development was followed by a 20 per cent rate cut.[45] Rates between Montana and the Missouri and Mississippi River valleys were thus disturbed. Because of an understanding between the Union and the Northern Pacific, the rates between Montana points and Chicago over the former were the same as to Chicago via St. Paul over the latter. The Manitoba reduced the rates from Montana to Chicago. The Northern Pacific rate between Helena and St. Paul was $3.00; the Manitoba reduced this to $2.00. These rate reductions, according to one observer, created the "biggest disturbance" since the passage of the Interstate Commerce Act early in 1887.[46]

On the eastern end of the Manitoba–Northern Pacific battlefield rate reductions were also made. The sale of its railroad by the provincial government of Manitoba to the Northern Pacific required the latter to make rates between Winnipeg and Duluth lower than between Winnipeg and Port Arthur, a point reached by the Canadian Pacific.[47] The Northern Pacific also was enjoined from entering into any agreement with the Canadian Pacific to maintain rates. The Canadian Pacific meanwhile was building a line to connect with another being built by an independent company north from Seattle. The Canadian Pacific could then cut rates against the Northern Pacific in the west, while the Northern Pacific did the same in the east.

Trouble meanwhile was brewing also in the lower Missouri River gateways in the area covered by the Southwestern Railway Association. That pool, which, had continued to operate so smoothly through 1886 and for a short while in the following year, began to weaken under the impetus of a number of corrosive forces. The completion of the St. Paul's line to Kansas City made that road a strong competitor for the lumber traffic from the Northwest, and what was even more significant, for the profitable hog and cattle business. A substantial part of the latter originated on the Atchison. The business at Kansas City was distributed on the basis of the allotment made in the Southwestern Railway Association to the roads running east and north from that point. Much of this traffic was delivered to the local packing houses and shipped east in the form of dressed beef and hog products. A director and large stockholder of the St. Paul, Philip D. Armour, also owned one of the nation's largest meat-packing establishments. It should occasion no surprise to learn that soon after the St. Paul reached Kansas City most of the beef and hog products traffic moved east over the lines of the St. Paul.

Competitive complications were intensified by the completion of the Atchison's Kansas City–Chicago extension. The Association could no longer distribute its eastbound Atchison business among its member lines. The Atchison naturally retained its eastbound traffic for its own line. One of the roads most seriously damaged was the Alton. That road had been a friendly connection of the Atchison; it did not compete with the Atchison for the movement of business west of the Missouri River. With the Atchison in control of its own line to Chicago the service of the Alton was no longer needed. The two roads became business enemies.

By the end of 1887 these competitive factors led to an outbreak of rate cuts. The Southwestern rates were "demoralized" and within a few weeks thereafter it became clear that the rates via Omaha would also weaken.[48] In mid-January Hughitt asked Perkins to call a meeting of Blackstone, president of the Alton, Cable, and himself, to consider the Southwestern problem. Perkins wrote to Blackstone suggesting such a meeting, and

Blackstone replied that unless the Burlington and the Wabash could agree on changes acceptable to the competing roads he was unable to see any good that might come from such a meeting. Perkins informed Hughitt that the Alton had some undisclosed motive "for letting the low rates continue for the present."[49]

By the beginning of 1888, accordingly, competitive forces were approaching a climax in the West, between the Canadian boundary and the lower Missouri Valley and between Chicago and the Rocky Mountains. Flour and grain rates from the Twin Cities to the seaboard were reduced approximately 25 per cent below the rate of the Chicago lines.[50] The Burlington–Burlington and Northern combination now decided to take the decisive step and come out in the open. In January, 1888, the route reduced its seaboard flour and grain rates to the newly established level.[51] Soon thereafter the rates broke between Chicago and the Missouri River.

The rate war spread to almost all parts of the Missouri and Mississippi Valleys. The regional interdependence of the railroad rate structure was clearly established. What happened to rates in the Northwest affected the rates in the West and Southwest, and any reduction in the Southwest affected the rates in the other areas. Railroad men questioned the necessity of such retaliatory interregional rate disturbances. "I do not see," wired Perkins to Hughitt, "why rates to the Southwest and to Council Bluffs should be dependent on rates to St. Paul. . . ."[52] Rate wars, it was evident, now differed from previous ones. War could no longer be confined to one area. To a considerable extent in previous disturbances, rates could be maintained by a number of roads in the Southwest, even though they were not maintained in the Northwest. By 1888 this was no longer possible. Roads in the Northwest had now penetrated deep into the Southwest. The St. Paul and the Stickney road, for example, now had lines between the Twin Cities and Chicago, as well as between the Twin Cities and Kansas City. The Atchison was no longer confined to the Southwest. Neither was the Rock Island confined to the territory east of the Missouri River; it now had lines to Denver and through Kansas. The rate war of February, 1888, was described by a contemporary writer as "chaos."[53]

The war was followed by the dissolution of the associations. The St. Paul gave notice of its intention to withdraw from the Western and the Northwestern Associations. The chairman of the Southwestern, as well

23

as of the Western and the Northwestern bodies, authorized their members to meet the low rates in accordance with market conditions. This in effect meant the dissolution of these associations.

Charges and countercharges soon appeared. To one railroad journal, the Burlington and Northern and the Stickney Line appeared to be "the most aggressive combatants in the war."[54] To the Burlington officials, the Stickney Line and the Wisconsin Central were the irresponsible culprits. A St. Paul official accused the Burlington of making secret contracts for the New York–St. Paul business at rates lower than those charged by other lines.[55] Perkins condemned the refusal of the Alton and the St. Paul to come into the Southwestern Association, thereby indicating, as he claimed, "where the responsibility lies for this present demoralization."[56]

The transcontinental rate war meanwhile ended with the help of a concession to one of the combatants. The Canadian Pacific had steadily refused to associate itself with any agreement. Efforts to reach an understanding continued, however, throughout 1887. One problem was the refusal of the Canadian Pacific to accept any settlement to maintain a uniform rate schedule. Its route between San Francisco and the East was circuitous. In order to balance the slower delivery line it believed it was entitled to charge a lower rate. Its views were finally accepted. In January, 1888, the Canadian Pacific enrolled as a member of a new Transcontinental Association. Rates were increased from existing levels on traffic between Chicago and the East. On traffic between Chicago and the East over the Canadian Pacific, a differential of from 5 to 10 per cent was deducted from the rates charged by other lines. The Canadian Pacific agreed to maintain rates. The differential did not apply to business to and from the Missouri River. The Canadian Pacific virtually withdrew from that traffic.[57]

The differential was not well received by railroad officialdom. The general manager of the Southern Pacific described it as a means of preventing the Canadian Pacific "from practically destroying the through traffic of the United States roads. . . ."[58] Another railroader was even more emphatic. The road, he asserted, followed "a sort of stand-and-deliver policy."[59]

The rate war in the West, however, continued to spread. Repeated efforts were made to effect a settlement. Attention was first turned in the direction of reorganizing the several associations. Cable's idea of replacing the western associations by a single body was revised. In February a committee was formed and approved such a plan in principle agreeing that one organization should be formed and that it should be under the control of a central authority. Objections were raised by Miller, president of the St. Paul. The Northwestern moved that rates be restored to the level of January 1. All voted in favor of the latter except the Burlington, whose representative argued against the proposal to maintain rates. A permanent peace was desirable, it was argued, and money lost was well spent if such a permanent peace actually was achieved; but the money was wasted if only a spurious "patch-work, upon the old bases of organization" was created, to be followed by another rate war. "Having been reluctantly compelled to fight," one official wrote, "we did not feel safe to lay down our arms till a treaty of peace seemed probable."[60]

The deadlock continued, and so did the rate war. A revealing justification of the war and of the necessity of its continuance until a definitive settlement could be reached was again presented by a Burlington official. Money, it is true, was being lost in the present war; but "no money which we have spent on construction account in building new lines in Nebraska or elsewhere during the last few years, will be as productive of net revenue to the company as the money which we are now being forced to spend to clear up the relations between the lines." Nothing would more certainly prevent the building of private lines than to make sure that they would lose a good deal of money.[61]

The search for peace went on. "Like you," wrote a banker interested in railroad securities, "I am anxious to secure a permanent peace. How to aid in bringing it about I don't know."[62] A few weeks later another railroad leader made an approach toward a settlement. Coolidge, a large stockholder in both the Burlington and the Atchison, declared that a rate settlement under existing conditions would be broken by Stickney or some underling. Honest railroads would then be cheated out of their business, and another war would soon follow. Coolidge learned through an agent of another road that Strong would be delighted to enter into a rate-maintenance agreement, but that no manager or superintendent could be trusted. They were too eager for business. Presidents, however, in contact with stockholders could, in Strong's opinion, effect a satisfactory arrangement.[63]

Not until September was another concerted effort made to restore rates. Early in that month the general managers of the roads, formerly members of the various associations, met. A renewed move to set up one association was again rejected. The St. Paul again refused to join the Southwestern Association until the problems in the Northwest had been solved. The major obstacle there was the refusal of the Burlington and Northern to accept an agreement until the St. Paul withdrew its milling-in-transit rates. Despite the inability to reorganize the associations, the managers did restore rates between Chicago and Kansas City, and between St. Paul, Minneapolis, and Southwestern Missouri River points.[64] This agreement did not last long, and within a few weeks the rates of the Southwestern roads were reported to be in a "more demoralized state" than in any other area.[65]

After these failures to settle the wars by the formation of new associations the roads acted informally, and by mid-March apparently agreed to a restoration of rates. A number announced publicly an advance to become effective on March 26. Although the St. Paul and Duluth continued its refusal to join and though the Soo Line insisted upon a differential rate as a price of joining, the rates were nevertheless restored in late March, except for those of the Burlington and Northern, which agreed to restore rates early in April. By that time the rates over most of the West were increased to the level of February 1. Authoritative opinion expressed skepticism over the permanence of the arrangement. One railroad periodical, for example, declared bluntly that it was "quite safe to agree with those people who believe that the present peace will be shortlived."[66] In the face of this general agreement the Burlington and Northern, apparently contrary to the wishes of the Burlington, declined to maintain the higher rates. This drew strong condemnation from responsible stockholders and directors of the Burlington. One banker-stockholder, for example, complained to Perkins that the regulatory commission in Iowa (under terms of a proposed law then under consideration) would compel the Burlington to carry freight in that state at rates as low as those charged by the Burlington and Northern in the St. Paul–Chicago business. Other roads would follow and the war would be revived.[67]

Further negotiations among the northwestern lines finally led to an agreement in late May to maintain uniform rates. There was, of course, no pooling provision; this was now illegal. There was, however, an agreement by which money would be deposited in a fund from which fines would be paid by the violators. Rates were to be raised on June 4.

The Burlington and Northern refused to ratify and, instead, reduced rates on the St. Paul–Chicago business from 60 to 40 cents on first class.[68] This cut was followed by a momentous step by the Stickney line. That road declared that while it would reduce the Chicago–St. Paul rate to this new level it would not be bound by the short haul clause of the Interstate Commerce Act.[69] The Wisconsin Central followed with a similar statement of policy. By early June the prospects for a peace settlement had disappeared. In other areas, meanwhile, the rate cutting also continued. Throughout the West, related one financial observer, between Chicago and St. Paul, between Chicago and the Missouri River, between that River and the Pacific Ocean, the story was the same. There "are so many roads to divide the traffic among, all inducement to take the through business is gone." Between Chicago and St. Paul the rate on the lowest classification dropped to 8 cents per hundred pounds; and on the Chicago–St. Paul haul of over four hundred miles the rate produced a return of 0.4 cent per ton-mile.[70]

Negotiations for the settlement of the Northwestern war continued, off and on, throughout the summer months. A major obstacle was the insistence of the St. Paul on its proposal to continue its transit privilege. It was "impossible to abolish transit," asserted a St. Paul official late in August. By this time the St. Paul had passed dividends, and stock control was lodged in the hands of an eastern banking group led by Drexel-Morgan. Under pressure from this source, the St. Paul finally gave way. It agreed to modify its transit system and give the other roads a share of the transit freight at Minneapolis, the proportion to be decided by the chairman of the Association. Rates would then be increased.[71] For the first time in railroad history investment bankers had intervened in Western affairs to settle a major rate dispute. Bankers had displaced management, and in a decisive way and on a major business problem. Thus was set a precedent for many developments along the same pattern in years to come.

But this agreement again proved to be delusive. There was no means of enforcing its provisions. There was no binding cement, and not long thereafter railroad managers agreed to take other measures to maintain the rate structure. In mid-November presidents and other top executives of the Northwestern, Rock Island, St. Paul, and Burlington agreed to place the movement of eastbound grain, livestock, and packing-house products from Omaha in the hands of the manager of one of the western

Associations. He would decide the share of the traffic to be carried by the participating roads. He would instruct the lines to take measures necessary to accomplish such a division. If a road exceeded its percentage of allotted traffic, the manager would request it to stop soliciting business, to refrain from supplying sufficient rolling stock, or to raise rates without the rates of other lines being increased. There was no record of the agreement. One of the railroad periodicals, however, suspected the existence of such an understanding, and observed that, while in spirit it was in violation of the law, in substance probably it was not. The law applied to the railroads and not to their officials individually. [72]

Despite these agreements the rates were not maintained. They remained lower than the level necessary to meet expenses and produce some slight margin of profit. "We cannot," wrote a railroad official, "live with substantially lower rates than we are now receiving; it is even a question whether we can live at the present rates." [73] There was general recognition that the agreements were no substitute for pools. Though pools were not always successful they did frequently lead to the maintenance of stable rate structures over short periods, and occasionally over longer ones. Rate-fixing agreements and allied schemes produced no satisfactory results, and to an increasing degree they were condemned by railroad officers. Hughitt stated flatly that "all the schemes proposed [were] chimerical." [74] Another railroad man said that they exerted only "a temporary and evanescent effect" in increasing rates. Nearly everybody, he continued, regarded the agreement as not binding upon him, "or, at least, binding no longer than he thinks it for his interest to be bound by it." For example, he asserted, the Wisconsin Central and the Stickney line, with circuitous roads in the Chicago–St. Paul traffic, would agree with the St. Paul and the Northwestern, with direct routes, to maintain equal rates. The former two lines, however, knew "perfectly well" that it was "utterly impossible" for them to do this. With similar rates they could not compete for business with the direct lines. When they were asked to make agreements with "merely good faith" as a basis, he wrote, they did so with the same "mental reservation." That is, "we will defend ourselves, if attacked, notwithstanding we have agreed to tie our hands." Nothing permanent, he concluded, could be accomplished "until there is a radical change in the methods and the underlying principle of these traffic agreements." [75] The man who made these observations was destined to become president of the reorganized Atchison in the late 1890's. The change he hoped for in the traffic agreements was not to be realized. Regional agreements, which had been made so rapidly in the previous two years, were soon to be replaced by industry-wide agreements. The understandings reached under the leadership of railroad operating managers and executives, furthermore, were to be replaced by those made under the leadership of investment bankers. The progress of such efforts and the results achieved will be sketched in the following two chapters.

Notes for Chapter XVII

[1] State of Missouri, Statements and Testimony of Railroad Managers and others before Committee on Railroads and Internal Improvements of the Extra Session of the 34th General Assembly of Missouri, Jefferson City, 1887, p. 13.

[2] *The New York Times*, Jan. 28, 1888.

[3] Hedges, p. 154.

[4] Burlington Archives, George B. Harris, of the Burlington and Northern, to Perkins, Jan. 6, 1888.

[5] M. E. Ingalls, president, Cleveland, St. Louis and Chicago Railroad, cited in *R. R. Gaz.*, April 17, 1885, p. 241.

[6] Burlington Archives, Perkins to Geddes, May 25, 1886. For this conflict over passenger fares between the Rock Island and the other roads, see *Chicago Tribune*, Feb. 26, 1886.

[7] A discussion of these rate reductions is found in *Bradstreet's* April 17, 1886, p. 242; and in somewhat less detail in *R. R. Gaz.*, April 16, 1886, p. 274.

[8] *Ibid.*, April 30, 1886, p. 304.

[9] *Ibid.*, April 30, 1886, p. 307.

[10] *Bradstreet's* Oct. 16, 1886, p. 256.

[11] *Ibid.*, July 3, 1886, p. 9.

[12] *Ibid.*, July 17, 1886, p. 42.

[13] The details on the progressive weakening and final dissolution of the Western Freight Association and the recommendations of the Committee are based upon Burlington Archives, Potter to Perkins, July 16, 1886.

[14] Details on the settlement are in *R. R. Gaz.*, Sept. 17, 1886, p. 645.

[15] This statement was made by Peter B. Shelby, assistant general traffic manager, Union Pacific, in Pac. Ry. Commission, p. 2147.

[16] Burlington Archives, Potter to Perkins, Dec. 21, 1885.

[17] *R. R. Gaz.*, Feb. 26, 1886, p. 159.

[18] *Ibid.*

[19] Burlington Archives, Palmer to Perkins, Feb. 16, 1886.

[20] *R. R. Gaz.*, Feb. 26, 1886, p. 149.

[21] This is the language used by Adams in the 1886 Annual Report of the Union Pacific, p. 25.

[22] *Chron.*, April 2, 1886, p. 237.

[23] *Chicago Tribune*, Feb. 28, 1886.

[24] *Ibid.*, Mar. 2, 1886.

[25] *Ibid.*, Mar. 18, 1886.

[26] Burlington Archives, Perkins to Palmer, June 4, 1886.

[27] Relations with Canada, Senate Report No. 1530, Part 1, 51st Congress, 1st Session, 1889, p. 905, Joseph Nimm Jr.

[28] Burlington Archives, Harris to Perkins, Feb. 26, 1887.

[29] *Ibid.*, Touzalin to Perkins, April 25, 1887.

[30] *Ry. Review*, May 7, 1887, p. 263.

[31] *R. R. Gaz.*, April 22, 1887.

[32] Burlington Archives, Stone to Perkins, Aug. 6, 1887.

[33] *Ibid.*, Dec. 30, 1887.

[34] *Ibid.*, Ripley to Perkins, Nov. 2, 1887. Ripley was the general freight agent of the Burlington.

[35] *Ibid.*, Ripley to Henry B. Stone, Dec. 29, 1887.

[36] *Ibid.*, Geddes to Perkins, Oct. 26, 1887.

[37] John J. Lipsey, *Hagerman and the Midland in the West* (Boulder, Colorado, 1955), p. 106. Jackson was at that time president of the Rio Grande, and Adams of the Union Pacific.

[38] Burlington Archives, Stones to Perkins, Nov. 26, 1888.

[39] *Ibid.*, Holdrege to Perkins, Dec. 17, 1888.

[40] *Ry. Review*, June 29, 1889, p. 371.

[41] Burlington Archives, Stone to Perkins, March 25, 1889.

[42] This statement was made to J. W. Midgley, the veteran Commissioner of the Southwestern Railway Association, according to a letter in the Burlington Archives, Midgley to Stone, June 7, 1889.

[43] Overton, p. 194.

[44] The description of the conflict between the Panhandle Route and its competitors is based on Burlington Archives, J. W. Midgley to H. B. Stone, June 7, 1889.

[45] *Ry. Review*, Nov. 19, 1887, p. 667.

[46] *The New York Times*, Oct. 24, 1887.

[47] *Chicago Tribune*, Aug. 3, 1888.

[48] The word "demoralized" is used by Perkins to Hughitt, in a letter of Feb. 17, 1888, in the Burlington Archives.

[49] *Ibid.*

[50] *Bradstreet's* Feb. 11, 1888, p. 90.

[51] *R. R. Gaz.*, Feb. 3, 1888, p. 82.

[52] Burlington Archives, Perkins to Hughitt, telegram, Feb. 4, 1888.

[53] *Bradstreet's* Feb. 11, 1888, p. 90.

[54] *R. R. Gaz.*, Feb. 17, 1888, p. 114.

[55] *Chicago Tribune*, Feb. 24, 1888.

[56] Burlington Archives, Perkins to Hughitt, Feb. 4, 1888.

[57] For details on the Canadian Pacific differential see 2 Reports Interstate Commerce Commission (1888), pp. 19-20.

[58] Towne, 3rd vice-president and general manager, Southern Pacific, cited in *Ry. Review*, June 15, 1889, p. 333.

[59] The United States and Canada, Senate, Report No. 847, 51st Congress, 1st Session, 1889, J. M. Hannaford, traffic manager, Northern Pacific, p. 569.

[60] Burlington Archives, Ripley to Stone, Feb. 18, 1888.

[61] *Ibid.*, Stone to Perkins, Feb. 18, 1888.

[62] *Ibid.*, Geddes to Perkins, Feb. 25, 1888.

[63] *Ibid.*, Coolidge to Perkins, Mar. 12, 1888.

[64] *Chicago Tribune*, Sept. 12, 1888, and Sept. 26, 1888.

[65] *Chron.*, Nov. 3, 1888, p. 514.

[66] *R. R. Gaz.*, April 13, 1888, p. 238.

[67] Burlington Archives, Geddes to Perkins, April 26, 1888.

[68] *Bradstreet's* June 2, 1888, p. 358.

[69] *R. R. Gaz.*, June 8, 1888, p. 371.

[70] *Chron.*, June 9, 1888, p. 721.

[71] *R. R. Gaz.*, Oct. 5, 1888, p. 661.

[72] The agreement is summarized in a letter, Stone to Perkins, Nov. 15, 1888, in the Burlington Archives, and the railroad comment is in *R. R. Gaz.*, April 5, 1889, p. 228.
[73] Burlington Archives, Stone to Perkins, Nov. 27, 1888.
[74] *Ibid.*, Nov. 30, 1888.
[75] *Ibid.*, Ripley to Stone, Nov. 6, 1888.

XVIII

Stabilization by Industry-wide Action
Interstate Commerce Railway Association

THE RATE wars had by the fall of 1888 brought western railroads to a dangerous point. It seemed almost impossible for individual railroad managements to look forward to a remedy. There was widespread opinion that the rate wars, even though they were accompanied by lower rates, did more harm than good. The selling prices, in terms of ton-mile rates, had throughout the 1880's declined almost uninterruptedly. Ton-mile rates, however, were not an accurate reflection of the extent of such reductions. A change in these rates reflected then, as it does now, in part changes in the composition of traffic, the length of haul, and the proportion of through and local traffic. Some commodities carry high rates, while others, particularly bulky commodities such as wheat, coal, and lumber, carry relatively low rates. Accordingly a rise or fall in ton-mile rates might be the result only of a change in the composition of traffic. An increase in the percentage of the higher-rated traffic, for example, would increase the average ton-mile rate. Specific evidence on the deficiency of the average ton-mile rate in disclosing the full effect of rate wars is furnished by the 1890 Annual Report of the Stickney road. For that year the average rate per ton-mile was 0.72 cent, for the previous year, 0.95 cent; and in 1888, 0.80 cent. During these years the ton-mile rate on flour between Chicago and Minneapolis, however, was only 0.35 cent. "The war of rates," reported the management in its 1890 Report, "has been fierce and continuous throughout the year, . . ."[1] Another example might be pertinent. One of the small northwestern roads reported for the year 1890 a slight rise in its ton-mile rate as compared with the preceding year. Yet its "through or competitive traffic . . . of the territory through which the line runs, has . . . been transported at

338

lower rates than have obtained during any period of equal length in the history of western railways and unquestionably a large proportion of it has proven very unremunerative to the lines transporting it."[2]

There is some evidence available on reductions directly produced by the rate wars. The first-class rates on the Chicago–St. Paul business per hundred pounds, according to a tabulation of one source, for example, moved as follows: May, 1887, 75 cents; February, 1888, 25 cents; June, 1888, 50 cents; September, 1888, 60 cents. In 1889 the rates fluctuated between 60 and 34 cents.[3]

The adverse effects of the rate competition on earnings and finances were generally recognized, both by railroad businessmen and by exponents of the public welfare. Railroad annual reports lent eloquent testimony to the belief by corporate management of "the evils of reckless competition."[4] Similar references to the pernicious effects of rate wars were found in the annual reports of almost all of the western roads in the late 1880's and early 1890's. The newly organized Interstate Commerce Commission added its voice to the managerial criticism. Some emotionally charged comments featured its statements. Retaliations by one road against another for "supposed grievances or for the punishment of supposed wrongs correspond to the methods whereby in a barbarous age a rude redress by force is sought for individual injury."[5]

These cumulative rate reductions by the fall of 1888 had impaired the financial strength of almost all of the western roads. Dividend reductions by roads whose securities were considered of high investment quality introduced a note of emergency. In some quarters a feeling of gloom pervaded the industry. Railroad construction programs that had been forecast in 1887 and for some months in 1888 were discarded. It was impossible to raise the necessary funds.

Reductions in stock prices accompanied the decline in earnings and dividends. The widespread financial losses led to severe condemnations of management. A surprising attack against the more conservative western railroads was delivered by the *New York Sun*, a paper long friendly to the railroad industry. The attacks in this journal were particularly bitter. "There is nothing in our commercial history so disgraceful," was an editorial comment, as the record for 1888 of the Burlington, St. Paul, Northwestern, Rock Island, and Burlington and Northern. Hughitt, Perkins, and Cable "have squandered millions of the property intrusted to their care, and they stand preeminent today as types of the very worst and most pernicious element that has ever become identified with a great commercial interest." The same writer, in referring to the failure of one of the numerous agreements made in the western railroad business—this one between Cable and Perkins, further expounded his views: "Things have come to an evil pass when the trustees of the greatest public trusts are the most conspicuous examples of chicanery and profligacy in high office that the history of the country affords."[6]

An even stauncher representative of the financial community, a leading weekly financial journal, was critical of the inability of management to maintain reasonable rates. "The controlling power in each corporation has been wholly selfish, bristling all over with hostile purpose towards every other. No right of territory, no settlement of rates, no adjustment of business, stood for a moment as a hindrance to the insatiable craving of getting business. There is a certain state of society when the freebooter is tolerated; there is a state of railroad development when the system of each man for himself, without respect to word or method, is endured. But as with the development of society new obligations and new bonds spring up, so with the vast and varied growth in railroad interests and property, a situation is reached which demands that the ambitions of each road must be subordinated to a union and comity in action which community of interests require."[7]

The advisability of industry-wide action, as a means of stabilizing the rate structure and restoring to the industry a reasonable earning power, had been recognized for a number of years. There was considerable difference of opinion over the way in which co-operation could displace railroad rivalry. Many were convinced that only pools could end rate wars. This remedy had been made illegal in 1887, but many still insisted that pools under government regulations would terminate the rate wars. "There may be other ways of preventing the ruinous competition that has brought so many roads to the verge of ruin," wrote Adlace F. Walker, a man with long railroad experience and one who was selected as a leader on an industry-wide basis in western railroad territory, "but I have not heard them."[8]

Efforts made to induce the Congress to modify the pool provisions of the law failed. Some form of industry co-operation was believed essential. Accordingly most of the major associations through which the pools were operated were not dissolved. They were subsequently used as a basis for efforts to stabilize western rates. During the late 1880's and the 1890's (until they were declared illegal in 1897) they performed a number of important functions—they diverted traffic from one road to another for the purpose of equalizing business in accordance with prior understandings; they constituted media through which agreements for the division of territory among the various roads was carried out; and they acted as channels for applying differential rates on a particular road or roads to offset some disability, such as excessive distance or unusually difficult physical handicaps. Roads were, however, still free to quote lower rates as a means of getting business or as a retaliatory device to retrieve losses to a rival.

Proposals to eliminate rate wars came more and more in 1888 to concentrate upon agreements to unify the rate-making activities of western roads. Informed opinion increasingly expressed itself in the direction of limiting the scope of free and open competition. A member of the Interstate Commerce Commission declared: "It is a fact now as well known as any fact of human experience that free and active competition is inconsistent with regulation; that, in the language of Judge Cooley, it kills the remedy."[9] Railroad officials, even those most active in competitive life, began to think in terms of the partial suppression of competition.

The outbreak of the violent war early in 1888 led Perkins to enter into confidential discussions with Albert Fink, the Eastern Railroad Commissioner. While the rate war was just beginning, asserted Perkins, it was "a good plan in time of war to prepare for peace." Perkins thought it wise to communicate with Fink because most of the stock ownership of western roads was concentrated in the East. Perkins credited Hughitt with the belief that "companies who inaugurated the existing disastrous conditions should immediately call a halt and invite the co-operation of all competing interests in an effort to adjust differences and restore rates to a remunerative standard." Perkins questioned the outcome of such a move. He was unable to understand what steps could be taken after the existing rate disturbance had been terminated. "I have been unable, so far," wrote Perkins, "to think of any plan for maintaining rates west of Chicago, unless we can agree upon some common agency, representing all the lines, which shall have the sole rate making power." Perkins suggested that a plan should come from Fink's office and that the roads west of Chicago should put their traffic questions into the hands of a commission composed of such men as Judge Cooley, a member of the Interstate Commerce Commission, and of traffic officials familiar with western railroad affairs. Perkins suggested further that the commission be empowered "to decide what proportion of competitive traffic each line ought to carry, and to vary rates to produce the desired result."[10] Many railroad executives agreed with Perkins that, though such a move was desirable, it was not practicable. There were many small roads that refused to enter into such an arrangement. Perhaps most of these independently minded properties owned roundabout lines. The circuitous transportation facilities that were to cause so many complicated railroad problems over the next half a century were for the most part built in the 1880's. They could not hope to secure a share of the business sufficient to meet their expenses on the basis of uniform rates. They could get traffic only by reducing rates. A few illustrations might clarify the problem. Between Council Bluffs and St. Paul the short line was 370 miles; the longest was 732 miles. Between Chicago and Des Moines the short line was 354 miles; the long line was 666 miles. Between Omaha and San Francisco there were five routes ranging from 1,865 miles to 2,724 miles. All these were operating, workable routes. Many included a number of small roads, or portions of such roads, and the revenue to each was frequently "ridiculously small."[11]

By the summer of 1888, thinking among railroad men and others in public life closely associated with the railroad industry finally led to the emergence of specific plans for industry-wide agreements. Probably the earliest was submitted jointly by Gould and Huntington. The proposal was presented after consultation with Adams, Strong, and others. The plan was "almost breath-taking in its universality. Nothing like it had ever been presented. All existing freight and passenger associations were to be abolished and their functions taken by a clearing house. Each road west of the Mississippi River would be represented, and the clearing house would take over the rate-making authority of all the roads. It would also prescribe the divisions on all through business. The suggested agreement struck at the very root of the stabilization problem by declaring that the bidding for business by means of private concessions shall cease. "[12] The proposal received the support of perhaps the most distinguished member of the Interstate Commerce Commission—Judge Cooley: "It hasn't the slightest thing in common with a trust."[13]

Other railroad men meanwhile had also been thinking along parallel lines. E. F. Winslow, president of the Frisco, had been conferring with "certain parties representing large interests" in some of the Western roads. Since the situation admitted "of no delay," a committee, of which

Winslow was chairman, worked out a platform embodying a plan for a clearinghouse. The plan would set up a board of Managers, which would devote its "entire attention" to the affairs of the clearinghouse. The authority to make rates and regulations on traffic would "be taken from the officers of the several railroads as such and be vested absolutely in the Clearing House." It was proposed, furthermore, that all rate concessions be disallowed, "unless authority therefore shall be given by the Board of Managers or the Executive Board." The proposed plan, indeed, went so far as to empower the executive board "to secure to each member such share of the business for which it can legitimately compete as they may conclude it is entitled to receive."[14]

When Winslow presented this plan he discovered broad differences of opinion. Hughitt thought it was too strong; the president of the Alton, too weak; while Cable might "be said to view it as insufficient or lacking in permanency." It is clear that the plan would not be accepted. Meanwhile, Winslow was fearful of the results of neglecting to act upon some comprehensive plan.[15]

In the interim a number of other ideas for industry-wide agreement were submitted. The plans of Gould and Winslow had been based on the idea of setting up a formal organization with an administrative machinery. Another, marked "Strictly Confidential," unsigned, and dated December 20, 1888, called for a company with the name of the United Railway Association. The Association would issue stock of which 15 per cent would be preference, to be held by banking firms, and not less than 85 per cent "by the railroad companies whose co-operation is desired." Railroads contracting with the Association would receive for the transportation of its passengers and freight a gross sum per month or per year to be agreed upon. The directors and officers of the Association would have "the power to supervise traffic; ... [to] prescribe the rates, rules and regulations which shall govern in the conduct of the ... passenger and freight traffic, and insure their strict maintenance by all members; and shall prescribe the character of the service and the conveniences which shall be offered for travelling and shipping public." The board of directors would comprise one person from each road and five named by the banks. Furthermore, the railroads "shall construct no new lines of railroad except by and with the unanimous approval of the Directors of the Association first had and obtained." Finally, the extraordinary provision was suggested that, when the Association had contracted with the

railroad, the latter's officers and agents would be "debarred from inter-
fering with the movement of the business, or from deviating from the
rates ordered to be charged and collected thereon."[16] One's imagination
is stirred by contemplating the state of mind of any railroad executive
who believed that such a plan could ever be accepted by the railroad
community or be seriously supported by public opinion.

Another proposal, couched along informal lines and based upon good
faith in the promises of railroad executives, was suggested by Strong.
No employee of the subscribing companies should depart "from the
established rates, rules and regulations governing competitive traffic
transported,—the word 'competitive' . . . intended to include traffic
competitive by reason of markets or contiguity of stations as well as traffic
to or from common points,—either by the payment of commissions,
drawbacks, bonuses, salaries, rebates by 'manipulation' so called, or in
any other way." To enforce the agreement it was proposed that if any
member had "reasonable grounds" for believing that action had been
taken "contrary to the spirit and intent" of the agreement, it would lay
the facts before the subscribers, and by a majority vote they would "require the withdrawal of any and all authority from the offending person
or persons to in anyway thereafter make, establish or quote rates, rules
or conditions on traffic subject to this agreement."[17] Adams approved
unconditionally, and Perkins approved "with the understanding that it
is to become operative if other competing lines which are material also
join."

The clearinghouse plan was condemned as a scheme of Gould[1]. It was
a rate-fixing device. It was monopolistic. It put many communities in
the power of a small group. A western newspaper asserted that Gould, as
part of his efforts to push through the clearinghouse plan, was "devoting
his attention to bulldozing tactics by demoralizing the securities of those
roads he considered unfriendly to his plans and working up a hostile
feeling against the management of those roads among their stockholders."
The clearinghouse plan was attacked in other quarters. "In less than a
week after its publication, its doom was certain. Gould, quick to learn,
saw the light and tried to evade responsibility for its failure. He had not
invented the scheme, he said: he had only approved a trial test."[18]

In the final event the railroad executives decided to accept no leadership from among their own members. They turned instead to the banking
community. Late in November they met at the New York City home of

Morgan, where a preliminary draft was drawn up. Morgan had already registered a number of important financial achievements. Another meeting was held on December 19 and 20, 1888, when the preliminary draft was presented. The meeting adjourned and was followed by another on January 8, 1889. This meeting was called by Drexel-Morgan, in conjunction with two other bankers—Brown Brothers and Kidder Peabody. The meeting continued for three days. A general plan was agreed upon, to become effective only when signed by a sufficient number of western roads. Another meeting, lasting seven days, was held in Chicago. There the agreement reached in New York early in January was changed in a number of particulars. The final meeting, held in Chicago, February 19 to February 22, was, according to a Burlington representative, a "stormy one." Miller, president of the St. Paul, resumed his attack on the Burlington and Northern. For two years he had complained that this road, supported by the Burlington, was the chief sinner in the Chicago–St. Paul rate wars. At this meeting, Miller "made the most violent and savage attack" on the Burlington and Northern and on the Burlington that the latter's representatives had ever heard. Miller suggested that no vote be taken on the adoption of a plan until a number of roads had agreed to sign. The plan was approved, however, and a new organization, the Interstate Commerce Railway Association, was set up. It was charged with the responsibility of maintaining "reasonable uniform and stable rates. Power was given to punish any employee found guilty of rate cutting and the railroad presidents pledged themselves to discharge this responsibility."[19] A number of western roads refused to sign, including the conservative Illinois Central.

The plan finally adopted was drafted under banking leadership. The bankers represented their clients. They were concerned primarily with one immediate problem: to end the rate wars. They apparently accomplished their immediate objective. One of them declared exuberantly, "You will hear of no more rate wars."[20] A nominal agreement had been reached including an understanding among the railroad presidents to restore rates for a period of sixty days. The underlying troubles, however, were not changed. They were soon to lead to further difficulties. Meanwhile, business harmony prevailed and the way was open for a rise in rates and a showing of presumptive rate stability.

The regional associations continued to function in the presence of the new association. Appeals were made from the decisions of the regional

24

associations to the Interstate Association on significant matters of policy affecting rates, rules, and regulations. The combinations worked well in stabilizing the rate structure for about six months. A good summary of the favorable effects produced by the new administrative organization was well presented in the 1889 Annual Report of the St. Paul. The Association, related this report, "has hitherto proven a benefit, although the failure to secure the co-operation of important lines, has . . . impaired its usefulness . . . . it has been demonstrated, however, to be the best form of agreement that has been devised."[21]

The six-month interlude of peace was broken in June of 1889. Cuts occurred in the Northwest and the Southwest. In the former the competition between the St. Paul–Chicago lines and those serving the Lake Superior ports grew more tense. The Hill system had organized an integrated lake-rail service via Duluth and had increased the standard of service. This channel of trade enabled eastern merchants to ship from Buffalo to the area served by the Hill lines, independent of the eastern trunk lines. Hill, president of the Great Northern—the road that had leased the Manitoba—decided to continue his independent line of action.

The competitive complexities in the Northwest were intensified by the refusal of the Burlington and Northern, the Wisconsin Central, and the Canadian Pacific's affiliates to join the new association. A substantial diversion of traffic from the Chicago lines to the Canadian Pacific–Soo route was effected. The Chicago lines were thus confronted by the alternative of either retiring from the Twin Cities traffic or of reducing rates.

The first shot in the new battle was fired by the Burlington and Northern. Late in May, 1889, that road announced a rate reduction to apply only on westbound through traffic—that is to say, on traffic coming from territory east of Chicago, through Chicago, and northwest to St. Paul and Minneapolis. It decided, furthermore, to maintain local rates. The first cut was from 60 to 34 cents. Successive reductions cut the rates to 15 cents. By September the 15-cent rate had spread to all the participating roads. To Judge Cooley the war appeared to be a waste of corporate funds. "The officials of the Northwestern Roads," declared the Judge, "are acting like a parcel of fools. Of course, Canadian Pacific competition has eaten deeply into their earnings, but that is no reason why illegal tariffs should be made to meet the situation."[22] The charge of illegality was based upon the low Chicago–Twin Cities through rate, with local rates remaining unchanged. This appeared to be a violation of the long and short haul clause of the Interstate Commerce Act.

In the Southwest, meanwhile, the festering sore that had developed since the completion of the Atchison's Kansas City–Chicago extension opened up again. By the summer of 1889 both the St. Paul and Stickney lines had finished their Kansas City extensions. These two roads, in addition to the Alton, commanded routes between Kansas City and Chicago but had no lines west of Kansas City. The Atchison's business between Chicago and Kansas City was relatively light. It was a new line and had had little time to build up a profitable local traffic. West of Kansas City the Atchison was a well-established route and commanded a substantial tonnage, particularly livestock. The Atchison encouraged the movement of its eastbound business over its own lines to Chicago. In August, in furtherance of this policy, it announced it would make through livestock rates to Chicago only over its own system.[23] The three Kansas City–Chicago lines with no extension of their own west of Kansas City presented a common front against their rival. Unfortunately the front was broken by the competition between the Alton and the St. Paul. Armour on the St. Paul directorate, persisted in moving his meat and cattle business over the St. Paul. The Alton thus lost business; it accordingly brought this competition to the attention of the new Association. On June 10, the latter directed the St. Paul to restrict its livestock traffic from Kansas City to a maximum of two trainloads weekly "until the then existing irregularity should be corrected." Should this remedy not suffice to produce a more equal competitive balance, the Association could either increase the rates of the St. Paul or reduce those of the Alton. If this failed, it could "take charge of the entire traffic through a joint agency." The St. Paul accepted this decision and for a number of weeks took no livestock from Kansas City to Chicago. The livestock traffic of the Alton and of the other Kansas City–Chicago lines increased.[24] The Alton was not satisfied and on June 15 announced its withdrawal from the Association. The St. Paul, it insisted, was securing traffic by making secret inducements.

To complicate matters there was added the policy of the Rock Island line between Omaha, Pueblo, and Denver. The Rock Island, upon reaching Denver, reduced rates on bullion from Denver and Pueblo to the Missouri River. Both the Rock Island and the Missouri Pacific were competitors of the Burlington west of the Missouri River. A Burlington official complained that the buyers on the Rock Island and the Missouri

Pacific had "paid more than the market warrants on tariff rates." He thought it advisable to wait a week or more to see what the Association would do in response to the demand of the Alton for a fair division of the Kansas City livestock traffic, and to the demand of the Rock Island for a redistribution of the Denver bullion traffic. The latter, according to this official, was getting more of the grain traffic at the Burlington's expense; and by "illicit means."[25]

By July of 1889 many of the roads were disillusioned. They looked upon the Association in the light of their inability to solve traffic problems in line with their own business interests. The Association denounced the recalcitrant roads, and they in turn denounced the Association. The latter declared that the Alton had determined to buy "what it pleased to consider its proportions of Kansas City traffic by reducing the rates. If the Alton buys business, the other lines must also buy it."[26] The Alton in turn denounced the Association as "a colossal fancy of some Eastern bankers whose sole excuse for foisting it upon the practical Managers of the West was the supposed necessity of doing something to satisfy demands of Wall Street."[27] The Association, said the Alton's vice president, did "not amount to a hill of beans."[28] A number of other roads became restless; they were losing business and could not afford to wait for what they considered to be the slow-moving decisions of the Association— decisions which were bound to cause some loss to one road or another.

The peace interval lasted for only a few months. As the Great Northern penetrated further south from its east-west main line between Duluth and Montana it afforded to an increasing number of shippers the opportunity to move their traffic east at lower rates via the Lake Superior Ports. The St. Paul and the Burlington were the chief losers. Officials were concerned over this competition. Perkins declared early in 1890 that "the tendency of grain to go to St. Paul and Duluth seems to be increasing," and that a "very large part" of the traffic carried by the Great Northern came from the Burlington territory west of the Missouri River. How, he asked, could this diversion from the Chicago to the Duluth lines be stopped.[29]

There appeared to be little hope of inducing Hill to adopt a policy of rate stabilization. He declined to attend a meeting held in New York to discuss the relationship of lake and rail rates. "Rates from Buffalo to Duluth," Hill insisted, "have always been higher than from Buffalo to Chicago, although the distance is about the same. I believe that there will be no trouble when they put them on the same basis. Of course that would give our St. Paul and Duluth lines an advantage—but shouldn't we have it? It is only 150 miles from Duluth to St. Paul, while it is 400 between Chicago and St. Paul, which is 250 miles in our favor. Why shouldn't we carry freight cheaper?"[30] Hill moved rapidly to build up a strong rail-water haul between the seaboard and the Missouri River via Duluth. By April this new route was perfected and rates reduced. On a lake-rail haul to Duluth from Boston, New York, and Philadelphia, for example, rates were quoted at 55 cents per hundred pounds, as compared with the Chicago lake-rail haul of 81 cents.[31]

In February, 1890, under the leadership of the Burlington and Northern, an open break in northwestern rates occurred. The Burlington announced a rate reduction on local traffic between Chicago and St. Paul to 40 cents and on through traffic to 30 cents. The Western Freight Association met in session for a week. Its efforts to stop or limit the effects of the impending war were of no effect. Other roads followed.[32] Rate cuts spread to points west of the Missouri River. A proposed reduction of 50 per cent in corn rates by Adams led Perkins to use strong language. If, he declared, Adams had made these lower rates on condition that the Burlington would agree, "it was an outrage which it is difficult to characterize in polite language. The U. P. is getting to be a public nuisance."[33]

In the Northwest, meanwhile, personal feelings between the St. Paul and the Burlington's officials over the Chicago–Twin Cities traffic grew bitter. The Burlington's executives complained, as they had for a number of years, over the other's milling-in-transit privileges on the wheat business. Miller, president of the St. Paul, was not much interested in the grain business. "There is no money in the traffic," he asserted. Grain rates remained low merely to protect the road's extensive territory. Miller added, "I do not care a snap of my fingers for the through grain or its products from Minneapolis to Chicago or to the lake." The St. Paul, he declared, was mostly interested in westbound merchandise and miscellaneous traffic. The Burlington wanted to force the St. Paul to share its local revenue with the Burlington and Northern; and while demoralizing the northwestern traffic, the latter hoped "to tie us [the St. Paul] up on the South-west."[34]

Acrimony accompanied the spread of the rate disturbances. The Association was in fact disrupted, though no formal action had yet been taken. Efforts made to restore rates failed. It appeared that "a reckless return to underhand practices and secret cuts" had been effected.[35]

By April, 1890, the competitive situation was again demoralized. Passenger fares between eastern Colorado and Kansas City were slashed. Lumber, dressed beef, and livestock rates between Chicago and Missouri River points were again reduced to unprofitable levels. The pattern of rate retaliation of road against road and of region against region was again traced. And again there were discussions between businessmen in an effort to secure a stable rate structure. The Association was ignored. Efforts to reach a solution failed. According to one observer, Gould requested a division of traffic to aid the Missouri Pacific lines west of the Missouri River, and threatened, should he not secure such a concession, to "fight it out for a permanent peace."[36] This is the kind of reasoning in which many railroad men—Perkins, Adams, Cable, and Blackstone—had from time to time indulged. The war, indeed, was growing hotter and general chaos seemed to prevail.

Suddenly the picture brightened and an agreement to terminate the war was reached in July, 1890. A report of a committee of presidents and general managers, agreed to by all the interested roads, provided for restoration of eastbound rates from the Missouri River to Chicago on cattle, hogs, dressed beef, and packing-house products. The agreement did not reflect the desires of all the railroad managements. Indeed, according to the Alton president, the understanding was entered upon "with reluctance but as a duty with the hope of arresting the prevailing demoralization."[37] The war was terminated without the help of the defunct Association. It was a regional settlement, achieved nominally through the Southwestern Association with the active partnership of four other associations. The roads promised, as they had many times before, to maintain rates and eliminate rebates. No rate changes could be made, except with the unanimous approval of a five-man executive committee.[38] A novel concept was added to this conventional provision. It was proposed to make adjustments of such a character as to "insure to each line in interest, a proper share of the competitive freight traffic between the Southwest Missouri River points, Mississippi River, and Chicago."[39] Though pools were illegal, it seems clear that this provision for traffic diversion would divide the business in somewhat the same way that the pools had done. The mechanism of traffic diversion had been used in many pools for purpose of correcting deficiencies.

In fact considerable diversion from one road to another was directed by the supervisory organization set up under the July agreement. A board consisting of five chairmen of the traffic associations, with Walker, secretary of the defunct Association, as chairman, directed the Burlington to divert fifty car loads each to the Alton and to the Missouri Pacific. It also directed the Atchison to divert to other roads; but in the opinion of a majority of lines, that road continued to obtain an excessive percentage. It diverted some, but not all. The Atchison insisted that only the receipt of an equivalent tonnage of westbound business would justify it in surrendering its eastbound business to others. Accordingly it was "slow about accepting the decisions of the arbitrators, and the belligerent expressions of its officers indicate that this dilatory action is not accidental."[40]

The failure of the Atchison to divert led the Burlington to question the desirability of obeying any such orders. The Atchison "has not turned over any freight that I know of. We don't want to turn over any freight if no one else does," wrote a Burlington officer.[41]

The Association obviously did not function satisfactorily. The same difficulties were encountered with traffic associations as with pools. The new lines west of the river, particularly the Rock Island and the Missouri Pacific, moved less traffic than the board deemed essential in order to provide for that equitable division necessary to the maintenance of the rate structure. The result of a reasonable, relatively profitable rate was, at least over a short period, a sense of resentment and complaint by the deficient roads, that their traffic volume was not heavy enough, and by the other roads, that the advantages gained through the arrangement were not commensurate with their loss in earnings through diverting traffic to other roads.

The termination of the rate wars by the fall of 1890 was the work of regional associations. The settlements were in the form of truces. The agreement in the Southwest was for ninety days, while in the North the term was indefinite. The settlement was helped by a large flow of traffic. The Union Pacific, for example, according to its president was suffering from "a plethora of riches." Traffic offered for transportation was 30 per cent higher than capacity.[42] And Hill declared that a leading railroad man in the Northwest told him that roads "were literally crushed with business."[43] The incentive to reduce rates was therefore minimized. The opinion however was widespread that a permanent rate stabilization in western territory must still be based on an industry-wide agreement. The first effort, through the Interstate Association, had failed. It was accordingly essential that another attempt be made. The next move reflected the acceptance of certain new ideas, some of which had already been adopted in various regional agreements. The following chapter will present a discussion of this renewed industry-wide effort to achieve a reasonable rate structure.

Notes for Chapter XVIII

[1] Annual Report, Chicago, St. Paul and Kansas City Railroad, 1890, p.2.
[2] Annual Report, Minneapolis and St. Louis, 1890, cited in *Chron.*, Sept. 27, 1890, p. 425.
[3] *Bradstreet's,* April 26, 1890, p. 265.
[4] Annual Report, Wabash Western, 1888, p. 6.
[5] Interstate Commerce Commission Reports, 1888, p. 28.
[6] *New York Sun,* Dec. 4, 1888.
[7] *Chron.,* Jan. 12, 1889, p. 49.
[8] *R. R. Gaz.,* Dec. 12, 1890, p. 868.
[9] August Schoonmaker, cited in *Ry. Review,* Aug. 15, 1891, p. 528.
[10] These quotations and the summary of the views of Perkins are taken from Burlington Archives, Perkins to Fink, Feb. 9, 1888. The letter was headed "Strictly Confidential."
[11] *Ry. Review,* July 19, 1890, p. 422.
[12] *Gould,* pp. 560-561.
[13] *New York Herald,* Dec. 2, 1888.
[14] The text of this plan for a clearing house was sent by Winslow to Perkins as an enclosure of a letter Nov. 23, 1888, in Burlington Archives.
[15] *Ibid.,* Winslow to Perkins, Dec. 4, 1888.
[16] This plan is found in the Burlington Archives.
[17] This plan is found in *Ibid.,* as part of a letter from Perkins to Strong, Dec. 8, 1888.
[18] *Gould,* p. 561.
[19] For summary of the plan, see *Chron.,* Jan. 12, 1889, pp. 67-68.
[20] *Iron Age,* Jan. 10, 1889, p. 63.
[21] Annual Report, St. Paul, 1889, p. 12.
[22] *R. R. Gaz.,* Aug. 30, 1889, p. 578.
[23] *Ibid.,* Aug. 9, 1889, p. 534.
[24] The quotations and the discussion of the actions of the Association are taken from and based on an address made by Chairman Walker, of the Association, as reported in *Ry. Review,* July 20, 1889, p. 421.
[25] Burlington Archives, Holdrege to Perkins, June 3, 1889.
[26] *R. R. Gaz.,* July 26, 1889, p. 502.
[27] *Stockholder,* July 20, 1889.
[28] *Boston Herald,* July 20, 1889.
[29] Burlington Archives, Perkins to Holdrege, Jan 6. 1890.
[30] *Ry. Review,* March 1, 1890, p. 124.
[31] *New York Sun,* May 3, 1890.
[32] A summary of these rate cuts is presented in *R. R. Gaz.,* Feb. 21, 1890, p. 136.
[33] Burlington Archives, Perkins to Ripley, March 26, 1890.
[34] *Ibid.,* Harris to Perkins, July 18, 1890.
[35] *Bradstreet's,* April 26, 1890, p. 264.
[36] *The New York Times,* May 17, 1890.
[37] *R. R. Gaz.,* Feb. 27, 1891. This language is a paraphrase of the views of Blackstone.

[38] *Ibid.*, Oct. 3, 1890, p. 691, for provisions of the agreement.
[39] Annual Report, Alton, 1890, p. 13.
[40] *Chron.*, Oct. 24, 1890, p. 740.
[41] Burlington Archives, W. F. Merrill to Harris, Sept. 6, 1890.
[42] *Ry. World*, Nov. 18, 1890, p. 1069.
[43] *Chron.*, Dec. 6, 1890, p. 787.

XIX

Stabilization by Industry-wide Action
Western Traffic Association

T HE FAILURE of the Interstate Association to stabilize rates led to a rash of industrial self-criticism and proposals for improvement. The critical conditions demanding heroic measures were well summarized in the 1890 Annual Report of the Interstate Commerce Commission in the form of a reported interview with a railroad officer. He declared that "the situation in the West is so bad it could hardly be worse. Rates are absolutely demoralized, and neither the shippers, the passengers, the railways, or the public in general make anything by this state of affairs. ... Certain shippers are allowed heavy rebates, while others are made to pay full rates. ... The management of rates is dishonest on all sides, and there is not a road in the country that can be accused of living up to the rules of the Interstate Commerce Law."[1] Walker, president of the dead Association, addressed a letter to the presidents of the member roads. Competition as it then existed among the roads, he said, was "simply war," and added that in fighting each other the roads were "rapidly destroying themselves." He denounced the use of "wild and reckless business methods" such as discriminatory long-term contracts with shippers, the use of commissions, free transportation and other inducements to influence business, and collusion with shippers who "have learned to cunningly obtain concessions which they know to be illegal."[2]

Suggestions for improvement took a number of forms. Gould, supported by Walker, proposed the elimination of the competitive soliciting agencies and their replacement by a joint agency. This would suppress the possibility of cutting rates. Rates would be established by a central agency responsible to the presidents and directors of the co-operating roads. The agency would also cut expenses and unnecessary facilities,

354

such as an excessive number of trains between competitive points. It could divide traffic in such a way as to equalize the volume among competing roads, and thereby further minimize the motive for rate reductions. This plan, though supported by many roads, was not adopted.

Another suggestion, included in most of the 1890 regional rate agreements, was the diversion of traffic from one road to another. A novel proposal made by Gould, and characteristic of his wide-ranging suggestions, was one calling for the elimination of railroad construction into the territory of another road.

A number of meetings of railroad presidents between October and December of 1890, again under the leadership of Morgan, culminated in the setting up of a new body, known as the Western Traffic Association, designed "to promote the equality of rates, and so far as possible secure a fair distribution of traffic."[3] It was also authorized to divert business from one road to another; and, probably in order to provide a legal justification for this provision, the new agreement conditioned such diversion "upon such basis and upon such lawful manner" as was deemed advisable. There was also set up an Advisory Board consisting of the president and a director of each railroad. An administrative agency, subject to the supervision of the Advisory Board, was clothed with power to secure "uniform, reasonable and stable rates." Commissioners were empowered by unanimous vote to decide the volume of traffic each road should have. An appeal from this decision could be taken to the Advisory Board. No decisions of the Commissioners nor of the Board could be construed as depriving the directors of their responsibilities to determine rates for their own roads.

This agreement, as finally ratified, did not obtain the endorsement of all the roads. The Burlington was reluctant in giving its approval. There was little love lost between the Burlington management and Gould. They had been violent business enemies for almost two decades. Since Gould was a "prime mover" of many of the meetings of the railroad presidents in the months preceding the final agreement, the Burlington was not particularly happy. Forbes, however, concluded that "an agreement through the agency of Gould seems better than drifting along.... In short it is better perhaps to assent to Gould's proposal than to continue the present state of things."[4] The Alton, still dissatisfied with its status in relation to the Atchison, and the St. Paul refused to sign.

The new Association supplemented the existing regional associations.

At this time, according to the Interstate Commerce Commission, there were sixty-eight such associations. Their combined efforts, again according to the Commission, exerted little if any influence upon the action of carriers in the prevention of rate wars, secret concessions in rates, and other demoralizing practices. These regional organizations exercised authority over the rates and practices of individual railroads. They held their own meetings subject to their own rules, though they were "in duty bound not to take any action in violation of the obligations" assumed by reason of their membership in the Western Traffic Association.[5] Their actions, however, frequently conflicted with the philosophy of that Association. It had already become well recognized that the railroads, each and all, were interdependent. Rate adjustment along the 32nd Parallel route, for example, affected business over the other transcontinental routes. They would be forced to take counteraction in response to any move made, let us say, by the Southern Pacific Sunset route. To take another illustration, the adjustment made to meet the competition of the Lake Superior rail-water routes tended to disturb the movement via Chicago from the Dakotas, Nebraska, and even Montana. It was therefore realistically impossible to expect roads to co-operate with the new Association in a spirit of harmony. The interests of particular railroads promised to clash with the interests of the western railroad industry as a whole. For the first year of its operation, however, affairs ran smoothly. There was a remarkable absence of rate wars; so much so, indeed, that a leading railroad periodical was led to describe the era as one "without parallel in history"; even more significant was the fact that the writer credited this phenomenon to the influence of the new Association.[6] And a journalistic observer interpreted this era of good feeling in prophetic language. The western railroads, ran this comment, were "gradually but surely abandoning belligerency in their inter-relations and substituting amicable methods of settling disputes and regulating rates."[7]

The rate stability can be interpreted to a considerable extent in terms of the heavy traffic. The year 1891 was marked by a prolific corn and wheat crop, as well as by a substantial movement of livestock. There was also a heavy tonnage of coal and lumber. Satisfactory volume led to increases in earnings. Some roads that had previously reduced their dividends increased them in 1891. In the Northwest and Southwest, where rate reductions were so prevalent for the first three-quarters of 1890, increases were introduced early in 1891.

Rate relationships were not, however, completely harmonious. Hill dropped no hint of his willingness to co-operate either with the Chicago roads or with the Lake Superior lines. He insisted upon making the same grain rates to Duluth as to St. Paul and Minneapolis. The Minneapolis miller, on the basis of a shorter distance, requested a differential of 5 cents per hundred pounds. Such an adjustment would have favored the Minneapolis–Chicago roads, and Hill, with no line to Chicago, declined the request. The Great Northern as well as the Soo— the latter refusing to join the new Association—continued to reduce rates on seaboard–Lake Superior traffic. Indeed the through rates from the East over the Canadian Pacific and the lake-rail routes had by the summer of 1891 become "practically demoralized."[8]

Rate competition also characterized the area centering around Kansas City. There the Alton continued to maintain its belligerency. This relatively small property thus dictated "the terms to roads that operate thousands of miles where it operates hundreds. The Western Traffic Association is practically inoperative until the Alton joins it";[9] and the Alton refused to join. It also refused to accept orders of the regional Passenger Association. A direction by its chairman to increase fares was accepted by all the roads involved in the business, except the Alton. The latter reduced rates, thereby increasing its passenger business. Additional orders of the Association to increase rates were again ignored. "We do not intend," asserted an Alton representative, "that you or your Association shall dictate to us."[10]

On the transcontinental traffic, meanwhile, business relations were not entirely pleasant. Both the Northern and Southern Pacific complained that the Canadian Pacific differentials were excessive. From February, 1888, when the differential was first granted, the traffic of the Canadian Pacific from San Francisco to the Atlantic seaboard increased month by month. In July, 1889, both the Northern and Southern Pacific announced that unless the differentials were reduced they would withdraw from the Association. The Southern Pacific demanded a cut of 50 per cent.[11] Indeed it proposed the elimination of the differential, and offered the Canadian Pacific a guaranteed percentage of the business if it would charge the regular rate; but agreement on the precise amount of the guaranteed business could not be reached.[12] In August both roads cancelled their withdrawal notices, and agreed on a lower differential for the California business. The Association was saved.

The lower differentials in favor of the Canadian Pacific, arranged in the summer of 1889, eased the conflict between that road and its competitors in the United States. In 1889, unlike 1888, the Northern Pacific had few complaints of loss of business. In that year about 60 per cent of the tonnage from the Pacific Coast terminals north of San Francisco moved over the Northern Pacific. The Canadian Pacific gave it "comparatively little annoyance."[13] This comparative freedom from Canadian Pacific competition was due in some degree to the Northern Pacific's Winnipeg extension. Rate cuts on the Pacific Coast by the Canadian Pacific would probably have led to retaliatory action by the Northern Pacific on the Winnipeg line. "I have no doubt that if we did not have that line into Winnipeg," said the latter's president, "we would have had to pay the Canadian $500,000 a year to maintain rates to the Pacific Coast."[14]

The rate peace that characterized such a large area in the West did not spread to the transcontinental business. Cutting continued there for most of 1890. In the fall, one of those informal approaches to the problem of rate stabilization outside the province of any association was made. Executives of three leading transcontinental roads memorialized the presidents of the other roads in an effort to re-establish rate stability. A form letter asked members of the Transcontinental Association to agree "upon their personal good faith and honor to strictly observe the rates and rules," and "to cooperate in securing an equally strict observance of the same by their respective connections and competitors."[15] This move met with some success, for late in November the Association ordered a 10 per cent increase in rates to take effect in January, 1891.[16] For the balance of that year transcontinental affairs paralleled the conditions in the rest of the West. With the increasing volume of business there were few rate disturbances.

By the summer of 1892, however, rate cutting had again spread over most of the West. The year and a half era of peace came to an end, though as usual the signs were not clearly foreseen by contemporary observers. As late as the last week in May a conservative eastern journal editorialized that a rate demoralization of the kind which had occurred in the late 1880's "does not exist now and is not likely to recur again in the near future."[17] Even while these lines were written the Burlington and Rock Island were requesting the Western Traffic Association to reduce rates to Colorado and Utah to the level created by secret rebates.

The refusal to grant permission was followed by notice that the lower rates would nevertheless be made effective in ninety days.[18] Chicago and Colorado rates were cut sharply. Roads west of the Missouri River in turn accused each other and denied the charges. Late in August the chairman of the Southwestern Association called a meeting to discover the identity of the roads carrying grains at secret concessions; but, wrote a railroad journal, "the prospects of success in this line are no better than heretofore."[19] In the Northwest both the Canadian Pacific and the Hill line resumed their rate cutting.

The competition of the Hill System, furthermore, became increasingly severe because of the introduction into the lake business of improved steamships. The Hill line met the Canadian Pacific–Soo cut by an even greater reduction. It was by that time recognized that lake rates had become a permanent regulator of the rates between the eastern seaboard and the Mississippi and Missouri valleys. The Chicago roads could retain a share of this business only by meeting these rates.

An entirely new factor meanwhile developed in the transcontinental business. A group of San Francisco merchants had long fought for a rate structure to place them on an equality with eastern competitors. They were denied competition with the Huntington System both by water and rail. The Pacific Mail, in exchange for a monthly subsidy of $75 thousand, still maintained rates.[20] Competition by rail did not as yet seriously disturb the Huntington monopoly. The Atchison, by virtue of its Mojave–San Francisco trackage agreement, received only a nominal tonnage; nor did the Canadian Pacific get much. Even with the aid of the rate differential, its share of the transcontinental traffic from San Francisco via Vancouver to United States ports amounted in 1888 to only $1\frac{1}{3}$ per cent of the total.[21] In October of 1891 the merchants decided, as a means of obtaining a more favorable rate structure, to engage on their own account in the business of transportation. To carry out their objective they organized the Traffic Association of California under the administration of J. S. Leeds, a former traffic manager of the Missouri Pacific. They first memorialized the State Railroad Commissioners for the purpose of securing lower rates. After their failure in this effort they chartered a number of ships from a major steamship line. By this means the traffic association moved a large tonnage at rates 50 per cent lower than those formerly quoted by the Southern Pacific.[22] The latter proposed to meet this competition with a sweeping rate reduction. It accordingly asked the Transcontinental and the Western Traffic Associations for approval.

Competition among the railroads and between them and steamship lines was meanwhile accelerating. In view of the low rates established by the San Francisco merchants there was no point in continuing the Pacific Mail subsidy. Indeed, all the roads, with the exception of the Southern Pacific, had always paid it reluctantly. Only the Southern Pacific benefited from the disappearance of the Pacific Mail as a rate-stabilizing factor. (The subsidy permitted Southern Pacific to compete more effectively for the eastern seaboard business.) Accordingly, the Transcontinental Association at its August meeting voted to cancel the subsidy.[23] The rate-stabilization function of the Pacific Mail was ended. With its subsidy gone and its earning power impaired, the price of its stock declined. To the Huntington railroads, however, it still had a value. In the contest with the San Francisco merchants combination the Pacific Mail was a valuable ally. It could be used as a tool in the rate war with the Association. Huntington therefore took control of the company and early in 1893 was elected president. The Pacific Mail became "a mere attachment to the Southern Pacific Railroad system."[24]

The Transcontinental Association soon began to crumble. The Canadian Pacific started a procession of withdrawals. The Great Northern soon followed. By the end of September, 1892, the Union Pacific, Northern Pacific, Atchison, Burlington, and Rock Island had acted similarly. Only the Southern Pacific and the Rio Grande still remained, and by the end of the year they had also withdrawn. The Transcontinental Association was dissolved. This was followed by the dissolution of the Trans-Missouri Association, covering the traffic between the Missouri River and the Colorado-Utah area.

The rivalry that swept through the ranks of the members of the Transcontinental Association infected also the relationships between the roads in the Western Traffic Association. First to express its resentment over the actions of the Association was the Burlington. Its appeal to reduce its Utah-Colorado rates was rejected. Since the Association thus "slapped our faces" by refusing to consider its request, there was, declared Perkins, nothing left but to withdraw.[25] A few days later the Burlington gave its withdrawal notice. Dissatisfaction with the Association's policies came also from the Great Northern. Hill's rate reductions had been contrary to the Association's stabilization policy. By September the Great Northern had also withdrawn and the Missouri Pacific soon followed. The latter's directors resolved that the Association appeared "to have outgrown its usefulness."[26] The Association was dead. It had performed valuable services, particularly in 1891. Hughitt paid tribute, in this respect, to the Association. "Deficient as the contract had proven," he remarked, it had saved the railroads "some millions of dollars" by preventing rate cuts that year. A final meeting was held in October and the formal obsequies were duly recorded. Gould, according to Palmer, was present at the final meeting, "looking more chirruppy than ever, and with a tone of injured innocence that was lovely to behold."[27]

By the end of 1892 the major associations were gone. All efforts to maintain uniform and stable rates had failed. Formal arrangements with committees, boards, and experts had been of no avail. Competitive forces overthrew all administrative organizations. Informal approaches made in the spirit of good faith had been no more successful. Co-operation between competing roads, in short, was a dead letter. What could replace the co-operative efforts, either in the form of associations or otherwise, was not clear. "Is there no alternative but anarchy?" was the query of Palmer. "Are the freight solicitors and scalpers to continue at the helm?"[28]

The answer was soon forthcoming. As the year 1892 drew to a close the western railroad industry was almost entirely disassociated from any industry-wide rate supervision. Between Chicago and the Twin Cities, on the routes pointing to the Lake Superior ports, along the Missouri River interchanges between Omaha and Kansas City, in the Southwest dominated by the Huntington, Gould, and Atchison empires, in the trans-Missouri area in Colorado and Utah, and along the transcontinental routes, corporate managements were confronted by the necessity of fashioning a strategy in line with competitive rate-determining policies. The immediate effect was a severe rate pressure on California transcontinental traffic.

A new competitive force was signaled by the completion of the Hill Line to the Puget Sound early in 1893. This was followed by a drop in eastbound lumber rates. Lumbermen in Washington had for some time pressed the Northern Pacific to reduce rates. As a member of the Transcontinental Association, the road resisted the pressure. It declared that such a reduction would lead only to a war of rates and that with lower rates, lumbermen in competition with others in different areas would be no better off. Hill promised that when his road was finished he would cut rates. He was true to his word. Shortly after his line was finished, he reduced lumber rates to the Middle West from 90 to 40 cents. The preponderant flow of traffic at that time was westbound; hence the lower rate on eastbound traffic saved the expense of returning empty eastbound cars.[29]

Transcontinental roads, unhampered for the most part by pools or traffic associations, resorted to a novel and what may perhaps be called a savage competitive device. A road would refuse to interchange business with connecting lines. The first step in this direction was taken by the Union Pacific early in 1893 when it decided to interchange passenger business only with the Northwestern and the Alton and declined to perform a similar service for the Atchison, Rock Island, and Burlington.[30] The Union Pacific later extended this policy of interdiction to the Great Northern for passengers coming from the Montana Central, the Great Northern subsidiary in that state. The intimate business friendship between the Union Pacific and the Hill property in the late 1880's, prior to the latter's Puget Sound extension, was now replaced by a deadly rivalry. Business friendships vary with changing circumstances.

The strategy of closing routes on one line to the business of another was also adopted by the Southern Pacific in its struggles with the Canadian Pacific. The former had by this time completed a line to Portland. It thus controlled the only line between Portland and California. The Southern Pacific closed this route to the Canadian Pacific—that is to say, it would not honor tickets sold by the Canadian Pacific for trips between Portland and San Francisco. The Canadian Pacific retaliated by reducing rates from San Francisco east via Puget Sound points reached over its line. The journey from Victoria, British Columbia, a Puget Sound port on the Canadian Pacific, to San Francisco was made by steamer. In November, 1893, for example, the Canadian Pacific quoted a rate over this indirect route between Chicago and San Francisco of $41.50 compared with one of $65.50 over the direct rail route. The Southern Pacific eventually modified its policy and opened its route to passengers from the Canadian Pacific. The Canadian Pacific, then restored the higher passenger rate.[31]

The fight for the diminishing volume of traffic, associated with the growing depression beginning in 1893, led to severe rate cuts. In the earlier stages of this struggle a renewed effort was made to introduce stability through a new form of industry-wide co-operation. The roads, formerly members of the Transcontinental Association, proposed to set up two rate committees—one for passenger fares and one for freight rates.[32] The scheme died aborning, and for the balance of the year competitive rivalries, unhindered by association or pool management, dominated the rate structure. Individual corporate strategy again destroyed efforts to maintain industry-wide rate structures.

In the Southwest another move to stabilize rates through a traffic association was frustrated by a new competitive force. This was the Rock Island—a property seeking more business to feed its recently completed light traffic-density line. To get more through business it tied up its fortunes with the Texas and Pacific. This route established a rate sufficiently low to divert the business from the older lines. The Atchison then announced that unless the tariffs were withdrawn it would leave the new association.[33]

The repeated attempts to restrain competitive forces by industry-wide agreement had by 1893 produced no permanent results. As a measure to stabilize rates, improve earnings, and maintain a credit structure sufficient to stimulate the flow of capital so essential to the health of a dynamic industry, co-operation failed as a means to restrain competition. Other means of avoiding competition were the consolidation of roads into fewer systems and the establishment of alliances between independently owned roads for the promotion of mutually beneficial traffic routes. Both these methods were adopted in the late 1880's and early 1890's. In some areas they proved somewhat successful in suppressing the forces leading to excessive rate cuts. They were not, however, sufficient to arrest, particularly in a period of declining business, rate reductions of a magnitude that contributed to financial difficulties and to railroad insolvencies in the middle 1890's. The efforts on the part of corporate management to effect consolidations and to establish traffic alliances and agreements will be examined in the following chapter.

Notes for Chapter XIX

[1] Interstate Commerce Commission Reports, 1890, pp. 355–356.

[2] *R. R. Gaz.*, Dec. 12, 1890, p. 859.

[3] This is the language used by the Association in a decision on a particular case, cited in *Ry. Review*, June 27, 1891.

[4] Burlington Archives, Forbes to Perkins Dec. 3, 1890.

[5] Board of Commissioners, Western Traffic Association, cited in *R. R. Gaz.*, Feb. 27, 1891, p. 154.

[6] *Ry. Review*, Jan. 2, 1892, p. 9.

[7] *Bradstreet's*, May 14, 1892, p. 307.

[8] *Ibid.*, May 31, 1891, p. 338.

[9] *R. R. Gaz.*, Feb. 27, 1891, p. 146.

[10] *Ibid.*, July 24, 1891, p. 522.

[11] The United States and Canada, Report No. 847, Senate, 51st Congress, 1st Session, 1889, pp. 347, 364.

[12] *R. R. Gaz.*, Aug. 2, 1889, p. 518.

[13] Annual Report, Northern Pacific, 1889, p. 27.

[14] H. V. P., statement of Oakes before the Master in the Northern Pacific receivership case, 1894; Box 34.

[15] This was a form letter in Burlington Archives, October 11, 1890, addressed to Perkins, with "Dear Sir" written in ink.

[16] *Iron Age*, Nov. 27, 1890, 959; and Dec. 18, 1890, p. 1087.

[17] *Chron.*, May 28, 1892, p. 872.

[18] *Ibid.*, May 14, 1892, p. 801.

[19] *R. R. Gaz.*, Sept. 2, 1892, p. 662.

[20] Report No. 778, Huntington, p. 126.

[21] The United States and Canada, Report No. 847, Senate, 51st Congress, 1st Session, 1889, p. 509.

[22] Details on these rates in *R. R. Gaz.*, Aug. 19, 1892, p. 626; *Bradstreet's*, Sept. 14, 1892, p. 611.

[23] *R. R. Gaz.*, Sept. 2, 1892, p. 655.

[24] *Bradstreet's*, June 10, 1893, p. 359.

[25] Burlington Archives, Perkins to Harris, July 19, 1892.

[26] *Chron.*, Oct. 1, 1892, p. 545.

[27] Burlington Archives, Palmer to Dodge, Oct. 14, 1892.

[28] *Ibid.*

[29] Hill explained this reasoning in the government's suit against the Northern Securities Company in 1902, as summarized in *Bradstreet's*, Oct. 25, 1902, p. 674; and in hearings before a Congressional Committee in 1905, Regulations of Railway Rates, Document No. 243, Vol. 2, 59th Congress, 1st Session, pp. 1474–5.

[30] *Bradstreet's*, Jan. 28, 1893, p. 50.

[31] For details on the struggle between Southern Pacific and Canadian Pacific, see *R. R. Gaz.*, Dec. 1, 1893, p. 880; and Dec. 15, p. 918.

[32] *Ibid.*, March 17, 1893, p. 218.

[33] *Ibid.*, Aug. 25, 1893, p. 646.

XX

Stabilization by Corporate Action

To MANY thoughtful people in the railroad industry in the late 1880's, reasonable rates and earnings could come only from consolidation of railroads into a limited number of systems. Competition was so all-embracing, however, that it was difficult to believe that independent businessmen could or would submerge their individual needs in the interests of a common purpose. There were many small roads, with high unit costs, in control of indirect routes between important traffic sources and major markets. They could not be expected to impair their earnings for the purpose of achieving a stable rate structure. Larger roads, under a stable and uniform rate structure, would carry most of the business. Their service would be better than that of the smaller roads; their profits would be greater; and since these profits would be invested in more efficient equipment they would be able to render a still higher standard of transportation service. This, in turn, would enable them to command even more traffic and to compete even more favorably with their smaller competitors.

Even among the major railroad properties there was no unity of interest. The construction program of the 1880's extended many lines into the territories of their competitors. To secure a share of the existing business, the invaders reduced rates and other roads followed suit.

The device of pooling, to limit rate reductions, was made illegal in 1887. Railroad men agreed that without some kind of associated endeavors it was impossible to maintain the price of railroad transportation. Many railroad men believed it was essential to make pooling legal again. "Without some method of effective co-operation competing lines must become bankrupt, and in the end consolidated," Perkins informed his stockholders in 1891.[1] Huntington, a strong expansionist, had arrived at the same conclusion. He expressed this opinion in an article in the *North American Review*.[2] Consolidation between two or more roads would furthermore avoid the necessity of constructing new roads. By combining, existing roads could in many cases produce the same channels of transportation as could be created by new building.

Over a large section of the West consolidation had by the late 1880's already gone to considerable lengths. In the Southwest east of California, west of the Mississippi, and south of Nebraska and Colorado, the transportation business was controlled largely by the Huntington lines, the Atchison, and the Missouri Pacific. Between Chicago and eastern Colorado competition was more intense. Western extension of lines from points east of the Missouri River and eastern extensions of lines from points west of the river intensified and complicated this competition.

Competition was also intense between Chicago and the Twin Cities and between the Twin Cities and the Lake Superior ports. Here the competition prevailed in part between the major railroad systems; and, to an increasing degree, between them and a growing number of smaller roads. The St. Paul and Duluth, for example, bereft of its traffic from the Manitoba by reason of the latter's extension to Lake Superior, discovered it could compete for business over its direct St. Paul–Duluth line only by reducing the rates below the Manitoba's level. The Manitoba in turn did not hesitate to cut its rates. Here, as in the Central West, there were many similar competitive complications.

In the territory west of the Twin Cities the competition was largely between the major railroads. These roads in 1887, with the exception of the Northern Pacific, terminated either at or near the Missouri River. The Northern Pacific, after the fall of 1883, had a through line via the Navigation to Portland; and after the fall of 1887 it had another under single ownership to Tacoma. The competition in this area was rapidly increasing. All roads, with the exception of the St. Paul, were building new lines. And many were planning to build to the Pacific Coast.

In the far Northwest, in western Idaho, and in Oregon and Washington furthermore, railroad rivalry threatened to develop into a war of railroad building and rate demoralization. The major stake was the control of the Navigation. Its control, after the departure of Villard, in December 1883, was uncertain. Villard's control of the company had lain in his holdings in the Transcontinental. That company owned a large block of the former's stock. The stock had been deposited as collateral to secure loans by the Transcontinental from Drexel-Morgan. In 1884 the controlling interest in the Navigation was held by the Morgan firm, as trustee, to secure the interests of the Transcontinental creditors. It was proposed, under Morgan's leadership, to lease the Navigation to the Northern Pacific on the basis of an 8 per cent dividend guarantee.[3] There was considerable opposition to this lease. After more than a year of discussion and negotiation the proposal of a single lease control was replaced by the idea of a joint lease. In the fall of 1885 approval was given to the principle of leasing the Navigation jointly to the Union Pacific and Northern Pacific.[4] By this time, however, a new factor had emerged that modified the relationships between the projected lessor and lessee roads. The Northern Pacific had begun the construction of its own line to the Pacific Coast—the so-called Cascade branch to Tacoma. This would destroy the Navigation's monopoly. To the extent that the Northern Pacific increased its business from the Puget Sound the Union Pacific would receive less from the Navigation. The latter would be tempted to extend north into the area served by the Northern Pacific, and the Northern Pacific south into the region served by the Navigation. To make the competition even more complex, another railroad under the leadership of George W. Hunt was building new roads in the Navigation territory. Wright, a director and large stockholder of the Northern Pacific, was reported to be financing and abetting the Hunt road. The Navigation accordingly believed that the Northern Pacific was invading its local territory. The Northern Pacific, of course, denied the claim, but competitive bitterness continued. After long discussion the Northern Pacific board in December, 1886, approved the joint lease, accompanied however "by an agreement for the division of the business in Oregon and Washington Territory."[5] In the following month, the Northern Pacific board changed its mind. A resolution declared that it was "not expedient" to participate in such a lease, "on the proposed basis of rental." The president was directed to negotiate with Adams "for the purpose of securing an equitable division of traffic, and a continuation of harmonious relations between the Union Pacific and the Northern Pacific Companies."[6]

By this time the problem had again changed. The Union Pacific, in the face of the reluctance of the Northern Pacific to negotiate a joint lease, had completed a lease of the Navigation on the basis of a 6 per cent dividend, effective January 1, 1887. Open war between the Union Pacific and the Northern Pacific for the control of the Navigation now broke out. The Union Pacific had leased the road but it did not own the stock. Though Transcontinental was the largest stockholder, it did not hold a majority. The Transcontinental president was Elijah Smith, long active in western railroads and a capitalist of considerable means with a substantial, largely speculative, following. Though the president of a company with the largest stock interest in the Navigation, he was unable to secure representation on the latter's board. Smith was a determined business enemy of the Northern Pacific. In 1885 and again in 1886 he endeavored to line up enough proxies to secure a majority of the Navigation's stock. In both years the Smith ticket was defeated.

As the date for the annual election of the Navigation in September, 1887, approached, Smith on behalf of the Transcontinental took comprehensive measures in an effort to acquire a majority interest. He decided first to buy more Northern Pacific. By controlling that road, as well as the Navigation, the Transcontinental could harmonize the relations between the three fighting roads: Northern Pacific, Union Pacific, and Navigation. The Transcontinental bought seventy thousand shares of Northern Pacific stock, largely on margin, with the aid of advances by the Navigation. The latter decided to raise funds by the issue of bonds and the Transcontinental arranged to sell them through a Boston firm, Chase and Higginson. Due largely to a stock market break, the bank could not sell the bonds. Transcontinental loans were called and the company was faced with bankruptcy.

By a fortunate circumstance, Villard was in this country. He had, what is even more important, secured the confidence of some leading German financial interests. He was equipped with a letter of recommendation from the Deutsche Bank to Drexel-Morgan and Company, which stated that "we would bespeak for him as our confidential friend and advisor the good will of your firm of which Mr. Morgan gave us verbal assurance."[7] Between the fall of 1886 and the late summer of 1887 Villard had been engaged in a combined program of speculating and investing.

When Transcontinental loans were called in August, 1887, Villard was there. Smith and the Boston banker called on Villard. The sum of $5 million was needed to save the Transcontinental. Through his foreign associations Villard raised the funds in forty-eight hours. Villard proposed to the Deutsche Bank that it buy the Navigation stock and also the bonds

at substantial discounts. The announcement of this purchase thrilled
Villard and recalled for him the halcyon era of 1879–1881. "We turned
whole market, restored general confidence and making greatest sensation
throughout country. Crowds of people congratulate and thank Villard
for relieving situation," wired Villard to his German client.[8] For raising
the money and saving the Transcontinental, Smith gave Villard the
Northern Pacific proxies.

Villard was confident that he could settle the differences between the
railroad rivals. The price of the Navigation stock would then rise. He
therefore urged his German client to buy the stock and, he stressed, not
to sell it quickly. But if the bank, attracted by a price increase, did decide
to sell, Villard requested that it sell "only through me. I expect great
movement in market next weeks."[9]

Villard now was back in his home territory and he began to make
business friends. Wright, with his large Philadelphia stock-holding
following, was impressed. Villard, he thought, could arrange an "amicable settlement"; he therefore decided to vote his stock in his favor.[10]
Villard and four of his business friends were elected to the Northern
Pacific board.

Villard was now ready for business. On September 15 the Northern
Pacific board met and Villard introduced a resolution to instruct the
president to appoint a committee to make a study of the differences
between the Northern Pacific, Navigation, and Union Pacific. Within
one month the committee presented a report which renewed the proposal
of a joint lease with a 6 per cent guaranteed dividend on the Navigation
stock. Provision was again made for a division of the territory south and
north of the Snake River between the Navigation and the Northern
Pacific, and rates were to be adjusted in such a way that the traffic could
move either to Portland via the Navigation or to Tacoma via the Northern Pacific.[11] The way now seemed open for a reconciliation of all interests. The lease was approved by the boards of both the proposed lessees.

Villard, satisfied that intercorporate harmony between the three roads
had been achieved, left for Germany. Soon afterward Adams grew suspicious of Villard. Hunt's road, Adams discovered, was planning to build
a line in territory which the Navigation had always called its own. The
plan was supported, Adams believed, by some Northern Pacific directors.
Hunt was buying rails in Chicago and selling bonds in Philadelphia—
largely to Wright's friends. Wright, asserted Adams, "was cutting the

vitals out of the Oregon Navigation as fast as he could."[12] If the Hunt System invaded the territory of the Navigation, Adams would retaliate and invade the country of the Northern Pacific. "Obviously my duty," declared Adams, is "to meet threatening movements, made with the knowledge and apparent concurrence of directors of the Northern Pacific with such counter movements as the exigency of the situation plainly dictate."[13] Adams also objected to the selection of the Navigation board members suggested by Villard.

There appeared to be a misunderstanding between Villard and Adams. The property interests were so great and the long delays incidental to the negotiation of agreements between the two roads so prolonged and frustrating that tempers became heated and calmness of judgment waned and almost disappeared. In August, 1888, Adams informed Villard of the withdrawal by the Union Pacific from the joint lease. Embittered language on both sides followed. Adams insisted that the Northern Pacific had engaged in "aggressive movements." This, declared Villard, was "absolutely unfounded and false."[14] He accused Adams of lack of faith and of a violation of contract. "I am more especially at a loss to concede how any understanding I had with you could justify the attempt to withdraw on the part of your companies."[15] Perhaps one more statement of Villard will suggest the intensity of feeling that characterized the relationship between these two: "You come and claim that I constituted myself both a fool and a knave by consenting, or seeming to consent, whichever way you may put it, to a course of action . . . directly contrary to my above-mentioned record. I must beg leave to denounce this as an absolutely unwarranted piece of perversion and grossly insulting to me."[16]

In the face of this unfriendly personal relationship, the leading actors in this corporate drama again resumed negotiations. Avoiding a construction war was so clearly necessary that the participants were once again able to sink their personal differences. By February, 1889, a so-called Arbitration Contract was concluded. This was an agreement with an elaborate administrative machinery. A board of five managers was set up to represent the interests of the Union Pacific and its Oregon Short Line. Also a scheme was presented to finance the sale by the Transcontinental of its $12 million (par value) Navigation stock to the Union and Northern Pacific. Again, superficially, the plan was a solution of all corporate differences. A Northern Pacific director expressed his enthusiasm with the arrangement. "The settlement will insure harmony in the extreme Northwest for many years and end the reckless building of branch lines."[17]

Alas, fate decreed war instead of peace. Again Adams changed his mind. Early in April he pronounced the plan impracticable. He suddenly turned bold. He had a new ally— Hill of the Manitoba—and a new plan as well. Adams decided to acquire control of the Transcontinental and thereby determine the policy of the Navigation. Smith joined Adams and Hill. As part of the plan Adams would build a 25-mile extension to connect the Union Pacific system with Spokane. He would then grant the Manitoba trackage rights from Spokane to Portland. Hill at this time was disturbed over the expansion plans of the Northern Pacific; this road, he declared, was "pursuing a very aggressive course almost regardless of permanent cost and business judgment. . . ."[18] The Hill-Adams understanding was designed to meet this competition.

Both contestants squared away for the battle. The prize was control of the Transcontinental and, through it, of the Navigation. In May, 1889, each group asked for proxies. The circular requesting proxy support for the Union Pacific contained the name of General Samuel Thomas, representing the Manitoba. The Villard appeal was signed by Colby, of the Wisconsin Central, with whom Villard had close business relationships. There was apparently here a *quid pro quo*. His support of Villard in the Navigation fight was later paid for, presumably by the Northern Pacific lease of the financially decrepit Wisconsin Central.

The position of Adams in this bitterly fought battle to acquire control of the Transcontinental is not entirely clear. Adams, it appears, was not enamored of the value of the Navigation. He thought the Union Pacific's traffic officials had not correctly analysed the value of the business accruing to the Union Pacific through the Navigation lease. The Union Pacific, in fact, related Adams, gave more passenger business to the Navigation than the latter gave the Union Pacific. "Very few emigrants come from Oregon to the east. A great many go from the east to Oregon . . . we give to the Navigation company two where they give us one." On freight business, continued Adams, about the only traffic delivered to the Union Pacific to points east of the Missouri River was some wool. The other freight, consisting of lumber and heavy articles did not go beyond the Missouri River; they were destined to points on the Union Pacific and could not be routed through any competitor. The Union Pacific, on the other hand, delivered freight to the Navigation from all points east of the

Missouri River destined to Portland. "We would be in as good position to compete for it on Portland rates without a lease as we are with it." Indeed, Adams concluded, he would prefer to lose the lease. "We would like nothing better than for them [the Navigation] to break the lease, leaving us to force our way into Portland either over them or in competition with them."[19] He was sure, however, the Navigation would do no such thing.

In face of this opinion about the slight value of the Navigation, Adams decided to acquire control through the Transcontinental. Adams' judgment must have been warped by the frustrations arising from the prolonged delays in reaching a settlement with the Northern Pacific. He believed that that road had repeatedly disregarded territorial agreements. If Villard maintained control of the Transcontinental and Navigation, he would, Adams believed, make changes in their management unfavorable to the Union Pacific. Accordingly in April, shortly after Adams withdrew from the Arbitration Contract, he informed Harris that "the time for delay was over, and we now propose to take care of ourselves."

Adams now seized the initiative and proposed to Harris a comprehensive set of traffic agreements. The Northern Pacific would go to any competitive point in the Navigation area by buying trackage from that company. The Union Pacific similarly would go to any competitive point in the Northern Pacific country in Washington and Idaho by buying trackage rights from it. Such an arrangement would carry the Union Pacific into the mining country of northern Idaho and to Puget Sound points, the richest sources of traffic in the Northern Pacific territory, "without the cost of competitive construction."

Harris informed Adams that his proposal would be carefully considered, but Adams would tolerate no delay. The Union Pacific had already delayed "to the utmost limit of safety." The Union Pacific meanwhile would take care of itself. If the Northern Pacific did not approve the arrangement, the Union Pacific would make an alliance with Hill and the Manitoba.[20] With that road, a through line could be made from Portland to important outlets in the Northwest. The Manitoba, declared Adams, "was the strongest card in our hands."[21]

After weeks of delay Villard declined to accept the proposal of mutual trackage concessions. Indeed he presented one in which, according to Adams, he took "the back track on everything except the points which touch his vanity." Villard was confident of success in the proxy fight; he insisted that he controlled more than a majority of the Transcontinental stock and he therefore offered a basis for settlement which accorded more largely with his interests. The central point was the establishment of a Transcontinental board in accordance with the proportion of share ownership. The board would consist of seven of Adams' group and eight of Villard's. The directors would be interested only in the Navigation and would have no connection with the Northern or the Union Pacific. Villard, "for purpose of vindication merely," would be chosen president, with the intimation that he would be willing to resign after he was vindicated. With the exception of Villard's presence on the board and his assumption of the presidency, it was a plan for which Adams had been contending, so Adams declared. The plan was "a complete theft of my thunder with a view to smiting me with my own lightning." Though he was inclined to consider the plan favorably he was fearful of public opinion. There was so much discussion over the suppression of competition and the establishment of a monopoly that "a popular conflagration on the subject of monopolies" might develop. It would be wise to reach a settlement, thought Adams. "I do not care whether Villard has the credit of it or not. That is immaterial. What we want is peace, traffic and money."[22]

The background for a peaceful settlement was not satisfactory. The proxy battle for the control of the Transcontinental was being carried out both in the stock market and in the law courts. Both sides were fighting for proxies.

Meanwhile Adams made a move opposed by the Villard party. The Navigation in 1889 had barely earned its operating expenses. It would probably, in the opinion of Adams, earn $1 million less than the rent paid by the Union Pacific. Adams therefore proposed that the guaranteed rent be reduced from 6 to 4 per cent. The proposal was condemned in a number of public sources. A New York newspaper looked upon this effort of Adams as "an example of conspicuous lack of the quality of common sense." If there were any more fights involving the Union Pacific, continued the same writer, "it might be judicious for the Directors to suggest to Mr. Adams the expediency of a short trip to Europe."[23]

Both sides meanwhile were buying Transcontinental stock. Villard in 1889 was assuming the same risks that he incurred in 1881. He bought Transcontinental from Drexel-Morgan on margin and borrowed from

Sage, with Transcontinental collateral, using the borrowed funds to purchase additional stock.[24] By mid-May an acute scarcity of the Transcontinental stock had developed. A corner had been created.[25] The Villard group had secured slightly more than a majority of Transcontinental stock and Adams had lost his battle to drive "Villard and his gang out of all the companies with which we are connected, including the Northern Pacific."[26]

It was now clear that co-operation between the Union and Northern Pacific in the affairs of the Navigation was impossible. Numerous plans had been suggested on both sides. They had all failed. In these negotiations Adams had allied himself with the Manitoba—perhaps the strongest rival of the Northern Pacific. The proposed agreement between the Union Pacific and the Manitoba would put the latter into the Northern Pacific country in Washington and Oregon. A peaceful arrangement with a road that lent itself to the support of a business enemy was out of the question. Villard decided to expand and enlarge the Northern Pacific and forget both the Manitoba and the Union Pacific. The sale of the Navigation stock at a high price of about $90 per share would furthermore give his clients a handsome profit. This would improve his ability to raise substantial sums for improving and extending Northern Pacific. Villard was then engaged in a number of non-railroad financial transactions, and his ability to attract capital from satisfied investors would enable him to carry out his plans successfully. Early in June, accordingly, he sold the Transcontinental's 120,000 shares of Navigation Company stock to the Union Pacific at $90 a share. The Union Pacific, furthermore, exchanged all its Transcontinental stock at cost in exchange for the Navigation stock, also at a price of 90.[27]

All the efforts over a three-year period to agree upon peace and avoid a war of construction and of rates had met with failure. The Union Pacific, now in control of the Navigation, was free to invade the territory of the Northern Pacific, and the latter was equally free to invade the territory of the other. Responsible thinking in the industry suggested "that it would be a financial crime if a failure to agree should be allowed for some years to come to compel any unnecessary railroad building in the Pacific Northwest."[28] In business, as in politics, what is logical or reasonable, what everybody agrees is needed, is frequently the very thing that is not done. Virtually all the railroad businessmen in this area wanted peace. What they got was war.

At the eastern end of the northern transcontinental routes the competitive problems were different and in a sense more complicated than in the West. The corporate conflicts in Washington and Oregon were more dramatic than those that took place between Chicago, the Twin Cities, and Lake Superior. There were here no legal or stock market battles. Four major railroad systems were involved. Of these, the St. Paul and the Northwestern had lines between the Twin Cities and Chicago, while the other two, the Northern Pacific and the Manitoba, did not. Of these properties, only the St. Paul lacked control of a route to the Lake Superior ports. Between Chicago and St. Paul, in addition to the direct lines of the St. Paul and the Northwestern, there were a number of others. The Stickney Line was the latest entrant, and it engaged in competition for traffic by the conventional medium adopted by weaker roads. Another was the Wisconsin Central, controlled by a group led by Colby, allied with Villard in the Transcontinental contest. The most roundabout Twin Cities and Chicago route was the Rock Island multi-line arrangement. Still another route was the Burlington and Northern, the Burlington System's outlet from Chicago to the Twin Cities.

The two St. Paul lines without a Chicago connection considered ways and means of remedying this situation. The completion of the Burlington and Northern's line in 1887 led to close business relationships between the Manitoba and the Burlington. There was only slight temptation by the Manitoba to build its own Chicago line. There was, however, the possibility that it might enter into a preferential agreement like the Tripartite of 1883. But the Burlington was skeptical about the value of such a transaction. It might disturb the relationship between the Burlington and the other St. Paul–Chicago lines. Forbes was clear in his mind about the inadvisability of such a business policy. "No such Companies as the C. B. & Q. and the St. P. M. & M. can afford to tie themselves up to the exclusion of other great Trunk Lines," he declared. Instead, as a basis for developing a mutual interest "a large amount" of the Manitoba stock was sold to the Burlington's stockholders, including both Perkins and Forbes. By this means Forbes hoped that the Burlington would secure a "fair share" of the business coming from the Northwest; and felt that "none of the Trunk lines can reasonably complain of our taking it for our own benefit and for that of the population along our well settled lines."[29]

Though the Burlington had secured a large block of the Burlington

and Northern Stock, there was by no means a harmonious business relationship between the two properties. The president of the latter was a
former vice-president of the Burlington. Its stock, moreover, was held
largely by some major stockholders of the Burlington, and some of them
were more interested in increasing the earnings of the Burlington and
Northern than those of the Burlington. Conflicts of interest developed
between the two properties, The contractual relations between the two
roads were such as to lead the former to submit heavy claims for damages
to the other. Curiously enough the independent traffic and rate policy
of the Burlington and Northern—a policy which appeared to be so
belligerent—was ascribed to the Burlington. The latter therefore began
to consider the advisability of acquiring full control of the other. Some
objections were made because of the low value of its property. One of the
directors and a large stockholder objected to the proposed acquisition.
"I have my doubts about the road being worth its bonds," was his
conclusion.[30]

Despite these objections the Burlington management thought it best to
follow a policy calculated to stabilize the northwestern railroad industry.
It was worth the heavy financial cost of taking over the ownership of the
other. The road, in fact, was in serious financial straits, and not many
months after the purchase of control by the Burlington, it was obliged
to borrow money to pay the October, 1890, interest.[31]

The purchase of the stock was made in March, 1890. The price was
$40 a share. To minimize the risk of an outbreak of rate troubles, an
understanding was reached to share the purchase on an equal basis with
Hill. It was agreed that the Burlington would supply the Chicago terminals for the St. Paul–Chicago route, and the Great Northern, would
supply the St. Paul and the Minneapolis terminals. According to Perkins,
Hill had agreed to a plan of joint ownership but after many procastina-
tions and evasions had declined to carry out the agreement.[32] The Burl-
lington accordingly took over the stock alone, for its own account. A
rate disturber had been removed. The more conservative Burlington
management was now in charge of the Twin Cities–Chicago rate
structure.

The Northern Pacific, the major competitor of the Great Northern,
adopted a more expansionist policy with respect to its Chicago outlet.
The leading financial interest in the Wisconsin Central was held by
Colby, long a business friend of Villard. In 1882, when Villard was riding

high in railroad circles, there had been some understanding that the Northern Pacific would take over the Wisconsin Central. The increasing financial strain on Villard property made it impossible, if such an understanding really existed, to carry it into operation.

Through the Transcontinental, Villard had bought a block of the Wisconsin Central stock, and according to one report Colby had worked with Villard with the intention of uniting the two roads.[33] The reappearance of Villard in affairs of the Northern Pacific in 1887 led to a resumption of the friendly relations. Colby voted his Transcontinental shares and those of his financial followers in support of Villard. At first the contact between the Northern Pacific and the Wisconsin was made in the form of a traffic agreement. The Wisconsin Central in early 1889, through contracts with other corporations, secured access to Chicago terminals, and soon thereafter permitted the Northern Pacific to utilize these facilities. The Northern Pacific–Wisconsin Central agreement created a preferential traffic exchange between Chicago, St. Paul, and Ashland, a Lake Superior port.[34] This loose arrangement was not satisfactory to the Wisconsin Central. It did not bind the Northern Pacific, at that time a prosperous enterprise whose earnings were rapidly increasing, to assume its obligations. According to the reports of an investigating committee three years later, the Northern Pacific in 1890 "relieved the backers of the Wisconsin Central from an impending bankruptcy."[35]

For the traffic agreement was replaced in January, 1890, by a lease based upon a fixed percentage (35 per cent) of its gross. This was followed by the organization under Villard's auspices of a terminal corporation in Chicago. Villard thereby unified a number of separately owned terminal properties into a larger company with a demonstrable earning power. This enabled him to raise funds by the sale of securities. He sold bonds of the terminal company, as well as a minority stock interest. The Wisconsin Central, like the Burlington and Northern, had also been a rate disturber. It thus appeared that another such disturber had been eliminated.

Still another unstabilizing influence remained, in the St. Paul and Duluth road. Though it controlled the short line between these two points, it had not regained the earnings lost by the construction of the parallel line of the Great Northern. Plans to build its lines west of St. Paul were frustrated by inability to raise capital. And of course the competition of the United States affiliates of the Canadian Pacific also remained. The Canadian Pacific itself was still free to use its outlets by rail, and also by water, to cut rates.

In the area west of Chicago and north of Kansas City the competition remained intense. There many of the smaller roads had been absorbed in the expansion program of the 1880's. Others remained. Some had once been enclosed in the arms of major railroads, but later, in the process of financial reorganization, had been dropped.

A notable independent road east of the Missouri was the Alton. In the 1880's its mileage remained unchanged. It therefore commanded no through traffic of its own from beyond the river. West of the river the Rio Grande was another independent line. The Burlington, after the completion of its Denver extension, had entered into close traffic relationships with that road. The line of the Rio Grande, however, was not satisfactory. The road was built with narrow gauge and the property was not in good physical condition. Its standard of service was not commensurate with the necessities of the Burlington. The Burlington management was therefore forced into consideration of a policy designed to improve the Rio Grande as part of a transcontinental route. There were strong influences in favor of the purchase of the property. One important board member believed it would diversify the traffic of the Burlington. The latter was strong in agricultural traffic, and the Rio Grande, in mineral. Perkins agreed that "it would be a good thing if we could own or control the D. & R. G. System, including the Western."[36]

The Rio Grande was desirable primarily to improve the standard of through service. If that could be accomplished in any other way than through the acquisition of the Rio Grande, the problem would be solved. In the late 1880's the western part of the route controlled by the Rio Grande Western took steps to improve its property. By 1889 both that road and the Rio Grande had become standard gauge. The former reduced its grades to the standard of the Union Pacific and eliminated a number of curves. In the language of its president, it now had a line that "even the C. B. & Q. may feel proud to connect with."[37] Perkins urged upon the president of the Rio Grande, the eastern end of the route, the adoption of a similar policy. If, he wrote to the president, the distance of the latter's line were reduced and the road made standard gauge, the Burlington would postpone "for the present and perhaps indefinitely" the building of a new line over the range.[38]

By the end of 1890 both the Rio Grande and the Western had changed their lines to standard gauge. Both properties had been improved. The Rio Grande route could now compete on a reasonably competitive basis with the Union Pacific. The Burlington, as well as the Rock Island, agreed to utilize this improved route. The latter, long friendly to the Union Pacific, had by this time become a determined rival.

In the Rocky Mountain area traversed by the Rio Grande, new competition had appeared in the form of the Colorado Midland. That road, with a line from Colorado Springs to the western Colorado boundary, had cut into some of the local business of the Rio Grande. It also competed for transcontinental traffic. At the Colorado–Utah boundary line it connected with the Rio Grande Western, and since the Western under Palmer's leadership was operated independently of the Rio Grande, the Western and the Colorado Midland joined to form a rival transcontinental route. The Rock Island, connecting with the road at Colorado Springs, looked forward in 1889 to the possibility of buying control.

It was, however, not with the Rock Island that the Midland had close traffic relationships. Its most important interchange business was with the Atchison.[39] The Midland had agreed to give its Denver and Kansas City business to the Atchison. In the summer of 1890 that agreement was broken. Rivalry for the acquisition of the Midland between the Rio Grande, Rock Island, and Atchison culminated in the latter paying a price in excess of its value based upon earnings. The Rio Grande was set to acquire the Midland, but shortly before the completion of the sale the Atchison stepped in and paid a higher price.[40]

The Midland–Atchison union formed a new transcontinental route via the Rio Grande Western–Central Pacific. It was questionable, however, whether the new route could offer a high standard of service. The Central Pacific was a part of the Huntington System. To the extent that the new route carried more traffic over the Central Pacific, the Southern Pacific division of the Huntington System carried less. Since the latter secured a longer haul by the Southern Pacific than by the Central Pacific, it was improbable that the latter would encourage the movement of business over a rival of the system. Its acquisition in 1890, however, did remove the Midland as a high-cost rate cutter.

In the Southwest the dominant position occupied by Huntington, Gould, and the Atchison was not seriously disturbed by developments in the late 1880's and early 1890's. After a prolonged battle involving many disputes with rival bond-holding groups, Gould's transcontinental line, the Texas and Pacific, emerged from receivership under his control.[41] The Kansas and Texas, after a prolonged battle and to the surprise of most informed observers passed from Gould control.[42] The Gould System thus lost the western hinge of its north–south lines between St. Louis and the Gulf Coast. The loss was partly offset by the acquisition of another line nourishing the Missouri Pacific with a substantial volume of northbound traffic. Though this road was not entirely controlled by Gould, his holdings were sufficient to make his son Edwin vice-president —"and thereafter the reorganized company—the St. Louis and South-western—became a friend, not a foe."[43]

The Huntington System was little changed. It had built with great speed between 1881 and 1884. The only significant major extension thereafter came after Villard's initial failure in 1883. Villard's efforts to extend the California and Oregon Railroad from Portland to a connec-tion with the Huntington lines met with failure. The loss to the Trans-continental was heavy. The holding company sold out to Huntington. Huntington pressed forward with the construction program, and by 1887 he completed the line to Portland. Portland now had another transcon-tinental connection with the East.

One of the few remaining independent southeastern properties offering competition to the three dominant systems was the Frisco. It had not participated in the extension of the 1880's. Its conservative policy was probably associated with the threat of Gould to retaliate. An extension would involve an invasion of Gould territory in Arkansas and Texas. In the second expansion phase of the 1880's, however, the Frisco did build a competitive line. The Frisco also enjoyed the strategic advantage, poten-tially of some importance to the Atchison, of a line to St. Louis. Both roads since 1880 had been partners in the Atlantic and Pacific venture. Relations cooled in 1886–1887. The Frisco threatened to violate its terri-torial agreement in Kansas. It also received stockholder approval for the increase of the authorized amount of bonds. The management informed its stockholders that the company was now free "to make such extensions and additions . . . as may . . . be judicious, profitable and necessary. . . ."[44] A construction program would strengthen the forces of rate instability, and would lead to an invasion of the Atchison's territory. The effect of the Frisco's threats upon the Atchison's decision to acquire the road is only inference. There is no factual basis for the determination of the truth. In announcing the purchase of control, the Atchison pointed to "many advantages": the road, "besides taking care of itself, will furnish the Atchison lines a vast traffic not had before the acquisition. . . . It takes care of its own finances and is in every way a benefit to Atchison stock value."[45] A stock exchange was effected in the summer of 1890. Later acquisitions gave the Atchison almost complete ownership of all common and preferred stock.

The control of the Huntington and Gould Systems, meanwhile, remained securely in the grip of their creators. Huntington, as well as Stanford and Crocker, did little trading in the Southern Pacific. In the face of repeated financial reversals they held on to their stock ownership. Gould did trade in the Missouri Pacific. Yet, despite many press reports to the contrary, he never relinquished control. The stock of the Atchison, on the other hand, was widely distributed. Unlike the stock of the two other roads, a large percentage had been sold for cash. As the financial strength of the Atchison waned, much of the stock found its way to the open market. Both Huntington and Gould became large holders. (According to one informed source, Huntington in 1890 was the largest individual holder.)[46] Though the amount of Gould's holdings are not known, a close student of western railway affairs remarked that Gould's holdings were probably sufficient to enable him to assume control. "Unless I am mistaken, [Gould] will yet have the Atchison."[47] Control of the Atchison by Gould, assuming that such a project was ever considered, was never consummated. He had, however, just completed another bold strategic move—the re-acquisition of the Union Pacific. That moved him into a host of complex financial problems. It is probable indeed that Gould sold the Atchison stock in order to finance other requirements.

Both the Atchison and the Huntington Systems had through routes to the Pacific Coast. A number of other major railroads were unable to realize this ambition. Of these, the St. Paul had, after completion of its extension to Kansas City, set aside its trans-Missouri hopes. Four other major roads—the Great Northern, Rock Island, Burlington, and Northwestern—were pushing their construction plans. All had plans to move on to the coast. The rate wars, with the accompanying decline in earnings and dividends, made it difficult to raise capital. Railroad managements accordingly looked forward to an alternative to further construction without sacrificing the possibility of participation in the transcontinental business. The answer was a system of traffic alliances and agreements and the cultivation of joint ownership of railroad facilities. Hill considered both of these measures. In 1890, according to Burlington officials, he entered into an understanding for the assumption of joint ownership of the Burlington and Northern. There was also the agreement between Hill and Adams. Hill soon changed his mind and decided to push his own line to the Pacific Coast. Business friends became business enemies. The Union Pacific retaliated by diverting to another line traffic which formerly moved over the Hill line. It ordered "all its business routed by Canadian Pacific," related a Burlington official.[48]

While the Manitoba thus rejected the mechanism of the traffic alliance, other railroads systems adopted a contrary policy. In the spring and early summer of 1889 press reports and informed comment united in the prediction that the Northwestern would extend its line west.[49] By the fall of the year, however, the Northwestern had surrendered its construction plans.

The Union Pacific, since the complition of its Omaha line in 1869, had pursued varying policies for traffic interchange with its eastern connections. The Rock Island and St. Paul had since 1883 been its favorite outlets. The Rock Island, however, by building west of the Missouri to a connection with the Rio Grande, had become a business rival. It appeared that the St. Paul and the Northwestern would now become the Union Pacific's preferred associates. The Northwestern had a strategic advantage denied to the St. Paul. It had a Lake Superior line. A traffic understanding between these two lines would enable the Union Pacific, in the opinion of a Burlington official, to establish such Lake Superior rates as "will dominate all that country."[50] The Union Pacific until the late 1880's had expanded little, while its transcontinental business was assailed from many directions. The year 1889 was marked by a revolutionary policy change—in June the Navigation stock was bought.

The Union Pacific and the Northwestern complemented each other. While the former had no outlet to Lake Superior and Chicago, the latter had none to the Pacific. The Northwestern had neither a line nor a reliable traffic associate for the transcontinental business.

The way was thus opened for an agreement. Each surrendered the idea of building into each other's territory. Each agreed to use the property of the other. The agreement was consummated in October, 1889. Eastbound traffic of the Union Pacific, so far as possible, would flow over the Northwestern; and the Northwestern's westbound, over the Union Pacific.

Each company would furnish its proportion of the required equipment. The Northwestern would make the rates on westbound business and the Union Pacific on eastbound. Adams was enthusiastic: "The Chicago & Northwestern and the Union Pacific become in all essential through traffic respects one company. They will protect and sustain each other; and, in case of attack, make common cause."[51] The new form of competition—the use of alliances instead of construction of parallel lines—is well illustrated by Adams' justification of the Northwestern treaty. It was, he said, "forced on the Union Pacific to a degree by the action of the Atchison, Topeka & Santa Fe in constructing its own line to Chicago, and that of the Northern Pacific in connecting itself with the Wisconsin Central . . . the Union Pacific has endeavored to reach the same point without incurring the liabilities of the Atchison. . . ."[52]

The agreement, so satisfactory to Adams, was received with open hostility by the officialdom of the other Union Pacific connections. The St. Paul, in the expressive language of one railroad man, was "bottled up."[53] In view of its newly established policy of prudence, however, the road made no countermove. The Burlington considered various measures to counteract the loss of traffic, excluding, however, any thought of new construction. Only a few months before Perkins had explained the policy of his road: it "would not at present want to bring out any new scheme involving the construction of additional mileage."[54] Consideration was given to a contract for preferential interchange between the Union Pacific and the Burlington via Kansas City. This, according to a Burlington officer, would be "practically worthless" to his road. After the Union Pacific gave the Northwestern its traffic at Omaha there would be left only "a lot of remnants." Such an alliance, furthermore, would antagonize the lines east of the Missouri and west of Denver.[55]

The Burlington neither arranged traffic alliances nor acquired new property. It did, however, enter into informal understandings with both the St. Paul and the Rock Island for the interchange of business at the Missouri River. The St. Paul did all it could "to encourage" lines at the Missouri River to give to the Burlington traffic competitive with the Union Pacific. This policy would be continued so long as the "Union Pacific–Northwestern trade continues to be carried out."[56]

The Northwestern–Union Pacific alliance also met with opposition in the Interstate Commerce Railway Association. Divisions of joint rates and the apportionment of competitive traffic, insisted an Association

official, should be arranged through the Association. To this decision
the Union Pacific objected. The objects accomplished through this
arrangement, declared the Union Pacific, were realized by other roads
through corporate union, either by lease or stock control. The contract
merely protected the contracting railroads "against an impending redistribution of traffic" by the other roads. The Union Pacific notified the
Association of its withdrawal.[57]

To the opposition of the Burlington and the Association must be added
the strong, even bitter, resentment by Gould. The Missouri Pacific's
lines to Kansas City and Omaha would be expected to lose most of the
Union Pacific business. Gould was dissatisfied not only with the arrangement with the Northwestern but with another by which the Union Pacific
permitted the Rock Island and the St. Paul to use its bridge at Omaha
and some auxiliary tracks southwest of Omaha. By this contract, executed
in May, 1890, these roads could use the Union Pacific facilities for the
more efficient movement of their business to Denver and beyond. In the
struggle for this business the competitive position of these roads, as against
the Missouri Pacific, was strengthened. Gould thus looked upon the
Union Pacific as a business enemy to the Missouri Pacific–Wabash
System. In November, 1890, taking advantage of a stock-market break,
Gould again secured control of the Union Pacific.[58]

The Rock Island was also a loser because of the Union Pacific–Northwestern alliance. Its plans for construction of its own lines west, toward
the coast, had been frustrated by the decline in earnings in the late 1880's.
Upon completion of its lines to Colorado Springs in 1888 it decided not
to build, and instead concluded an agreement with the Rio Grande for
the use of its tracks, north to Denver and south to Pueblo.

The Union Pacific–Northwestern alliance was a challenge to the Rock
Island. New building was not considered. Yet the new rivalry must be
met. And the countermove was another alliance—a traffic agreement
with the Atchison. The two roads connected at Dodge City, Kansas. The
Rock Island promised to deliver to the Atchison all unconsigned westbound traffic, while the Atchison agreed to turn over to the Rock Island
its eastbound business. Both roads would maintain rates to competitive
points. The agreement was regarded by Cable, the Rock Island president, as a satisfactory challenge to the Union Pacific alliance. "I regard
this as a stronger agreement in every way than the Chicago & Northwestern–Union Pacific agreement. It makes a powerful alliance which

will command respect."[59] There promised, however, to be more difficulty in preserving harmony between these two roads than between the Union Pacific and the Northwestern. Both the Rock Island and the Atchison had lines of their own between the Missouri River and Chicago. There was no such complexity in the relations between the Union Pacific and the Northwestern, since the former had no lines east of the Missouri River.

In all these 1889 negotiations Adams consulted with General Dodge. Adams placed great reliance upon his judgment. Dodge, in fact, made the purchase contract for the Navigation stock in June. He also worked with Adams in the negotiations over the Northwestern alliance. He was also the policy maker of the Panhandle Route between Denver and Fort Worth. Dodge convinced Adams that the Union Pacific could wisely make an arrangement with the Panhandle Route, and in this way move traffic from the eastern seaboard by water to the Gulf, and north via rail over a multi-line route to Colorado and Montana. The Union Pacific could thereby secure a long haul over its own lines. In May of 1889, accordingly, the Union Pacific and the Denver, Texas and Fort Worth entered into an alliance "offensively and defensively."[60] The Union Pacific agreed to give the other road its unconsigned freight at Denver and a maximum volume of business moving between New York and the Northwest. This alliance lasted for only a few months. It was superseded in November by an agreement for the acquisition by the Union Pacific (through a subsidiary) of the controlling stock interest in the various corporate members of the Panhandle System. The new corporate subsidiary of the Union Pacific was known as the Union Pacific, Denver and Gulf Railway.[61]

These acquisitions and alliances reversed the elaborate Far West construction programs of the late 1880's. The Rock Island and the Northwestern remained within the boundaries set by the completion of their programs. The Atchison later did reach the Pacific Coast, but without the building of any substantial new mileage. The Burlington abandoned its projects of building across the mountains. Only the Manitoba pushed through a new line to the Pacific.

A campaign of competitive building of feeders and branches meanwhile went on feverishly between the competing systems of the Union Pacific and the Northern Pacific. They also purchased other roads in the rapid-expansion years of 1889 and 1890. The sellers and lessors took financial advantage of the necessities of the buyers and lessees, and exacted high prices in a period of prosperity. The Atchison also acquired strategic properties at the high costs characteristic of business booms. All these three roads, furthermore, assumed heavy financial burdens. And in all three the burdens proved insupportable. Within a few years thereafter they fell into receivership. The Burlington, Rock Island, Northwestern, and St. Paul—the properties that refrained from new construction and acquisitions in the late 1880's and early 1890's—escaped financial disaster. They maintained their dividend payments throughout the depression years of the 1890's. Only one major competitive building program in the nineteenth century remains for discussion. It will be the subject of the following chapter.

Notes for Chapter XX

[1] Annual Report, Burlington, 1890, p. 18.
[2] *North American Review*, Sept. 1891, pp. 272–282.
[3] Northern Pacific Archives, Harris to Billings, June 27, 1884.
[4] *R. R. Gaz.* Sept. 4, 1885, p. 574.
[5] Northern Pacific Archives, Harris to Adams, Dec. 17, 1886. The quotation is from the resolution approved by the Northern Pacific board of directors.
[6] *Ibid.*, Harris to Adams, Jan. 7, 1887.
[7] H. V. P., Deutsche Bank to Drexel-Morgan & Company, Sept. 29, 1886.
[8] *Ibid.*, Villard to Deutsche Bank, Sept. 1, 1887.
[9] *Ibid.*, Sept. 4, 1887.
[10] Hedges, p. 149.
[11] The provisions of the lease are detailed in Hedges, pp. 158–159.
[12] *Philadelphia Press*, June 15, 1888, quoting a letter of Adams' to Colby.
[13] Hedges, pp. 174–175.
[14] H. V. P., Villard to Adams, no date but probably early in September, 1888, Box 128, Letter Book 59.
[15] *Ibid.*, Aug. 3, 1888.
[16] Hedges, p. 180.
[17] *R. R. Gaz.*, Mar. 1, 1889, p. 151.
[18] Pyle, I, 451.
[19] Dodge Papers, Adams to Dodge, June 3, 1889.
[20] The above quotations other than the one from Burlington Archives are taken from Dodge Papers, Adams to Dillon, April 10, 1889.
[21] *Ibid.*, Adams to Dodge, June 5, 1889.
[22] *Ibid.*, Adams to Dodge, May 28, 1889.
[23] *The New York Times*, May 19, 1889.
[24] For the loan from Sage, see H. V. P., Charles H. Collis to Villard, May 29, 1889, Box 66.
[25] *Bradstreet's*, May 18, 1889, p. 318, for details.
[26] Dodge Papers, Adams to Dodge, May 15, 1889.
[27] Hedges, p. 201.
[28] *R. R. Gaz.*, July 5, 1889, p. 446.

[29] Burlington Archives, Forbes to R. W. Cutler, August 26, 1885.

[30] *Ibid.*, Geddes to Perkins, Feb. 27, 1889.

[31] *Ibid.*, T. S. Howland to Perkins, Sept. 26, 1890.

[32] *Ibid.*, Perkins to Forbes, Jan. 22, 1891.

[33] *Chron.*, Aug. 27, 1887, p. 204.

[34] *Ibid.*, May 4, 1889, p. 590.

[35] *Bradstreet's*, Feb. 25, 1893, p. 115.

[36] Burlington Archives, Perkins to Griswold, Aug. 25, 1890.

[37] *Ibid.*, Palmer to Perkins, Nov. 16, 1889.

[38] *Ibid.*, Perkins to D. H. Moffatt, Jan. 30, 1890.

[39] *Chron.*, Nov. 1, 1890, p. 608, presents some details.

[40] Burlington Archives, D. H. Moffatt to Perkins, Sept. 28, 1890.

[41] For details on the receivership and subsequent reorganization, see *Gould*, Chap. XXI, pp. 423–424, Chap. XXII, pp. 440–445.

[42] For details see *Gould*, Chap. XXVII, pp. 545–546.

[43] *Ibid.*, 551.

[44] Annual Report, Frisco, 1887, p. 9.

[45] J. W. Reinhart, president, Atchison, to Boston News Bureau, cited in *Chron.*, Aug. 16, 1890, p. 205.

[46] *Bradstreet's*, Oct. 11, 1890, p. 649.

[47] Burlington Archives, Geddes to Perkins, Mar. 1, 1891.

[48] *Ibid.*, Harris to Perkins, Nov. 18, 1889.

[49] See, for example, *Ry. Review*, April 13, 1889, p. 205; *R. R. Gaz.*, May 10, 1889, p. 312; and July 5, 1889, p. 448.

[50] Burlington Archives, Harris to Perkins, Nov. 10, 1889.

[51] Dodge Papers, Adams to Dodge, Oct. 23, 1889.

[52] *Ibid.*

[53] Burlington Archives, Stone to Perkins, Oct. 28, 1889.

[54] *Ibid.*, Perkins to Geo. B. Roberts, Aug. 7, 1889.

[55] *Ibid.*, Harris to Perkins, Nov. 10, 1889.

[56] *Ibid.*, Perkins to Harris, June 20, 1890.

[57] Adams to Walker, Jan. 18, 1890, cited in *Ry. Review*, Feb. 1, 1890, pp. 66–67.

[58] For details, see *Gould*, pp. 577–578.

[59] *Chron.*, Nov. 23, 1889, p. 689.

[60] Overton, p. 232.

[61] For details on these contracts, see *Ibid.*, pp. 237, 258.

XXI

Final 19th Century Transcontinental Building Program

THE STABILIZING forces—both industry-wide and corporate—in the late 1880's were reinforced by the cessation of railroad building in the Southwest, the Central West, and in most of the Northwest. No new through lines were completed in the former two areas, and only that of the Great Northern in the latter. In the Southwest and Midwest, except for some branch-line construction designed to serve local areas or to fill gaps in existing through lines, virtually no new mileage was built or planned. The decline in new construction to such a low level was a logical outcome of the forces arising from the expansion of 1886–1887. Duplicate and parallel lines led to rate reductions, earning decreases, and dividend suspensions and eliminations. These untoward financial consequences of the building programs characterized the careers of both weak and financially strong railroads. Adverse financial results blocked the flow of long-term capital into the industry. The stoppage of new building thus tended to restrain any increase in transportation capacity. It was a force that would aid, other things remaining unchanged, in maintaining a stable rate structure.

The major southwestern railroads had indeed virtually completed their expansion programs in the early 1880's. The southwestern divisions of the Missouri Pacific system fell into financial difficulties before the second expansion wave began in 1886. The Texas and Pacific and the International added almost nothing to their mileage in the latter 1880's and early 1890's. The Kansas and Texas, divorced from Gould control, extended its line from a small point in southern Texas to a connection with Houston. Branch lines were built in a number of areas on the northern end of its line near Fort Worth, and another served the east Texas lumber areas. The Kansas and Texas thereby was able to establish its own through line between the Mississippi Valley and Houston.

The Southern Pacific had by 1883 completed its through route between San Francisco and New Orleans. Thereafter it built no new through lines, though it did build some local branches in California. The Atchison had by the end of 1888 completed the most ambitious expansion program of any of the western roads. Since September, however, it had built "practically no new mileage,"[1] The Rock Island, the other Chicago line which in the late 1880's had crossed the Missouri River, also by the end of the decade brought its construction activities to a halt. It did however build a number of lines south from Indian Territory into Texas and to the Gulf Coast. In the Northwest, east of the Missouri River to the Great Lakes, railroad building also came to almost a complete halt. The St. Paul, under the Morgan leadership, built little. It even refused the opportunity to build branch lines. "It is impossible," wrote the president in 1892 to a resident of a South Dakota town, "for us to extend any of our lines in the Dakotas this year. The road we already have has been so greatly a burden that it has been somewhat discouraging and we must wait for more development of the country."[2] The Northwestern, under a conservative administration, terminated its expansion career in 1889 with the conclusion of the Union Pacific Traffic Alliance.

Both the St. Paul and the Northwestern, as well as all the other roads between Chicago and St. Paul, had by the end of the decade abandoned any plans for the building of new lines. Two of the smaller roads, indeed, changed their ownership, with the hope thereby of strengthening their position financially. The Wisconsin Central leased its line to the Northern Pacific, while the owners of the Burlington and Northern sold out to the Burlington. It was hoped that thereby their rate-cutting tactics would be eliminated.

The Burlington moved cautiously further into west Nebraska and Wyoming. There was some high-grade coal reserves in this area, and rail transportation facilities would aid the Burlington in getting a supply of low-cost fuel. Most of the country west of the Rocky Mountain Range in Colorado had by this time been "pretty completely" occupied by the Rio Grande, the Union Pacific, and the Midland. A line into northwestern Nebraska and eastern Wyoming was, in the opinion of the Burlington management, the one remaining opportunity for extension into a large area unoccupied by others. This construction was carried out somewhat gingerly. Adams, of the Union Pacific, was advised that it was "entirely outside of territory tributary to his line."[3] The Burlington board cautiously appropriated funds to finance this 100-mile extension. Perkins declared that in this area there was a profitable cattle traffic and that the Burlington should "take advantage of the hold we have now secured up there, and not let the Northern Pacific cut us off by building branches." Nevertheless he was not able to secure funds for the quick building of the line. He pleaded with members of the finance committee to make available $200 thousand for grading purposes.[4] This Wyoming line—competitive with the Northern Pacific—was criticized by a railroad journal as a move which "can hardly be called . . . justifiable."[5] A further extension in 1893 and early 1894 appeared to indicate the prospect of the construction of another transcontinental line to the Pacific Coast. The necessity of rate stabilization, however, overcame the imperial ambitions of system builders. Early in 1894, at a meeting between officials of the Burlington and the Northern Pacific, a trackage-traffic agreement between the two roads was negotiated. Provision was made for interchange of business at Billings, Montana, and for a division of the rates on through traffic. The contract, including subsequent changes, was applied to business moving to and from points west of the Mississippi River. Neither party could require the other to participate in a war of rates.[6] The Burlington, like the Northwestern, could now reach the Pacific Coast over the tracks of another road. Construction of duplicate and parallel mileage was thereby avoided.

In California there was some significant local building. Though Huntington did little in Texas and Louisiana, he found it profitable to provide new local lines in California. A "long and difficult piece of work" involved a 110-mile extension—a line that traversed a thriving country and also gave the Southern Pacific a second Los Angeles–San Francisco connection.[7] Some other branch construction was undertaken, none significant. The difficulty of providing funds is well illustrated by an observation of a Southern Pacific vice-president: "We have never been able to build a branch railroad out of the profits of the company, but we have been compelled to issue bonds for all of them."[8]

Branch building continued beyond the nineteenth century and well into the third decade of the twentieth century. This construction responded largely, though not entirely, to local requirements. Such projects did not reflect any system strategy. They did not create the necessity for the investment of large amounts of capital in risky enterprises. They did not involve the entrance into lightly settled territories. Branch line construction did not lead to competitive overbuilding of railroad facilities— the kind that led to the profit-depressing rate wars of the 1880's.

It was only in the Far Northwest, primarily in the state of Washington and to a lesser degree in Oregon, Idaho, and Montana, that an old-fashioned construction war developed. A curious paradox of this construction war—the last of the 19th century—was the leadership assumed by a businessman who had refrained from participation in the earlier wars. Adams had in 1888 denounced a construction war as "a folly amounting even to a crime."[9] The Union Pacific in the 1880's had not built lines to develop the fertile country in Nebraska "until the best of the territory had been occupied by other companies."[10] It was the Union Pacific lease of the Navigation in June, 1889, that led to the competitive construction war. For about a decade prior to this time there had been a succession of invasion threats and counterthreats, punctuated by apparently stable intercorporate relationships, in the lower Columbia River Valley. The Northern Pacific in 1887 finished a transcontinental route of its own to Tacoma, thereby competing with the Navigation line to Portland. This extension strengthened the competitive rivalries between the two properties. However, it appeared probable that a war of construction would not break out. The Northern Pacific, under the leadership of Morgan, chairman of the Northern Pacific finance committee, entered into negotiations with Adams, an equally conservative fashioner of Union Pacific policies, to work out a compromise solution. The re-entry of Villard in the fall of 1887 into the affairs of the Northern Pacific led to another joint effort to avoid the invasion of each other's territory. These efforts finally failed.

After a lengthy intercorporate struggle the Navigation line to Portland was brought under the domination of one of the major transcontinental systems. This in turn brought the short-lived Adams-Hill friendship to a quick end. Hill was denied any interest in a Coast line. Adams had acquired the Navigation for the exclusive use of the Union Pacific. In order to acquire an alternative line, Hill looked into the possibility, in cooperation with the Canadian Pacific, of acquiring control of the Northern Pacific. His purpose, Hill declared, was to remove "all expensive rivalry and competition. . . ."[11] Hill failed to make any headway, and the lease of the Navigation to the Union Pacific spelled out the impossibility of securing a friendly alliance with the latter. In the fall of 1889, accordingly, Hill decided to build his own coast line. He informed its stockholders that "the great extension of this company's lines and the rapid growth of the entire West have, in the opinion of your Directors, made it indispensable to provide, on a larger scale, for the development of your business."[12] In order to provide an adequate financial plan for the projected enlarged organization, Hill set up a new company, the Great Northern Railway Company. This company secured control of the Manitoba in exchange for $20 million of new preferred stock; each Manitoba stockholder received Great Northern stock share for share. For each share ($100 par), the Great Northern paid $50 in cash and the balance by the transfer to the new company of the property of the Manitoba. The latter then leased its road to the Great Northern for a guaranteed 6 per cent dividend on its stock.

Shortly thereafter, Villard, now the undisputed head of the Northern Pacific, announced his determination to expand in the Northwest. He dropped his cautious spending program, based upon his desire to avoid the losses incurred in the earlier program that culminated so disastrously.

A new competitive factor, in the form of the renewed expansion plan of the Canadian Pacific, appeared at about the same time. That road had bid for the transcontinental business moving to and from Portland and Puget Sound points, through the media of steamship connections between these points and the western terminus of the Canadian Pacific in British Columbia. The Canadian Pacific now proposed to build a land connection south from this terminus to the international boundary line, there to join up with another road coming north from the state of Washington. An independent line—the Seattle, Lake Shore and Eastern—was the suitable partner of the Canadian Pacific. This company had built part of a short line between Seattle and the boundary. It also owned an uncompleted line from Seattle east toward Spokane. This east and west extension had little value. The projected northern extension, however, threatened to set up a strong rival to the northern Pacific. The property was for sale—but as a whole, not in parts. The property was offered for sale to the Union Pacific. Adams declined. "I often wish," he wrote, "that I had about a hundred million of dollars at my disposal to effect necessary arrangements, or else that enterprises like the Lake Shore, Seattle and Eastern, [sic] were at the bottom of Puget Sound. There seems to be no end to the railroad cats and dogs lying round loose."[13]

Adams, despite his criticism of railroad warfare, now decided to enter the intercorporate building fracas. There is some evidence to suggest that Dodge, an advisor on corporate policy to Adams since 1887, was responsible for Adams' change of front and his decision to replace conservatism by a policy of business boldness. In January, 1890, Dodge was prodding Adams to retaliate against the Rio Grande for some slight construction by that road near Trinidad in an area served by the Union Pacific, Denver and Gulf—the line controlled by the Union Pacific that bought the property owned by the Panhandle Route. The Union Pacific, Dodge informed Adams, was not protected at one point in this area. Such protection would require the building of a 15-mile line. Dodge informed Adams that the Rio Grande had planned to occupy this area. "Under no circumstances," insisted Dodge, should this be allowed. "If I find any attempt towards that by them I should occupy it for the Fort Worth."[14] From time to time over the next few months Adams repeated his previously expressed opinion that the Union Pacific had no expansion plans. The company, Adams believed, was in good financial shape. Dodge had been in poor health for sometime, but by April he apparently had recovered, and Adams expressed his gratification that Dodge was on his feet again. "For reasons which I fancy you fully appreciate," he wrote to Dodge, "I find more effective co-operation in you than in most of the others connected with the company's direction."[15]

Shortly thereafter Adams traveled through the Northwest. By June he decided to build from Portland to Tacoma and Seattle, subject, of course, to the approval of the board.[16] The board approved, and by the end of the summer a new company was organized to build the line at a cost of approximately $8 million.[17] This would parallel the Northern Pacific line—a duplication of the sort that had characterized the classic building program of the previous decade. The company also made surveys for the building of new lines both into northern and southern California, and laid plans for an extension of about 145 miles southwest into Nevada.[18]

Thus four transcontinental lines—Union Pacific, Northern Pacific, Canadian Pacific, and Great Northern—all decided by 1890 to expand in the Far Northwest. All these roads by the summer of the year moved to the fulfillment of their projects. The short independently owned lines recognized their favorable bargaining power; they enjoyed the unique position of being both weak and strong. They were weak financially; they were in debt; they paid no dividends; and, upon a proper recording of accounts, they probably did not earn their interest charges. This weakness was balanced by the strength of their strategic positions. They connected important lines of traffic; they controlled uncompleted lines which could serve as the basis, when completed, of through routes desired by one or more of the transcontinental rivals. The Seattle, Lake Shore and Eastern was in a particularly fortunate position. The Canadian Pacific, the Great Northern, and the Northern Pacific all made bids for control. The Northern Pacific carried most of the Puget Sound traffic to St. Paul and Chicago. Both the Union Pacific and the Canadian Pacific, however, through steamers plying the waters of Puget Sound, competed for the business. The purchase of this small line would enhance their competitive strength. The road was finally bought by Villard, for the Northern Pacific. The purchase was a typical offensive-defensive piece of business strategy. The eastwest uncompleted line was of no value to the Northern Pacific. It already had such a line, and an investment in this extension would produce no earnings. The entire property was eventually bought at a stiff price. The 6 per cent bonds of the acquired road were guaranteed and for $3 million out of the $5 million par value stock the Northern Pacific paid a substantial cash consideration.[19]

Villard also moved rapidly to acquire control of additional local territory, in part through the acquisition of existing roads and in part through the building of new lines. The so-called Hunt System in northeastern Oregon and southeastern Washington—the road which had entered so significantly into the Villard-Adams discussions over the control of the Navigation in 1888 and 1889—was in 1890 still under control of Hunt, its promoter. The road penetrated some valuable wheat fields. Both the Navigation and the Great Northern bid for control. The property early in 1891 was bought by Wright, of Philadelphia. Wright, a member of the Northern Pacific board, then resold the road to the Northern Pacific for cash and a guarantee of bond interest. This acquisition gave the Northern Pacific the wheat traffic of the road for movement to Tacoma. Business was thus lost to the Navigation's Portland line.

In Northern Idaho, the Northern Pacific in the fall of 1888 had acquired the ownership of a small road serving a rapidly growing mining area. In the summer of 1891 it built a 120-mile extension, which, together with the acquired line, afforded the Northern Pacific a direct route into this territory.

On its main line, furthermore, the Northern Pacific completed a cut-off which reduced by 104 miles the distance between St. Paul and the copper mining area centering around Butte. On the far western end, in Washington along the Pacific Coast, the Northern Pacific built other lines—one to Grays Harbor and another northwest from that point to a suburb of Tacoma. It also built some mileage to form, in conjunction with the newly acquired Seattle, Lake Shore and Eastern, a belt line around Seattle and some neighboring territory.

This expansion program was expensive. The branch lines in Washington, Montana, and Idaho alone called for an investment of not far from $30 million. Villard in his *Memoirs* observed with a tinge of sadness that they hardly earned their operating expenses. "The acquisition and building of these disappointing lines had in a few years absorbed the large amount of consolidated bonds set aside for construction purposes, which had been assumed to be sufficient for all needs in that direction for a long time."[20]

The ambitious plans of the Union Pacific meanwhile were suddenly frustrated by an unexpected development. In November of 1890 control was acquired by Gould. By early December the executive committee abandoned virtually the entire expansion program. Work on the Portland–Seattle line was suspended. A shortage of labor early in the year was succeeded by an excessive supply. The men working on the Portland and Puget Sound road were discharged, and tragic personal suffering ensued. Many of the discharged workers were fed and lodged by city authorities in Portland.[21] Shortly thereafter the proposed 145-mile extension into and through Nevada was abandoned. Adams' confidence in the ability of the Union Pacific to take care of the road's floating debt proved to be ill founded. The credit of the company was impaired, and the management found itself confronted by the necessity of selling an expensive short-term collateral note. More than a year later the Northern Pacific was faced with the same problem. It solved it in the same way— through the sale on expensive terms of a short-term collateral obligation.

None of these problems confronted Hill. The brighter outlook of the Great Northern, as compared with that of its two rivals, reflected in large part the differences between the business personality of Hill and those of Villard and Adams. Hill's Great Northern and its corporate predecessor, the Manitoba, had been continuously under the *operating* leadership of Hill: as general manager between 1879 and 1882 and as president after that time. The Manitoba, as a financial reorganization of the St. Paul and Pacific, furthermore enjoyed a financial advantage as compared with the Northern Pacific and the Union Pacific. In the reorganization the common stock and a substantial percentage of the bonds of the St. Paul and Pacific were eliminated. Therefore the debt and the fixed charges per mile of the newly reorganized Manitoba were substantially lower than those of the other two roads. The Northern Pacific was also reorganized in the middle 1870's. Its mileage at that time, however, was relatively small in comparison with the amount completed in the high-cost period of the early 1880's. In 1878 the St. Paul and Pacific, while still in receivership, built a substantial mileage at the low costs then prevailing. Between 1879 and 1882 the Manitoba built additional mileage in the Red River Valley. In accordance with the agreement made with the Northern Pacific, it did not build west into the relatively unsettled, low traffic-producing territory. The Northern Pacific, under Villard, on the contrary, pushed boldly west in one of the most widespread expansion programs of the early 1880's.

A large part of the Northern Pacific was thus built in a period of high costs. The Manitoba's extension from the Red River Valley to Manitoba, on the other hand, was built in 1887, in a period of low costs. The Union Pacific, unlike the Northern Pacific and the Manitoba, did not enjoy the advantage of low costs at the expense of the pioneer investor, through the medium of a financial reorganization. This company was financed in the post-Civil War inflation. Labor and capital were scarce and costs high. And finally a number of emergency plans in the early 1870's were necessary, in order to save the company from receivership. These included the sale of 10 per cent bonds at heavy discounts. Both the Union Pacific and the Northern Pacific were burdened with higher fixed charges than the Great Northern.

The Great Northern was also the beneficiary of an outstanding managerial cost-reducing factor. Hill, unlike Villard, Adams, and Gould, was by profession a skilled transportation technician. He spent his early and mature years on the ground, mastering the details of railroad building and operation. In addition to lower fixed charges there were lower operating costs. Hill built his line carefully, with attention to grades and curves. It was not necessary for him, as it was for his competitors, to assign the responsibility for construction and operation to others.

Under a given rate structure, accordingly, Hill's road, operating at lower costs, could make a profit while his higher-cost competitors incurred losses, His road was able to pay dividends, while the Union Pacific, after 1884, paid nothing, and the Northern Pacific paid only an occasional dividend. The superior earning and dividend-paying power of Hill's road enabled him to sell securities at higher prices. The advantages Hill enjoyed in a sense constituted a continuing spiral—the initial advantage of lower capital costs in part paved the way for lower operating costs, which in turn kept down the cost of securing new capital. In the late 1880's, upon the eve of the extension of the Great Northern to the Pacific Coast, Hill could say with reference to the per-mile amount of stock and bonds outstanding, "I think it is lower than any other road in the country. That amount represents the actual capital of private individuals that has been put into the road."[22] The debt of the Manitoba was slightly more than $18,000 and the stock, approximately $6,800 per mile. The Interstate Commerce Commission placed the corresponding figures, for the Group Four of railroads, in which the Manitoba was included, at $23,600 for the debt and $22,500 for the stock.

Contrary to general expectations a low-cost passage through the Rocky Mountains was discovered. Actual construction to Everett was begun in 1890 and completed in January of 1893. Hill informed his stockholders that upon its completion the line from the Pacific Coast to the Twin Cities would be "shorter than any existing transcontinental railway, and with lower grades and less curvature."[23] The expectations of Hill were confirmed by the chief engineer, who reported that the Pacific extension was the finest ever built across the continent. "It has the lightest grades and the least curvature of any transcontinental line."[24] Financing was easily arranged. Bonds and stock were sold to the company's stockholders at substantial discounts, on a privileged subscription basis. A bond issue of $10 million was also sold in London.

The new line needed a connection with the Canadian boundary. In order to make this possible, Hill in 1889 had organized two subsidiaries and had also acquired a third small enterprise. By this program and the building of a number of small lines, the Great Northern secured a connection between Seattle and British Columbia, there joining with the Canadian Pacific. Thus a physical connection between the Canadian Pacific and the Great Northern System was effected. The former could run its trains through to Seattle and the latter to Canada.

The relation between the two roads, however, were not harmonious

The Great Northern expected business from the Canadian Pacific, and the latter in turn expected something from the Great Northern, particularly a part of the business moving to the Twin Cities. The Great Northern controlled the short line for this business. In accordance with sound business strategy it declined to permit the Canadian Pacific to participate in the profitable long haul to the Twin Cities. It refused to prorate— that is, to give the Canadian Pacific a reasonable division of the through rate, so as to enable both roads to charge approximately the same rates for the long haul. The Canadian Pacific was equally as firm as the Great Northern. The refusal of the Great Northern to prorate was followed by the decision of the other to build a line under its control to the Twin Cities. This it accomplished through the Soo system, in which the Canadian Pacific now had a substantial interest. The extension between the Soo in North Dakota to a connection with the Canadian Pacific at Regina, a total of approximately 320 miles, was completed in 1893. It was advertised as "the shortest line from Minneapolis and St. Paul to the Pacific Coast."[25]

Now that the Canadian Pacific had successfully retaliated the way was open for a mutual exchange of benefits. Both roads discontinued their warlike threats and agreed to restore the traffic arrangements which had been so abruptly broken upon completion of the Great Northern to the Pacific Coast.[26]

The pattern of American transcontinental lines was now set. No more through routes were built in the nineteenth century. Two more, however, were added in the first decade of the twentieth—the St. Paul on the northern route and the Western Pacific on the central. The equity money put in both of these roads was lost. They were financial failures. The other transcontinental roads, after the crisis in the middle 1890's, were outstanding successes in the following two generations. The pioneering capital that built these systems was mostly lost in the crises of the late 1880's and the middle 1890's. The exception was the Southern Pacific; and here the shares were held together under the control of Huntington. Huntington was saved by a bare margin in 1893, as he had been in 1873 and again in 1884.

The transcontinental system, so indispensable to the national economy, with the single exception of the Union Pacific, was built between 1879 and 1893. Through lines were provided on the north, in the center, and in the south. Besides the short one-line routes, many additional multi-routes were provided, affording in this way an opportunity for many towns to participate in the advantage of overland communication. The Frisco connected with the Atchison, to afford cities in Missouri and Texas access to the transcontinental highways. The Burlington, by its connection with the Northern Pacific, opened up a vast country to similar advantages. The Missouri Pacific, by its connection with the Rio Grande in eastern Colorado, afforded such privileges to many communities in its territory. The Texas and Pacific, through its connection with the Southern Pacific, also was able to offer service to Texas and Louisiana. The Northwestern, Rock Island, and St. Paul connected with many roads both east and west, thereby furnishing long-haul service to hundreds of additional communities.

All this was accompanied by sharp and almost continuous reduction in selling prices. Some investors secured reasonable returns—others lost. Some speculators received substantial, even exorbitant, profits—and many, particularly the very early pioneers, lost much more. Whoever gained and whoever lost, the public was the gainer. Some of the roads were efficiently operated and gave good service; others were less efficient and gave poor service. This outcome was the essence of competition. Competition served the public well.

Notes for Chapter XXI

[1] Annual Report, Atchison, 1891, p. 14.

[2] *R. R. Gaz.*, Mar. 11, 1892, p. 198.

[3] The above quotations are taken from Burlington Archives, Holdrege to T. S. Howland, Jan. 5, 1889.

[4] *Ibid.*, Perkins to Griswold, Oct. 9, 1891.

[5] *R. R. Gaz.*, Feb. 10, 1893, p. 112.

[6] For details on this contract see Interstate Commerce Commission Docket No. 12964, Consolidation of Railroads, pp. 1497–1502. The report of the Commission is in 159 I. C. C., p. 522 (1929).

[7] *R. R. Gaz.*, May 23, 1890, 369; and May 20, 1892, p. 379.

[8] *Ibid.*, Aug. 21, 1891, p. 589.

[9] H. V. P., Adams to Villard, Aug. 3, 1888, Box 35.

[10] *R. R. Gaz.*, May 13, 1892, p. 353.

[11] William J. Wilgus, *The Railway Interrelations of the United States and Canada* (New Haven: Yale University Press, 1937), p. 129.

[12] *Chron.*, Oct. 5, 1889, 435.

[13] Dodge Papers, Adams to Dodge, Dec. 13, 1889.

[14] *Ibid.*, Adams to Dodge, Jan. 11, 1890. Fort Worth was another name for the Panhandle Route.

[15] *Ibid.*, Adams to Dodge, April 8, 1890.

[16] *R. R. Gaz.*, June 20, 1890, p. 447.

[17] *Chron.*, Sept. 3, 1890, p. 348.

[18] *R. R. Gaz.*, Oct. 17, 1890, p. 727; interview with the road's chief engineer.

[19] For details on this transaction see, *Bradstreet's*, Mar. 4, 1893, p. 142, and *R. R. Gaz.*, June 25, 1890, p. 534.

[20] Henry Villard, *Memoirs* (Boston, 1904), II, pp. 259–260.

[21] *R. R. Gaz.*, Jan. 9, 1891, p. 35.

[22] The United States and Canada, Report No. 847, Senate 51st Congress, 1st Session, 1889, p. 182.

[23] Annual Report, Great Northern, 1890, p. 13.

[24] *Ry. World*, July 30, 1892, p. 737.

[25] *R. R. Gaz.*, Nov. 18, 1892, p. 871.

[26] *Ibid.*, Aug. 11, 1893, p. 614.

XXII

Profit and Loss

THE EXPANSION and building program of the 1880's, the most extensive for a similar period in American railroad history, was on the whole unprofitable. The rate wars, unleashed by competition, were the main cause. There were others. Poor crops and labor disturbances combined with the more fundamental cause of rate reductions to reduce earnings in the late 1880's. To these factors there should be added another, which in the opinion of railroad management exerted a decisive influence. This was the Interstate Commerce Act passed at the very time when the expansion program was in full swing. The prohibition of pooling and the provision that, except under special circumstances, a rate for a haul could not be lower than that for a longer haul in the same direction, were the major legal obstacles.

Though the railroad construction boom did not mature until 1886, and did not reach its zenith until 1887, the plans for the boom were made in discussions beginning as early as 1885. Of the roads in poor financial condition in 1884, the Union Pacific and Northern Pacific participated little in the expansion of 1886–1887. The major exception was the building of the Cascade line of the Northern Pacific. The Texas and Pacific never renewed its transcontinental ambitions. Neither the Central nor the Southern Pacific did much building. The Huntington system did improve its property and it did spend large sums for this purpose. Except for its line to Portland, however, its growth through these years was confined to the building of branches and the improvement of facilities. Huntington, indeed after a last-gasp effort in 1885, relinquished his ambitions to establish a through rail transcontinental route between the Atlantic and the Pacific.

Besides the major properties involved in the expansion, there were a number of others, smaller in size and weaker in financial strength. Some of them were strategically located and commanded positions of traffic strength. Their policies could weaken the finances of the larger lines. Such lines as the Stickney road and the Minneapolis and St. Louis long remained trouble spots and continued to plague the competitive life of major western railroads.

The financing of the expansion began in the summer of 1886. By this time the western railroads had passed their pioneering stage. Building was now carried on by roads with a record of dividends and earnings. It was therefore no longer necessary to capture the funds of the more speculative type of investors. Construction companies were no longer needed to entice their funds. Roads involved in this building program, moreover, had many stockholders.[1]

The building program was financed largely by bonds. Some roads—the Southern Pacific, Northern Pacific, Manitoba, Frisco, and Union Pacific —issued no stock. Some of the dividend payers in the early 1880's did sell stock—the Atchison, Burlington, Rock Island, Missouri Pacific, and St. Paul. Two dividend payers—the Manitoba and the Northwestern—sold no stock. But none of the roads that had passed their dividends prior to 1884 succeeded in selling stock in the expansion boom of 1886–1887.

The collateral trust bond used so widely in the earlier 1880's, retained its popularity. Many of the new lines were built by subsidiary corporations under the laws of particular states, because of legal requirements. Included are roads such as the Atchison, Rock Island, Missouri Pacific, and Northwestern. On the Manitoba, according to Hill, "a large part of the railway extensions, made under the auspices of this company, has been made by other corporations . . . and this company now holds such securities and other property, to the amount of over $22,000,000 par value, of which $11,750,000 have been deposited as security for $8,000,000 collateral trust mortgage bonds."[2]

The restrictions in the second mortgage securing the loan of the United States Government bonds continued to force the Union Pacific to use the collateral bond for its borrowing vehicle. Adams in a picturesque verbal explosion explained the effects of these restrictions upon the road— ". . . the construction of competing lines is now going on because we cannot defend ourselves. Our means of defense are taken from us. We stand in the position of a tradesman whose creditor holds his arms while his competitor robs his till. The Government says we shall not borrow; we shall not lease; we shall not guarantee except within very narrow limits."[3] So the Union Pacific leased the Navigation through the Short Line, and, in order to secure the funds to purchase the Navigation stock from Villard, it issued collateral trust bonds secured by Navigation stock. These "complex and involved methods arising from branch guaranteed collateral trust and indorsed bonds," declared a government agency, "has cost the company a vast amount of money, fairly stated in millions, which may have been in a large degree saved if it had been permitted to issue its own direct obligations, secured by direct mortgage upon its own property."[4]

Another unusual phase of bond financing was carried out by the Manitoba. This road sold bonds not through investment banking channels but by subscription rights offered to its own stockholders. This practice, first introduced in 1883, was again adopted in the later 1880's. Funds needed were obtained by collateral trust bonds sold to the stockholders at 75 in amounts equal to 40 per cent of their holdings. A first-mortgage bond, to raise funds for the Montana lines, was also sold to the stockholders at 80 cents on the dollar. Part of the Montana extension bonds guaranteed by the Manitoba were offered by advertisements to the investors. Tenders were received at the Central Trust Company in New York, to "be opened in the presence of bidders who may desire to be present. . . . The company does not bind to itself accept the highest or any bid."[5] The sale of bonds direct to stockholders was possible because the stock was closely held by relatively few investors.

The phenomenon of debt structures with a variety of bonds outstanding in small amounts, with different maturities, interest rates, callable and sinking-fund provisions, continued to plague the financial managers as in the early 1880's. With such a miscellany of mortgage liens on various segments of the property, it was difficult to use the full financial resources of the system as a means of borrowing long-term funds.

It was therefore necessary to devise some new financial instruments to utilize to the maximum advantage the debt-creating possibilities of a large railroad system. This is the kind of problem that stimulated the imagination of Villard. Shortly after his reappearance in Northern Pacific affairs he moved in the direction of relieving the road from restrictions on its borrowing power by the preferred stockholders. The Northern Pacific carried a floating debt; and it needed additional funds to complete the Tacoma extension. Villard secured the consent of the stockholders to remove the $25,000-per-mile bond limitation and to approve the creation of a third mortgage at 5 per cent with a 40-year term. The approval of these measures included also the authorization to sell $12 million of the bonds. By the summer of 1888 the entire amount was sold through a group of New York and German bankers.[6]

The system had also a number of branch-line bonds, some secured by a third mortgage. The expansion program of the Northern Pacific made it necessary, in Villard's view, to create still another financial mechanism to lure the attention of the investor. It was difficult to popularize a fourth-mortgage bond; and it was presumably equally unwise to create new branch-line mortgages. Until the fall of 1888, Villard had restrained his financial imagination; he had in fact placed some self-imposed limits on his expansion plans and the creation of debts. "The great confidence reposed in me by my business friends abroad," he declared in October, 1888, "makes it incumbent upon me to exercise great caution in my investments."[7]

A year later improved earnings, combined with the decision to expand, led Villard to relax his sense of prudence and restraint. He now proposed the creation of a consolidated mortgage to cover the entire Northern Pacific property. He proposed that there be authorized $160 million of bonds with a 100-year maturity; that $77,439,000 be reserved to retire the outstanding first, second, and third mortgage bonds; that $26 million more be set aside to retire the branch-line bonds; that another $20 million be used to acquire additional branches at not more than $30,000 per mile; that another $20 million be dedicated to property improvements; that $10 million be used, subject to some restrictions by the board, for premiums on bonds exchanged, and that another $9 million be set aside for general purposes. All this was necessary for "the inception and the carrying out of this successful effort to put the company's finances upon a strong and favorable foundation."[8] The mortgage furthermore placed only slight limitation upon the creation of debt for purposes other than bond retirement. To validate the issue of bonds there was needed only a certification by the management or the board of directors. There were no provisions requiring the company to certify to the trustee that the money raised from the sale of the bonds had been used for construction or improvement; nor was there any provision directing the management to issue bonds for property acquisition at a price not in excess of the fair value of an acquired property.

Villard's plan met with opposition. According to a source in Philadelphia, a city with substantial holdings of the road's securities, the finance committee did not view the Villard Plan "seriously."[9] For a number of years there had been two factions on the board. One was led by Villard. It included the capitalists interested in the Wisconsin Central. The other party was led by Wright, the leader of the Philadelphia investors. Wright had a substantial investment in Tacoma real estate and would be benefited by a local terminal-improvement program. To enlist Wright's support, Villard included a provision to expend a substantial sum of Northern Pacific funds in that area. To make his financial plan more attractive to the stockholders Villard proposed to redeem some outstanding bonds with proceeds to be realized from the sale of the consolidated bonds. The existing bonds carried a heavy sinking fund; the new bonds would have no sinking fund. This financial legerdemain would save $1 million annually, thereby creating dividend nourishment for the stockholders. Villard also proposed that the proceeds of land sales formerly devoted to bond retirement be used for corporate needs—perhaps for dividends. In view of the three main-line mortgages, borrowing through another fourth-mortgage bond was out of the question.

The arguments of Villard were persuasive and in mid-November the stockholders approved his proposals. Villard was optimistic. The Northern Pacific's earnings at that time were on the upgrade. The Northern Pacific, he declared "forms almost the only exception to the general decline in income that Western railroads have of late experienced."[10] For a short time Villard's optimism was justified by events, just as in the early 1880's. For the first time since the 1883 debacle, the road early in 1890 put its stock on a dividend-paying basis. Observant critics were as skeptical as ever, and one of the leading metropolitan newspapers renewed its attacks upon Villard. Villard, it said "seems to have no faculty but that of borrowing, and in that he has such genius he could borrow the United States Treasury in six months, and bankrupt it in six more."[11]

Another mortgage of a type similar to that of the Northern Pacific was created at about the same time by the St. Paul. On this road the new instrument was called a General Mortgage. The authorized bonds amounted to $150 million and of this amount $121,819,000 was set aside to retire debts at maturity. The mortgage was more restrictive upon management than the Northern Pacific's.

The Northern Pacific, soon after stockholders' approval, sold a large issue of its bonds. Not so on the St. Paul. Except in the far Northwest, earnings of western railroads were dropping. As early as the fall of 1887 money could be procured only under more onerous conditions than formerly. "Money continues to be difficult to get," wrote a Boston capitalist-banker.[12] By the following year the difficulties had increased. Reduced rates and a poor crop year had not made things any better. For the first six months of 1888 the earnings of western railroads declined. "Such a remarkable contraction in one single year on a large body of roads is probably without a parallel in railroad history," observed a leading financial journal.[13] Lowered earnings were reflected in lowered dividends. The shock to investor confidence came from the passage of the St. Paul dividend in September. Early in 1885 a vice-president declared the company would continue to pay its regular semi-annual $3\frac{1}{2}$ per cent dividend; and that "the company was never in better condition, physically and financially, than it now is."[14] The company had reduced its dividend to an annual 5 per cent rate in 1886; but in September of 1888, the dividend was passed. The company had had a satisfactory dividend history. Though its financial structure was heavily weighted with bonds in comparison with stocks, the debt per mile was relatively low. The company, furthermore, had been able to pay a high dividend on its relatively few number of shares of stock. Much of the stock was held in England. Morgan of the firm of Drexel-Morgan, with the aid of his father J. S. Morgan, who was in charge of the destinies of an English banking house of that name, had distributed the St. Paul securities to English clients. The stoppage of the St. Paul dividend was followed by organization of its stockholders. A meeting was held two weeks after the dividend suspension. The depth of investor reaction is well reflected by the remarks of the managing director of the English Association of American Bond and Shareholders: "I venture to say there has scarcely ever been an announcement made in the city of London, either in connection with American or English railways, that has created a greater sensation than that unexpected announcement."[15]

J. S. Morgan and Company meanwhile moved to unite the English shareholders. The firm requested both English and European stockholders to deposit their shares with the firm in exchange for certificates. Through this concentration of stock a member of the English Morgan firm would qualify for representation on the board of directors.

The discussion incident to the St. Paul's dividend action led to some bitter comments about American railroad management. At a London meeting of the American Bond and Shareholders railway managers were described as despots, many of whom "had used their power wisely and well; but when they took it into their heads to act otherwise, the shareholders were entirely at their mercy." The deposit of shares with Drexel-Morgan and Company was characterized as a helpful gesture, but it was nevertheless an exercise of paternalistic government of the affairs of the shareholders and the Morgan offer amounted to an assumption that "some gentleman of position and wealth should take the position of paternal despot."[16]

The deposit of securities with the Morgan firm led to some revival of confidence. The reduction of dividends by so many western roads, however, soon spread gloom in the ranks of both management and investors. There was still an ample supply of capital, and money rates were still low. The redemption of United States Government bonds in the summer of 1888 added to the supply of funds. Call-money rates of $1\frac{1}{2}$ to 2 per cent continued to prevail. But the investor was not disposed to commit his funds to the railroad industry. The rate wars continued, though efforts were underway to organize an industry-wide co-operation scheme, the success of which might, it was hoped, make possible the resumption of dividends. Nevertheless, leaders of the industry in the fall of 1888 and for some two years thereafter expressed themselves in the language of defeatism. Gould in 1889 said that the rate war then in progress was the worst in thirty years.[17] Perkins, though confident that the value of railroad property would not be destroyed, conceded that some board members of the Burlington thought it would take "a large stock of faith to feel so, and I agree that the immediate outlook is rather dark."[18]

Surprisingly enough, the slash in earnings and dividends was accompanied by an expansion in the Pacific Northwest. In Oregon, Washington, and Montana a building and mining boom maintained the earnings of the Northern Pacific, the Union Pacific, and the Manitoba. In the rate-cutting year of 1888 the earnings of these roads increased. They appeared to have a bright future. Optimism characterized the remarks both of railroad managers and outside commentators. In the fall of 1889, on the basis of the rise in earnings of the previous two years, the Northern Pacific announced its intension of paying a preferred dividend. Villard was certain that the dividend could be maintained. There was "every indication," he said, "that the growth of the business of the road will continue right along."[19] A leading financial weekly, whose view reflected the judgment of conservative investors, repeated *ad nauseum* its bubbling optimism over the progress of the Northern Pacific. In the fall of 1888, in the very week when the St. Paul dividend was passed, the Northern Pacific's growth and future was described in flattering language. Only a year before, in 1887, when the newly constructed division to Tacoma was completed, the prospects of the Northern Pacific had not been bright. The road was then barely earning its fixed charges and its debt was increasing. Long-term funds were needed to finance improvements and to pay the floating debt. There were fears over the prospects of a fight with the Navigation and of the effect of the Manitoba's Helena extension. By 1888, however, all these fears had been confounded, and by the following fall the prospects were even more flattering. Between 1886 and 1889 the gross revenue had increased from $11,730,000 to $19,707,000. This expansion observed the weekly already mentioned had "few parallels in the whole history of American railroad undertakings."[20]

Similarly happy results flowed in the following year. There were some local crop failures, but in the opinion of the management these were of little consequence in view of the rapid development of the Pacific Coast and of the mines in Manitoba and Idaho. The expansion of business continued into 1891. This achievement was credited to Villard. The record of that road after Villard took hold "has been a record of continuous, we might also say phenomenal growth. And the growth is still in progress, reflecting in this the careful and intelligent way in which the property's interests are being fostered."[21]

The shock to investor confidence arising from the dividend casualties of 1888 left a number of roads with uncompleted capital-expenditure programs. A number cut down their expansion programs almost immediately. Some of these roads were in good financial condition. Other western roads, however, were not so fortunate. The Missouri Pacific was in the midst of a construction and improvement program involving an expenditure of more than $37 million. Of this amount, more than $31 million had already been raised by the end of 1888. When the expansion program was ordered, so read the 1888 Annual Report, a ready market existed for railway securities, the capital stock of the Missouri Pacific Railway Company was selling above par, and it was the reasonable expectation to repay these expenditures by allotting shares to the stockholders at par. . . . The general decline in railway securities has postponed the carrying out of this plan, and the financial depression of the past year [1888] was so great that, to avoid any sacrifice of the assets of the Company, several of the Directors, who are the largest stockholders of the Company, advanced the necessary amount to complete the lines. . . ."22 The company thus entered 1889 with a large floating debt. This was a prelude to financial trouble; indeed, it was an invitation to financial disaster. It was not so regarded in 1889. There was plenty of collateral so it was urged, to secure the debt. The collateral, however, consisted largely of system securities, of the bonds and stocks of the branch and auxiliary roads, whose value lay largely in the earning power of the system as a whole.

The menace of the floating debt—short-term obligations that could be called for payment at an unpropitious time—raised the specter of insolvency. The floating debt was a by-product of uncompleted expansion programs in the midst of a sudden decline in earnings. The Missouri Pacific, as well as the Northern Pacific, was unexpectedly confronted by the menace of such a debt. The Union Pacific sharply expanded its capital requirements by the purchase of the Navigation stock. This was followed by the acquisition of the Panhandle Route and the merger of the Oregon Short Line and the southern Montana line into a new corporation—the Oregon Short Line and Utah Northern. These moves were accompanied and followed by a number of other expansion programs. The decline in security prices and the increase in interest rates led the Union Pacific to refrain from carrying out a program of long-term financing. Instead, it borrowed on short-time loans, and hoped that as the security markets improved long-term bonds could be sold on a more favorable basis. Adams was concerned over this sudden appearance of a floating debt. He had inherited one in 1884, and prided himself on its elimination in the following two years. The road early in 1890, he recognized, was "loaded" with unfunded debt; the management was "extremely loath to engage in any new work of construction not absolutely necessary. You know how easy it is," he wrote to Dodge, "to pile up a large floating debt through disconnected bits of construction each small in itself but in the aggregate soon running into the millions."23 Adams was nevertheless hopeful that the floating debt would soon be wiped out. The company, like the Missouri Pacific, had collateral in the form of the stock of system companies. The company by May, 1890, would receive nearly $10 million from the sale of securities recently offered to the stockholders on a privileged-subscription basis. "Under these circumstances," wrote Adams, "we do not feel like hurrying the negotiation of the bonds secured by the Navigation."[24]

Adams was prepared to postpone long-term financing pending increases in earnings of the Oregon Short Line and the Navigation companies. Their earnings had been adversely affected by the dry winters of 1888 and 1889. Such an event, thought Adams, was not likely to recur. The Short Line, furthermore, would have earnings in 1890 from extensions in Washington and Idaho. A survey, made at the suggestion of a Senate committee, "astonished" Adams: he found that the amount earned by the Union Pacific on traffic interchanged with the Oregon Short Line was such that "the Union Pacific would not to-day be earning any surplus over its interest charges, but for the business done with the Oregon Short Line system." And further to assure the investor of the conservative character of the management, Adams said that the road did not "propose, at present, to try and cover the earth." This rhetorical comment was designed to defend the Union Pacific against the criticism of unduly expanding its system lines.[25]

The floating debt thus remained. And with historical irony Adams passed on to Gould in the fall of 1890 the same gift of a floating debt that Gould had passed on to Adams in the summer of 1884.

The prospects of a continuous growth in business in the Pacific Northwest led Villard, as it had led Adams, into a heavy capital-spending program and to the creation of a floating debt. And on the Northern Pacific, as on the Union Pacific, the results were disastrous. The Northern Pacific debacle of 1883 had been followed by the emergence of a prudent financial management under the Morgan leadership. At the road's 1885 annual meeting, a Morgan resolution was adapted to the effect that no new construction would be undertaken except such as could be paid out of available assets.[26] This interdiction of a floating debt was observed until 1889. Harris, prior to his replacement as president by Oakes, a long-time associate of Villard, was a careful administrator. In his railroad career his actions were characterized by a meticulous attention to managerial details and by an avoidance of risks incidental to imaginative expansion. His replacement by Oakes in 1889 revealed Villard's dominant position in the road's affairs. Villard made his views clear in a St. Paul address in the following April. Within four years, he declared, the road would expend between $50 million and $60 million in the Pacific Northwest.[27] The expansion in earnings created a receptive market for the sale of the road's securities. The demands of long-term investors, however, was insufficient to absorb the heavy flow of Northern Pacific securities, even in the prosperous years of 1890 and 1891. By June, 1891, the floating debt had jumped to $20.8 million, although only a few weeks prior to that time officials of the road had declared publicly that its finances had "hardly ever been better."[28] Late in 1891, after prolonged negotiations, the road managed to reduce its floating debt temporarily by an expensive piece of long-term financing. Through a syndicate of New York and German bankers it sold $6 million of 5 per cent bonds at 78, plus a stock bonus of 25 per cent. But the floating debt continued to mount.

The same pattern of accruing short-term liabilities, in the wake of an inability to finance an extensive expansion program in a weakening securities market, was revealed in the affairs of the Atchison. That road by the summer of 1888 had completed a major program—perhaps the largest in the country. It had recorded an enviable financial history. Its rise from a financial weakling in the late 1870's to one of the western giants in the middle 1880's was equaled only by the growth of the Hill system. Its financial structure was conservative. There was little of that distribution of stock for services rendered so characteristic of the pioneering stages of railroad construction financing.

Despite this prudence, the Atchison was hit badly by the widespread rate wars, to which were added a number of other unfavorable factors. "Droughts, failure of crops, excessive competition, continually decreasing rates, unwise legislation, strikes and other calamities have befallen us as they have other Western roads," declared the Atchison in its 1888 Annual Report; "But your Directors could not know in advance that any of these unfavorable conditions would have to be met—much less that they would all have to be met, at one and the same time."[29] The future cannot be predicted, and in the inability to do so lies the explanation of many of the losses, and, for that matter, many of the successes, of business management.

The Atchison, like the Missouri Pacific, was loyally supported by its shareowners—but with a difference. The sums needed to complete the financing of the Missouri Pacific program were secured through advances of a few major stockholders—Sage, Gould, Dillon. The needs of the Atchison were met by a $10 million guarantee fund secured by second-mortgage notes. It was expected that this advance would be temporary.

Criticism of the apparent recklessness of the Atchison now appeared. In particular, the paralleling of the Alton's Chicago–Kansas City line was condemned.

The problems confronting the Atchison, which reached such a sudden climax in 1888, were more serious than those facing the other western roads. Many of its extensions were built across territory originating but little traffic. Such was the case with the 35th Parallel line and with those in California. The Chicago extension, moreover, invaded a territory infected with the hottest kind of competition. This competition contributed to rate declines that spelled heavy losses for the Atchison. These in turn led to dissatisfaction with the work of Strong, the creator of the Atchison empire. In 1889 he was succeeded by Allen Manvel, a former executive of the Manitoba, who had frequently clashed with Hill. Manvel, conservatively inclined, had represented the Boston interests of the Manitoba management. His departure from the Manitoba afforded the Boston interests of the Atchison the opportunity of putting a man of their choice into the affairs of that property.[30]

The new management was confronted not only with the problem of the floating debt but also with that of the fixed charges on the funded debt. Operating losses in that year were another critical problem. By fall, the new management presented a plan for the exchange of some of the existing mortgage bonds for new income bonds, plus a lesser amount of fixed-interest bonds. The outstanding bonds were exchanged for new mortgage bonds with a lower interest rate, but the holders were given some income bonds, interest on which was payable only if earned. If the income bonds paid interest the bondholders would get the same income on the new bonds as on the old ones. The bonds with inferior liens were given smaller amounts of first-mortgage bonds and larger amounts of income bonds. The plan was intended to solve at one stroke both of the company's critical problems: to eliminate the floating debt and reduce the company's fixed charges. The stock was placed in a ten-year trust, thereby giving bankers, who largely represented the bondholders, the opportunity of restraining the management. It was an ingenious plan; but it did not, of course, solve the problem of achieving earnings sufficient to pay interest on the income bonds, to say nothing of dividends on the stock. The plan was approved, and by the end of the year most of the outstanding bonds had been deposited.

By 1890, accordingly, the Atchison under new management was relieved of its short-term debts. It was also equipped with a substantial bond reserve ready to be used to finance its future capital programs. The immediate outcome of the 1889 capital readjustment was favorable. The earnings over the next two years increased. A financial weekly referred to the "marvellous transformation" as "one of the most noteworthy occurrences in American railroad history . . . every vestige of financial difficulties has been removed; the physical condition of the property raised to very high standards; the geographical position of the system strengthened; its business developed and extended, and all its varied interest and requirements down to the minutest particulars, studied and attended to."[31] But the floating debt problem persisted. It continued to plague the company's finances; only the subsequent receivership furnished a solution.

The major building programs of the western railroads were by 1890 drawing to a close. The nineteenth century transcontinental routes had by this time, with the notable exception of the Great Northern, been completed. And the completion of that line was only a few years away. The country had been provided with competitive transcontinental routes and with an extensive branch system. Railroad management in a free competitive battle, had supplied the country with an adequate railroad system—indeed with one substantially more than adequate.

The transformation of the transcontinental railroad industry from a single line between Chicago and the Pacific Coast in 1879 to the multiline competitive system in 1890 was carried out with almost no government control or regulation. What reward did the investors receive in exchange for these results? They provided the funds. What were their profits? The picture can perhaps be most effectively presented as a comparison between the miles of road built, the amount of business in physical terms and in dollars, the interest paid to creditors for their capital contributions, and finally the profits to the stockholders. Profits reflected the realization of those alluring hopes of munificent returns in exchange for the risks of total loss. Table VI is presented in an effort to show the profits and loss. A comparison is made between the 1879 and the 1890 year-ends. This is the period of railroad construction and expansion. To carry the comparison to 1893, the year of the completion of the Great Northern, would present an inaccurate picture. The results of that year reflect depression influences; 1890, on the other hand, was a year of normal economic conditions, of reasonable prosperity—indeed, of boom and

expansion in the Pacific Northwest. The results of the comparison correspond to this situation. *Miles of road* requires no explanation; *Ton-miles*
reflects the physical volume of business; *Gross Revenue* represents its dollar
value; *Interest* is the price paid to creditors and to landlords of leased
properties; and *Dividends* indicate the returns received in exchange for
the risk capital contributed by the stockholders. The table discloses for
the western railroads included in this study the profit and loss realized in
the 1880's by the railroad risk-takers. The country received its railroads;
the shippers received their service in ton-miles; the railroad companies
received their revenues from the sale of services rendered; the creditors
received their interest; and the stockholders received their dividends.
Who got most and who got least? Some light will be thrown on this question by an examination of Table VI.

Table VI

PROFIT AND LOSS OF MAJOR WESTERN RAILROADS IN EXPANSION DECADE, 1879–1889

Atchison, Topeka, and Santa Fe

	1879	*1889*	Percentage of Change
Miles of road . . .	996·9	7,110·2	+613·2
Ton-miles (in millions) .	133·0*	1,769·0	+1230·1
Rate per ton-mile . .	2·122c*	1·228c	−42·1
Gross revenue (in thousands)	$6,381·4	$31,004·3†	+385·9
Interest (in thousands) .	$795·4	$6,208·2†	+680·5
Dividends (in thousands) .	$691·3	——	−100·0

* For 1878; 1879 not available.
† Interest for 9 months ending June 30, 1890, under plan of reorganization.

Chicago, Burlington and Quincy

	1879	*1889*	Percentage of Change
Miles of road . . .	1857·2	5,140·0	+176·8
Ton-miles (in millions) .	1139·0	1,727·0	+51·6
Rate per ton-mile . .	3·15*	1·60	−49·2

	1879	1889	Percentage of Change
Gross revenue (in thousands)	$14,779·7	$26,778·3	+81·1
Interest (in thousands) .	$2,110·9	$5,425·6	+157·0
Dividends (in thousands) .	$3,081·9	$3,055·7	−·9

* Data for 1880 on Burlington lines west of Missouri River.

CHICAGO, MILWAUKEE AND ST. PAUL

	1879	1889	Percentage of Change
Miles of road . . .	1,996	5,678	+184·5
Ton-miles (in millions) .	401·5	1,842·7	+359·0
Rate per ton-mile . .	1·72c	0·99c	−42·5
Gross revenue (in thousands)	$10,012·8	$26,405·7	+63·7
Interest (in thousands) .	$2,284·4	$7,214·1	+215·8
Dividends (in thousands) .	$1,244·6	$756·5	−39·2

CHICAGO AND NORTHWESTERN

	1879	1889	Percentage of Change
Miles of road . . .	2,798	4,250	+51·9
Ton-miles (in millions) .	865·9	2,000·1	+131·0
Rate per ton-mile . .	1·49c	0·98c	−34·2
Gross revenue (in thousands)	$15,912·8	$27,164·8	+70·7
Interest (in thousands) .	$3,797·8	$5,826·9	+53·4
Dividends (in thousands) .	$2,405·5	$3,141·9	+30·6

CHICAGO, ROCK ISLAND AND PACIFIC

	1879	1889	Percentage of Change
Miles of road . . .	1,257	3,266	+156·6
Ton-miles (in millions) .	664·8	1,157·4	+74·1
Rate per ton-mile . .	1·21c	1·02c	−15·7
Gross revenue (in thousands)	$11,061·6	$17,639·0	+59·5
Interest (in thousands) .	$856·9	$4,429·6*	+416·9
Dividends (in thousands) .	$2,097·9	$1,846·2	−12·0

* Includes rentals.

Denver and Rio Grande

	1879	1889	Percentage of Change
Miles of road . . .	337	1,493	+343·0
Ton-miles (in millions) .	N.A.	260·3	——
Rate on ton-miles . .	3·62c*	2·10c	—42·0
Gross revenue (in thousands)	$1,157·4	$8,046·6	+595·2
Interest (in thousands) .	$870·6†	$1,654·6	+90·1
Dividends (in thousands) .	——	——	——

* For year 1881; data for 1879 and 1880 not available.
† For year 1880; data for 1879 not available.

Missouri Pacific

	1879	1889	Percentage of Change
Miles of road . . .	421·5	5,019·0	+1,090·5
Ton-miles (in millions) .	N.A.	1,428·5	——
Rate per ton-mile . .	1·19c	1·13c	—5·1
Gross revenue (in thousands)	$3,922·8	$23,493·4	+498·9
Interest (in thousands) .	$1,139·8	$2,458·4	+115·7
Dividends (in thousands) .	——	$1,574·1	——

Northern Pacific

	1879	1889	Percentage of Change
Miles of road . . .	1,193	3,778	+216·7
Ton-miles (in millions) .	88·9	1,095·8	+1,132·6
Rate per ton-mile . .	2·59c	1·40c	—46·0
Gross revenue (in thousands)	$2,230·1	$21,741·0	+874·9
Interest (in thousands) .	$159·5	$8,549·0	+5,259·9
Dividends (in thousands)	——	——	——

St. Paul, Minneapolis and Manitoba

	1879	1889	Percentage of Charge
Miles of road . . .	656	3,006	+358·2
Ton-miles (in millions) .	N.A.	554·7	——
Rate per ton-mile . .	2·88c*	1·27c	−55·9
Gross revenue (in thousands)	$2,885·3	$9,582·9	+232·1
Interest (in thousands) .	$824·0	$3,431·0†	+316·4
Dividends (in thousands) .	——	$1,200·0	——

* Data for 1880. Data for 1879 not available.

† For year ending June 30, 1889. Data for year ending June 30, 1890, not available.

Southern Pacific

	1879*	1889	Percentage of Change
Miles of road . . .	2,360·0	6,052·4	+156·5
Ton-miles (in millions) .	392·9	1,117·1	+184·3
Rate per ton-mile . .	2·75c	1·768c	−35·6
Gross revenue (in thousands)	$17,153·1	$46,343·2	+170·2
Interest (in thousands) .	$4,206·3	$13,582·2	+222·9
Dividends (in thousands)	——	——	——

* Data for 1879 included the Central Pacific and roads operated under lease or contracts, including Southern Pacific.

Union Pacific

	1879	1889	Percentage of Change
Miles of road . . .	1,042	6,996	+571·4
Ton-miles (in millions) .	436·0	1,671·5	+283·3
Rate per ton-mile . .	1·99c	1·37c	−31·2
Gross revenue (in thousands)	$13,201·0	$31,070·1	+135·4
Interest (in thousands) .	$3,390·5	$9,747·3*	+187·5
Dividends (in thousands) .	$2,204·7	——	−100

* Includes deficit of leased and jointly controlled line.

The growth of the western railroad net in physical terms is clearly disclosed by the increase in miles of road and in ton-miles. The heavy increase in ton-miles reflects the growth in the production sector of the national economy. Only a relatively slight proportion of the transportation service was performed by a non-railroad agency. Hence the growth of the economy as measured in total output is well reflected in the expansion in the ton-mile traffic. The price of ton-mile service declined on every road included in the tabulation, and it is a safe generalization that there were no major exceptions to the decline in railroad selling prices in the 1880's. With the exception of the Missouri Pacific, the decline ranged from approximately 30 per cent to 55 per cent, with the sharpest drop registered on the Manitoba. This is a tribute to the operating genius of Hill, the promoter and guiding hand in the affairs of that property.

In order to create the physical property and carry the expanding ton-mile business, a sizeable debt was incurred, with a corresponding growth in interest. This represents the price paid by prudent investors in search of a return upon what was considered an investment with relatively little risk. Henry Clay Frick, one of the industrial leaders closely associated with Andrew Carnegie, described railroad bonds as the Rembrandts of Investment, while Vanderbilt was reputed to have regarded railroad bonds as superior to government bonds. Railroads, declared this leading businessman, would always be necessary even if governments should fall. With some relatively unimportant exceptions the interest was not received by the promoters and the active business administrators. These men of business pledged their personal fortunes, concentrated their energies, and assumed a heavy burden of risks in exchange for the common stock. Huntington, Gould, Villard, Mitchell, Forbes, and others maintained stock control of their major properties during their lifetimes and they passed on their stockholdings to their heirs. Their compensation was in the form of dividends. In a number of cases no dividends were received during the entire decade of the 1880's; or, for that matter, in the year prior to the 1880's and for ten years or more afterwards. The Rio Grande and the Southern Pacific are included in this category. The Northern Pacific paid no dividends during the entire decade, though a number of dividends were paid in the early 1890's, only to be followed by a receivership in 1893. The Atchison started out in the 1880's with a good dividend, only to be overtaken by adversity. The Missouri Pacific, though it paid no dividends in 1879, went on a dividend basis in the early 1880's and continued to pay until 1890. The dividend, however, in the late 1880's was reduced and was finally passed in the 1890's. A similar calamity, somewhat different in timing, overtook the Union Pacific. That company entered into the decade of the 1880's as a high-grade dividend payer. Its stock sold at a high price and returned an exceptionally low yield to the investor. In 1884 the dividend was passed and was destined not to be resumed for almost a quarter of a century.

The steady dividend payers among the major western roads, at least during the 1880's and for a generation thereafter, were the central, western, and northwestern properties, embracing the Burlington, St. Paul, Northwestern, Rock Island, and Manitoba. The latter, financially speaking, was the sensation of the decade. The other dividend payers enjoyed the support of business flowing from a well-established territory with a well-settled population. The heavy volume of traffic in southern Kansas, arising from such a situation, financed in large part the expansion program of the Atchison.

The profit of the risk-taking promoters and businessmen were distributed largely in accordance with the results that normally emerge in a free enterprise system. Some businessmen profited extensively and permanently, such as Hill and his followers on the Manitoba, and Keep and Hughitt and their followers on the Northwestern. Others received benefits in the form of irregular dividends, and were subject to shocks such as those experienced by the St. Paul stockholders. Still others received no sustained rewards for their services in creating and maintaining a useful public service. In this category are included Palmer and his investor following on the Rio Grande, and Villard and his army of investors, including many in Germany. The high hopes of a permanent flow of dividends entertained by the stockholders of the Atchison were rudely upset by the cessation of dividends late in the 1880's. Dividends of the Burlington were well maintained for most of the decade, but they were reduced later in that period amidst an environment of fear and impending disaster.

There is no purpose to be served in building up a statistical record of averages and percentages. Taking the western roads as a whole in the period of their most rapid growth, the profit paid in the form of dividends was a relatively slight price for the public benefits in the form of an efficient transportation agency. The system of free-enterprise capitalism created this agency and rendered a public service in western railroad territory in return for a surprisingly small proportion of the gross revenue in the form of dividends to the stockholder risk-takers.

Notes for Chapter XXII

[1] Burlington Archives, Forbes to L. Z. Leiter, May 18, 1889, for example, disclosed that 85 per cent of the stockholders in the Burlington at that time had less than 100 shares, and over 50 per cent of the stockholders held 25 shares or less. The average number of shares held per stockholder were 67. More than half of the stockholders were women, trustees, and institutions.

[2] Circular of J. J. Hill to shareholders of the Manitoba, cited in *Chron.*, Oct. 5, 1889, p. 435.

[3] Pac. Ry. Commission, p. 989.

[4] Report of Government Directors, Union Pacific, cited in *R. R. Gaz.*, Oct. 2, 1891, p. 692.

[5] *The New York Times*, Jan. 31, 1888.

[6] *Chron.*, July 7, 1888, p. 21; and Aug. 25, 1888, p. 227.

[7] H. V. P., Box 24. These remarks were made in a speech before the St. Paul Chamber of Commerce, Oct. 8, 1888.

[8] Annual Report, Northern Pacific, 1890, p. 8.

[9] *Philadelphia Inquirer*, Aug. 15, 1889.

[10] *Chron.*, Nov. 30, 1889, p. 719.

[11] *The New York Times*, Nov. 16, 1890.

[12] Burlington Archives, Coolidge to Perkins, Sept. 16, 1887.

[13] *Chron.*, Oct. 6, 1888, p. 395.

[14] *Boston Transcript*, Mar. 28, 1885.

[15] *London Railway News*, Sept. 29, 1888, p. 549.

[16] *Ibid.*, p. 550.

[17] *Philadelphia Press*, Mar. 14, 1889.

[18] Burlington Archives, Perkins to Forbes, Aug. 9, 1890.

[19] *Ry. Review*, Sept. 21, 1889, p. 554.

[20] *Chron.*, Aug. 10, 1889, p. 158.

[21] *Ibid.*, Oct. 17, 1891, p. 546.

[22] Annual Report, Missouri Pacific, 1888, p. 3.

[23] Dodge Papers, Adams to Dodge, Jan. 11, 1890.

[24] *Ibid.*, Adams to Dodge.

[25] *London Railway News*, Jan. 11, 1890, p. 73.

[26] *Chron.*, Sept. 19, 1885, p. 331.

[27] *Ibid.*, Aug. 30, 1890, p. 263.

[28] *Ibid.*, April 25, 1891, p. 619.

[29] Annual Report, Atchison, 1888, p. 17.

[30] For clashes between Hill and Manvel, see *The New York Times*, Sept. 1, 1889.

[31] *Chron.*, Dec. 19, 1891, p. 898.

XXIII

Conclusion

THIS REVIEW of the evolution of the transcontinental railroads leads to a clear conclusion. The western railroad network was built quickly and at a relatively low cost to the travelling and shipping public and the profits to the investors and to the risk-taking promoters were on the whole relatively slight.

The single transcontinental line between Omaha and San Francisco, the combined Union Pacific–Central Pacific route, which had been finished by 1869 remained the only through line a decade later. Investments made by bondholders, stockholders, and promoters in competitive lines during this decade were largely lost. The Northern Pacific was a financial failure; the Atlantic and Pacific met a similar fate; and so did the Texas and Pacific. The feeder lines to the Union Pacific at its eastern end also encountered heavy losses. The Kansas Pacific and the Central Branch Union Pacific defaulted on their interest payments; the St. Joseph fell into receivership; the corporate predecessors of the Kansas City and Northern and the Missouri Pacific also passed their interest payments and remained in receivership for a number of years. Nor were the investors more fortunate with their commitments in the southwestern lines designed to connect the Missouri Valley with the Gulf Coast. In this area the Iron Mountain, the International, and the Kansas and Texas, were all unable to meet their interest obligations and fell into financial difficulties.

Of the trans-Missouri River railroads, only the western wing of the single completed transcontinental road prior to 1875, the Central Pacific, was able to pay a dividend. And in that year, the Union Pacific followed. The three major eastern connections of the latter, controlling the direct

421

Omaha–Chicago route, were in a more fortunate condition. Both the Burlington and the Rock Island were dividend payers, though the third road in this category did not pay any dividends until 1879. The two dividend payers were by 1869 well-established properties. They controlled growing local traffic carried at relatively high rates.

And it is by no means unimportant to point out that the promoters, those who received a large share of the railroad stock for services rendered, with only a nominal cash consideration, personally lost most of their commitments. This observation applies to the promoters of the Northern Pacific, the Atlantic and Pacific, the Texas and Pacific, the International, the Missouri Pacific, and the Kansas and Texas. It also covers the activities of the pioneer investors in the Atchison and the Union Pacific.

By the fall of 1872 construction in these pioneer transportation ventures had ceased. Funds invested in stocks had been almost completely lost, and those invested in bonds had also suffered substantial deterioration. Under these unfortunate conditions new capital for further construction could not be obtained. The loss of invested capital was even more pronounced in many of the smaller and local lines. Their promoters and their financial followers penetrated the American frontier in many cases even earlier than the major through trunk lines. They moved beyond the line of then-existing settlements and into territories with light populations, supported by only slight agricultural resources. Beyond these assets there was little available for transportation. Almost all the funds invested in the stocks and in a large proportion of the bonds were lost. Most of these local lines were acquired by the major systems, as part of the expansion boom between 1879 and 1883, while a smaller number were merged in the middle and late 1880's.

The prolonged period of construction inactivity in the western railroad field was brought to an end in the winter of 1878–1879. From that time until 1890 there followed the greatest and most sustained railroad-building program in the country's history. Railroad lines that had been under consideration for many years were suddenly completed in an astonishingly short time. In about three years competition sprang up along all transcontinental routes. The Northern Pacific, the Burlington–Rio Grande, the Frisco–Atchison–Atlantic and Pacific, the Texas and Pacific–Southern Pacific, and the Southern Pacific line between San Francisco and New Orleans were all completed during these few years. "Never before in the history of the world was so vast a territory made accessible in so short a time," declared a leading railroad journal.[1] These roads for the most part were not planned carefully, in accordance with the advancing tide of population. Rather, they were built mostly in advance of settlement. Investors furnished funds with the hope of profiting in the future, with full recognition that losses, temporary though they might be, would have to be incurred for the present. Railroad managements expressed hope over *ultimate* results. In the Northwest, the St. Paul management, the leader in the area's expansion surge, described the rapid settlement in Dakota as "a marvel of the times."[2] In the single year of 1883 this road reported that more than twelve million acres were taken up for cultivation. And the Northwestern, second only to the St. Paul in this expansion, stressed in its Annual Reports the light traffic-density in the area through which new mileage had just been acquired. The 1882 Report observed that immigration into and cultivation of this land had "immensely increased."[3] Railroad mileage in the early 1880's was growing at a rate substantially in excess of the growth of the national economy. The industry was expanding and, characteristic of the pattern of industrial growth, paradoxical as it may seem, it tended to grow too rapidly. In the eyes of observers, then as now, rapid expansion was charged with dangerous possibilities. "We may safely say," declared a railroad journal, "that the construction now is at a rate which cannot be possibly kept up for many years without grave disaster."[4] The country was increasing in population, production, and wealth, but not as rapidly as the expansion of 40 per cent in the railroad network in a four-year period. In the Rocky Mountain territory, embracing New Mexico, Arizona, Utah, Colorado, Montana, Idaho, and Wyoming—the center of the transcontinental area —the increase in railroad mileage was 165 per cent.

To a considerable extent the light traffic density in the frontier areas was balanced by lower construction costs. The fixed charges per mile on these frontier roads were lower than on the more sturdily built roads in the more populous areas. Furthermore these new lines were fed with traffic largely from agricultural production. Crop failures could and did reduce railroad profits and not infrequently they led to substantial losses. This was particularly the case in the late 1880's in the rich agricultural regions of Kansas and Nebraska.

This multiplication of railroad mileage, making accessible to the national economy such a large area of fertile land, was accompanied by a steady decline in railroad rates. Decreasing prices in a rapidly growing industry are normal. The decline was partly the result of the same influences that reduced the price level between 1873 and 1893. In this respect the railroad industry operated in the familiar pattern of increasing sales, lower prices, and reduced profits per unit of sale so characteristic of American industry.

This crossing of the American frontier, this supply of low-cost technologically efficient transportation facilities, this opening up of vast supplies of raw materials, food, energy, metals, and lumber was carried out under the leadership of active businessmen—entrepreneurs, as they are called in the lingo of economic theory. A variety of business abilities participated in this business task, so essential to the development of the country. Careful conservatism, and careless, perhaps even reckless, speculation combined to produce the final product. Some business leaders attracted the funds of savings institutions and of individuals anxious to secure a reasonable return. There is a tendency to favor this kind of capital, partly on moral and ethical grounds, as against funds in search of extraordinary profits. Such spectacular profits are frequently castigated as unearned increments, as profits to which the holders are not legitimately entitled. Be that as it may. Suffice it to say that such speculative funds were essential to railroad building. The pioneering funds, the funds committed to uses involving high degrees of risks, were provided by men of business who were willing and able to risk potential losses in exchange for the possibility of extraordinary profits. Such businessmen-investors did not look for a reasonable profit upon carefully invested capital. They thought in terms of creating personal fortunes. In this competitive race there were many outstanding and widely publicized successes. There were many, many more failures. Successes in fact, were to a considerable extent based upon failures. The expansion programs of Hill, Huntington, Cable, Mitchell, Forbes, Keep, Gould, and Nickerson involved in part the acquisition of properties bought at heavy losses to the pioneer risk takers. Little has been written about this last-named group. Though they were financially unsuccessful they performed notable public services. Many threw improved transportation facilities across the American frontier. In Minnesota, Iowa, Wisconsin, Illinois, Kansas, California, and Dakota, the early railroads were built by unnamed and unsung risk takers. They wasted both their funds and many years of their time and energy in losing ventures. But the railroads they built remained; and they were sold, in most cases, at prices reflecting only a fraction of their original cost.

Much of the success of the major railroads and of their business leaders resulted from the purchase of these smaller properties at the right time— at the end of a period of poor business, when prices were still low and before they had advanced in the wake of an ensuing business boom. Good "timing" produced low capital costs. It gave the businessman an advantage in an industry in which capital costs constituted a substantial proportion of total costs. The acquisition of the St. Paul and Pacific in 1878, at low prices reflecting depression influences, was a major cause of the prosperity of the successor Manitoba. Similarly Villard's entrance into the railroad business in 1879, just before the boom in the Northwest, laid the foundation for the subsequent success of the Navigation, though Villard personally lost in 1883 what he gained in 1879. Even more impressive was the acquisition by Gould in 1879 of low-priced stocks with little or no earning power. A relatively small amount of cash obtained through the sale of Union Pacific stock was invested in the earliest stages of a strong security market in the stocks of financially weak, one might say financially desperate, railroads. Part of these capital gains were later invested, through the purchase of bonds and stock, in new construction and improvements. The channels of finance are devious and indirect, and, strange as it may seem, a substantial part of the funds realized from security trading found their way into productive capital.

Further illustrations of fortunate timing in corporate expansion are afforded by the program of the St. Paul initiated late in 1878 and the Huntington forward push at the same time despite the heavy debts and the reluctance of his associates.

On the other hand, poor timing—the acquisition of assets at high prices during prosperity, just prior to a decline in prices—was a major cause of heavy financial losses. A word of caution may, however, be in order. It is not correct to state that high prices were the only cause of failure, nor that failure would not have intervened had the assets been purchased at lower price levels. It is sufficient to observe that poor timing is a serious handicap in the race for business success. Cooke, in the expansion of the Northern Pacific, was victimized by high prices. The losses incurred so quickly in 1873 permanently eliminated him as a factor in the railroad industry. A similar disaster overtook T. A. Scott in his expansion program in the Southeast, Southwest, and Midwest. He laid the foundations of two continental systems for the benefit of the Pennsylvania Railroad, only to fail overwhelmingly. Poor timing was associated with the incurring of financial obligations maturing before the development of adequate earning power.

In "timing" purchases, the successful businessmen are usually, though not exclusively, found in the so-called speculative group. They are willing to assume heavy risks at a time when the more cautious businessmen decline to act. An interesting contract between these two classes of businessmen was afforded in 1879. Gould, acting individually with the support of no financial groups, bought successively a number of roads in competition with Forbes: the St. Joseph, the Central Branch Union Pacific, the Kansas and Texas, and a number of other smaller properties. Villard at the same time took speculative chances in the purchase of properties incorporated into the Navigation. The same observations can be applied to Hill and his associates. They used their credit and resources to finance the purchase of the St. Paul and Pacific. A great part of Huntington's success in the creation of the Southern Pacific's San Francisco–New Orleans line came from the purchase of securities and from new construction in the years of low prices. These were transformed into low capital costs and thus conferred a cost advantage in comparison with competition that installed their facilities in periods of higher prices. With a given reasonable rate structure the low-cost properties earned higher profits; and in a war of rates they remained solvent when competitors met with failure.

This, of course, is only one phase of a complicated problem. Roads built quickly at low cost in periods of depressed prices were frequently not constructed in accordance with the best physical standards. In subsequent years it was necessary to rebuild, to modernize, to improve, in order to put the property in a more suitable physical condition. Much of the benefits of low capital costs were lost by the additional cost incurred in making improvements at higher prices in subsequent years.

The risks assumed by business leaders normally involved heavy personal financial responsibilities. The dividing line between corporate and personal obligations was not usually respected. Frequently, indeed, outstanding and constructive financial services were performed without any compensation. A leading example is afforded by the reorganization of the West Shore Railroad and the accompanying elimination of the costly competition between the Pennsylvania and the New York Central in

1885, under the Morgan leadership. The reward to this business leader came in the form of higher market values for his clients' holdings of stocks and bonds. The complexity of properly appraising the worth of such a service is not well recognized in much of the business literature. An interesting illustration of unrealistic interpretation is the observation of an American historian that "a great part of Morgan's fortune was built up by sheer manipulation of stocks."[5] Morgan made heavy commitments in many pioneer companies, including, for example, those set up to finance the inventions of Thomas A. Edison. As a whole there were more losses than profits in these ventures. Stocks received in connection with the railroad reorganizations constituted the products neither of speculation nor of manipulation. They were compensations for important services—services furthermore, that involved no adverse public interests. The compensation was in exchange for a service that gave the railroads access to additional supplies of capital. Financial structures were so arranged that new capital, not forthcoming under old financial setups, was made available under new dispensations.

The risks assumed by such businessmen as Hill, Huntington, Gould, Forbes, Villard, T. A. Scott, Nickerson, and many others, though not so designed, were more than corporate risks. They involved potential personal losses, balanced of course by the possibility of capital gains in the event of success. Hill invested all his personal assets to facilitate his entrance into the railroad business through the reorganization of the St. Paul and Pacific. Villard twice risked and lost personal fortunes in an effort to sustain his tottering railroad creation. Upon resigning from the directorate of the Northern Pacific after his second major collapse in 1893, he left an account of his personal tribulations. His association with the road, he related, was "a constant source of exhausting work, wearing anxiety and heavy pecuniary loss." Between 1889 and 1893, he declared, he saved the company twice from "disaster" by raising many millions of dollars. His confidence in the road made him the "greatest sufferer as a stock and bond holder."[6]

Heavy also were the financial burdens assumed by Huntington. The ingeniousness of his financial practices, his numerous loans, the slight margin by which he averted defaults during financial disasters in the 1870's and in 1884 have been sketched in previous chapters. These hair-raising experiences were again repeated in 1893. Again he overextended himself personally in raising funds to expand and improve railroad facilities. The Southern Pacific, through which Huntington controlled his railroad empire, owed the banks large sums, secured, furthermore, by his notes and those of his associates. Huntington enjoyed a high credit standing and it was with the help of a bank (on which Huntington served as director) and with the aid of a banking syndicate that he was able to raise approximately $4 million to avoid both personal and corporate default.[7] Help was also furnished by a businessman with whom Huntington had done business from time to time—James G. Fair, who made a fortune from the Comstock silver mines in the 1870's. Again in 1893, as in 1873 and in 1884, Huntington survived; but, in the language of a contemporary observer, he "passed through the fight of his life. . . ."[8]

At this critical period Huntington was also aided by the fortunately timed desire of the Illinois Central to buy control of his Louisville–New Orleans line. Though it was not essential to the Huntington System, it had a strategic value to the Illinois Central. Huntington's desperate need for cash at this time was disclosed by his refusal to grant the Illinois Central an option for its purchase. He insisted upon an immediate sale. The road was sold late in 1892 and provided $5 million in cash and $20 million in Illinois Central bonds.[9] Almost until the end of his days Huntington borrowed in order to expand and improve his wide-flung system.

The early history of the powerful competitor of the Huntington System —the Atchison—was also featured by the assumption of financial risks by a small group of Boston capitalists under the Nickerson leadership. Nickerson, a successful man of business, was brought into the property in 1873. The company was then in financial difficulties. He solved the problem by personal advances by himself and his associates. The road was thus enabled to construct rapidly and at then-prevailing low costs the western extension to the Kansas–Colorado boundary. The Atchison was thereby also able to secure a valuable land grant. The Kansas extension thus built at low costs was the mainstay of the company's earning power in the following decade—an earning power that was well exploited in order to finance in part the transformation of this relatively small property into one of the major transcontinental systems. A typical illustration of the inability of a cautious businessman to "time" a business transaction is the failure of Forbes in 1877–1878 to purchase control of the Atchison. The purchase was considered by his board and informally by conversation and correspondence between Forbes, Perkins, and other

Burlington officials. The risks, however, were too great. The funds were available, but they were not committed, as they were by the more speculative type of businessmen, to the purchase of properties in a period of poor business, when earnings were low and losses high.

Enough has been presented here to suggest, if not to establish definitively, the conclusion that business leadership in the early western railroad industry involved the assumption of extraordinary risks. In these pioneer times the building of roads, the creation of jobs, the supply of low-cost transportation services, the creation of conditions to facilitate immigration into unsettled territory, and the pushing back of the American frontier—all these boons and more—flowed largely from the willingness of businessmen to invest their funds and commit their energy to the risky business of pioneer railroad transportation. Most of the pioneers were financial failures. Only a few survived. To all of them, however, goes the credit, in the words of a contemporary railroad writer, for "the enormous construction west of the Mississippi," which he described as "one of the greatest industrial feats in the world's history."[10]

Notes for Chapter XXIII

[1] *R. R. Gaz.*, Aug. 1, 1884, p. 569.
[2] Annual Report, St. Paul, 1883, p. 12.
[3] Annual Report, Northwestern, 1882, p. 23.
[4] *R. R. Gaz.*, Aug. 1, 1884, p. 569.
[5] Allan Nevins, *John D. Rockefeller* (New York: Scribner's, 1941), II, p. 342.
[6] H. V. P., Villard to Oakes, March 1, 1893, Box 23.
[7] *Ry. World*, July 24, 1897, p. 740.
[8] *San Francisco Chronicle*, Aug. 31, 1893.
[9] *Bradstreet's*, June 11, 1892.
[10] *R. R. Gaz.*, Aug. 8, 1884, p. 587.

Index

VERMONT COLLEGE
MONTPELIER, VERMONT.